After Confucius

After Confucius

Studies in Early Chinese Philosophy

Paul R. Goldin

University of Hawai'i Press Honolulu

Printed in the United States of America

10 09 08 07 06 05 6 5 4 3 2 1

Library of Congress Cataloging-in-Publication Data

Goldin, Paul Rakita.
After Confucius : studies in early Chinese philosophy / Paul R. Goldin.
p. cm.
Includes bibliographical references and index.
ISBN 0-8248-2842-9 (alk. paper)
1. Philosophy, Chinese—To 221 B.C. 2. Philosophy, Chinese—221 B.C.–960 A.D.
I. Title: Studies in early Chinese philosophy. II. Title.

B126.G65 2005
181'.11—dc22
2004017241

University of Hawai'i Press books are printed on acid-free paper and meet the guidelines for permanence and durability of the Council on Library Resources.

Designed by University of Hawai'i Press production staff
Printed by IBT Global

Gilbert L. Mattos (1939–2002)
in memoriam

魚貫終何益
龍門在苦登
有成當作雨
無用恥為鵬
激浪誠難泝
雄心亦自憑
風雲潛會合
鬐鬣忽騰凌
泥滓辭何濁
煙霄見海澄
迴瞻順流輩
誰敢望同升

元積

Contents

Acknowledgments

The debts that I have accumulated in the course of writing this book are numerous, but I owe the most to my parents and to my wife, Edilma. Little Andrew Samuel arrived in time to observe and applaud some of the final revisions while perched on the author's knee.

The title is intended to recall *Before Confucius,* by Edward L. Shaughnessy, who first encouraged me to take excavated manuscripts seriously. I hope in this way to convey to him how much of an effect that conversation has had on my work.

My arguments have been sharpened and refined by discussions with the following colleagues: William H. Baxter, Wolfgang Behr, E. Bruce Brooks, Alvin P. Cohen, Chen Ning, Constance A. Cook, Scott Cook, Mark Csikszentmihalyi, Donald Harper, Kenneth W. Holloway, Martin Kern, Terry F. Kleeman, Paul W. Kroll, Joachim Kurtz, Whalen Lai, Victor H. Mair, John S. Major, Michael Puett, Sarah A. Queen, Moss Roberts, David Schaberg, Nathan Sivin, Xing Wen, Xu Shaohua, and Robin D. S. Yates. Special thanks are due Bryan W. Van Norden, who read the entire manuscript, offering many helpful comments, and also suggested the title of chapter 8.

I am grateful to Eric Henry for sharing his unpublished index of *Shi* references in the *Zuozhuan* and to Command Sergeant Major Eugene B. Patton III, Defense Language Institute Foreign Language Center and Presidio of Monterey, for information about language instruction at that famous school. Many thanks, finally, to Patricia Crosby and the staff at the University of Hawai'i Press for continuing to accommodate the peculiar demands of an academic author.

This book is dedicated to the memory of Gilbert L. Mattos, who knew more about Chinese writing than anyone I have ever met. We became research collaborators within a week of our first meeting and friends not a day later. The final portion of this manuscript was composed with the benefit of his nonpareil library—the greatest gift that one scholar can receive from another.

Most of the chapters in this book were presented as conference papers or public lectures. I would like to thank the audiences at each of these events for helpful questions and criticism. Some of the chapters were originally published elsewhere in preliminary versions:

"Toward a Thick Description of Chinese Philosophy": contains material from research notes published in *Journal of the American Oriental Society* 120.1 (2000): 77–81, and 122.1 (2002): 83–85.

"Xunzi in the Light of the Guodian Manuscripts": *Early China* 25 (2000): 113–146.

"Han Fei's Doctrine of Self-Interest": *Asian Philosophy* 11.3 (2001): 151–159.

"Li Si, Chancellor of the Universe": *The Human Tradition in Premodern China,* ed. Kenneth J. Hammond (Wilmington: Scholarly Resources, 2002), 15–25.

"Rhetoric and Machination in *Stratagems of the Warring States*": *Sino-Platonic Papers* 41 (1993): 1–27 (with the title "Miching Mallecho: The *Zhanguo ce* and Classical Rhetoric").

"Insidious Syncretism in the Political Philosophy of *Huainanzi*": *Asian Philosophy* 9.3 (1999): 165–191.

"Those Who Don't Know Speak": *Asian Philosophy* 12.3 (2002): 183–195.

Introduction

Toward a Thick Description of Chinese Philosophy

In his *Critique of Stammler,* Max Weber (1864–1920) presented the following scenario:

> Let us suppose that two men who otherwise engage in no "social relation"—for example, two uncivilized men of different races, or a European who encounters a native in darkest Africa—meet and "exchange" two objects. We are inclined to think that a mere description of what can be observed during this exchange—muscular movements and, if some words were "spoken," the sounds which, so to say, constitute the "matter" or "material" of the behavior—would in no sense comprehend the "essence" of what happens. This is quite correct. The "essence" of what happens is constituted by the "meaning" which the two parties ascribe to their observable behavior, a "meaning" which "regulates" the course of their future conduct. Without this "meaning," we are inclined to say, an "exchange" is neither empirically possible nor conceptually imaginable.[1]

Weber's dated vocabulary (we no longer need to speak of "races" and of "darkest Africa") should not prevent us from recognizing the importance of his argument to both history and anthropology. A witness—that is to say, an anthropologist or historian—who wishes to describe an "exchange" cannot be satisfied with relating the observable phenomena of the event, for this would be to ignore the underlying logic that Weber calls the "'essence' of what happens." From the point of the view of the agents themselves, the significance of the exchange lies not in their "muscular movements" but in the "meaning" that they attribute to the exchange and that, for the exchange to be completed, they must expect their colleagues to share. In short, the onus is to explain not the mere "muscular movements" but the "essence." This methodology is often called Weber's *Verstehen* thesis.

Verstehen in this sense is comparable to what Gilbert Ryle dubbed "thick description":

> Two boys fairly swiftly contract the eyelids of their right eyes. In the first boy this is only an involuntary twitch; but the other is winking conspiratorially to an accomplice. At the lowest or the thinnest level of description the two contractions of the eyelids may be exactly alike. From a cinematograph-film of the two faces there might be no telling which contraction, if either, was a wink, or which, if either, was a mere twitch. Yet there remains an immense but unphotographable difference between a twitch and a wink. For to wink is to try to signal to someone in particular, without the cognisance of others, a definite message according to an already understood code.[2]

A twitch is not a wink, but the only way for an outsider to come to understand the difference between the two is to investigate the "understood code" that informs conspiratorial winking. It is not surprising that anthropologists have seized upon the concept of thick description for their own discipline. And the paradigm is equally useful in the study of cultural history, for the position of an ethnologist observing natives engaged in "exchange" is analogous to that of a historian trying to make sense of the scattered evidence found in historical sources. No less than in cultural anthropology, thick description in the domain of cultural history entails "sorting out the structures of signification . . . and determining their social ground and import."[3]

In this book I present piecemeal attempts at the thick description of classical Chinese philosophy. This approach is only indirectly concerned with such considerations as the viability of Chinese philosophy today and its similarity or dissimilarity to Western philosophy, which animate most discussions of the subject within the framework of academic philosophy. The question of whether Chinese philosophy qualifies as genuine philosophy, seriously addressed by several scholars,[4] depends entirely on the scope of one's definitions. If philosophy is made out to be an entity inseverable from the post-Platonic world,[5] then classical Chinese philosophy is not and never can be "philosophy." But it certainly was something, and thick description is the best preliminary method to determine how Chinese thinkers conceived of their own enterprise. This book is not about whether Chinese philosophy is philosophy but about how Chinese philosophy is Chinese.

Who were the ancient Chinese philosophers? What was their intended audience? What were they arguing about? How did they respond to earlier thinkers and to each other? What rhetorical devices did they use to convey their ideas persuasively? Why did those in power wish to hear from them, and what did they claim to offer in return for patronage? Such questions are essential to a broader understanding of the milieu in which Chinese thinkers flourished. Some scholars have begun to address the social aspects of these problems;[6] but at the level of ideas, contemporary inquiries often submit descriptions that are too thin. Much ink has been spilled, for example, over the Procrustean question of whether Mohist ethics is deontological or consequentialist.[7] The answer will matter only to a philosopher who is prepared to deracinate Mohism by disregarding what the ancient Chinese themselves thought was significant about Mohist philosophy.[8] The purpose of the Mohists was not to work out a formal taxonomy of moral philosophy but to provide an alternative to Confucian ethics, which they regarded as objectionably partial in that it mandated obligations to other people in proportion to their proximity to oneself. The Mohists did not want to live in a world in which people treated their brothers with greater care than they did their neighbors. If such anachronistic terms as "deontological" and "consequentialist" must be imposed on Chinese thought, the only satisfactory assessment of Mohism is that it belongs to both categories: actions are right if and only if they produce material benefit, and actions that produce material benefit are right because Heaven mandates them. This would be a thicker understanding of what Mohism meant, both to its adherents and to its opponents.

Before proceeding to some concrete examples of what I mean by a thick description of Chinese philosophy—involving the significance of names and of paronomasia in Chinese philosophical literature—let me note that the necessary inquiries are difficult for technical reasons alone. Thus what is offered here is only a collection of illustrative studies, not a comprehensive disquisition.[9] Chinese has never been considered an easy language (along with Arabic, Japanese, and Korean it is commonly reckoned as one of the hardest languages for an American to learn),[10] and the archaic idiom in which classical Chinese philosophy has been transmitted is more demanding than the modern vernacular. Raising the cost of admission even further is the extraordinary series of archaeological discoveries in China since the 1970s. The artifacts that most directly affect the study of early Chinese thought are manuscripts, inscribed primarily on bamboo and silk, of which dozens have been found and which present unprecedented problems of interpretation. The basic work of deciphering the texts (and, in the case of bamboo texts, piecing the documents together strip by strip) is arduous, as they are written in a script that is older than the standard characters used in China today and that is not perfectly understood. Making sense of these materials requires an array of specialized skills (including epigraphy and linguistics, not the traditional strengths of Chinese studies in the United States), rendering progress slow under the best of circumstances and impossible without the ongoing cooperation of researchers across the globe.[11]

But if research has become more challenging, it has also become proportionally more rewarding. The changes in the field that have been brought about by the archaeological discovery of ancient manuscripts are profound. First, the many recent discoveries suggest that texts recorded on manuscripts circulated more widely in Warring States and Han China than was previously believed. When the documents from the tombs at Mawangdui 馬王堆 were first reported some thirty years ago, they produced a worldwide sensation, because nothing like them had ever been seen before.[12] While Mawangdui must still rank as one of the greatest textual hoards in the archaeological record, we have today a much richer context in which to place these extraordinary finds. It is now apparent that feudal lords, and even well connected private citizens, could amass substantial and diverse libraries.

Moreover, the value of manuscripts is now more finely appreciated. Written texts were surely rare and valuable—they are rarer in tombs than bronzes, for example—but they were commodities that members of the elite commonly collected. This is a new insight. The older view of the nature and function of a text was influenced by the accounts of the transmission of the canons in such histories as the *History of the Han* (*Hanshu* 漢書).[13] According to that understanding, texts were sacred revelations; they were transmitted in secret from master to disciple and were safeguarded among doctrinal lineages.[14] But the archaeological record does not square with that model. Excavated texts show influence from a multitude of intellectual sources, and, even more important, libraries are typically eclectic: that is to say, most collections of texts found in tombs include materials from several intellectual camps, many of which espoused beliefs incompatible with those of other represented schools.

A more likely thesis would hold that, by Warring States times, a national literary culture had begun to emerge in China in which members of the highest classes participated by collecting a wide variety of texts. Ideology and region seem to have played a minor role in shaping the habits of bibliophiles.[15] One finds commentaries on the *Canon of Changes* 易經 together with medical treatises at Mawangdui, demonological and hemerological almanacs together with legal handbooks at Shuihudi 睡虎地, and Confucian texts together with the *Daode jing* 道德經 (or *Laozi* 老子) at Guodian 郭店. Similarly, Confucian materials have been recovered not only from Qi 齊, where one might have expected them, but also from Chu 楚, which was never famous as a bastion of Confucianism.[16] To this extent, the ancient Chinese intellectual world was more like our own than we, as cautious spectators of the "other," have recognized. The precise mechanisms by which manuscripts were copied and acquired are still unclear, but we may have to start thinking of Warring States China as a vast philosophical marketplace, with new and classic books readily available in all subjects and for all sufficiently affluent tastes.

A more specific example: The state of Qin 秦, widely disparaged as a semibarbaric frontier territory in earlier times, developed into a fearsome world leader in the late Warring States period. For centuries, the rise of Qin was normally explained as a consequence of its cruel administration: Lord Shang 商君 (d. 338 B.C.) was often credited with transforming Qin into a fighting machine by emphasizing agriculture and war and by reorganizing the populace into a system of subdivisions inspired by military command structure.[17] Through its terrifying laws, Qin was supposedly able to make its people more productive and docile. But the details of these laws were never known.

Our understanding of the Qin dynasty was utterly transformed in 1975, when a substantial collection of statutes and legal manuals was discovered in a tomb at Shuihudi.[18] Dating from the mid–third century B.C., these were the oldest legal texts ever discovered in China. The newfound Qin laws are difficult to read, because they use many unglossed technical terms and routinely allude to statutes whose content we can only guess at. Nevertheless, the laws are clear enough to explode the received image of the Qin state. Though they may appear harsh indeed to a modern reader, they were not extraordinarily severe for the times and were by no means arbitrary.

On the contrary, the laws from Shuihudi display a sophisticated awareness of such concepts as criminal intent, judicial procedure, defendants' rights, and the difference between what we would call common law and statutory law. Defendants were even allowed to appeal for a second inquest if they or their families disagreed with the results of the first. From our point of view, the most alienating aspects of the Qin laws are probably the mutilating punishments that they countenance, the instruments of collective responsibility, and the right of a father to demand the death of an "unfilial" son.

But even from our modern perspective, conditioned by our more liberal juridical traditions, it is impossible to deny the basic justice of the Qin laws. If a man or woman was to be punished, it could not be simply at the whim of an invidious magistrate. Every subject of the Qin state could expect to be treated according to unambiguous and predetermined protocols—and that is precisely the judicial environment that every viable law code must bring about.[19] In sum, if these laws allow us any opportunity to speculate about the rapid ascendancy of Qin, then we must acknowledge that their outstanding feature is not their cruelty but their fairness.[20]

To be sure, some traditional scholars were able to arrive at similar conclusions on the basis of materials that had always been available,[21] but statements about the Qin legal system had to remain tentative before the excavation of the tomb at Shuihudi. The continuing excavations in the People's Republic of China and the unimagined artifacts that they produce invite us to construct a thicker description of the early Chinese intellectual world than would have been feasible in previous generations.

What would a thick description of Chinese philosophy look like? It would begin by focusing on cultural phenomena that appear strange or surprising to us today.[22] Consider Chinese names. Few accounts of classical Chinese thought have discussed or appreciated the fact that many early Chinese names reveal distinctive characteristics of the people they refer to.[23] We do not normally think of "Descartes" or "Hobbes" as names that shed any particular light on Descartes or Hobbes as people. But Chinese names of this type are widespread. Two famous examples are the strikingly appropriate names Wen 文 (Cultured) and Wu 武 (Warlike), which refer to the founding kings of the Zhou 周 dynasty.[24] The former is regularly praised for his moral and administrative accomplishments, the latter for his martial prowess and terrifying visage. Traditionally, Wen and Wu have been understood as posthumous names (*shi* 謚/諡), but recent evidence suggests that the kings may have acquired those names during their lifetimes.[25] What is noteworthy, in either case, is that the names Wen and Wu seem to say something about the kings who bore them. Wen and Wu are hardly exceptional in this respect; they belong to a large class of early Chinese names that convey a definite meaning. Some further examples are presented below.[26]

The *Mozi* contains this story:

> 昔者宋文君鮑之時，有臣曰祝觀辜固嘗從事於厲，祩子杖楫出，與言曰：觀辜，是何珪璧之不滿度量，酒醴粢盛之不淨潔也，犧牲之不全肥，春秋冬夏選失時，豈女為之與？意鮑為之與？觀辜曰：鮑幼弱，在荷繈之中，鮑何與識焉？官臣觀辜特為之。祩子舉楫而槁之，殪之壇上。當是時，宋人從者莫不見，遠者莫不聞，著在宋之春秋。諸侯傳而語之曰：諸不敬慎祭祀者，鬼神之誅，至若此其憯遬也。以若書之說觀之，鬼神之有，豈可疑哉。[27]

> In the past, in the time of Bao, Lord Wen of Song [r. 610–589 B.C.], there was a functionary named Priest Guangu, who was following the service for a ghost.[28] The medium[29] emerged with a staff and said to him: "Guangu, why are the jade tablets and disks not up to their full measure? Why is the wine and millet unclean? Why are the sacrificial victims not unblemished and fat? Why are the offerings of spring, autumn, winter, and summer not timely? Did you do this, or did Bao do this?"
>
> Guangu said: "Bao is young and immature; he is still in his diapers. What could Bao know about this? This was done expressly by the functionary in charge, Guangu."
>
> The medium lifted his staff and beat him, killing him on top of the altar. At the time, those people in Song who were participating in the ceremony all saw it; those who were far away all heard of it. It is written in the annals of Song. The feudal lords transmitted [the story] and commented: "For whoever is not reverent and cautious about sacrifices, the punishment of the spirits is even as swift as this." Seeing that the story is in several books, one can hardly doubt that ghosts exist.[30]

The name Guangu 觀辜 means, literally, Faulty Observance. In a parallel account in a different text, the priest's name is given as Yegu 夜古, which does not have any obvious meaning.[31] This evidence indicates that there was a popular ancient story in which a negligent priest was said to have been bludgeoned to death by a medium possessed by an irate spirit. In at least one version of the story, the name of the offending cleric was transmitted as Faulty Observance, which someone must have found fitting. Even if the story is not entirely fictitious, it is difficult to believe that the name Guangu was given at birth. We must take it as an epithet.[32]

There was a well-known jester in the fourth century B.C. named Chunyu Kun 淳于髡.[33] This figure is noteworthy because he is one of the most famous early examples of a *zhuixu* 贅婿 (excrescent son-in-law), that is, a husband who is forced on account of indigence to reside with his wife's family.[34] He is usually referred to as Chunyu Kun,[35] but Kun is best understood as an epithet: Shaved (like a slave).[36] Like Guangu, Kun is probably not a name that was given at birth.

In *Analects* 13.18, we read:

> 葉公語孔子曰：吾黨有直躬者，其父攘羊，而子證之。孔子曰：吾黨之直者異於是，父為子隱，子為父隱，直在其中矣。[37]
>
> The Lord of She said to Confucius: "In our village there is one Upright Gong. His father stole a sheep, so the son testified against him."
>
> Confucius said: "The upright people of my village are different from this. The fathers are willing to conceal their sons; the sons are willing to conceal their fathers. Uprightness lies therein."

Most commentators agree that *zhi* (upright) is an appellation, but Gong is usually accepted as a genuine name. *Gong* means "self," however, and is not common as a personal name. Taking the entire phrase as an epithet—Self-Righteous—recasts the entire dynamic of this exchange. For then the Lord of She would be saying: "In our village there is one Self-Righteous..."—an implicit criticism in line with Confucius' response. As the passage is usually read, Confucius is understood to be rebuking the Lord of She for respecting a man who would testify against his father.

The origin of such a nickname is related in *Springs and Autumns of Mr. Lü* (*Lüshi chunqiu* 呂氏春秋):

> 襄子謁於代君而請觴之，先令舞者置兵其羽中數百人，先具大金斗。代君至，酒酣，反斗而擊之，一成，腦塗地。舞者操兵以鬥，盡殺其從者。因以代君之車迎其妻，其妻遙聞之狀，磨笄以自刺，故趙氏至今有磨笄之山與反斗之號。[38]
>
> Viscount Xiang [of Zhao, r. 474–425 B.C.], being visited by the Lord of Dai, proposed a banquet. He ordered several hundred dancers to place weapons in their plumed costumes and also prepared a large metal ladle. The Lord of Dai arrived, and when he was intoxicated with liquor, [Viscount Xiang] turned the ladle over and struck him; with one blow, his brains were spattered on the ground. The dancers grasped their weapons and attacked, killing all of his followers. Then [Viscount Xiang] used the chariot of the Lord of Dai to welcome the latter's wife [who was Viscount Xiang's sister],

> but when his wife heard the report from a distance, she sharpened a hairpin and stabbed herself with it. Thus to this day the House of Zhao has the mountain called Sharpened Hairpin[39] and the appellation Overturned Ladle.

We are given to understand that Zhao finally annexed the territories of Dai. To my knowledge, Fandou 反斗 does not occur in any other context as a wry appellation of the Zhao clan. But the examples of Self-Righteous and Faulty Observance show that nicknames of this kind were not uncommon. One can imagine detractors referring to Overturned Ladle and his ill-gotten gains.

The supposed personal name of Sun Bin 孫臏, the famous military strategist, is also an epithet.

> 孫臏嘗與龐涓俱學兵法。龐涓既事魏，得為惠王將軍，而自以為能不及孫臏，乃陰使召孫臏。臏至，龐涓恐其賢於己，疾之，則以法刑斷其兩足而黥之，欲隱勿見。[40]

> Sun Bin used to study military methods together with Pang Juan [d. ca. 341 B.C.]. When Pang Juan began to serve Wei, he became a general under King Hui [r. 370–335 B.C.] but did not consider his own abilities equal to those of Sun Bin. Thus he secretly summoned Sun Bin. When Bin arrived, Pang Juan was afraid that [Bin] was more talented, and, because he hated him, he used the penal laws to cut off [Bin's] two feet and have him tattooed, desiring thus to keep him hidden and unseen.

Since *bin* means "to amputate the feet," the name Sun Bin means precisely Sun Whose Legs Were Cut Off (or, perhaps more humorously, Kneecaps Sun). In a stimulating article, Jens Østergård Petersen contends further that the supposed surname Sun should be taken as *xun* 遜, "to flee"; thus Sun Bin is The Legless One Who Fled. Following the earlier suggestion of Jaroslav Průšek,[41] Petersen argues that the name of Sun Bin's famous ancestor Sun Wu 孫武 (Warlike), the putative author of the *Sunzi,* is also "as fictitious as [it] is meaningful."[42]

Petersen presents several other instances of meaningful personal names in early China, which, for the sake of concision, are not rehearsed here. He has found, among other impeccable examples, a dissimulating poser named Deceptive and a presumptuous retainer named Reckless.[43] One other obvious example that defies easy explanation is the personal name of Lord Wen of Jin 晉文公 (r. 635–627 B.C.): Chonger 重耳 (Double Ears), which apparently refers to some distinctive physical feature.

Lord Wen is also noted for his "linked ribs" (*pianxie* 駢脅), but it is not clear how the name Chonger could refer to his unusual ribs.[44]

These examples demonstrate that it was common in early China to refer to people by appellations that could not have been birth names but must be interpreted as meaningful epithets. Other examples could doubtless be added to the above.[45] Recognizing this problem has consequences for an assessment of early Chinese texts. Once we see, for example, that the name of the negligent priest means Faulty Observance, we may be inclined to treat the entire story more like one of those lovely allegories in the *Zhuangzi* 莊子 (with such fabulous characters as Nag the Hump 哀駘它 and Fancypants Scholar 士成綺)[46]—and less like history *wie es eigentlich gewesen.* The fact that these names can even appear in works pretending to be historical only underscores our obligation to be aware of them. Students of early China may wish to make a habit of asking themselves whether the personal names that they encounter in their research might be construed as meaningful epithets like Faulty Observance and Kneecaps Sun.

Ancient writers were aware of such names; indeed, they approved of them. There was a general sense that personal names, like all names, should reflect reality. For example, we read in the "Shifa" 謚法 (a manual on selecting appropriate posthumous names):[47]

> 謚者行之跡也。號者功之表也。車服者位之章也。是以大行受大名，細行受細名。行出於己，名生於人。[48]
>
> Posthumous names are traces of conduct. Appellations are indications of accomplishment. Chariot and dress are displays of status. Therefore great conduct receives a great name; trifling conduct receives a trifling name. Conduct emerges from the self; the name is born of others.

The beginning of this passage is not surprising; most historians of early China would readily agree that posthumous names were chosen to encapsulate a judgment about the deceased's conduct in life. However, the text says more than that: it is not only posthumous names that should be appropriate; *every* name should "indicate" or "display" the accomplishments and status of the person in question. In technical terms, the passage is saying that a person's several names—the *shi,* the *hao* (appellation), and the *ming* (personal name), which, in later times at least, are kept strictly distinct[49]—are all essentially of the same kind. Choosing the right appellation for someone was conceived as simply another species of "rectifying names" (*zhengming* 正名), a primary concern of early Chinese philosophy.[50] Naming was an essentially philosophical act.

Another name whose significance has often been misunderstood is Xi Wangmu 西王母, which denotes the goddess of immortality. The stock translation of Xi Wangmu is Queen Mother of the West, but this reflects a misprision. "Queen mother" in everyday English refers to the mother of a ruler, but it is not suggested in any of the traditions concerning Xi Wangmu that she earned her title by virtue of being the mother of a king.[51] The translation "Queen Mother" may be intended as something similar to "royal mother"—but if this is what translators have in mind, they should say "Royal Mother" rather than "Queen Mother."

However, "Royal Mother" would still be imprecise, because *wang* in this context probably does not carry its basic meaning of "king, ruler." *Wangmu* is a cultic term referring specifically to a deceased paternal grandmother. This usage is explained in the classical glossary called *Erya* 爾雅:

> 父為考，母為妣。父之考為王父，父之妣為王母。王父之考曾祖王父，王父之母為曾祖王母。[52]
>
> One's father is one's *kao* [i.e., "deceased father"]; one's mother is one's *bi* [i.e., "deceased mother"]. One's father's *kao* is one's *wang*-father; one's father's *bi* is one's *wang*-mother. One's *wang*-father's *kao* is one's ancestral *wang*-father; one's *wang*-father's *bi* is one's ancestral *wang*-mother.

The precise meaning of *wang* in this passage is not obvious. The commentator Guo Pu 郭璞 (A.D. 276–324) suggests, plausibly, that "one adds *wang* in order to honor them" 加王者尊之. The opinion of Hao Yixing 郝懿行 (1757–1825) is similar: "*Wang* means 'great,' 'lordly'; it is an appellation honoring one's superiors. Thus *wang*-father and *wang*-mother are also called 'great father' and 'great mother'" 王，大也，君也，尊上之稱。故王父母亦曰大父母也.[53]

Although this nomenclature is rare in received texts,[54] excavated manuscripts reveal that it was standard in ancient formulaic language. In the almanacs 日書 from Shuihudi, various diseases are said to be cured by offerings to *wangfu* or *wangmu*, as in the following example:

丙丁有疾，王父為祟。得之赤肉、雄雞、酒。庚辛病，壬有閒，癸作。若不作，煩居南方，歲在南方，赤色死。戊己有疾，巫堪行，王母為祟。得之於黃色索魚、堇酒。壬癸病，甲有閒，乙作。若不作，煩居邦中，歲在西方，黃色死。[55]

If there is an illness on *bing* and *ding* days, it is a calamity caused by *wangfu*. One gets it[56] from red meat, roosters, and liquor. On *geng* and *xin* days, [the subject will still be] sick; on *ren* day he will begin to be cured; on *gui* day there will be activity [i.e., the subject will arise from bed]. If there is no activity, then those who dwell in the south will have headaches; those who are in the south will be injured; and those associated with the color red will die.

If there is an illness on *wu* and *ji* days, Shaman Kan carries it out [?];[57] it is a calamity caused by *wangmu*. One gets it from yellow dried fish and tawny liquor. On *ren* and *gui* days, [the subject will still be] sick; on *jia* day he will begin to be cured; on *yi* day there will be activity. If there is no activity, then those who dwell in the center of the state will have headaches; those who are in the west will be injured; and those associated with the color yellow will die.

It is crucial to keep in mind that *wangfu* and *wangmu* refer to one's grandfather and grandmother after they are deceased and not while they are still alive—in other words, only when they have entered the spirit world. This is significant, because in other contexts, *wang* is used more generally to denote spirits of any kind. A good example appears in an offhand comment by the philosopher Xunzi 荀子 (third century B.C.):

郊者，并百王於上天而祭祀之。[58]

In the suburban sacrifice, one unites the many *wang* with Heaven Above and sacrifices to them.

The commentary of Yang Liang (A.D. 818) notes, reasonably, that *baiwang* should be understood as *baishen* 百神, "the many spirits."[59] Indeed, there is a similar passage in the *Ritual Records* (*Liji* 禮記) that reads *baishen* instead of *baiwang*.[60] The use of the term *wang* to denote a spirit may not be common, but it should not be considered exceptional either, because lofty terrestrial titles—such as *jun* 君, "lord"; *gong* 公 "lord, duke"—frequently appear in the names of spirits and deities, including those that are construed as female.[61]

There seems to be abundant textual support, then, for taking the *wang* in Xi Wangmu in the sense of "spirit, divinity." After all, she is a goddess, not a queen. If we apply the terminology of *Erya* and the Shuihudi almanacs, then Xi Wangmu means precisely "Deceased Paternal Grandmother of the West." But since the implication of her title is evidently that she is a powerful spirit—like a deceased paternal grandmother—a more general rendering, such as "Spirit Mother of the West," may best capture the sense of Xi Wangmu.[62]

Why is *wang* used in this sense of "powerful spirit"? There are several defensible explanations. One was offered by Guo Pu and Hao Yixing: *wang* is simply an honorific epithet. But there are other possibilities. In this sense, *wang* might be understood as *wang* 往, "to depart": thus *wangmu* 王/往母, "departed mother";[63] after all, *wang* 王 is used in place of *wang* 往 in the *Odes*.[64] Moreover, Edward H. Schafer demonstrated in a brilliant article that *wang* 王 belongs to a series of words with strong connotations of shamanism, including *kuang* 狂, "maniacal, possessed"; *wang* 尪, "(crippled) shaman"; and *kuang* 匡, "male shaman." Schafer concludes: "this group of words suggests strongly the shamanistic character of the prehistoric Chinese king, and probably also the delirium of the great shaman when possessed by a spirit."[65]

Finally, *wàng* 王 can function as a verb of obscure meaning that is occasionally used as the predicate of a subject *shen* 神: spirits naturally *wang*. The most familiar example appears in the *Zhuangzi:*

> 澤雉十步一啄，百步一飲，不蘄畜乎樊中。神雖王，不善也。[66]
>
> The swamp pheasant must take ten steps for one peck and a hundred steps for one drink, but it does not ask to be kept in a cage. Although its spirit will *wang*, it will not be in its element.

In other words, even though the "spirit" of a caged pheasant will be well nourished, the bird is more content wandering along the marshes—a more difficult life, but a freer one. (Zhuangzi's diction implies subtly that a caged pheasant is dead, like an ancestral spirit that one feeds with sacrifices.) This *wang* is usually glossed as the equivalent of *wang* 旺/暀, "to flourish, to gleam."[67] Thus if *wang* was understood in the ancient language as an attribute of satiated spirits, *wangmu* 王/旺/暀母 may mean something like "*wang*ing mother, numinous mother."[68] This is surely closer to what devotees understood by the name than the conceptually thin title, "Queen Mother of the West," that sinologists have conferred on the goddess.

The interrelations among all these words pronounced *wang* may remind one of another pervasive feature of Chinese philosophical literature, namely, its use of "paronomastic glosses," by which certain essential terms are explained by homophones (or near homophones) with more accessible meanings.[69] The most frequently cited example is the phrase *Ren zhe, ren ye* 仁者，人也, which appears in the *Application of Equilibrium* 中庸, one of the central texts in the classical tradition.[70] The first *ren* (humanity) denotes the virtue that Confucius singled out as the most important goal of self-cultivation.[71] Understandably, people wanted to know precisely what *ren* meant, and Confucius was generally unwilling to explain it simply. The Confucian *Analects* are replete with episodes wherein one or more of the Master's disciples ask whether such-and-such an action or attitude qualifies as *ren;* Confucius' answers are typically vague, and he is careful never to give a neat definition.[72] (In practical terms, Confucius' *ren* means something close to acting with respect to another as one would want another to act with respect to oneself if one were in that other person's situation.)[73]

The second *ren* means "person," "human being."[74] These characters are not simply homophones today; rather, they probably represent two different ways of writing the same word. (The reconstructed Old Chinese pronunciation for both characters is *nin.)[75] *Ren* 仁 came to be the special character used in those instances where the "state of being human"—or the virtue of "humanity"—was intended. So the *Application of Equilibrium* defines the term as follows: "'Humanity' is 'human.'" This paronomastic gloss is more informative than it may seem: it tells us that the virtue of *ren* originates among people and that its very etymology is bound up in the word for "human being."[76] In giving its own pithy definition of *ren,* the *Application of Equilibrium* appeals to the reader's eagerness to be provided with a simple and memorable explanation of a concept that frustrated Confucius' own disciples.

Such paronomastic glosses, however, cannot always be taken to be etymological in nature. For example, the scholastic text known as *Comprehensive Discussions in the White Tiger Hall* (*Baihu tong* 白虎通) uses paronomasia to explain why there are nine conventional groups of kinfolk:

> 尚書曰：以親九族。族所以有九何？九之為言究也。親疏恩愛究竟，謂之九族也。[77]

> It is said in the *Exalted Documents:* "Thus he was intimate with the nine branches of his kin."[78] Why is it that there are nine branches of kin? "Nine"

> (*k^{w}u:) is as if to say "end" (*kuw:).[79] The kindness among relatives persists to the end, so one refers to the nine branches of kin.[80]

Such casuistry has earned the *Comprehensive Discussions* a dubious reputation among modern readers, but this posited connection between "nine" 九 and "end" 究 rests on one of the basic convictions of Chinese philosophy. Language corresponds to reality; words that belong together consequently ought to denote concepts that belong together. Though "nine" and "end" are not obviously cognate, they happen to be nearly homophonous in Old (as in Modern) Chinese and are represented by two characters that share the same graph: 九. How is a translator supposed to convey all this? The case of "humanity" presents less of a problem, because there we can safely use two words with the same English root (e.g., "humanity" and "human") to capture the intended etymological thrust. But to capture all the dimensions of this gloss, the translator would have to find two unrelated words for "nine" and "end" that not only sound similar but actually appear similar when written out. The force of this statement transcends language, because it derives from the very shape of the written characters. One can appreciate how the translator of ancient Chinese philosophy attempts to translate not merely a different language, but an aesthetic sensibility that must be completely alien to readers of languages written in an alphabetic script.[81]

Other instances of paronomasia in ancient Chinese philosophical writing fall into yet a third category. Consider the following example from the *Mencius:*

> 孟子曰：君子之於物也，愛之而弗仁。於民也，仁之而弗親。親親而仁民，仁民而愛物。[82]
>
> Mencius said: The noble man is kind to animals, but does not treat them with humanity. He treats people with humanity, but he is not intimate with them. He is intimate with his parents and treats people with humanity; he treats people with humanity and is kind to animals.

In other words, the noble man treats different kinds of creatures according to a scale of moral obligations, ranging from "being kind" to animals to "being intimate" with his own parents. The crux of the statement comes in the phrase *qinqin,* translated above as "being intimate with one's parents." The basic sense of *qin* is "close"; the specialized sense of "parent" (or "agnatic relative") is derived from the fact that one's parents are the people who are closest to oneself. So *qinqin* incorporates a variety of meanings: "being close to those whom one ought to be close to"; "treating one's parents as one ought to treat one's parents"; and so forth. Classical readers would have recognized these several meanings instantly, as have most commentators through the centuries.

What is no longer obvious—and what translators rarely convey—is that the words *ren* (humanity) and *qin* (intimate) are cognate in Old Chinese. The reconstructed Old Chinese pronunciations are *nin and *snin,[83] respectively. This point is essential to understanding the rhetorical aspect of Mencius' statement: he is saying that we should treat people with *ren,* or "humanity," for this is what they deserve—but we should treat the people who are closest to us in a way that is related to *ren* but reserved for our parents and intimate relations. The link between *ren* and *qin* would have made this seem like a perfectly natural claim to an ancient Chinese audience. This is an example of a third type of paronomasia: words that sound similar but are written with characters whose forms do not reveal these connections. Such cases can be more problematic for the translator still, because centuries of sound change have frequently obscured the paronomasia.

Mencius plays on this family of words on a number of occasions.[84] Elsewhere, he declares:

> 不信仁賢，則國空虛。[85]
>
> If [the lord] does not trust men of humanity and talent, the state will become empty and void.

The word for humanity here is the same *ren* discussed above. The new term is *xin* 信, or "trust." The graphic composition of this character is telling: the grapheme on the left is a form of *ren* 人, "human," and is borrowed for its phonetic value. For it turns out that *xin,* too, is cognate with *ren* 人 and *ren* 仁. The Old Chinese reconstruction of *xin* is *snins, which represents the same root *nin with a prefix and the prolific Old Chinese suffix *-s. The etymology of the word *xin* is not lost on Mencius. He juxtaposes the two words so as to highlight why it is natural that "men of humanity" should be "trusted": the word for "trust" is simply a derivative of the word for "humanity."

Mencius then proceeds further in this vein by bringing in *xian* 賢, or "men of talent." The Old Chinese pronunciation of *xian* is *gīn, and the reigning assonance among *ren, xin,* and *xian* is no coincidence: *nin, *snins, *gīn. *Xian* is not cognate with *ren* and *xin,* but the manifest similarity in sound sufficed for Mencius' purposes. We are to infer that we should implicitly "trust" men of "humanity," because *xin* and *ren* share the same root and also that we should "trust" men of "talent," because *xian* belongs to the same rhyme group. These ideas are conveyed in Old Chinese entirely by suggestion and association. Mencius is tapping into fundamental linguistic connections that would have been second nature to a speaker of Mencius' language.

Ancient Chinese writers themselves were aware that the words with which they expressed their ideas could be skillfully chosen to resonate with correspondences ingrained in the audience's mind. Xunzi once remarked:

> 名有固善，徑易而不拂，謂之善名。[86]
>
> Names have intrinsic goodness. If they are direct, easy, and not contrary [to their meaning], they are called good names.

Scholars are often perplexed by this statement, since it comes at the end of a long and insightful discussion that anticipates Saussure in demonstrating the intrinsic arbitrariness of names. How could Xunzi suddenly shift his ground and argue that good names bear some elemental relation to their meanings? It seems that Xunzi went even beyond Saussure and recognized a linguistic phenomenon similar to the "nonarbitrariness theory of language" of Roman Jakobson: the names of objects are indeed absolutely arbitrary, but from the point of view of speakers, certain names may still seem especially appropriate. (To use Jakobson's example: when a German-speaking woman was told that the word for "cheese" in French is *fromage,* she replied, "*'Käse' ist doch viel natürlicher!*")[87] Thus Xunzi well understood the power of Mencius' arguments, which built on the ancient Chinese reader's sense that such words as "humanity" and "trust" belong together.[88] *Nin and *snins sound right.

Translators cannot hope to preserve this dimension of Mencius' writing, precisely because the essential linguistic connections would not exist in any other language. Similarly, it is impossible to "translate" the gloss on "nine" and "end," because the connection between the two concepts exists only in the context of the Chinese writing system. So the best that we can do in such instances is to translate the text as faithfully as possible and then explain the dimensions of the original in the form of annotation. But the annotation is crucial.[89] If we fail to highlight these problems, we fail to convey to a foreign reader the world of concerns of the original text in its culture. The result would be the transmogrification —not translation—of a complex Chinese statement into specious and facile English.

"Translation" must entail more than that. As Quine demonstrated long ago,[90] the problem of translation is at root an ontological problem: it is not merely the routine transposition of a set of words in one language into another set in another language but the attempt to recreate a speaker's entire world view in an idiom that fits an observer's entirely separate world view. We must translate worlds, not words.

—1—

The Reception of the *Odes* in the Warring States Era

A thick description of Chinese philosophy requires, in addition to the desiderata outlined in the Introduction, the breakdown of certain anachronistic disciplinary boundaries. Ancient Chinese thinkers did not have to choose among fields such as philosophy, history, or literature; they were equally conversant with all these branches of learning and produced works that cannot be comprehended by focusing merely on their philosophical, historiographical, or literary contributions. The early reception of the *Canon of Odes* (*Shijing* 詩經) is a case in point. Students of Chinese literature have long recognized the towering status of this text in all periods of Chinese literary history, but accounts of Chinese philosophy rarely consider its use in philosophical disputation. The reason is that the typical academic curriculum treats the *Odes,* because they are poems, as literature, not philosophy. But Chinese philosophers continually found philosophical meaning in the *Odes* in a manner so peculiar and alien to modern tastes that a reader today cannot appreciate the character of early Chinese philosophy without seriously investigating the place of this text in their world.

Traditional commentators to the *Odes* were known for their attempts to explicate the abstruse moral and political import of that collection. For centuries, their efforts were considered respectable, but some twentieth-century critics, both in China and the West, vilipended such commentary as "exegetical debris" obscuring the supposed simplicity of these songs. Herbert A. Giles, for example, complained: "Early commentators, incapable of seeing the simple natural beauties of the poems, which have furnished endless household words and a large stock of phraseology to the language of the present day... set to work to read into country-side ditties deep moral and political significations. Every single one of the immortal Three Hundred has thus been forced to yield some hidden meaning and point an appropriate moral."[1]

Presumably, the "early commentators," whom Giles declined to identify more closely, are to be understood as the author or authors of the so-called Minor Prefaces (*xiaoxu* 小序) preceding each piece in the canon. The attribution of these prefaces is another disputed matter, but it is widely accepted that the later portions of these prefaces (the *houxu* 後序) were written either by "Master Mao" 毛公—a reference to Mao Heng 毛亨 or Mao Chang 毛萇 (both second century B.C.), who redacted the received version of the text—or perhaps by Wei Hong 衛宏 (A.D. first century).[2] The fact that all of these figures lived during the Han dynasty raises a crucial point: revisionist commentators like Giles, who fault earlier interpreters of the *Odes* for reading too much into what appear to be straightforward poems, seem to view this hermeneutic tradition as an objectionable phenomenon of imperial times. The idea is that the ancient poems were originally mere "country-side ditties," which the ancients understood as such but which imperial commentators, for political or perhaps doctrinal reasons, distorted and misrepresented.[3]

One important area of research that has been neglected is the reception of the *Odes* in pre-imperial times.[4] While no complete and systematic exegesis of the *Odes* like that of the Prefaces has been transmitted from Zhou times, the extant texts still contain many interpretations, both implicit and explicit, of particular pieces. A survey of pre-imperial citations of the *Odes* demonstrates that already in Zhou times these poems were normally interpreted in the politicized manner that the later tradition enthusiastically adopted (and eventually ossified). These Zhou texts, which contain the oldest readings of the *Odes* available to us, do not always agree with the later Prefaces on specific details,[5] but there is strong evidence of a consensus that a thoughtful and persuasive interpretation of a canonical ode was one that elucidated its moral or political dimensions. If we are to believe that the traditional commentators have misunderstood the *Odes,* then we must acknowledge that this kind of "misunderstanding" goes back to high antiquity—perhaps even as far back as the time of the *Odes* themselves.[6]

The following pre-imperial texts (listed roughly in chronological order) contain references to or quotations from the *Odes: Analects, Mozi, Mencius, Xunzi, Zuo Commentary to the Springs and Autumns* (*Zuozhuan* 左傳), *Discourses of the States* (*Guoyu* 國語), *Canon of Filial Piety* (*Xiaojing* 孝經),

Springs and Autumns of Master Yan (*Yanzi chunqiu* 晏子春秋), *Springs and Autumns of Mr. Lü, Han Feizi* 韓非子, *Guanzi* 管子, *Application of Equilibrium,* and *Stratagems of the Warring States* (*Zhanguo ce* 戰國策). There are as yet but two archaeologically excavated texts that make substantive use of the *Odes: The Five Forms of Conduct* (*Wuxing* 五行) and *Jet-Black Robes* (*Ziyi* 緇衣).[7]

Altogether, these works include some 520 references[8]—a considerable total to be sure, but not an astonishingly large one given that a single Han text, the *Outer Commentary to the Hán Odes* (*Han-Shi waizhuan* 韓詩外傳), contains approximately 315. Moreover, the vast majority of these 520 references are not helpful to the project of reconstructing the Zhou understanding of the *Odes.* This is because references to the *Odes* come in various conventional forms. Most commonly, a speaker will simply borrow a well-known phrase or apposite line from the canon, and while these quotations can be rhetorically effective (when not overused), they rarely shed any light on the author's interpretation of the *Ode* itself.

For example, in the midst of a disquisition on ritual, the philosopher Xunzi wishes to prove that "when a feudal lord summons his ministers, the ministers do not wait for their horses to be yoked but rush off, having donned their clothing upside-down" 諸侯召其臣，臣不俟駕，顛倒衣裳而走.[9] Ode 100 in the Mao sequence ("Dongfang wei ming" 東方未明) furnishes a matchless precedent for this argument, and Xunzi does not hesitate to recite it:

顛之倒之	I was donning my clothing upside-down;
自公召之	there was a summons for me from my lord.

This kind of quotation tells us nothing about how Xunzi interpreted Mao 100 (which happens to be a particularly enigmatic poem). He is merely invoking the canonical status of the text in order to buttress an argument to which it is not otherwise germane.

This manner of citation is very common. In the same passage, Xunzi quotes Mao 168 ("Chuju" 出車) in order to prove that when the Son of Heaven summons his vassals, they drag their carriages to their horses (rather than waiting for the horses to be brought to them):[10]

我出我車	We went out with our carriages
于彼牧矣	to that pasture ground.
自天子所	From the seat of the Son of Heaven
謂我來矣	we were called to come.

Some other typical examples:

Mencius and Xunzi both cite the same lines from Mao 154 ("Qiyue" 七月) to describe the life of the common folk:[11]

晝爾于茅	The days you spend among the *mao* grasses;
宵爾索綯	at night you twist it into cord.
亟其乘屋	Quickly mount the roof!
其始播百穀	Start sowing the many grains!

Mencius cites Mao 179 ("Jugong" 車攻) to demonstrate that even a charioteer must drive according to the right protocols:[12]

不失其馳	They do not fail as they drive [the horses] to a gallop;
舍矢如破	they loose their arrows and[13] crush [the game].

In the *Zuo Commentary,* the Marquis of Jin 晉侯 cites Mao 193 ("Shiyue zhi jiao" 十月之交) as a preamble to a question about the significance of eclipses:[14]

此日而食	Now that the sun has been eclipsed—
于何不臧	Oh, what discord!

A different portion of the same poem is quoted elsewhere in the *Zuo Commentary* in an argument on the futility of prognostication in the absence of virtue:[15]

下民之孽	The depravity of the base people
不降自天	does not descend from Heaven.
噂沓背憎	Jabbering and babbling, hatred behind the back—
職競由人	strife simply arises from people.

Considering that this poem articulates an attitude toward Heaven and human beings comparable to the view later defended by Xunzi, it is not surprising that he too quoted these lines.[16]

The narrator of the *Zuo Commentary* cites Mao 198 ("Qiaoyan" 巧言) to illustrate the principle that treaties are of no use when there is no good faith:[17]

君子屢盟	The gentleman makes frequent covenants;
亂是用長	this is only an occasion for the growth of disorder.

Mencius quotes Mao 212 ("Datian" 大田) in order to prove that hereditary emolument was the custom in antiquity.[18]

雨我公田	Let it rain on our communal fields,
遂及我私	and then extend to our private ones.

Mozi is said to have cited Mao 235 ("Wenwang" 文王) with the intention of proving one of his favorite tenets, namely, the existence of ghosts.

文王在上	King Wen is above;
於昭于天	oh, how he shines in Heaven.
周雖舊邦	Although Zhou was an old nation,
其命維新	its mandate has renewed it.
有周不顯	Is the possessor of Zhou not illustrious?
帝命不時	Is the mandate of Di not timely?
文王陟降	King Wen ascends and descends,
在帝左右	on the left and the right of Di.

Mozi observes that King Wen, long dead, could hardly be "on the left and the right of Di"—unless he were a ghost.[19]

In an anecdote included in both the *Springs and Autumns of Mr. Lü* and *Springs and Autumns of Master Yan,* Yan Ying 晏嬰 (d. 500 B.C.) cites the following lines from Mao 239 ("Hanlu" 旱麓) before declaring that he will not seek fortune by betraying his lord:[20]

莫莫葛藟	Lush are the dolichos and *lei* creepers,
施于條枚	spreading[21] among the branches and stems.
豈弟君子	The serene gentleman
求福不回	will not seek fortune by crooked means.

Several early passages dealing with the construction of towers or pleasure parks make use of the ready canonical precedent in Mao 242 ("Lingtai" 靈臺), wherein it is recorded that King Wen did not oppress his populace when he built his magnificent tower.[22]

Similarly, both the *Discourses of the States* and the *Mencius* cite the last lines of Mao 255 ("Dang" 蕩) when they wish to refer to an age of doom preceding the transferal of Heaven's Mandate:[23]

殷鑒不遠	The mirror of Yin is not distant;
在夏后之世	it is in the age of the lords of Xia.

One could go on rehearsing such cases. But these ten examples suffice to show that citations of this sort, however skillful, do not necessarily disclose anything about the speakers' interpretations of the poems themselves. Yan Ying's anecdote is instructive. The first line of the quotation "Lush are the dolichos and *lei* creepers" 莫莫葛藟 is usually taken by commentators to have some kind of metaphorical or allegorical meaning: one must cling to the virtuous example of one's forefathers as a creeper clings to a tree.[24] But Master Yan is interested only in the aphorism that a gentleman does not seek fortune by crooked means.[25] One might argue that the dolichos and *lei* creepers constitute a meaningful image for Master Yan as well: for example, one could say that just as a vine cannot survive without its host, Master Yan cannot prosper if he betrays his lord. But his utterance would still be comprehensible without a creative reading along those lines. He might simply be taking advantage of the coincidence that Mao 239 contains a line providentially relevant to his own condition. In that respect, the example imparts no definitive hermeneutical information whatsoever.

The vast majority of pre-imperial references to the *Odes* are of this genus: because the text is cited as a canon or apophthegm rather than as a poem, the speaker simply does not reveal his personal interpretation—if he even has one. Moreover, such citations could become banal. For example, thinkers of various backgrounds intoned the famous lines from Mao 205 ("Beishan" 北山) when describing the supremacy of the Son of Heaven:[26]

溥天之下	Under billowing Heaven,
莫非王土	there is nothing that is not the king's land.
率土之濱	Along the sea boundaries of the land,
莫非王臣	there is no one who is not the king's servitor.

But few writers seemed to bear in mind that in the original poem the references to the king's power are bitter and ironic. Mencius stands out for rebuking an interlocutor who cited this ode as though it were simply a formulaic exaltation of the king's position; the real meaning of the ode (*shi zhi wei* 詩之謂), Mencius declares, is that "in toiling at the king's business, [the speaker] was unable to nourish his parents" 勞於王事，而不得養父母也.[27] Nevertheless, in remembering the original context of the odes that he quoted, Mencius was decidedly in the minority; most pre-imperial texts disregarded such concerns entirely.[28]

There is another inhibiting feature of the evidence: the distribution of the cited poems is significantly uneven. Specifically, there is a pronounced tendency among Zhou texts to cite poems in the sections of the *Odes* called "Elegantiae" 雅 (especially the "Greater Elegantiae" 大雅) and "Hymns" 頌 rather than those in the "Airs of the States" 國風.[29] The most frequently quoted "Air" is Mao 152 ("Shijiu" 鳲鳩), which is cited ten times in the literature.[30] By contrast, the most frequently quoted "Elegantiae," namely, Mao 235 ("Wenwang" 文王) and Mao 256 ("Yi" 抑), are cited twenty-five and twenty-six times, respectively; together, these two poems account for almost 10 percent of all the references. Moreover, only 107 of the 520 total references are from the "Airs," even though that section contains more poems than the others combined. (The "Airs" make up the first 160 of the 305 poems in the collection.) This means that a given poem in the "Elegantiae" or "Hymns" is roughly four times more likely to be cited than one in the "Airs."

Sometimes it is suggested that because the "Elegantiae" and "Hymns" deal with loftier themes than the "Airs," they were considered more suitable for citation.[31] On the one hand, there may be some merit to this explanation: it would be understandable if an author thought it perhaps safer to quote a grandiloquent paean titled "King Wen" (Mao 235) than an aubade called "The Girl Said, 'The Cock Croweth'" (Nü yue ji ming 女曰雞鳴, Mao 82).[32] There must be more to the issue, however. Pre-imperial texts still refer to the "Airs" regularly and without any hint of pudency. While they acknowledge the frank nature of the poems,[33] they do not assert that the "Airs" are shameful or inappropriate to elegant discourse.[34] The attitude expressed by Xunzi is characteristic: "There is a tradition about the lustfulness of the 'Airs of the States': 'They are replete with desire but do not seep beyond the [correct] stopping-point'" 國風之好色也，傳曰：盈其欲而不愆其止.[35]

It is less commonly observed that the "Airs" are more difficult, from a hermeneutical point of view, than the "Elegantiae" and "Hymns." The "Airs" are, after all, among the most opaque and powerful lyrics in world literature.[36] While the later sections are brimming with stately and self-contained pronouncements on virtue and ritual, the "Airs" present quotidian themes laced with pregnant natural imagery. A citation of an "Air" in the course of an argument requires a degree of critical attention that might overwhelm the rest of the passage. Consequently, when a quotation from the "Airs" does appear in a pre-imperial text, it usually forms the centerpiece of discourse. Rhetorically speaking, the "Elegantiae" and "Hymns" are more versatile, because one can refer to them casually without having to fear that they may prove so profound as to lead the reader astray. But for precisely this reason, we are most likely to learn about how early readers interpreted the *Odes* by studying their citations from the "Airs."

For material with which to confront the view of Giles and readers of a similar mindset, one can begin with an anecdote in the *Springs and Autumns of Mr. Lü:*

> 晉人欲攻鄭，令叔嚮聘焉，視其有人與無人。子產為之詩曰：子惠思我，褰裳涉洧；子不我思，豈無他士？叔嚮歸曰：鄭有人，子產在焉，不可攻也。秦、荊近，其詩有異心，不可攻也。晉人乃輟攻鄭。孔子曰：詩云：無競惟人。子產一稱而鄭國免。[37]
>
> The men of Jin wished to attack Zheng, so they ordered Shuxiang to go there as an envoy and see whether there were any [formidable] people there. Zichan recited an ode for him: "If you think kindly on me, raise your skirts and ford the Wei; if you do not think on me, are there no other men?" [Mao 87, "Qianchang" 褰裳].
>
> Shuxiang returned home and said: "There is a [formidable][38] man in Zheng: Zichan resides there, and [Zheng] cannot be attacked. It is near Qin and Chu, and his poem had a special intention. [Zheng] cannot be attacked." The men of Jin then ceased their attack on Zheng.
>
> Confucius said: "It is said in the *Odes:* 'Is he not mighty, he who is humane?' [Mao 256, "Yi"]. Zichan made one citation, and the state of Zheng was spared."[39]

This passage is important for several reasons. First, despite the prominent reference to Confucius, the text in which this anecdote is found, namely, the *Springs and Autumns of Mr. Lü,* is neither Confucian nor orthodox,[40] though the manner of citing and interpreting the *Odes* displayed by Zichan and Shuxiang may have been inspired by the Confucian tradition (more on this subject below). Furthermore, the text dates to the mid–third century B.C., several hundred years after the time of the *Odes* themselves but still long before those traditional commentators who displease modern critics. Finally, the two quotations from the *Odes* conform to the pattern of usage outlined above: the lines from Mao 87, a poem in the "Airs," represent the heart of the entire episode, whereas the verse from Mao 256, sententious but ancillary, serves only to summarize a point after it has already been brilliantly earned.

The key to the passage lies in the phrase *yixin* 異心 (literally "different heart"), the polysemous term that Shuxiang uses to characterize Zichan's poem. Shuxiang is able to discern that Zichan is a formidable man because his poem has significance beyond its literal meaning—rendered above as "special intention." So Shuxiang reports to his compatriots that Zheng cannot be attacked because it houses a gentleman who knows how to express himself in allusive verse. Someone as refined as that would surely be able to defend his homeland.

But in keeping with the amatory theme of Zichan's poem, *yixin* can also mean "inconstant heart," such as would be possessed by a lover who is about to confer his or her affections on someone else. In this affair of international diplomacy, Shuxiang deduces that the new mate would be either of two potent competitors: Qin and Chu. Zichan's quotation, therefore, has a twofold function: it demonstrates that Zheng is home to some redoubtable statesmen and at the same time sternly warns Jin not to abandon its former ally when there are other suitors to contend with.[41]

The figure of Confucius praises Zichan to the skies in the coda to this anecdote, but the cultured reader is probably supposed to admire Shuxiang as well. To understand a message as dense as Zichan's requires a schooled interpreter, and by correctly decoding Zichan's statement of intent, Shuxiang evidently prevented Jin from undertaking a disastrous invasion. Furthermore, Shuxiang himself exhibits the same facility with implicative language by describing Zichan's poem as having *yixin,* a phrase with two distinct, yet equally appropriate, senses.

This kind of deep reading, informed by the conviction that the verses of the *Odes,* however terrene their ostensible subject, must contain latent and sage meaning, is reminiscent of the Minor Prefaces.[42] The Minor Preface to Mao 87 is vague, but there can be no doubt that it too interprets the love relation in the poem as an emblem of a weightier matter of state:

> 褰裳，思見正也。狂童恣行，國人思大國之正己也。[43]
>
> In "Qianchang" there is yearning to be corrected. The "crazed boy" [the object of the speaker's recriminations] was acting recklessly, and the citizens yearned for a great state to govern them.

One would assume that according to this exegesis, the "crazed boy" refers to the debauched ruler of Zheng. The citizens are threatening to transfer their loyalty to a more deserving sovereign.[44] It is but a small step from the interpretive convention exemplified by Zichan and

Shuxiang to the systematic exegetical scheme that Giles detested: assigning "deep moral and political significations" to poems that do not seem to depict anything more remarkable than two lovers quarreling by a brook. As indicated above, only a small minority of the roughly five hundred references to the *Odes* in pre-imperial texts involve this degree of hermeneutic firepower. But where such references occur, the sources proceed consistently from the presupposition that the canonical poems lend themselves to multifaceted interpretations. No text ever claims that the poems are really just about work, love, and daily life.

Political interpretations of the "Airs," as in the anecdote about Zichan and Shuxiang, are common in the *Zuo Commentary*. In 583 B.C., we are told, the state of Jin required its weaker neighbor Lu 魯 to return the lands of Wenyang 汶陽 to Qi 齊 in order to placate the latter, even though it had but six years earlier asked Qi to hand over this same territory to Lu. A representative of the beleaguered state of Lu then addressed his counterpart from Jin:

> 大國制義，以為盟主，是以諸侯懷德畏討，無有貳心。謂汶陽之田，敝邑之舊也，而用師于齊，使歸諸敝邑。今有二命，曰：歸諸齊。信以行義，義以成命，小國所望而懷也。信不可知，義無所立，四方諸侯，其誰不解體？詩曰：女也不爽，士貳其行，士也罔極，二三其德。七年之中，一與一奪，二三孰甚焉？士之二三，猶喪妃耦，而況霸主？霸主將德是以，而二三之，其何以長有諸侯乎？詩曰：猶之未遠，是用大簡。行父懼晉之不遠猶而失諸侯也，是以敢私言之。[45]

> Your great state has come to preside over treaties by instituting righteousness; therefore, the feudal lords cherish your favors and dread your chastisements, without possessing a duplicitous heart. Regarding the fields of Wenyang: they were an old [territory] of our lowly fief; after you deployed your hosts against Qi, you brought about their return to our lowly fief. Now there is a second command; you say: "Return them to Qi." Trustworthiness in carrying out what is right and righteousness in consolidating your mandate—these are what our minor state admires and cherishes. But if your trustworthiness cannot be known and your righteousness has no foundation, then who among the feudal lords will not dissolve [their bonds with you]? It is said in the *Odes:* "The girl has not erred, but the gentleman has been two-faced in his conduct. The gentleman is unrestrained;[46] variable is his character" [Mao 58, "Meng" 氓]. Within seven years, you have granted us [the land] once and taken it away once—what can be more variable than this? When the gentleman [in the poem] was variable, he lost his mate; how

much more do you have [to lose] as a hegemonic lord? A hegemonic lord must apply virtue, but you are variable in this respect; how can you long retain [the allegiance] of the feudal lords? It is said in the *Odes:* "Your counsels have not reached far, and I greatly expostulate with you on this account" [Mao 254, "Ban" 板]. Fearing that Jin may lose [the allegiance] of the feudal lords through counsels that "have not reached far," I have ventured to speak to you privately about this.[47]

Whereas the quotation from the "Greater Elegantiae," for all its elegance, is once again entirely dispensable, the quotation from the "Airs" is central. The plenipotentiary from Lu compares the relationship between his state and Jin to that between the wronged speaker in Mao 58 and her faithless, desultory lover.[48] The consequence of dealing falsely with one's dependent neighbors is the termination of a liaison that ought to be mutually rewarding.

While it is evident that a free and open-ended approach to the *Odes* is essential to the speech above, the implicit interpretations are not so arcane as to make the argument difficult to follow. If we are to believe the pages of the *Zuo Commentary,* this sort of rhetoric, adorned with artfully chosen lines from the canon, was commonplace and plainly intelligible to all but the crudest participants in elite culture.[49] The disdain endured by those infamous characters who failed to comprehend the significance of an ode demonstrates that what we might term "Ode oratory" was considered to be a basic component of aristocratic education.[50]

Some of the more difficult citations of the *Odes,* in contrast, involve not political interpretations, which conform to familiar templates, but moral ones. A typical example is found in the *Springs and Autumns of Mr. Lü:*

詩曰：執轡如組。孔子曰：審此言也可以為天下。子貢曰：何其躁也？孔子曰：非謂其躁也，謂其為之於此，而成文於彼也，聖人組修其身，而成文於天下矣。[51]

It is said in the *Odes:* "I grasp the reins as though they were ribands" [Mao 38, "Jian xi" 簡兮].

Confucius said: "Examine this saying, and you can govern[52] the world."

Zigong [i.e., Duanmu Si 端木賜, b. 520 B.C.] said: "Why is he so impetuous?"

Confucius said: "[The poem] does not refer to his impetuousness but to his acting on what is near and bringing refinement to what is far. The

Sage cultivates himself as though he were weaving ribands and brings refinement to the world."[53]

The lesson of this exchange is that the moral meaning of the *Odes* cannot be found without penetrating to a layer of the language deep beneath the literal veneer. Zigong tries to understand why his master reveres this quote from Mao 38 and assumes that it must have something to do with the driver's evident haste. But Confucius replies that the fundamental meaning of the poem has nothing to do with the impetuousness of a charioteer: it lies instead in the basic Confucian notion that one influences the world by cultivating oneself.[54] While the details of his explanation are not entirely clear—does he mean that the driver will go on to accomplish great things because of the care with which he tends the reins?—his larger point about reading the *Odes* is unmistakable: Zigong will not understand the full import of the quote until he has broken out of a literal frame of mind.

Analects 14.39 is one of the most famous examples of moral reading:

子擊磬於衛。有荷蕢而過孔氏之門者，曰：有心哉，擊磬乎！既而曰：鄙哉硜硜乎！莫己知也，斯己而已矣。深則厲，淺則揭。子曰：果哉，末之難矣！[55]

The Master was playing chimes in Wei. Someone carrying a basket passed by Confucius' gate and said: "There is heart in the way he strikes the chimes!" Then he said: "It is vulgar, this sound of pebbles clanging! If there is no one who knows you, then just be by yourself. 'Where it is deep, they cross with their clothes on. Where it is shallow, they cross by lifting their clothes' [Mao 34, 'Pao you kuye' 匏有苦葉]."

The Master said: "Indeed! There is no refuting that!"[56]

This is a very dense passage. Commentators have debated its meaning for centuries (and there may also be some intractable problems of textual corruption).[57] Still, the basic elements are clear. The person "carrying a basket" reveals himself to be no simple peasant but a perspicacious anchorite who is able to discern the emotions that Confucius expresses through his music. Confucius is evidently distraught that he has not found anyone who knows him (*jizhi* 己知), that is, one who understands his philosophical outlook and lofty intentions. Then the critic cites a passage from Mao 34, suggesting that Confucius' anguish is comparable to that of the speaker in the poem, an unwed girl left waiting by a riverbank. Probably the hermit means to say that Confucius should simply cross his intellectual ford without worrying about who might accompany him.[58]

Another celebrated dialogue on the *Odes* appears in *Analects* 3.8:

> 子夏問曰：巧笑倩兮，美目盼兮，素以為絢兮，何謂也？子曰：繪事後素。曰：禮後乎？子曰：起予者商也！始可與言詩已矣。[59]
>
> Zixia [i.e., Bu Shang 卜商, b. 507 B.C.] asked: "'Oh, her artful smile is dimpled. Oh, her beautiful eye is black and white.[60] Oh, a plain [background] on which to apply the highlights' [Mao 57, "Shiren" 碩人].[61] What does this refer to?"
>
> The Master said: "In painting, everything follows the plain [background]."
>
> [Zixia] said: "Does ritual follow [in similar fashion]?"
>
> The Master said: "Shang, it is you who have inspired me. Finally I have someone to discuss the *Odes* with."[62]

Here too the interpretation of the ode is rarefied and confusing. Presumably Zixia means to say that the rituals, significant though they may be, still constitute nothing more than a set of embellishments that are effective only if practiced by those who have prepared themselves for the task. It is not the lady's makeup, but her pristine face, that makes her beautiful; by analogy, it is not our mastery of rituals, but the purity of our moral foundation, that indicates our moral worth. Devote yourself to self-cultivation, in other words, rather than to conspicuous propriety.[63]

Critics may contend that there is no trace of such a meaning in the original poem; indeed, if a verse devoted to a woman's cosmetics can be transformed into an epochal meditation on moral philosophy, what kind of reading would *not* be called for?[64] But Zixia is simply extending the liberal hermeneutic that was standard in his day and deriving a moral insight that even Confucius must applaud. If this example departs from the previous ones, the difference is only one of degree; what all these readings have in common is the idea that we have done the *Odes* justice when we can articulate an interpretation that is both instructive and unapparent.

This style of exegesis was congenial to the later Confucian Xunzi. For example, in the midst of excoriating sophists who enjoy perplexing people with paradoxes such as "Eggs have hair" 卵有毛, Xunzi declares:

> 君子行不貴苟難，說不貴苟察，名不貴苟傳，唯其當之為貴。詩曰：物其有矣，唯其時矣。此之謂也。[65]
>
> In his actions, the noble man does not esteem difficult acts if they are indecorous; in his speech, he does not esteem investigations if they are indecorous; in matters of reputation, he does not esteem traditions if they are indecorous. He esteems only what is appropriate. When it is said in the *Odes,* "The goods are in quantities, and yet they are timely" [Mao 170, "Yuli" 魚麗], this is what it refers to.[66]

A review of Mao 170 will reveal that the "goods"—fish and wine, perhaps gathered for a sacrifice—do not, in the context of the poem, pertain even remotely to indecorous casuistry (or any of the other targets of Xunzi's plentiful animadversions). Xunzi's motivation in quoting this line has to do with the word "timely" (*shi* 時): his point is that timely and suitable actions can bring about great quantities of goods without violating any moral principles. So the tactics of sophists and cozeners are not only disgraceful, but also unnecessary. One cannot take Xunzi literally when he says that Mao 170 "refers to" (*wei* 謂) this teaching. Rather, he means to say that he can illustrate his argument through a deep reading of the poem.[67]

In the same manner, he glosses the line "The crane squalls in the nine marshes;[68] the sound is heard in the skies" 鶴鳴于九皋，聲聞于天 (Mao 184, "Heming" 鶴鳴) as a reference to the ability of a moral paragon to influence the world even if his social position is base.[69] Here too, the original poem contains no manifest allegorical or metaphorical meaning,[70] but Xunzi invests it with profound moral significance. Transforming the world through the perfection of one's character is the highest aspiration of the early Confucian school.

The genius of the early Confucian masters for discovering complex moral attitudes in the formally simple language of the *Odes* is nowhere exhibited more fully than in *The Five Forms of Conduct,* a text that was lost in antiquity and remained utterly unknown until it was discovered at Mawangdui in the 1970s. Another manuscript of the work has recently been excavated in an elite tomb at Guodian, and most scholars now regard it as a revered Confucian document from the fourth century B.C.[71]

The Five Forms of Conduct weaves quotations from the *Odes* into its sustained moral discourse in a manner unparalleled by any other text.

> 不仁，思不能清；不智，思不能長。不仁不智。未見君子，憂心不能惙惙，既見君子，心不能悅。詩曰：未見君子，憂心惙惙，亦既見之，亦既覯之，我心則悅。此之謂。不仁，思不能清；不聖，思不能輕。不仁不聖，未見君子，憂心不能忡忡，既見君子，心不能降。[72]
>
> If one is not humane, one's thoughts cannot be clear. If one is not wise, one's thoughts cannot be extended. One will be neither humane nor wise. If one's "concerned heart cannot be agitated, not having seen one's lord," then one's "heart cannot be delighted, having seen one's lord." This is what is meant when it is said in the *Odes:* "Indeed when I have seen him, indeed when I have joined him, then my heart will be delighted" [Mao 14, "Caochong" 草蟲]. If one is not humane, one's thoughts cannot be clear. If one is not sage, one's thoughts cannot be light. One will be neither humane nor sage. If one's "concerned heart cannot be sorrowful, not having seen one's lord," then one's "heart cannot be calmed, having seen one's lord."

This argument is constructed around a series of intentional misquotations from Mao 14.[73] The poem, ostensibly a plaint of longing by an ardent woman, is typical of its genre:

喓喓草蟲	*Yao, yao,* chirp the insects in the grass.
趯趯阜螽	The hoppers jump about.
未見君子	I have not seen my lord,
憂心忡忡	and my sorrowful heart is agitated.[74]
亦既見之	Indeed, when I have seen him,
亦既覯之	indeed, when I have joined him,
我心則降	my heart will be calmed.
陟彼南山	I ascend that southern mountain,
言采其蕨	yea, and pick the ferns.
未見君子	I have not seen my lord,
憂心惙惙	and my sorrowful heart is sad.
亦既見之	Indeed, when I have seen him,
亦既覯之	indeed, when I have joined him,
我心則說	my heart will be delighted.
陟彼南山	I ascend that southern mountain,
言采其薇	yea, and pick the thorn-ferns.
未見君子	I have not seen my lord,

我心傷悲	and my heart is wounded with grief.
亦既見之	Indeed, when I have seen him,
亦既覯之	indeed, when I have joined him,
我心則夷	my heart will be at peace.

Even traditional commentators acknowledge the unvarnished eroticism of this song,[75] but *The Five Forms of Conduct* elevates it to the august plane of Confucian moral psychology by emphasizing that one would not be capable of feelings such as agitation and delight without the virtues of humanity and wisdom. To an uninitiated reader, the subject of the poem may appear to be amorous passion, but *The Five Forms of Conduct* advances a deeper interpretation: the poem is a statement of the power of properly stimulated emotions. (This attitude may remind us of Xunzi's assertion that the "Airs" are "replete with desire but do not seep beyond the [correct] stopping point.") The vivid affections of the speaker, far from being shameful, testify to the fervent development of her moral sense. A person who does not experience violent emotions—and struggle to keep them in check—must have stunted moral faculties. The technique of deliberately misquoting the lines of the canon has a striking effect: it allows the text to refer more forcefully to the putative spirit rather than the letter of the *Odes.*

The hermeneutical approach displayed by the texts surveyed above may not be unfamiliar to readers of Chinese literature, because, as we have noted, they rest on the same conviction that guided traditional critics and commentators into the twentieth century: a satisfactory interpretation of an ode must reveal its embosked wisdom. What is noteworthy, then, is not the nature of these interpretations, but their date: the latest texts examined above date to the third century B.C., while some of the oldest go back at least to the fifth. This is not yet the world of the *Odes* themselves—assuming that they are as old as the tradition holds them to be—but it is as close as we can come with the sources available today. We may never be able to discover what the *Odes* meant to the men and women in distant antiquity who composed them and first recited them, but at least we have some idea of how they were received by readers only a few generations later.

An instructive passage delineating the right way to read an ode appears in *Mencius* 5A.4 (the same scene, discussed above, in which Mencius admonishes his partner in dialogue for misapplying the lines "Under billowing Heaven, there is nothing that is not the king's land").

故說詩者，不以文害辭，不以辭害志，以意逆志，是為得之。[76]

> One who interprets the *Odes* does not take the words to distort the lyric or the lyric to distort [the poet's] intention. To engage this intention with one's own faculties—that is to comprehend it.[77]

The exhortation to avoid literalism would probably find favor among sophisticated readers today, whereas the duty to "engage the poet's intention" would be dismissed as a manifestation of the intentional fallacy.[78] But the aporia of the *Odes* renders Mencius' hermeneutic fruitfully indeterminate in practice.[79] To take the example of the crane calling in her paludal habitat: Xunzi's unique interpretation—that the sound of the crane symbolizes the noble man's transformative influence on the universe around him—emerged naturally from the culture of reading that flourished in his time. In that world, to insist that the poem had no larger significance would have been tantamount to diminishing the author's stature; for any poetaster can write a few lines about a bird calling in the wild, but only a sage can transmute such an ordinary image into a diuturnal instruction. No early reader would have dared to suggest that when the venerable authors of the *Odes* sang about a lovers' squabble, they did not expect us to infer a sublime moral.

Finally, when Confucius repeatedly accentuates the value of the *Odes* (as in *Analects* 16.13 and 17.9), his opinion is not to be taken lightly.[80] The intensity of the Confucian school's devotion to the *Odes* is revealed by their studied citations of that text. The overwhelming majority of pre-imperial references to the *Odes* appear in Confucian works, and it is to the Confucian tradition that we owe not only some of the most memorable examples of tropological reading but probably the very concept of interpreting the *Odes* in this manner. Participating in Confucian culture meant more than simply professing a congeries of ethical beliefs; Confucianism was also a distinct form of expression. Since Confucianism as an intellectual movement has been notoriously difficult to define, perhaps we might try a novel tack: the Confucians were philosophers who pondered the *Odes*. Other groups, such as the Mohists, may also have accepted the *Odes* as canonical, and writers with no partisan loyalties, such as the compilers of the *Lüshi chunqiu,* may have adopted the art of referring suggestively to the *Odes,* but it was the Confucians who made it the hallmark of their discourse.

—2—

Xunzi in the Light of the Guodian Manuscripts

Newly excavated manuscripts, as discussed in the Introduction, offer opportunities for a richer understanding of classical Chinese philosophy than was available to previous generations, even in China. After the discovery in 1993 of a cache of bamboo manuscripts in an elite tomb at Guodian, near Jingmen 荊門, Hubei province 湖北省,[1] the scholarly world celebrated the so-called Guodian *Laozi:* the three texts in the collection that are composed of material with close parallels in the received *Laozi.* Now that this initial period of excitement has begun to ebb, it has become clear that the other manuscripts from Guodian are at least as interesting as the *Laozi* texts from a philosophical point of view and probably even more important from a historical point of view. The Guodian tomb has yielded the earliest editions of two canonical Confucian texts: *Jet-Black Robes* (*Ziyi*) and *The Five Forms of Conduct* (*Wuxing*). Furthermore, the excavation yielded several previously unknown Confucian texts that shed light on the early history of the Confucian tradition.

This chapter will focus on several texts from this last category: *Cheng zhi wen zhi* 成之聞之;[2] *Honoring Virtue and Morality* (*Zun deyi* 尊德義); *The* Xing *Emerges from the Endowment* (*Xing zi ming chu* 性自命出); *The Six Forms of Virtue* (*Liude* 六德);[3] *Failure and Success Depend on Time* (*Qiongda yi shi* 窮達以時); *The Way of Tang and Yu* (*Tang Yu zhi dao* 唐虞之道);[4] *The Way of Integrity and Trustworthiness* (*Zhongxin zhi dao* 忠信之道); and some untitled miscellanies known as *Collections of Sayings* (*Yucong* 語叢). I believe that these works should be understood as doctrinal material deriving from a single tradition of Confucianism and datable to around 300 B.C. Of the surviving literature from the same period, they are closer to the *Xunzi* than to any other text and indeed anticipate several significant ideas in Xunzi's philosophy.[5] It is especially important to take note of these connections with Xunzi, in view of the emerging trend to associate the Guodian manuscripts with Zisi 子思,[6] the grandson of Confucius, whom Xunzi bitterly criticized.

These newfound Confucian texts contain a number of core ideas that distinguish them clearly from Mencian Confucianism and suggest the existence of a vibrant non-Mencian tradition of Confucianism that culminated in Xunzi's system of moral philosophy. Before the discovery of the Guodian tomb, there was very little evidence concerning Xunzi's intellectual antecedents, but it is apparent now that the Guodian manuscripts anticipate several characteristic themes in Xunzi's philosophy: (1) the notion of "human nature" (*xing* 性), including the controversy over whether the source of morality is "internal" or "external"; (2) the role of "learning" (*xue* 學) and "habitual practice" (*xi* 習) in moral development; (3) the content and origin of "ritual" (*li* 禮), by which human beings accord with the Way; (4) the conception of the ruler as the "mind" (*xin* 心) of the state; (5) and the psychological utility of "music" (*yue* 樂) in inculcating proper values. Each of these subjects will be addressed below.

One caveat before proceeding: for a number of reasons, the Guodian manuscripts are among the most difficult texts yet excavated. First, the writing of the Chinese characters presents more epigraphic problems than that of manuscripts recently excavated at sites such as Mawangdui. The manuscripts contain dozens of opaque graphs, including many that simply cannot be deciphered (so-called *daikao zi* 待考字).[7] Second, while the bamboo strips are well preserved, there are several lacunae, some of which occur, frustratingly, at crucial junctures in the argument of the texts. Finally, and most important, the texts had to be reconstructed strip by strip (since they were found, in the words of one Chinese expert, "in a pile"),[8] and determining the correct sequence is often a matter of educated guesswork. Consequently, the current arrangement of the material is often questionable.

For these reasons, the analysis and translations presented below are necessarily tentative. We can only hope that with more intensive study, and with the ongoing publication of the early Confucian texts housed at the Shanghai Museum, our understanding of the Guodian manuscripts will improve.

Famously, Xunzi believes that human nature is "evil" 惡 (or, more literally, "detestable")—by which he means that human beings naturally wish only to satisfy their appetitive and concupiscent desires. He is also famous for his distinctive use of the term *xing*, which is unlike that encountered, for example, in the *Mencius*. For Xunzi, *xing* means "what is so by birth" 生之所以然者,[9] or everything that we possess without having exerted any effort to obtain it. For Mencius, in contrast, *xing* represents the natural course of development that an organism may be expected to undergo given nourishing conditions, as has been persuasively demonstrated in a classic study by A. C. Graham.[10] This is no trivial point, because Xunzi's attempted refutation of Mencius is based on an understanding of the keyword *xing* that Mencius would not have accepted. The consequence of this difference in usage, as Dai Zhen 戴震 (1724–1777) pointed out, is that Xunzi uses *xing* to denote the characteristic that all members of a species have in common, whereas Mencius uses the term to denote the characteristic that distinguishes a species from all others.[11] (For example, all human beings have brains, but having brains does not distinguish human beings from all other species.)

The Guodian manuscripts consistently use *xing* in the same sense as Xunzi:[12]

> 四海之內其性一也。其用心各異，教使然也。[13]
>
> Within the four seas, [everyone's] *xing* is the same. That they use their minds differently is caused by teaching.

> 聖人之性與中人之性，其生而未有非之節於天[14]也，則猶是也・・・ ・・・此以民皆有性而聖人不可莫也。[15]
>
> The *xing* of a sage and the *xing* of a mediocre person are without exception regulated by Heaven at birth; thus they are as they are. . . . Therefore the people all have *xing*, and a sage cannot be without[16] one.

None of the Guodian manuscripts state explicitly that *xing* is evil, but it is evident that they regularly understand it to be naturally deficient of "morality" 義, which must be attained from "outside" 外. In this respect, the conception of *xing* in the Guodian manuscripts could hardly come closer to that of Xunzi. *The* Xing *Emerges from the Endowment* explains that our inborn nature is revealed spontaneously in our responses to the stimuli around us and that it is not naturally moral. We must strive to "bring morality inside ourselves":

凡人雖有性，心亡定志，待物而後作，待悅而後行，待習而後定。喜、怒、哀、悲之氣，性也。及其見於外，則物取之。性自命出，命自天降。道始於情，情生於性。始者近情，終者近義。知[情者能]出之，知義者能內之。[17]

Although everyone has a *xing*, the mind has no fixed will. It becomes operative only after [it encounters] objects; it becomes active only after [it encounters] pleasure; it becomes fixed only after habitual practice. The *qi* of happiness, anger, grief, and sorrow is the *xing*. Once it is apparent externally, objects take hold of it. The *xing* emerges from the endowment; the endowment is sent down from Heaven. The Way begins in the one's responses to reality;[18] one's responses to reality are born of one's *xing*. At first, one stays close to one's responses to reality; in the end, one stays close to morality. Those who know their responses to reality know how to express them; those who know morality know how to bring it inside themselves.

In other words, when presented with external stimuli, we exhibit our *qing* 情, our "responses to reality," which are simply a manifestation of our unsettled internal state. "Knowing one's *qing*" is identified here as a crucial first step toward moral development (and elsewhere, as described below, *The* Xing *Emerges from the Endowment* emphasizes the importance of speaking in accord with one's genuine *qing*). But the *qing* is only the beginning of the Way; specifically, it lacks morality, for morality can come about only after "habitual practice," the conscious and habitual reformation of the *xing*.

Other manuscripts in the corpus advance the same idea, affirming more explicitly that morality is not inborn.

仁生於人，義生於道。或生於內，或生於外。[19]

Humanity is born in human beings; morality is born of the Way. Some things are born inside [us]; some things are born outside [us].

仁，內也。義，外也。[20]

Humanity is internal. Morality is external.

This last statement must be astonishing to any student of Chinese philosophy, because it is attributed to the philosopher Gaozi 告子 in a debate recorded in the received *Mencius*. The consequences of this association will be discussed later. For now, let us observe that this idea, namely, that morality must be obtained from outside the self, is common to Gaozi, Xunzi, and the Guodian manuscripts—and to virtually no other known members of the Confucian school.

Xunzi postulates that, despite our natural evil, we can improve ourselves, namely, by what he calls "learning," which includes studying the canonical texts handed down by the ancient sages.[21] These texts are the *Rites,* the *Music,* the *Odes,* the *Documents,* and the *Springs and Autumns,* which incorporate the principles of the entire universe.

> 《禮》之敬文也，《樂》之中和也，《詩》、《書》之博也，《春秋》之微也，在天地之閒者畢矣。[22]
>
> The reverence and refinement of the *Rites,* the centrality and harmony of the *Music,* the expansiveness of the *Odes* and *Documents,* the subtleties of the *Springs and Autumns*—all that is between Heaven and Earth is fulfilled in them.[23]

And: "When learning comes to the *Rites,* it ceases. This is what is called 'the ridgepole of the Way and virtue'" 故學至乎禮而止矣。夫是之謂道德之極.[24]

In a similar vein, *The* Xing *Emerges from the Endowment* asserts that the Sages helped to imbue people with morality by teaching from the classics:

> 凡性，或動之，或逹之，或交之，或厲之，或絀之，或養之，或長之。凡動性者，物也，逹性者，悅也，交性者，故也，厲性者，義也，絀性者，勢也，養性者，習也，長性者，道也。凡見者之謂物，快於己者之謂悅，物之勢者之謂勢，有為也者之謂故。義也者，群善之蕝。習也者，有以習其性也。道者，群物之道。凡道，心術為主。道四術，唯人道為可道也。其三術者，道之而已。《詩》、《書》、《禮》、《樂》，其始出皆生於人。《詩》，有為為之也。《書》，有為言之也。《禮》、《樂》，有為舉之也。聖人比其類而論會之，觀其先後而格訓之，體其義而次序之，理其情而出內之。[25]
>
> As a rule, there is something that moves the *xing,* something that activates[26] it, something that engages it, something that whets it, something that impedes it, something that nourishes it, something that augments it. As a rule, objects are what move the *xing;* pleasure is what activates it; causes are what engage it; morality is what whets it; circumstances are what impede it; habitual practice is what nourishes it; the Way is what augments it. Whatever one sees is called "objects"; what is congenial to oneself is called "pleasure"; the circumstances of objects are called "circumstances"; what is efficacious is

> called "causes." Morality is the expression of the many forms of goodness; habitual practice is what one uses to train the *xing;* the Way is the Way of the many objects. (As a rule, regarding the Way, the techniques of the mind are primary. Of the four techniques of the Way, only the Way of Humanity can be taken as the Way. One does no more than speak of the other three techniques.)[27] The *Odes, Documents, Rites,* and *Music* are all originally born of humanity. The *Odes* were made efficaciously; the *Documents* were spoken efficaciously; the *Rites* and *Music* were undertaken efficaciously. The Sages compared the categories [of the classics] and, expounding on these, assembled [the people]; they observed the sequences [of the classics] and restrained and instructed [the people]; they embodied the morality [of the classics] and ordered [the people]; they organized their *qing* and expressed [what should be expressed] and brought inside [what should be brought inside oneself].

Although this account omits the *Springs and Autumns,* other Guodian manuscripts include that text in the canonical collection:

> 觀諸《詩》、《書》則亦在矣，觀諸《禮》、《樂》則亦在矣，觀諸《易》、《春秋》則亦在矣。[28]
>
> When one observes this [principle?] in the *Odes* and *Documents,* it is also present; when one observes this in the *Rites* and *Music,* it is also present; when one observes this in the *Changes* and *Springs and Autumns,* it is also present.

> 《易》所以會天道人道也。《詩》所以會古今之志[29]也者。《春秋》所以會古今之事也。[30]
>
> The *Changes* are what unites the Way of Heaven and the Way of Humanity. The *Odes* are what unites ancient and modern aspirations. The *Springs and Autumns* are what unites ancient and modern affairs.

The Xing *Emerges from the Endowment* presents a scheme very much like that of Xunzi: we use the Way to "augment" our inborn *xing,* and studying the canonical classics is recommended as one of the best methods of attaining the Way.[31]

Xunzi argues that the Sages established "ritual and morality" in order to bring about harmonious society:

禮起於何也？曰：人生而有欲，欲而不得，則不能無求，求而無度量分界，則不能不爭，爭則亂，亂則窮。先王惡其亂也，故制禮義以分之，以養人之欲，給人之求，使欲必不窮乎物，物必不屈於欲，兩者相持而長，是禮之所起也。[32]

Whence did rituals arise? I say: People are born with desires; if they desire and do not obtain [the object of their desires], then they cannot but seek it. If, in seeking, people have no measures or limits, then there cannot but be contention. Contention makes disorder, and disorder privation. The Former Kings hated such disorder, and established ritual and morality in order to divide [the people's responsibilities], in order to nourish people's desires and grant what people seek. They brought it about that desires need not be deprived of objects, that objects need not be depleted by desires; the two support each other and grow: this is what gives rise to rituals.[33]

"Ritual and morality" also help people overcome their evil natures and become good:

今人之性惡，必將待聖王之治，禮義之化，然後皆出於治，合於禮也。[34]

Since people's natures are evil, they must await the governance of the Sage Kings, the transformation of ritual and morality—then everything emerges with government and is in accord with ritual.[35]

Where Xunzi appears to be most original, however—or, more precisely, where he appeared to be most original before the discovery of the Guodian manuscripts—is in his insistence that only the rituals of the Sage Kings can bring about harmonious society and personal self-cultivation in this manner, because only the rituals of the Sage Kings conform to the essential characteristics of humanity that distinguish us from all other species. In referring to the distinguishing characteristics of the human species, Xunzi does not use the word *xing* (which, as we have seen, denotes in his parlance the characteristics that all humans naturally share), but the expression *ren zhi suoyi wei ren zhe* 人之所以為人者, literally "that by which humans are human."

人之所以為人者，何已也？曰：以其有辨也。饑而欲食，寒而欲煖，勞而欲息，好利而惡害，是人之所生而有也，是無待而然也，是禹、桀之所同也。然則人之所以為人者，非特以二足而無毛也，以其有辨也。今夫狌狌形笑[＝肖][36]，亦二足而無毛也，然而君子啜其羹，食其胾。故人之所以為人者，非特以其二足而無毛也，以其有辨也。夫禽獸有父子而無父子之親，有牝牡而無男女之別，故人道莫不有辨。辨莫大於分，分莫大於禮，禮莫大於聖王。[37]

What is it that makes humans human? I say: their making of distinctions. Desiring food when hungry, desiring warmth when cold, desiring rest when toiling, liking profit and hating injury—these [characteristics] are all possessed by people from birth. They are not things such that we must wait for them to be so. This is where Yu [a legendary sage king] and Jie [a legendary tyrant] are similar. This being the case, what makes humans human is not specifically that they have two feet and no pelt [i.e., that they are featherless bipeds]. It is their making of distinctions. Now the *xingxing* ape[38] resembles us, and also has two feet and no pelt. But the noble man sips his soup and eats his food cooked.[39] Thus what makes humans human is not specifically that they have two feet and no pelt. It is their making of distinctions. Birds and beasts have fathers and sons but no affection between fathers and sons. They have males and females but no separation between men and women. Thus the Way of Humanity is nothing other than to make distinctions. There are no greater distinctions than social distinctions. There are no greater social distinctions than rituals. There are no greater rituals than those of the Sage Kings.[40]

In other words, the rituals are right because they embody the Way of Humanity and not merely because the Sages dictated them. Other systems of social control—such as law codes established by human rulers—cannot bring about the same results, because they do not necessarily accord with the Way. The consequence of this view, which has not always been appreciated, is that for Xunzi the Way is paramount, not the rituals—for it is the Way that determines the rituals.[41]

It is noteworthy, therefore, that one finds much the same view presented in the Guodian manuscripts.

禮因人之情而為之。[42]

The rituals are made by according with humans' *qing*.

情生於性，禮生於情。[43]

Our *qing* are born of our *xing;* the rituals are born of our *qing*.

And most explicitly:

天降[44]大常，以理人倫。制為君臣之義，作[45]為父子之親，分為夫婦之辨。是故小人亂天常以逆天道，君子治人倫以順天德。[46]

Heaven lays down its great constancy; one uses it as a pattern for human relations. It regulates the moral [relationship] between ruler and subject; it fashions intimacy between father and son; it apportions the distinction between husband and wife. Thus the petty man disorders the constancy of Heaven, thereby opposing the Way of Heaven; the noble man orders human relations, thereby according with the authority of Heaven.

The last passage reveals that the Guodian manuscripts conceive of the Way as the appropriate pattern for human interaction on earth,[47] a point that forces a reconsideration of the supposed "Daoist" influence on Xunzi, much discussed in the critical literature.[48] It is now evident that *dao* was already well established as a term of Confucian discourse in Xunzi's time; he would not have had to borrow it from Daoist thinkers.

Xunzi posits an analogy between polity and personhood. Kingdoms, he argues, are made up of two parts: their initial resources and the policies that their rulers elect to follow. It is Xunzi's conviction that a state's initial resources play no appreciable role in its ultimate success or failure; all that matters is the ruler and his decision to follow (or not to follow) the rituals. Similarly, people are also made up of two parts: the *xing* that they are born with and their conduct—or, in his language, their "artifice" 偽. Like the policies of a state, the "artifice" of a human being must conform to the rituals to be successful. But like a state's initial resources, the evil *xing* plays no role in determining our ultimate success or failure as human beings; all that matters are the mind and its decision to follow (or not to follow) the Way.[49]

Xunzi articulates this view in a number of passages found throughout his book. He affirms that a state's initial power is irrelevant to its prospects for success by pointing out that "a state of one hundred *li* is sufficient to establish autonomy" 百里之國，足以獨立矣.[50] This is because a sage ruler can defend himself against his enemies by following the rituals:

刑范[＝範][51]正，金錫美，工合巧，火齊得，剖刑而莫邪已。然而不剝脫，不砥厲，則不可以斷繩；剝脫之，砥厲之，則劙盤盂，刎牛馬忽然耳。彼國者，亦有[52]彊國之剖刑已。然而不教誨，不調一，則入不可以守，出不可以戰；教誨之，調一之，則兵勁城固，敵國不敢嬰也。彼國者亦有砥厲，禮義節奏也。[53]

If the mold is regular, the metal auspicious, the workmanship and casting skillful, and the fire and alloying appropriate, then cut open the mold and there will be a Moye [the name of a mythical sword]. But if one does not pare and expose it [when it becomes rough], does not sharpen it with a whetstone, then it will not be able to cut a rope. If one pares and exposes it, sharpens it with a whetstone, then it can slice a pan or basin, and slash an ox or horse instantly. As for the state—there is also a "cutting open of the mold" for a strong state. But if one does not teach and instruct, does not attune and unify, then one cannot defend against invasions or wage war outside [i.e., on other states]. But if one teaches and instructs them, attunes and unifies them, then the soldiers will be firm and the fortifications secure; enemy states will dare not close in. As for the state—there is also a "sharpening with a whetstone." This is ritual and morality, and restrictions [enacted] in due measure.[54]

With such decisive influence over the complexion of his state, the lord is the absolute standard of conduct:

君者，儀也，儀正而景正；君者，槃也，槃圓而水圓；君者，盂也，盂方而水方。[55]

The lord is the sundial; if the sundial is straight, the shadow is straight. The lord is the bowl; if the bowl is round, the water is round. The lord is the basin; if the basin is square, the water is square.[56]

Many of the sayings in *Jet-Black Robes* display a similar spirit:

子曰：民以君為心，君以民為體，心好則體安之，君好則民欲。故心以體廢，君以民亡。[57]

The Master said: "The people take the ruler as their mind; the ruler takes the people as his body. What the mind is fond of, the body takes peace in; what the lord is fond of, the people desire. Thus the mind perishes along with the body; the lord is undone along with his people."

子曰：上好仁則下之為仁也爭先。故長民者，章志以昭百姓，則民致行己以悅上。[58]

The Master said: "If the superiors love humanity, then the inferiors will contend with each other to be first in practicing humanity. Thus the leader of the people displays his intentions in order to shed light on the commoners, and the people bring his conduct down to themselves in order to please their superiors."

子曰：下之事上也，不從其所以命，而從其所行。上好此物也，下必有甚安者矣。故上之好惡，不可不慎也。[59]

The Master said: "In serving their superiors, inferiors do not follow their commandments but follow their conduct. If the superiors are fond of a thing, there must be those among the inferiors who outdo them in that regard. Thus superiors cannot but be careful about their likes and dislikes."

The last passage is repeated verbatim in *Honoring Virtue and Morality*,[60] and the general idea recurs in several other Guodian texts:

行不信則命不從，信不著則言不樂。民不從上之命，不信其言，而能含德者，未之有也。[61]

If [a ruler's] actions are not trustworthy, then his commandments will not be followed; if his trustworthiness is not manifest, then his sayings will not be felicitous. It has never happened that people who do not follow their superiors' commandments, and who place no trust in their sayings, can yet internalize virtue.

I do not mean to suggest that the Guodian manuscripts were in any respect original in saying that a ruler's likes and dislikes necessarily influence the populace's emulous behavior. By 300 B.C., this was a well-worn theme in Chinese philosophy that was routinely used even by non-Confucian writers.[62] But the statement in *Jet-Black Robes* that the people take the ruler as their mind is nonetheless striking. After all, in Xunzi's philosophy, the role of the mind in human self-cultivation is perfectly analogous to that of the ruler in the government of a state.[63] Perhaps Xunzi deliberately alluded to *Jet-Black Robes* while expounding his philosophy of mind.

The Guodian manuscripts agree that an indispensable component of the ruler's behavior consists of his utterances, both verbal and musical. These must reflect his sincere will, so as to present a worthy model for the people to follow, as in *The* Xing *Emerges from the Endowment:*

凡聲，其出於情也信，然後其入撥人心也厚。[64]

As for sounds generally, if they emerge in a trustworthy manner from the *qing,* then they will enter and stir up people's hearts profoundly.

> 求其心有偽也，弗得之矣。人之不能以偽也，可知也。[65]
>
> If one seeks the mind [of the people] with artifice, one will not obtain it. We know that people cannot be [persuaded?][66] with artifice.

This usage of *wei* 為/偽 is reminiscent of Xunzi's tenet: "The principle of ritual is to make manifest what is genuine and to eliminate what is fake" 著誠去偽，禮之經也.[67]

Another fundamental idea in Xunzi's philosophy pertains to music:

> 夫樂者，樂也，人情之所必不免也，故人不能無樂。樂則必發於聲音，形於動靜，而人之道，聲音、動靜，性術之變盡是矣。故人不能不樂，樂則不能無形，形而不為道，則不能無亂。先王惡其亂也，故制雅、頌之聲以道之，使其聲足以樂而不流，使其文足以辨而不諰，使其曲直、繁省、廉肉、節奏足以感動人之善心，使夫邪汙之氣無由得接焉。[68]
>
> Music is joy; it is what humans cannot avoid in their *qing*. Thus humans cannot be without music. If we are joyous, then we must express it in sounds and tones, and give form to it in movement and quietude. And the Way of Humanity is fulfilled in sounds and tones, in movement and quietude, and in the changes in the techniques of the *xing*.[69] Thus humans cannot be without joy, and joy cannot be without form, but if that form is not [in accord with] the Way, then there cannot but be disorder. The Former Kings hated this disorder; thus they instituted the sounds of the "Elegantiae" and "Hymns" in order to make them *dao*. They brought it about that their sounds were sufficient [to give form] to joy but were not dissipated; they brought it about that their patterned [compositions] were sufficient to make distinctions but were not timorous;[70] they brought it about that the directness, complexity, richness, and rhythm were sufficient to move people's good minds; they brought it about that heterodox and impure *qi* would have no opportunity to attach itself.[71]

This is one of the most important passages in the history of Chinese aesthetics, because it brings together similar ideas that had been expressed in earlier sources (such as the *Zuo Commentary*)[72] but organizes these into the most comprehensive explanation of the origins of music in the irrepressible human urge to express emotions. Xunzi's framework was then adopted wholesale by such later works as the "Great Preface" to the *Odes* and the treatise known as "Record of Music" (Yueji 樂記), now found in the canonical *Ritual Records*. Xunzi's primary motive in composing this essay was to refute Mozi's notorious argument that music is wasteful; on the contrary, Xunzi claims, music is essential to the project of moral transformation, because music that conforms to the Way can influence human beings and lead them to morality.[73]

> 夫聲樂之入人也深，其化人也速。故先王謹為之文。樂中平，則民和而不流，樂肅莊，則民齊而不亂，民和齊，則兵勁城固，敵國不敢嬰也。[74]
>
> Sounds and tones enter man deeply; they change man quickly. Thus the Former Kings were careful to make them patterned. When music is centered and balanced, the people are harmonious and not dissipated. When music is stern and grave, the people are uniform and not chaotic. When the people are harmonious and uniform, the army is strong and the fortifications secure; enemy states dare not invade.[75]

Xunzi's final point is a calculated strike on Mohist policy, which was famous for its emphasis on territorial defense. Xunzi's message is that the Mohists do not even know what is good for them, inasmuch as music is essential to attaining their own goal.

Essentially the same scheme is at work in the account of music in *The* Xing *Emerges from the Endowment:*

> 凡聲，其出於情也信，然後其入撥人心也厚。聞笑聲，則鮮如也斯喜。聞歌謠，則陶如也斯奮。聽琴瑟之聲，則悸如也斯歎。觀《賚》、《武》，則齊如也斯作。觀《韶》、《夏》，則勉如也斯儉。[76]
>
> As for sounds generally, if they emerge in a trustworthy manner from the *qing,* then they will enter and stir up people's hearts profoundly. When one hears the sound of laughter, one will be as though refreshed and thus happy. When one hears singing and chanting, one will be as though jolly and thus excited. When one listens to the sounds of the lute and cithern, one will be as though perturbed[77] and thus full of sighs. When one observes the "Lai" and "Wu" dances, one will be as though even-tempered and thus stirred.[78] When one observes the "Shao" and "Xia" dances, one will be as though assiduous and thus frugal.

Where Xunzi recommends the "Elegantiae" and "Hymns," *The* Xing *Emerges from the Endowment* extols the power of the "Lai," "Wu," "Shao," and "Xia" dances.[79] But effectively, these all refer to the same kind of musical compositions that were handed down by the Sages for the purpose of inspiring human beings to embody the virtues conveyed in them.

To be sure, Xunzi's essay explains this process much more clearly than *The* Xing *Emerges from the Endowment*—but once again, the essential components of Xunzi's philosophical position seem to be anticipated by the Guodian manuscripts.

While it is possible to maintain that these broad similarities between the philosophy of Xunzi and that of the Guodian manuscripts may be coincidental, that position would have to be reconciled with the considerable evidence that Xunzi intended to refer (or at least allude) to the Guodian texts in his own writings.

Since the discovery of *The Five Forms of Conduct* at Mawangdui, it has become clear that Xunzi had this same tradition in mind—if not this very text—when he criticized Mencius and Zisi for "pretending that they were following early precedents in inventing their propositions, calling them the 'Five *Xing*'" 案往舊造說，謂之五行.[80] As early as A.D. 818, the commentator Yang Liang 楊倞 had a good idea of what Xunzi meant, for he tells us: "The 'Five *Xing*' are the 'Five Constancies': these are humanity, righteousness, ritual, wisdom, and trustworthiness" 五行，五常，仁義禮智信是也.[81] Twentieth-century scholars, however, assumed that Xunzi was referring to the so-called Five Phases 五行 of late Warring States and early Han philosophy.[82] It is clear now that Yang Liang was closer to the truth; the *Wuxing* manuscripts found at Mawangdui and Guodian enumerate these five virtuous forms of behavior as humanity, righteousness, ritual, wisdom, and sagehood 聖—and this set of virtues is doubtless what Xunzi refers to as the "Five *Xing*."[83]

Another example: the Guodian text *Failure and Success Depend on Time* is a parallel account of a story told in the *Xunzi* about Confucius' difficulties while traveling between the states of Chen and Cai.[84] In a recent study of the several "between Chen and Cai" stories in the ancient literature, John Makeham has suggested that the narrative in the *Xunzi* may be the oldest version of a cycle based on the brief notice in *Analects* 15.2:[85]

> 在陳絕糧，從者病，莫能興。子路慍見曰：君子亦有窮乎？子曰：君子固窮，小人窮斯濫矣。[86]
>
> When they were in Chen, they ran out of grain; the followers became ill, and none could get up. Zilu's resentment showed, and he said: "Does the noble man also encounter hard times?"
>
> The Master said: "The noble man is firm in hard times; when the lesser man falls on hard times, he becomes dissolute."[87]

In Xunzi's telling of the story, however, Confucius makes a different point, namely, that success and failure depend on one's position and opportunities, and that many virtuous heroes of the past were undone by circumstances beyond their control. As Makeham shows, this later counsel is typical of versions of the tale from the third century B.C. onward.

The lesson recorded in *Failure and Success Depend on Time* is not situated between Chen and Cai—nor is it even attributed to Confucius—but the language and argument contain striking echoes of Xunzi's account. Both texts mention the example of Wu Zixu 伍子胥, for example. Similarly, *Failure and Success Depend on Time* says: "Whether one meets or does not meet [with opportunity] depends on Heaven" 遇不遇，天也,[88] a phrase that recurs almost word for word in the *Xunzi:* "Whether one meets or does not meet [with opportunity] depends on time" 遇不遇者，時也.[89] Again, *Failure and Success* says:

> 有其人，亡其世，雖賢弗行矣。[90]
>
> If there is the right person, but not the right generation, then even one who is talented will not succeed.

The version in *Xunzi* says:

> 今有其人不遇其時，雖賢，其能行乎？[91]
>
> If the right person does not meet with the right time, then will even one who is talented be able to succeed?[92]

These and other similarities indicate that even if the account in the *Xunzi* is not modeled after *Failure and Success Depend on Time,* the two must share a common source or sources. Recalling that *Failure and Success* never refers to Confucius' difficulties between Chen and Cai, perhaps we may say that Xunzi was the first writer to combine this teaching about timeliness with the famous legend from *Analects* 15.2, where, as we have seen, the figure of Confucius gives a very different response to Zilu.[93]

Finally, it was noted above that Xunzi may have been inspired by a saying in *Jet-Black Robes* ("The people take the ruler as their mind," and so forth) while formulating his unique philosophy of mind. The editorial group from the Jingmen Municipal Museum has pointed out a specific case where Xunzi's language appears to be based on that of the Guodian manuscripts.[94] *The Way of Integrity and Trustworthiness* says:

忠之為道也，百工不楛。[95]

With the Way of Integrity, the many artisans do not make slipshod wares.

Compare the corresponding statement in the *Xunzi:*

如是，則百工莫不忠信而不楛矣。[96]

If things are as above, then among the many artisans, none will fail to have integrity and trustworthiness, and they will not make slipshod wares.[97]

One can only expect that as we come to understand the Guodian manuscripts more fully, we will find many more such correspondences, both philosophical and literary, with the writing of Xunzi.[98]

Since the similarities between the world view of the Guodian manuscripts and that of Xunzi are evidently profound and pervasive, it is important not to overlook the differences between the two.

First,.Xunzi addresses a great number of philosophical issues that are never broached in the Guodian manuscripts. The chapter called "Rectifying Names" (Zhengming), for example, lays down an intricate theory of naming that has attracted modern linguists and analytical philosophers as a valuable contribution to the philosophy of language.[99] His work also contains a sophisticated consideration of the famous ancient paradoxes ("Eggs have hair," and so forth)[100] and a sustained discussion of the reasons for rejecting this kind of semantic legerdemain.[101] While the authors of the Guodian manuscripts are also keenly aware of the persuasive power of language and literature, their writings, as we possess them, do not treat of such subjects as the appropriateness of names, the errors of falsidical paradoxes,[102] and the relationship between language and the Way.

Similarly, another well-known feature of Xunzi's philosophy is his excoriation of theurgists, omen seekers, and purveyors of supernatural theories. In his "Discourse on Heaven" (Tianlun 天論), Xunzi articulates a distinction between what he calls "material anomalies" 物之罕至 (or "transformations of *yin* and *yang*" 陰陽之化), on the one hand, and "human portents" 人袄 on the other. The former, such as yawping trees and falling stars, are essentially innocuous and inscrutable; they have occurred in all periods of history and have never exercised a decisive influence on human affairs. The latter, however, are "to be feared" 可畏. Examples of "human portents" are poor plowing, hoeing and weeding out of season, or governmental injustice: in other words, willful actions, undertaken by unenlightened human beings, that violate the order of the Way and spell disaster for the entire nation.[103] Xunzi's point is that if we must look for omens, we will find them not in the skies but in our own deeds—for it is we, and not Heaven, who forge our own destinies. While this manner of thinking is surely not incompatible with the conception of Heaven in *Cheng zhi wen zhi,* none of the Guodian manuscripts incorporates the distinctive idea of "material anomalies" and "human portents." That seems to be a purely Xunzian innovation.[104]

Finally, Xunzi uses his paradigm of rituals and the Way to attack other provinces of philosophical debate. In the "Discussion of Warfare" (Yibing 議兵), for example, Xunzi declares that the victor in any battle will not be the side with the superior tactics or weaponry but the side that has cultivated the rituals more assiduously:

> 古之兵，戈、矛、弓、矢而已矣，然而敵國不待試而詘；城郭不辨[=辦][105]，溝池不拑[=扣][106]，固塞不樹，機變不張，然而國晏然不畏外而固者，無它故焉，明道而分鈞之。[107]
>
> The weapons of the ancients were nothing more than halberd, spear, bow, and arrow, but enemy states recoiled without contest. Fortifications and battlements were not managed, pits and moats were not dug, strongholds and fortresses were not planted, machinery and surprise tactics not brought to bear; however, that the state, in peace, did not fear foreigners and was secure[108]—there was no other reason for this than that [the rulers] were enlightened with respect to the Way and divided the [responsibilities] of the people equitably.[109]

In effect, then, military science is viewed as one of the many areas in which the consequences of the Way can be worked out rationally and systematically. The "Discussion of Warfare" is not really about warfare at all; it merely uses the example of warfare to demonstrate the unparalleled efficacy of the rituals and the Way.[110] This example highlights a fundamental difference between Xunzi and the Guodian manuscripts. The latter may discuss various ideas—such as human nature, learning, music, and the Way—that are also basic to Xunzi's outlook, but in these earlier documents, those themes are not yet galvanized into an integral system. Rather, they appear to be a congeries of typically Confucian, but not apodictically interrelated, approaches to moral philosophy. For Xunzi, by contrast, all topics in philosophy are but aspects or reflections of the Way in its infinite applicability. In that respect, Xunzi's views on diverse subjects—language, warfare, ritual—are predetermined by his commitment to the Way as the Heaven-ordained plan and pattern of nature, the infallible standard of reason and conduct. In this respect he is, to borrow the useful paradigm of Isaiah Berlin, a hedgehog rather than a fox.[111]

Since several of the Guodian manuscripts can be shown to anticipate Xunzi in so many respects, it is worthwhile to ask who may have written them.[112] The above discussion touched on one important clue, namely, the tenet that "humanity" is internal and "morality" external. As far as I know, there are only two places in the received literature where this position is espoused. First, it is attributed to the philosopher Gaozi in his celebrated debate with Mencius (recorded in *Mencius* 6A); and second, it appears in a curious fragment now included in the "Jie" 戒 chapter of the *Guanzi,*[113] which, as A. C. Graham has demonstrated, is probably "a surviving document of the school of Gaozi."[114] Therefore, it is reasonable as a first hypothesis to suppose that the Guodian manuscripts may have something to do with Gaozi or the branch of Confucianism that he represented.[115]

The Six Forms of Virtue gives a unique and coherent explanation of the principle that humanity is internal and morality external. The text starts by assigning six separate virtues to the six cardinal social roles. Morality 義 pertains to the lord 君, integrity 忠 to the subject 臣, wisdom 智 to the husband 夫, trustworthiness 信 to the wife 婦, sagehood 聖 to the father 父, and humanity 仁 to the son 子.[116] Then we read:

> 仁，內也。義，外也。禮樂，共也。內立父、子、夫也，外立君、臣、婦也 ⋯ ⋯ 為父絕君，不為君絕父。為昆弟絕妻，不為妻絕昆弟。為宗族殺朋友，不為朋友殺宗族。[117]
>
> Humanity is internal; morality is external; ritual and music are shared. Inside are established the father, the son, and the husband; outside are established the lord, the subject, and the wife. [The text then justifies this schema by describing the various funerary rites observed on the death of different relations.][118] One breaks with one's lord on account of one's father, but one does not break with one's father on account of one's lord. One breaks with one's wife on account of one's brothers, but one does not break with one's brothers on account of one's wife. One reduces[119] [the number of] one's friends on account of one's clan relations, but one does

> not reduce [the number of] one's clan relations on account of one's friends.

In other words, when the text says that humanity is internal and morality external, it means that when moral dilemmas arise, the social role pertaining to humanity is to be privileged over the social role pertaining to morality. We protect our clan members before we protect "outside" relations.[120] This idea is clearly in line with *Analects* 13.18 (examined in the Introduction, above):

> The Lord of She said to Confucius: "In our village there is one Upright Gong. His father stole a sheep, so the son testified against him."
>
> Confucius said: "The upright people of my village are different from this. The fathers are willing to conceal their sons; the sons are willing to conceal their fathers. Uprightness lies therein."[121]

The impulsive young man, struggling to live up to his epithet, should have known that his obligations to his father outweigh his obligations to his lord.

Is this what Gaozi meant when he said that humanity is internal and morality external? Perhaps, but nowhere in *Mencius* 6A does he make an argument even remotely resembling this one. On the contrary, his justification of his famous tenet is shown by Mencius to be thoroughly untenable. Gaozi argues that morality is external, because we naturally venerate people who are older than ourselves, and the fact that they are older is an objective circumstance external to ourselves. So moral behavior is determined by factors outside the self. Mencius responds, compellingly, that our tendency to venerate our elders is actually internal, for we do not venerate aged horses, only aged humans. *We* decide when and where "age" is a factor that we must take into account in moral behavior. The significance of age is subjective.[122]

What Gaozi really believed and whether the editors of the *Mencius* included his best arguments are, at least at present, unanswerable questions. Nevertheless, *Cheng zhi wen zhi* and *The* Xing *Emerges from the Endowment* shed great light on an enigmatic passage in the debate between Mencius and Gaozi as recorded in *Mencius.*

> 告子曰：生之謂性。
> 孟子曰：生之謂性也，猶白之謂白與？
> 曰：然。

白羽之白也，猶白雪之白；白雪之白，猶白玉之白與？
曰：然。
然則犬之性猶牛之性，牛之性猶人之性與？[123]

Gaozi said: "What is inborn is called *xing.*"

Mencius said: "Is what is inborn called *xing* in the way that white is called 'white'?"

He said: "It is so."

"Is the whiteness of white feathers like the whiteness of white snow; is the whiteness of white snow like the whiteness of white jade?"

He said: "It is so."

"Then is the *xing* of a dog like the *xing* of an ox; is the *xing* of an ox like the *xing* of a human being?"[124]

It has never been clear to commentators precisely what Mencius believes he has accomplished in this exchange. If anything, by referring to such questionable hypostatizations as "the whiteness of white feathers," his argument may remind one of the notorious sophistic technique of *jianbai* 堅白 ("the separation of distinct but mutually pervasive properties").[125] But the Guodian manuscripts reveal what is at stake. Gaozi is presenting a definition of *xing* like that of *The* Xing *Emerges from the Endowment: xing* is the name that we use to denote the inborn characteristics shared by all members of a single species. Mencius simply cannot accept Gaozi's definition because of his own peculiar usage, which we have examined above. This is why he raises the issue of the dog's *xing* and the ox's *xing:* in his world view, *xing* refers to the special characteristic that distinguishes one species from all others. As far as Mencius is concerned, by asserting that "what is inborn is called *xing,*" Gaozi is effectively denying that there is a fundamental difference between human beings and animals. The debate is best understood as a scholastic dispute: Gaozi stands for a group that understands the keyword *xing* in a manner intolerable to Mencius. (And the Guodian manuscripts suggest, contrary to all subsequent orthodoxy, that it may have been Mencius' usage of *xing,* and not that of Gaozi or Xunzi, that was considered misguided in ancient times.)[126]

Similarly, Mencius' disciple Gongduzi, in discussing Gaozi, refers to a position that is explicitly avowed by *Honoring Virtue and Morality:*

公都子曰：告子曰：性無善無不善也。或曰：性可以為善，可以為不善，是故文武興則民好善，幽厲興則民好暴。[127]

> Gongduzi said: "Gaozi said: 'There is no inherent goodness or lack of goodness in the *xing*.' Some say: 'The *xing* can be made to be good and can be made to be not good. Thus when Kings Wen and Wu arose, the people were fond of goodness; when Kings You and Li arose, the people were fond of violence.'"[128]

Honoring Virtue and Morality (manifestly following the lead of *Jet-Black Robes*) agrees that people are, by nature, morally indeterminate; they simply take on the characteristics exhibited by their ruler.

> 桀不謂其民必亂，而民有為亂矣。[129]
>
> Jie did not tell his people that they must be disorderly, but the people became disorderly.

> 下之事上也，不從其所命，而從其所行。上好是物也，下必有甚焉者。[130]
>
> In serving their superiors, inferiors do not follow their commandments but follow their conduct. If the superiors are fond of a thing, there must be those among their inferiors who outdo them in that regard.

There is another historical figure with whom the Guodian manuscripts can be plausibly associated: Gongsun Nizi 公孫尼子, a native of Chu who is sometimes said to be the author of *Jet-Black Robes*[131] and whose works are listed in an ancient bibliography as comprising twenty-eight chapters.[132] Unfortunately, we know even less about Gongsun Nizi than we do about Gaozi; it is not even clear when he lived.[133] We are told by some commentators that he was the compiler of a "Record of Music,"[134] but there are several reasons why it is doubtful that this can refer to the extant chapter by that name in the *Ritual Records*. More plausible is the hypothesis that Gongsun Nizi wrote a lost essay about music, which may have ultimately contributed to the philosophical view that informs the received "Record of Music." It is not farfetched to view *The* Xing *Emerges from the Endowment* as a possible remnant of Gongsun Nizi's tradition.[135]

Another useful reference to Gongsun Nizi is provided by the curmudgeonly author Wang Chong 王充 (A.D. 27–ca. 100). Wang places him in the same category as certain other early Confucians who believed that the *xing* contains both goodness and evil in it and that human beings can be made to augment one or the other aspect of their natures.[136] This position is similar to that attributed to Gaozi in *Mencius* 6A, which Wang

Chong also discusses.[137] Not coincidentally, it is also very much like the position that Xunzi defends with incomparably greater rigor.[138]

This is not to suggest that the Guodian manuscripts were necessarily written by Gaozi or Gongsun Nizi. Indeed, it is not impossible that these names refer to fictitious characters who never lived. However, the philosophical positions sketchily attributed to these two figures correspond well to what we read in the Guodian manuscripts. It cannot be a coincidence that the "humanity is internal, morality is external" apophthegm is elsewhere attributed to Gaozi and to no one else—just as it cannot be a coincidence that *Jet-Black Robes* is attributed to Gongsun Nizi of Chu, whose doctrinal views, as outlined by Wang Chong, fit with *The* Xing *Emerges from the Endowment* and the other manuscripts like it. Gaozi and Gongsun Nizi, therefore, are best understood as names representing a distinct branch within the Confucian tradition,[139] the same branch that produced such texts as *The* Xing *Emerges from the Endowment, The Six Forms of Virtue,* and *Cheng zhi wen zhi.* Their platform, insofar as it can be reconstructed, is as follows:[140]

1. *Xing* refers to what is inborn in an organism and thus to the features that all members of a certain species hold in common rather than the features that distinguish a certain species from all other species.
2. Although the *xing* is morally indeterminate, people can make themselves good through self-cultivation. The method to become good is to follow the Way (which is established by Heaven), and the Sages transmitted rituals and canonical texts in order to help us in this process. People can also be led to evil if they are given destructive examples to follow. The ruler, consequently, must be careful about the rightness of his own actions.
3. Thus it is said that humanity is internal but morality external.
4. Music is especially useful in the project of self-cultivation, because the sounds and tones of appropriate music can inspire human beings to emulate the virtues expressed in them.

In conclusion, it is evident that Xunzi did not arise ex nihilo, and we now have a better view than ever before of the intellectual world from which he emerged.[141] His positions may be more systematically argued than anything to be found in the Guodian manuscripts, but there can be little question that he descends from the same doctrinal sect. One can imagine that the Guodian texts are what Xunzi learned in school.

—3—

Han Fei's Doctrine of Self-Interest

Chapter 49 of the *Han Feizi,* titled "The Five Vermin" (Wudu 五蠹), includes one of the earliest discussions in Chinese history of the concepts of *gong* 公 and *si* 私. Influenced no doubt by the modern meanings of these terms, most translators render *gong* and *si* as "public" and "private," respectively,[1] but an examination of the original passage reveals the inadequacy of these translations:

> 古者倉頡之作書也，自環者謂之私，背私謂之公，公私之相背也，乃倉頡固以知之矣。今以為同利者，不察之患也。然則為匹夫計者，莫如脩行義而習文學。行義脩則見信，見信則受事；文學習則為明師，為明師則顯榮，此匹夫之美也。然則無功而受事，無爵而顯榮，為有政如此，則國必亂，主必危矣。故不相容之事，不兩立也。[2]

> In ancient times, when Cangjie invented writing, he called acting in one's own interest *si;* what opposes *si* he called *gong.* So Cangjie certainly knew already that *gong* and *si* oppose each other. To consider them now equally profitable is a calamity resulting from a failure to investigate [the issue]. Thus, if one calculates on behalf of common men, there is nothing better than cultivating humanity[3] and righteousness and engaging in literature and study. If they cultivate humanity and righteousness, they obtain an audience and are trusted [by the ruler]; if they obtain an audience and are trusted, they receive an appointment. If they engage in literature and study, they become brilliant teachers; if they become brilliant teachers, they will be prominent and honored. This is beautiful for common men. But those without merit receive appointments and those without rank are prominent and honored—if one practices government like this, the state will surely fall

> into disorder and the ruler will surely be imperiled. Thus incompatible things cannot stand together.

This passage requires some unpacking. First, Han Fei relies on the graphic correspondence between *gong* and *si* to suggest that Cangjie, the ancient sage who supposedly invented writing, understood these two concepts to be mutually antagonistic. Both *gong* and *si* share the element *si* 厶, which Han Fei takes to mean "acting in one's own interest." *Gong* is what "opposes" (*bei* 背, or *ba* 八, understood in the sense of 扒) *si* and is therefore written as *ba si* 公.[4] Han Fei's elucidation of the characters—which would be lost on readers who do not recognize that *gong* and *si* share the same graph—is designed to show that it is inexcusable today not to understand the difference between *gong* and *si,* when Cangjie pointed out their mutual incompatibility countless generations ago.

Han Fei then goes on to illustrate *si* with the example of "common men" who pursue a life of ostentatious morality and scholarship in order to impress the ruler and attain power and eminence—a "beautiful" outcome. The implication is that people become teachers and moral paragons for selfish reasons: they hope that a shining reputation will eventually be convertible into abundant material benefits. The ambitious throng competing for administrative positions is acting out of *si,* self-interest. No one should believe that the virtue of such men is anything but mercenary.[5]

However, self-interest is not inherently reprehensible in Han Fei's view; the problem is that a ruler simply cannot entrust important appointments to men with spotless moral records but no real merit. So the interests of the ministers and the ruler are diametrically opposed. Ministers hope to parlay their undeserved fame into a comfortable career; a ruler must weed out the posers in his search for those rare and invaluable adjuvants who are genuinely capable of administering the state. In short, if *si* is the self-interest of the minister, *gong* is the self-interest of the ruler.[6] Thus, while "private" may be defensible as a rendering of *si,* "public" is wholly misleading for *gong,* because the self-interest of the ruler need not coincide with the general interest of the public. Indeed, our modern concept of the "public interest" or "public good" hardly existed in ancient China. Han Fei was not James Madison.

Han Fei continues in this vein, turning his attention to hypocritical ministers who expatiate on the so-called Horizontal and Vertical Alliances 從衡.[7] Neither alternative is in the ruler's best interest. Joining the Horizontal Alliance means prostrating oneself before the might of Qin, and states that routinely prostrate themselves find their territory pared down until nothing is left. In contrast, joining the Vertical Alliance means rescuing impotent states that are about to be annexed by Qin, and states that routinely rescue their impotent neighbors find their own strength weakened until their armies are defeated. Han Fei concludes:

> 是故事強則以外權士官於內，救小則以內重求利於外，國利未立，封土厚祿至矣；主上雖卑，人臣尊矣；國地雖削，私家富矣。事成則以權長重，事敗則以富退處。人主之於其聽說也，於其臣，事未成則爵祿已尊矣；事敗則弗誅，則游說之士，孰不為用矰繳之說徼倖其後？故破國亡主以聽言談者之浮說，此其故何也？是人君不明乎公私之利，不察當否之言，而誅罰不必其後也。[8]

> Thus if they [advocate] serving the mighty, they mean to serve in the administration within [the state] by means of some power outside it; if they [advocate] rescuing the small, they mean to seek profit outside [the state] by means of their importance within it. Before any profit has come to the state, they have obtained their feudal territories and rich emoluments. Although the ruler above is despised, the ministers are esteemed; although the state's territory is pared away, private households are wealthy. If their affairs succeed, they become senior and important with their power; if their affairs fail, they retire to their homes with their wealth. In hearing proposals, rulers of men generally do not hold ministers responsible for their names and realities.[9] Before [the ministers'] affairs have succeeded, their emoluments are already estimable—and since they are not punished if their affairs fail, why should the wandering persuaders not use some "dart-and-string" proposal and count on luck?[10] Why are there such groundless proposals that would smash a state and ruin a ruler if one listened to them? It is because the ruler of men is not clear about the respective profits of *gong* and *si*, does not investigate appropriate and false speech, and is uncertain in administering punishment.

Han Fei counsels rulers to remember that ministers propose policies out of self-interest: they are concerned only with enriching themselves and look upon the ruler and his state as nothing more than a resource to be exploited in their quest for material aggrandizement. Only a fool, therefore, would follow a minister's advice uncritically. The ruler must use a rational system of rewards and punishments so that ministers can expect swift penalties if their plans fail; this will deter ministers from making frivolous proposals that do not promise at least some benefit to the state. Moreover, the ruler must always ask himself who stands to gain from a particular proposal and be sure to distinguish the personal interests of the ministers, or *si*, from the general interests of the sovereign, or *gong*.

This view is noteworthy in that it does not necessarily privilege *gong* at the expense of *si*. The issue is simply one of competing interests: a shrewd minister is intent on advancing his *si* just as a shrewd ruler takes care to protect his *gong*. Han Fei consistently implies that rulers have only themselves to blame for the consequences of adopting a ruinous strategy without first considering *gong* and *si*. In later writers, by contrast, *gong* typically refers to imperial control in accordance with the universal Way, and *si* denotes those troublesome areas where *gong* has failed to take hold.[11] To be sure, in this chapter, Han Fei does not show any sympathy for ministers and *si*, for he lists among the five vermin "those chatterers who engage in deceitful flattery, who borrow foreign power in order to complete their *si* and cause the profit owed to the Altars of Soil and Millet to be neglected" 其言古者，為設詐稱，借於外力，以成其私而遺社稷之利.[12] But this condemnation is explained by the fact that "The Five Vermin" is addressed to a ruler. Han Fei's understanding of the tension between *gong* and *si* raises the possibility that in recommendations intended for the ministerial class, he might advocate *si*.

And this is precisely what we find in chapter 12, "The Difficulties of Persuasion" (Shuinan 說難):

> 譽異人與同行者，規異事與同計者。有與同汙者，則必以大飾其無傷也；有與同敗者，則必以明飾其無失也。彼自多其力，則毋以其難概之也；自勇其斷，則無以其謫怒之；自智其計，則毋以其敗窮之。大意無所拂悟，辭言無所繫縻，然後極騁智辯焉，此道所得親近不疑而得盡辭也。[13]
>
> Eulogize other people who act in a manner similar to the ruler; take as a model those affairs of others that are similar to his plans. If there is someone as vile as he, you must use [that person's] greatness to prettify him, as though he were harmless. If there is someone who has had the same failures as he, you must use [that person's] brilliance to prettify him, as though there were no real loss. If he considers his own strengths manifold, do not cause him to regret[14] his [past] difficulties. If he considers his decisions brave, do not anger him by reprimanding him. If he considers his plans wise, do not diminish him [by citing] his failures. Only if there is nothing contrary[15] in your general import and nothing stringent in your speech will your wisdom and rhetoric gallop forward to the ultimate. This is the way of attaining both intimacy without suspicion and effectual speech.

Han Fei does not mean that a minister must always be a sycophant; the point is that one must craft one's speeches to complement the ruler's character. "The difficulty of persuasion always lies in knowing the mind of the one being persuaded, so that we can match it with our persuasions" 凡說之難，在知所說之心，可以吾說當之.[16] But rulers being habitually vain and impetuous, a fawning approach is usually safest.

It is remarkable that a minister who follows Han Fei's prescriptions in chapter 12 would be condemned by the Han Fei of chapter 49 as a "chatterer who engages in deceitful flattery." Scholars sometimes cite such ostensible contradictions as evidence that the *Han Feizi* could not have been written by one man.[17] The weakness of this theory is that it does not take into account the fundamental similarities of the two chapters. The basic issue in both contexts is the natural and inevitable antagonism between the ruler and his ministers, a topic more typical of the *Han Feizi* than any other Chinese text. There are no irreconcilable inconsistencies: Han Fei's avowed opinion simply changes with his intended audience. (He may write more often for rulers than for ministers, but that is only a consequence of his own context: he, too, has *si* and can expect to gain more from the favor of his suzerain than from that of mere career men.) Now he may excoriate duplicitous ministers; now he may explain how to gull a king. It is impossible to say which is the "real" Han Fei, because in neither authorial mode does Han Fei disclose his personal views.

Or perhaps we ought not assume that Han Fei had personal views at all. Textbooks generally aim to elucidate the philosophical system of a particular thinker, but Han Fei is unsuited to that kind of project. He simply does not affirm a belief in any absolute scale according to which one can rank objectively the disparate interests of all the actors on the stage. The only genuine force in the world is self-interest, the competing and interacting interests of rulers, ministers, and common men and women. His system is one of *gong* and *si,* not right and wrong. A. C. Graham's fitting description of this world view is "amoral."[18]

Scholars often point out that Han Fei was influenced by the political interpretations of the *Laozi* that were popular at the time and frequently invoked the Way in his discussions.[19] When these passages are scrutinized, however, it becomes evident that, unlike his predecessors, Han Fei does not conceive of the Way as the foundation of morality, but merely employs themes and phrases borrowed from the *Laozi* in order to further his arguments about the ongoing political struggle between a ruler and his ministers.

Chapter 5, "The Way of the Ruler" (Zhudao 主道), is illustrative. Han Fei opens with sententious pronouncements about the primordial Way:

> 道者，萬物之始，是非之紀也。是以明君守始以知萬物之源，治紀以知善敗之端。故虛靜以待令，令名自命也，令事自定也。虛則知實之情，靜則知動者正。有言者自為名，有事者自為形，形名參同，君乃無事焉，歸之其情。[20]
>
> The Way is the origin of the Myriad Things, the skein of right and wrong. Therefore, the enlightened lord holds to the origin in order to know the source of the Myriad Things and masters the skein in order to know the endpoints of gain and loss. Thus, in emptiness and tranquillity, he awaits commandment—the commandment for names to name themselves and for affairs to settle themselves. Since he is empty, he knows the essence of objects; since he is tranquil, he knows what is correct for everything that moves. One who speaks spontaneously makes a "name"; one who acts spontaneously makes a "form." When "forms and names" match identically, then everything returns to its essence without any action on the part of the ruler.

This exordium is a patchwork of ideas and keywords borrowed from earlier thinkers. "The Way is the origin of the Myriad Things" is a direct allusion to the discussion of the Way as the "origin of the world" 天下有始 in *Laozi* 52.[21] Most of Han Fei's other statements here are reminiscent of Shen Buhai 申不害 (fl. 354–340 B.C.),[22] the renowned administrative theorist whose influence Han Fei freely acknowledges.[23] The notion that the enlightened ruler must wait for names to name themselves and affairs to settle themselves is anticipated in Shen Buhai's essay "Dati" 大體 (The great body): "Names rectify themselves; affairs settle themselves. Thus he who has the Way accords with names but still rectifies them; he follows affairs but still settles them" 名自正也，事自定也，是以有道者自名而正之，隨事而定之.[24] Shen Buhai's point is that the ruler must practice *wu-wei* 無為 (nonaction), which means handling affairs in accordance with the Way and not engaging in any purposive action that may violate the natural order of things. Han Fei uses the phrase "emptiness and tranquillity" to express an equivalent view: the ruler rules by responding to things, rather than by acting on them.[25]

The end of the passage then focuses on "forms and names," another term associated with Shen Buhai in ancient times.[26] As H. G. Creel has shown, "forms and names" is a tenet of bureaucratic government: a minister is given a title or duty—his "name"—and is then judged according to his performance of that office—his "form." If "forms and names" match, the minister has discharged his obligations acceptably and should be rewarded. But if there is any discrepancy, the minister has failed and must be punished.[27] Shen Buhai refers to this idea in "The Great Body" in language inspired by legal convention: "One who is a minister grasps the tally, by which he is held responsible for his name" 為人臣者操契以責其名.[28] A tally was a promissory instrument in ancient China. An agreement between a debtor and creditor was embodied in a tally, which would be broken in half. Each party then retained one portion of the tally as proof of the creditor's claim.[29] The relationship of "form and name," in other words, is conceived as a covenant between a debtor and a creditor: the minister's performance must always tally with the ruler's expectations.[30]

Han Fei continues in "The Way of the Ruler" to write in this tradition. Immediately after the opening lines on the Way, we read:

> 故曰：君無見其所欲，君見其所欲，臣自將雕琢；君無見其意，君見其意，臣將自表異。故曰：去好去惡，臣乃見素，去舊去智，臣乃自備。[31]
>
> Thus it is said: The lord ought not make his desires apparent. If the lord's desires are apparent, the ministers will carve and polish themselves [to his liking]. The lord ought not make his intentions apparent. If the lord's intentions are apparent, the ministers will display themselves falsely. Thus it is said: Eliminate likes; eliminate dislikes. Then the ministers will appear plainly. Eliminate tradition; eliminate wisdom. Then the ministers will prepare themselves.

This is yet another pastiche of patent references to Shen Buhai and the *Laozi*. The admonition to eliminate desires and traditional wisdom reminds the reader immediately of comparable lines in the *Laozi*.[32] The first half of the passage, similarly, is adumbrated by Shen Buhai in "The Great Body":

> 故善為主者，倚於愚，立於不盈，設於不敢，藏於無事。竄端匿疏。示天下無為，是以近者親之，遠者懷之。示人有餘者，人奪之；示人不足者，人與之。剛者折，危者覆，動者搖，靜者安。[33]
>
> Thus one who is adept at ruling relies on [an appearance of] stupidity, erects himself in insufficiency, displays himself in cowardice, and conceals himself in lack of undertaking. He hides his reasons and covers his tracks.[34]

> He exhibits his inaction to the world; therefore those who are near are intimate with him and those who are distant cherish him. People snatch from those who exhibit their surpluses and cooperate with those who exhibit their shortfalls. Those who are hard are felled; those who are endangered are protected. Those who move sway [precariously]; those who are tranquil are secure.

With the idea that a ruler must present an expressionless face to the outside world, Han Fei's meandering and derivative introduction has finally led to the main argument. A wise ruler will not reveal any tendencies or emotions that his vulpine ministers might exploit in their tireless pursuit of *si.* The ideal ministers of "The Difficulties of Persuasion" thrive, we remember, precisely because they "know the mind" of their incautious lord and mold their speeches to conform to his transparent character. The basic struggle of *gong* and *si,* therefore, produces a related dynamic: the ongoing campaign of the ministers to discover "the mind" of the ruler and the concomitant measures taken by the ruler to remain aloof and unfathomable.[35] The method that Han Fei recommends to sovereigns is what he calls "the Way of the ruler." Respond; do not act; remain "tranquil" and "reserved"; do not reveal thyself. The rest of the chapter deals exclusively with the central problem of keeping ministers in check—or, in Han Fei's parlance, clearing the "five kinds of blockage" 五壅, or the five sets of circumstances under which a minister can wrest power from a ruler.[36] The Way has served as nothing more than an august pretext, a rhetorical ornamentation designed to attract rulers who have had a smattering of philosophy.

Han Fei reduces the Way to the Way of the ruler.[37] His real issue is not the mysterious source of the Myriad Things, but the urgent need of rulers to foil their subdolous ministers by imitating the attributes of formlessness and inscrutability commonly associated with the Way. Thus even in his most naturalistic moments, Han Fei does not display a definite belief in anything like natural law or universal morality. His sole purpose is to expound his doctrine of self-interest and to apprise his readers of the dangers of ignoring it.

—4—

Li Si, Chancellor of the Universe

Almost all the surviving information about Li Si 李斯 (ca. 280–208 B.C.), the Chancellor of the Qin empire, comes from his biography in the magisterial *Records of the Historian,* by Sima Qian 司馬遷 (145?–86? B.C.).[1] It is remarkable that were it not for this one document, we could say virtually nothing about one of the most pivotal figures in Chinese history. As it is, our view of Li Si is inevitably colored by the biases of Sima Qian, who, notwithstanding his deserved fame as a historian, incorporated into his writings a peculiar view of the empire and its legitimacy.[2] Still, the extant biography of Li Si admirably conveys his historical importance and furnishes a prism through which posterity can observe the momentous events accompanying the rise and fall of the Qin empire.

We are told nothing more of Li Si's origins than that he was born to a family of commoners from Shangcai 上蔡, in the state of Chu, and served as a minor functionary in the local administration. An amusing anecdote explains why Li Si was unsatisfied with this humble post:

> 見吏舍廁中鼠食不絜，近人犬，數驚恐之。斯入倉，觀倉中鼠，食積粟，居大廡之下，不見人犬之憂。於是李斯乃歎曰：人之賢不肖譬如鼠矣，在所自處耳！[3]
>
> He saw that the rats in the latrines and the functionaries' quarters ate refuse and would be terrified whenever people or dogs approached. When [Li] Si entered the granary, he observed that the rats in the granary ate mounds of grain and, living under a great portico, were not bothered by people or dogs. Therefore Si sighed and said: "People are worthy or ignoble just like rats: [one's fate] depends on where one is located!"

In the context of Li Si's biography, the apparent significance of this story is that it reveals the ambition of an undistinguished government clerk who would go on to become one of the most powerful men in all of China. However, Sima Qian was concerned with the question of why the virtuous suffer and the iniquitous prosper, and frequently used the commonplace (also encountered in the Guodian manuscripts) of "success or failure depends on one's circumstances." So this quotation may also be intended to show that Li Si had profound insight into the reality of life.

Next we read that Li Si became a student of Xunzi in order to master "the techniques of an emperor or king" and thus prepare himself for a more glorious political career.[4] This period of apprenticeship must have taken place between the years 255 B.C., when Xunzi was appointed magistrate of Lanling 蘭陵 (in Chu), and 247, when Li Si left Chu to seek his fortunes in the mighty state of Qin. Evidently sensing that his teacher was no longer useful to him, Li Si bade farewell: "I have heard that one must seize the moment and not be idle," he says, adding that he will find employment at the court of the King of Qin, who is about to conquer the world.[5]

In Qin, Li Si found favor with Lü Buwei 呂不韋, who was chancellor (*chengxiang* 丞相) and—so Sima Qian alleges—the illegitimate father of Zheng 政, then King of Qin and later First Emperor. With such a lofty patron, Li Si was granted the opportunity to speak to the king and seems to have excited him with hortatory flattery, asserting that victory and unprecedented power were within His Majesty's grasp. The king then followed many of Li Si's specific suggestions, which involved bribing those of his enemies who could be bribed and assassinating those who could not.

Some years later, in 237 B.C., Li Si faced his first political challenge: a faction at the Qin court, motivated more by fear of espionage than by xenophobia, urged the king to banish all foreigners currently serving in the Qin government. Li Si, as a native of Chu, would have been expelled under this resolution, and he argued against it in a flowery memorial that Sima Qian has preserved in its entirety, presumably as an example of effective rhetoric. In this oration, Li Si recalls several former rulers of Qin who employed foreign advisors, but the section that the hedonistic king must have found most persuasive discusses the many wonders and treasures that he has imported from alien lands—of which "the sultry girls of Zhao" were not the least delightful. It is incongruous that a king with such international tastes should consider banishing all the foreigners in his state. "You would seem to care more for sex, music, and gems than you do for people."[6]

The king had to relent, of course, because the proposal was incompatible with his own imperialistic aspirations. A ruler of the world had to be more than just the ruler of Qin. In taking such a prominent role in this debate, Li Si emerged as one of the leading politicians in the Qin court and rose rapidly through the ranks to the post of Commandant of Justice (*tingwei* 廷尉).

That same year, Li Si is said to have encouraged the King of Qin to annex the neighboring state of Hán 韓 "in order to intimidate the other states."[7] When Li Si arrived in Han to declare Qin's intentions, the King of Han was understandably upset and asked his relative Han Fei to save Han by diplomatic means. At this juncture, the details become sketchy. All sources agree that Han Fei was imprisoned in Qin and forced to commit suicide in 233 B.C. and that the state of Han was annihilated in the same year. Beyond that, the events are difficult to reconstruct. (By this point in his life, it is worth noting, Li Si had had dealings with Xunzi, Lü Buwei, the First Emperor of Qin, and Han Fei—the four most illustrious men of his day.)

The annals of the First Emperor of Qin in *Records of the Historian* inform us that Han Fei did not arrive in Qin until 233 B.C., four full years after Li Si first threatened the King of Han.[8] No extant sources explain what transpired in the interim.[9] Moreover, the surviving works of Han Fei include a number of documents pertaining to this affair that raise more questions than they answer. There is a memorial by Han Fei in which he argues that it is in Qin's own best interest to preserve the state of Han,[10] as well as a rebuttal by Li Si contending that an independent Han is like an infirmity of the heart or stomach plaguing Qin. Li Si goes on to outline a complex plan: he begs leave to return to Han in order to delude their king into thinking that Qin will aid its former enemy, whereupon Qin will seize the opportunity and conquer Han once and for all.[11] Then there is a third set of memorials, ostensibly recording Li Si's duplicitous speeches to the King of Han.[12]

But the situation is confused further by yet another memorial in the *Han Feizi;* here Han Fei addresses the King of Qin, urging him to become a "hegemon" by destroying the other states—including Han, Han Fei's own homeland![13] We must conclude either that one or more of these documents are spurious, or that Han Fei recognized the inevitable and switched his allegiance from Han to Qin. This change of heart would explain why it is alleged in Han Fei's biography that Li Si slandered Han Fei, caused him to be imprisoned on a trumped-up charge, and finally inveigled him into killing himself. The King of Qin, we are told, was impressed by Han Fei's writings and must have been contemplating his potential value as a minister of Qin. Thus Li Si may have considered Han Fei—whom he must have known, after all, from the days when they were both studying under Xunzi—as a dangerous rival and plotted to have him removed.

For the next two decades, Li Si's place in the Qin government was secure. When the King of Qin united China in 221 B.C. and declared himself the First Emperor, Li Si, as Commandant of Justice of the entire empire, had already attained more success than he could ever have imagined while contemplating the rats in the functionaries' privy at Shangcai. And as one of the new emperor's most trusted advisors, his future promised even greater dignities and honors.

History has not preserved the names of every commandant of justice in ancient China, and if it were not for Li Si's activities after the founding of the empire, he would hardly be remembered today. Li Si's first opportunity to influence the complexion of imperial government came soon after the King of Qin assumed the title of "emperor" (*huangdi* 皇帝) in 221 B.C. The chancellor, a man named Wang Wan 王綰, suggested that the sons of the emperor be granted fiefs so as to assist in the administration of the emperor's vast new realm. We are told that all the other ministers concurred in this opinion, but Li Si opposed it. He pointed out that the idea of dividing the realm into fiefs entrusted to relatives or trusted allies of the sovereign was obviously taken directly from the model of the Zhou, and it should not have taken much reflection to realize that the protracted period of warfare from which China had only just emerged was the consequence this very practice. Only a few generations after the establishment of the Zhou dynasty, the various feudal lords were able to cast off the yoke of Zhou sovereignty and rule their fiefs as independent states. It was therefore quite imprudent for the new emperor to follow the policies of the dynasty that he had just replaced. The emperor agreed.[14]

In place of the old feudal covenants, the First Emperor inaugurated an administrative system that revealed a fundamentally different conception of the empire—one that had been adumbrated by earlier political thinkers but had never been instituted on such a prodigious scale. The realm was divided into thirty-six "commanderies" governed by a bureaucratic administration under the direct control of the emperor himself. Then all the weapons in the empire were supposedly collected, melted down, and recast into bells and statues. The powerful families of the vanquished kingdoms were forcibly relocated to the new imperial capital, and simulacra of their palaces were built in the capital as well.

We are not told whether Li Si had a role in these particular reforms,[15] but they are plainly in line with the imperialist vision for which he was becoming famous. Already in 237, his memorial against the proposal to banish foreigners from Qin disclosed his view of the state as an entity that transcended regional differences by incorporating equally all the territories of the world. One might argue that because Li Si himself was an alien dwelling in Qin, this speech was written more out of self-interest than any grandiose ideals of political philosophy. But all of Li Si's proposals—at least until his last days, when, as we shall see, he was reduced to toadying to unworthy superiors—reflect a consistent and revolutionary view of Qin's mission: to unify the disparate kingdoms and implement a new centralized form of government, while eliminating divergent customs and resisting any policy that might lead to a recrudescence of territorial power.

At some point between 219 and 213 B.C., Li Si was promoted to chancellor and was now one of the two highest-ranking subjects in the empire.[16] In 213, a scholar named Chunyu Yue 淳于越 remonstrated with the First Emperor, repeating the old suggestion that the sons and younger brothers of the emperor, along with certain meritorious ministers, should be enfeoffed as feudal lords. The First Emperor handed the matter down to Chancellor Li Si, who was even more emphatic in his rejection of this proposal than when he first discussed the issue eight years earlier. In his reply this time, he did not even devote any space to refuting Chunyu Yue's suggestion, taking it as a matter of course that such ideas were hopelessly outdated. Instead, Li Si addressed what he took to be the real problem: men like Chunyu Yue took the liberty of criticizing official decrees on the basis of what he calls their "private learning" 私學 (or, read in Han Fei's terms, "self-interested learning"). This is unacceptable, Li Si argues, because in the new unified regime, only the emperor has the authority to determine right and wrong. If "private learning" is not prohibited, "the power of the ruler will decline above and parties will be formed below."[17]

Li Si then recommends that every subject who possesses works of literature, including the canonical *Odes* and *Documents* and the "sayings of the hundred experts," must remand these to the appropriate officials for burning. Anyone who wants to study must take an administrative official as his teacher. The only exceptions to this ordinance are books on medicine, divination, and agriculture; according to one version of the memorial, Li Si allows government-appointed academicians to retain their copies of canonical Confucian texts. The First Emperor, we are told, approved the measure.

This was the notorious Qin biblioclasm, the event with which Li Si has been most intimately connected in the minds of traditional Chinese literati. Generations of historians have criticized Li Si as an enemy of learning in general and Confucianism in particular. Indeed, he cannot be easily acquitted of these charges. Yet some modern scholars have suggested that the entire account is fabricated or at least exaggerated, because the memorial implies a massive campaign to collect books and burn them, but there is little evidence that texts were permanently lost. That observation, however, is not in itself compelling: texts were commonly memorized and recited in ancient China, so that even if all written copies were destroyed, they could still be reconstructed afterward (provided that enough people remained who knew the text by heart). In fact, the Han government made a concerted effort some decades later to locate the aged masters of the Qin era and have them recite what they could remember for scribes to record with brush and ink. Moreover, if we are to believe the account that official academicians were exempt from the ban, then it follows that the canons were never totally exterminated in the first place.[18]

Whether or not the "biblioclasm" really took place, it is clear that the proposal is in keeping with Li Si's political views. "Private learning," as Li Si put it, was antithetical to the pretensions of the unified empire, and eradicating all autonomous intellectual life was only the logical conclusion of the reforms that he had been advocating for years.[19] Any institution whose authority did not derive directly from the emperor inherently challenged the foundations of the empire and had to be destroyed. Philosophers and teachers, who routinely appealed to traditions, scriptures, and august precedents, would have constituted a conspicuous example of what Li Si feared most. The Qin empire was not merely an empire; it was a unified cosmos with a proper cosmology. The ruler of the cosmos, similarly, was not merely an emperor or great king; he was the center of the cosmos, the prime mover of all order and logic.

In short, Li Si was unable to conceive of a flourishing empire that countenanced free thought, let alone dissent. By imposing its rigid dictates on all aspects of human experience, the empire sowed the seeds of its own destruction. To Americans living in the twenty-first century, it may seem obvious that Li Si's attempts at thought control were to blame for the astonishingly rapid collapse of the Qin dynasty. But it took a long decade of intense bloodshed for the point to become apparent to observers in the third century B.C.

Li Si was now at the peak of his power, and Sima Qian includes a picturesque episode in his biography intended to show that the chancellor himself may have had a premonition that his fortunes were about to turn. At some point after the memorial on the burning of the books, Li Si held a feast at his home to welcome back his son, Li You 李由, who was serving as governor of Sanchuan 三川 (a commandery along the Yellow River, east of the capital). It is said that thousands of chariots and horsemen arrived at the gates of his residence as officials from all branches of government came to wish him long life. The chancellor then quoted his former teacher and compared himself to a useless carriage horse:

> 嗟乎！吾聞之荀卿曰物禁大盛。夫斯乃上蔡布衣，閭巷之黔首，上不知其駑下，遂擢至此。當今人臣之位無居臣上者，可謂富貴極矣。物極則衰，吾未知所稅駕也！[20]
>
> Alas, I have heard Xunzi say: "Do not let things flourish too greatly." I wore a commoner's clothes at Shangcai; I was an ordinary subject from the lanes and alleyways. The emperor did not realize that his nag was inferior, so he raised me to this [position]. No one with a ministerial position occupies a post higher than mine; one can call this the pinnacle of wealth and honor. When things reach their pinnacle, they decline. I do not yet know where my carriage will be halted.

Late in 211 B.C., the First Emperor decided to make one of his habitual circuits through his empire, accompanied by Li Si and two other men: Huhai 胡亥, his young son, and Zhao Gao 趙高, a eunuch who was Superintendent of the Imperial Carriage House. The First Emperor's eldest son, named Fusu 扶蘇, had irritated his father by criticizing him repeatedly for his denigration of Confucius. Consequently, the First Emperor sent Fusu to the camp of General Meng Tian 蒙恬, who was stationed at the frontier.[21] With Fusu far removed from palace politics, it seems that the aging First Emperor began to dote on Huhai.

Nine months into his grand tour, the First Emperor fell deathly ill and died at a place called Sand Hill 沙丘.[22] Before he died, he dictated a letter to Fusu, commanding him to come to the capital with Meng Tian's troops and bury his father there. The letter was sealed but still had not been sent when the First Emperor expired. Since no definite heir had been designated, Li Si decided to keep the matter secret, and only he, Zhao Gao, Huhai, and a handful of trusted eunuchs knew that the First Emperor had passed away. They placed the emperor's cadaver in a "warm-and-cool carriage" 轀輬車—that is, a carriage that could be opened or closed as the climate dictated[23]—and continued to conduct official business from within the closed carriage as though the emperor were still alive.[24] As one of the First Emperor's most intimate associates, Zhao Gao must have known that Huhai was a foolish and malleable lordling. He encouraged the young prince to seize the throne for himself, hinting darkly that the empire would not rebel if Fusu were to be assassinated.

After obtaining Huhai's consent, Zhao Gao approached Li Si with his plan, but the latter declined repeatedly to cooperate. Zhao Gao countered by remarking that Fusu trusted only General Meng Tian, his comrade in arms, and if Fusu were to succeed the First Emperor, Li Si would surely be replaced as chancellor. Li Si remained unmoved: he and his family had enjoyed great prosperity at the hands of the First Emperor and must remain loyal, come what may. Furthermore, Li Si cited several examples from history showing that such treachery always causes great harm to the state. Zhao Gao importuned Li Si relentlessly, until the latter finally "looked up to Heaven and sighed" 仰天而歎. With tears streaming down his face, he declared: "Alas, I alone have encountered this chaotic age. Since I cannot bring myself to die, to what shall I entrust my life?" 嗟乎！獨遭亂世，既以不能死，安託命哉？[25] Thereupon he obeyed Zhao Gao.

Modern readers are likely to be puzzled by all of Li Si's sighs and rhetorical questions; and whatever the implicit argument in "Since I cannot bring myself to die, to what shall I entrust my life?" it hardly persuades us that his actions were anything but disloyal. This passage probably tells us more about the author, Sima Qian, than it does about Li Si. Having characters gaze up to Heaven at crucial moments in history is a trope that Sima Qian uses on several occasions to suggest that the irresistible will of Heaven lies behind the inscrutable vicissitudes of human life.[26] We must remember that Sima Qian was writing for the emperor of the Han, a dynasty whose rise would not have been possible without the destruction of the Qin. For a Han audience, the conspiracy at Sand Hill was a matter of historical necessity. Li Si's protestations were gallant but ineffectual: in one way or another, Heaven was going to find a method for the plot to unfold. By gazing up at Heaven, Li Si, we are given to understand, recognized and accepted the role that fate had assigned him.

Huhai's reign as Second Emperor was an unmitigated disaster. A power struggle ensued between Li Si and Zhao Gao: both courtiers knew that Huhai was thoroughly incapable of standing on his own, so they competed for the opportunity to rule behind the scenes. This was a contest that Li Si was bound to lose, for Zhao Gao was more adept at manipulating the puerile emperor. With Zhao Gao's encouragement, the Second Emperor ushered in a reign of terror, executing influential men in government and confiscating their estates; the turmoil amused the Second Emperor but had the decisive consequence of destroying whatever power base he had at his disposal.[27]

The famous rebellion of Chen She 陳涉 and Wu Guang 吳廣 then erupted in Chu, and with the central government in such disarray, the imperial forces were powerless to quell it. When the rebels arrived at Sanchuan, Li Si's son You, who was still governor of the district, could not stop them from advancing westward toward the imperial capital. Zhao Gao immediately took advantage of this opportunity to accuse Li Si and his son of conniving at the insurrection. Before long, the chancellor was thrown into prison and brought to trial; once again, he gazed up fecklessly at Heaven, this time comparing himself to various celebrated ministers of antiquity who were wrongly condemned.[28]

The rest of Li Si's biography is devoted to his craven attempts to save his skin. He penned a long and fawning epistle laying out heavy-handed principles of government that he hoped would meet with the Second Emperor's approval. One of the authorities he cites in this disquisition is Han Fei, the great thinker whose downfall he himself plotted years before;[29] it must have galled him to memorialize his archrival in this manner, but such was the humiliating position to which he was reduced. Next he assailed Zhao Gao's integrity, asserting at one point that the eunuch was avaricious because of his lowly origins.[30] (Forensically, this was a doomed approach: after all, Li Si too was born a commoner, and his own ambition was of historic proportions.) Then, in a final act of desperation, Li Si wrote a direct plea to the Second Emperor from his jail cell, recounting his great services to the state of Qin and begging for mercy. But Zhao Gao intercepted the letter and refused to show it to the emperor. In the summer of 208 B.C., Li Si and his son were put to death and their clan exterminated.

Sima Qian records Li Si's last words, and they are characteristically disingenuous. On the way to the execution ground, he supposedly turned to his son and said: "I wish that you and I could take our brown dog and go out through the eastern gate of Shangcai to chase the crafty hare. But how could we do that!"[31] This quote has become famous, but, like his repeated perlustrations of Heaven, it is simply an expression of counterfeit pathos. While he was still living in Shangcai, Li Si felt nothing more for the place than intense desire to leave it, and a bucolic life would hardly have contented him while he was serving in the grimy municipal offices. But a life devoted to hunting rabbits might not have been cut short by the executioner's blade.

In the end, we must acknowledge that the vision of Li Si, the primary architect of early Chinese imperialism, affected the course of history of an entire subcontinent. Most later writers dispraised him as a traitor and an opportunist, but there is no doubt that the imperial institutions of every succeeding dynasty were indebted to Li Si's model of centralized bureaucracy. If, as some historians affirm, Chinese civilization was a bureaucratic civilization,[32] then a place must be reserved for Li Si as one of the nation's founding fathers.

—5—

Rhetoric and Machination in *Stratagems of the Warring States*

A critical consensus regarding *Stratagems of the Warring States* (*Zhanguo ce*), an iconoclastic collection of anecdotes gathered by Liu Xiang 劉向 (79–8 B.C.), has proven to be elusive. Henri Maspero (1883–1945) demonstrated that much of the material in the *Stratagems* is fictional,[1] and most historians have since rejected the text as a primary source of information, although it has been suggested that the *Stratagems* may be derived from some of the same sources that Sima Qian used in *Records of the Historian*.[2] Still, it is generally agreed that *Stratagems of the Warring States* is very unreliable as a history book and was probably never intended to serve as one.

Others see the *Stratagems* as a manual of persuasive speaking, filled with debates and speeches that serve as models of superior rhetoric.[3] Yet the value of the text as a handbook is dubious. There is no evidence of a conscious attempt by Liu Xiang (or the anonymous authors themselves) to classify the various items by style or theme. The anecdotes are ordered only by state of provenance and at that quite loosely. Readers of the *Stratagems* might sense that they are made privy to several gems of rhetorical strategy that can be employed when the appropriate situation should arise, but they discover neither a unified theory of rhetoric applicable to any occasion nor a systematic treatise that can be routinely consulted.[4]

By contrast, the most influential of the classical Western textbooks—such as the *Rhetoric* of Aristotle (384–322 B.C.), *De oratore* by Cicero (106–43 B.C.), or the anonymous *Rhetorica ad Herennium*[5]—share the advantage of clear organization: the discussions and examples are consistently arranged by topic. A primer should be coherent and lead the student's mind directly to the points it wishes to convey. But *Stratagems of the War-*

ring States, though it may be valuable as something else, is inadequate as a textbook. None of the rhetorical skills that are demonstrated so brilliantly in these speeches are ever identified explicitly, let alone analyzed or categorized.

The most prominent Western scholar in the study of the *Stratagems* is James I. Crump, Jr., whose critical works and complete translation stand out as fundamental contributions.[6] Crump's own interpretation of the *Stratagems* (which he calls *Intrigues*) is encapsulated in the following paragraph:

> Suppose a Chinese rhetorical tradition included some such device as the *suasoria* for training men in the art of persuasion: would that not explain much of what is most baffling about the Intrigues? If exercises by the masters or the disciples of such a "school" were part of the "school's" heritage it would not only explain many of the contradictions in the Intrigues, but it would account for many other facets of this delightful work. Why, for example, do so many persuaders so often speak their entire piece with no interruption from the ruler, who simply says "so be it" when the persuader is finished? Why are the pieces in the Intrigues so beautifully polished? And how did the men in the Intrigues invariably think of just the right thing to say for the occasion? These become understandable if the training a man underwent to pursue the career he hoped for (political advisor, emissary, and the like) included model advice which would or should have been offered at certain historic occasions, and somehow found its way into what we now call the *Intrigues of the Warring States.*[7]

This is the first formulation of a theory that has gained widespread popularity over the past forty years. David Hawkes, for example, agrees wholeheartedly, adding: "It is even arguable that *Chan-kuo ts'e* meant not 'Intrigues of the Warring States' but 'Imaginary Speeches on Warring States Themes.'"[8] The most significant dissenting voice is that of Jaroslav Průšek, who finds that the "stress on the anecdotal aspect is not by any means subordinated to the stress on rhetoric" (more on this problem below).[9] But neither Crump's supporters nor his critics have applied a study of the tradition of the Roman *suasoria* to the rhetoric of *Stratagems of the Warring States.* This involves a comparison of several aspects of Chinese and Roman rhetoric, such as the use of language and devices as well as the theory of rhetoric and its ultimate goal.

Suasoriae were Roman school exercises: pupils were reminded of a well-known historical event and asked to write persuasive speeches that might have been delivered by the personages involved. If a contemporary high-school student were required to write his or her own version of George Washington's address at Valley Forge, this assignment would be similar in spirit to the *suasoriae* of ancient times. *Suasoriae* are also considered a class of *prosopopoeiae,* or speeches in which a later writer "supplies the words which someone else, real or fictitious, might in agreement with the laws of necessity and probability have composed and delivered under a given set of circumstances."[10] The genre is not rare. The students of Seneca the Elder (54 B.C.–A.D. 39?) provided the exercises contained in the largest extant anthology of *suasoriae.*[11] Quintilian (b. ca. A.D. 35) discussed them at length in his *Institutio oratoria,* and both Juvenal (d. ca. A.D. 140) and Persius (A.D. 34–62) remembered with disdain the days they spent as schoolboys producing them.[12]

There can be little disagreement that the several hundred items in the *Stratagems* are fairly categorized as *prosopopoeiae.* They contain too many internal contradictions, both factual and chronological, to be true history. It is more likely that the speeches in the text are merely a later author's conjectures as to what the ancients may have said at certain moments of history. This is why some modern historians claim to find a kernel of truth in the *Stratagems:* the authors deliberately chose real events to embroider. But their compositions were intended as historical fiction or romanticized history, not as accurate accounts of the past.[13]

However, a *prosopopoeia* is not necessarily a *suasoria.* The latter genre is an idiosyncratic outcropping of classical Roman culture. Social advancement in Rome required the ability to speak well, and this entailed mastery of the complex rhetorical conventions of the day. Roman schoolmasters were aware that the stylized use of language typical of successful orators was an art that could be acquired only through intensive practice. The *suasoriae,* which furnished an unlimited selection of historical situations to re-create, represented one solution to the peculiar Roman problem of training youths to become competent statesmen in the classical mold.

But ancient China was another world, and although rhetorical ability provided material advantages in that society as well, some of the dissimilarities between the *suasoriae* and the *Stratagems* can be traced to the political contexts in which these two forms flourished. In both Greece and Rome, the main purpose of rhetoric was to convince masses of people.[14] It followed that the most popular and effective rhetorical devices were those designed to sway large audiences, and these were the techniques that students practiced in their *suasoriae.* The situation was radically different in Warring States China, where the final arbiter was the king alone. A minister who wanted to press his agenda needed above all to convince the sovereign, whose approval was required before any momentous decision could be carried out. This is why most of the arguments in the *Stratagems* are tailored to persuade a single figure of absolute authority.[15]

Thus the intended audiences of Chinese and Roman rhetoric had a differing effect on the structure of persuasive speech and orators' choice of devices. The manner in which Aristotle and Han Fei treated this problem is instructive. Aristotle devotes a substantial section of his *Rhetoric* (II.12–17) to a discussion of the psychological means by which speakers must match the character of the audience: the young, the old, those in the prime of life, the noble, the wealthy, and the powerful.[16] Han Fei is also interested in molding speech to suit the audience, but his analysis considers the range of nuances in the character of a ruler—impetuous, self-satisfied, sanctimonious, and so forth[17]—not a range of social classes that speakers address. For the only kind of oratory with real consequences is directed at a king.

However, there are indeed some remarkable similarities between the *suasoriae* and the *Stratagems*. For example, the following thoughts on *suasoriae*, by Quintilian, would be equally appropriate with regard to the Chinese material: "Consequently, as a rule, a *suasoria* is nothing other than a comparison, and we must consider what we shall gain and by what means, that it may be possible to form an estimate as to whether there is greater advantage in the aims that we pursue, or disadvantage in the means that we employ."[18]

One of the most readily identifiable traits of the *Stratagems* is precisely the sort of comparison of opposing arguments that, according to Quintilian, typifies the *suasoriae*. Consider, for example, the famous debate between Sima Cuo 司馬錯 and Zhang Yi 張儀. Where should the state of Qin attack? The renowned minister Zhang Yi advocates attacking Hán, which lies near the royal domain of Zhou. Eventually Qin should seize the Nine Cauldrons, arrest the Son of Heaven, and claim suzerainty over the world. But then Sima Cuo points out the adverse effects that such a brazen step would have on Qin's relations with its neighbors.

> 今攻韓劫天子，劫天子，惡名也，而未必利也。又有不義之名，而攻天下之所不欲，危！臣請謁其故：周，天下之宗室也；齊，韓、周之與國也。周自知失九鼎，韓自知亡三川，則必將二國并力合謀，以因于齊、趙，而求解乎楚、魏。[19]

> Now if you were to attack Han and capture the Son of Heaven—capturing the Son of Heaven makes for a bad reputation and is not necessarily profitable. Moreover, you would have a reputation for being immoral, and it is dangerous to attack what the world does not wish you [to attack]. I, your servant, beg leave to explain my reasons. Zhou is the premier house in the world, and Qi is a state that cooperates with Han and Zhou. When Zhou knows that it will lose the Nine Cauldrons, and Han knows that it will lose [the district of] Sanchuan, they will surely take their two states and combine forces and plot together. They will rely on Qin and Zhao, and will ask Chu and Wei to release them [from Qin's attack].

Sima Cuo argues instead for a campaign against the fecund but underdeveloped land of Shu 蜀, which Qin could take "as though one had set jackals and wolves to chase a flock of sheep" 譬如使豺狼逐群羊也. He adds that his plan promises immeasurable wealth and worldwide respect. The tension here is heightened by the great disparity in the influence of the two parties. Zhang Yi is one of the most revered advisors in the world, Sima Cuo (though later claimed by Sima Qian as an ancestor)[20] a relative unknown who does not appear anywhere else in the text. But the king follows Sima Cuo's proposal, which, judging from hindsight, history seems to have favored as well.[21] The author of this account, sensitive to the same concerns as Quintilian, recognizes that there must have been several reasonable points of view at the time. If Qin's object was world domination, the most obvious approach would have been to attack Zhou directly and assume control of the Nine Cauldrons, the traditional symbol of Heaven-ordained rulership. But the debate would have little rhetorical value if there were no other opinions to consider. Thus the author employs the same solution as the writers of *suasoriae* and presents two competing arguments for the king—and the reader—to weigh.

However, the similarities between the *suasoriae* and the *Stratagems* are evident only on this structural level. The two forms differ considerably, for example, in their use of rhetorical devices. One of the salient features of classical rhetoric is its heavy reliance on conventional devices, ranged in taxonomies found in much of the ancient theoretical literature: anaphora, asyndeton, chiasmus, hypallage (transferred epithet), litotes, hendiadys, and so on. Most of these devices are inapplicable to classical Chinese because of its grammar. Because it is (discounting certain fossilized forms) an uninflected language, the logic of Chinese appears exclusively in the syntax; that is to say, the different functions of words are indicated by their placement in a sentence. There is generally much less opportunity for variation with word order in languages of this type, as compared to Latin. The distinction is significant: while we may not be surprised to see very general devices—such as isocolon, simile, antithesis, assonance, or rhyme—in the literatures of all cultures, devices associated with liberal word order will tend to appear in inflected languages only. For this reason, many of the Latin figures, such as hendiadys and epithet transfer, are not likely to appear in Chinese rhetoric.

A typical example of chiasmus in Latin is found in the *suasoriae* of Seneca (VI.xxvi.24): *nostraeque cadens ferus Annibal irae.* In this clause, *cadens ferus Annibal* (literally "fierce Hannibal falling," or, in this context, "when fierce Hannibal fell") is in the nominative case and thus functions as the subject. *Nostraeque . . . irae* (and to our wrath) is in the dative case. Taken together, the words mean "and when fierce Hannibal fell to our wrath,"[22] although the chiasmus is lost in translation precisely because English is a largely uninflected language, and it is impossible to arrange the words in chiasmic form. Such a phrase could be found only in a language like Latin (or Greek, Sanskrit, and so on), whose complex nominal and adjectival declensions can accommodate the necessary word order.

And it is absent from the *Stratagems:* a Chinese sentence usually cannot be wrenched to form a chiasmus.[23] It is similarly inappropriate to speak of asyndeton in Chinese, since words are regularly connected without conjunctions. For example, the "jackals and wolves" invoked by Sima Cuo appear literally as "jackals wolves" 豺狼. Only in languages with habitual use of conjunctions can there be any discussion of asyndeton as a rhetorical device, because only in these languages does asyndeton have any unusual effect. When Shakespeare writes "hang, beg, starve, die in the streets" (*Romeo and Juliet* III.v.194), readers of English are struck by the stark desolation of the phrase. In classical Chinese, it would seem unnerving to coordinate a similar series of words in any other way.

Hendiadys, furthermore, is impossible in the language of the *Stratagems,* which makes no essential separations between parts of speech. (These are determined entirely by syntax.) Anaphora, wordy and repetitive, would normally be out of place in the terse style of the *Stratagems.* And transferred epithets, while readily identifiable in the five-case nominal system of Latin, would be unintelligible in Chinese.[24]

But do the Chinese speeches display rhetorical devices of their own? This question is rarely asked in studies of ancient Chinese rhetoric. Crump notes that the prose of the *Stratagems* "will be found to have very strong rhythm, a penchant for antithesis (or chiasm), parisosis (or symmetry of units), consonance verging on rhyme, and all the other devices peculiar to the orator's self-conscious and somewhat fulsome use of language."[25]

These are all, naturally, devices that fit an uninflected language like Chinese. Whatever chiasmus is found in the *Stratagems* is not semantic or syntactic chiasmus (as in the example from Seneca), but thematic chiasmus, where the explication of whole themes or concepts may form a chiasmus. This appears even in the Hebrew Bible,[26] and it is probably a universal feature of human expression.

Some other rhetorical devices known to Roman orators appear in the *Stratagems;* these are linguistic flourishes that can be employed effectively in Chinese. Sententia (a maxim or aphorism conveyed in a dense phrase) is a good example: the inherent power of such a pithy utterance is rendered even more forceful by the lapidary rhythm of classical Chinese.[27] Litotes (as in the ubiquitous "not a little" 不少) and other ornamentations appear as well.[28] But the most powerful Chinese devices involve not simply the use of language but entire methods of argumentation and thematic arrangement of material. These are comparable to the topoi or *loci communes* (commonplaces) of classical rhetoric.[29] The following is a representative overview.[30]

Historical Allusion. The direct reference to a historical incident, citing the circumstances that brought it about as well as the aftermath, serving the twofold function of displaying the speaker's erudition and providing historical justification for a position. Examples: (1) Su Qin 蘇秦 presents a catalog of opportunistic warriors who took up arms.[31] (2) Chen Zhen 陳軫 refers to Xiaoji 孝己 and Zixu 子胥, loyal men of old.[32] (3) Zhang Yi ventures to speak of "the past" 往昔.[33] This topic is very common and is so firmly identified in the Western mind with Chinese rhetoric as to have been labeled the "Chinese argument" by Jeremy Bentham (1748–1832) in his famous catalog of fallacies.[34]

Literary Allusion. The reference to a venerable work, serving much the same purpose as Historical Allusion. Examples: (1) From the *Odes.*[35] (2) From the *Documents.*[36] (3) From a commentary to the *Changes.*[37] (4) From *Laozi.*[38]

Apophthegm. Citing a proverb, with the implication that conventional wisdom is on the speaker's side. Examples: (1) "Those whose feathers are not abundant cannot fly high" 毛羽不豐滿者不可以高飛.[39] (2) "Three men make a tiger [if they all claim to see one]" 三人成虎.[40] (3) "When Qiji [a legendary thoroughbred] jades, a nag will pass it; when Meng

Ben [a warrior famed for his strength] is tired, a woman will defeat him" 騏驥之衰也，駑馬先之；孟賁之倦也，女子勝之.[41]

Induction. Asking questions of one's opponent in order to lead him or her to agree to certain premises, after which one's argument becomes irrefutable, because the opposing party has itself assented to the clinching proposition. Examples: (1) Su Qin leads the King of Qi to attack Song (even though it is hardly clear that this invasion would be profitable).[42] (2) Su Dai 蘇代 convinces the King of Wei to maintain Tian Xu 田需, a loyal vassal who has apparently fallen out of favor with his liege, in order to watch over two other followers, who, as the king himself admits, are not trustworthy.[43]

Dilemma. This versatile commonplace is found in three general forms.

Type A: Reducing the number of possible solutions to two and then refuting one, thereby affirming the other. Examples: (1) the debate between Zhang Yi and Sima Cuo (discussed above). (2) Zhang Gai 張丐 persuades the state of Lu to remain neutral for the time being, since one can attack now or later, and attacking later is better than attacking now.[44]

Type B: Showing that an action will have the same result in all possible sequences of events. Examples: (1) Queen Dowager Xuan of Qin 秦宣太后 should not insist that her lover, Wei Choufu 魏醜夫, be buried alive with her. If there is no life after death, she has no use for her paramour, and if there is life after death, then she will be busy appeasing her irate husband, with no time left for Wei Choufu.[45] (2) Zou Ji 鄒忌 (385–319 B.C.),[46] the Marquis of Cheng 成 and Prime Minister of Qi, can overcome his nemesis, Tian Ji 田忌, by recommending that the latter engage in battle: for if Tian Ji should succeed, the king would reward Zou Ji for his good counsel, and if Tian Ji should fail, Zou Ji would be rid of a troublesome competitor.[47] (3) Zheng Shen 鄭申, the envoy of the King of Chu, takes matters into his own hands by giving land to the embattled crown prince. Zheng has determined, through an intricate series of calculations, that the king will profit whether his son succeeds or fails.[48]

Type C (Scylla and Charybdis): Finding a clever solution to a Type B Dilemma by navigating through two apparently irreconcilable impediments. Examples: (1) Hui Shi 惠施 is an enemy of Zhang Yi but a friend of the King of Song 宋. So how should the King of Chu proceed? If he treats Hui Shi well, Zhang Yi will be offended, but if he treats Hui Shi badly, the King of Song will be offended. A counselor, Feng He 馮郝, hits on the solution: support Hui Shi well but then send him away to the

King of Song. This course of action will please both Zhang Yi and the King of Song.[49] (2) An adulterous wife plans to poison her husband, and a concubine learns of the plot. How can she now avoid betraying either her master or her mistress? The concubine knocks over the poisoned chalice, and is beaten for it, but manages to escape from the dilemma.[50] (3) Without an intermediary, a girl cannot be married. If her father does not show her to anyone, she will become an old spinster for lack of suitors, but if he displays her himself, she will be cheapened and remain unwanted. The intermediary is the only solution.[51]

Dilemma, especially of the third and most polished type, is a productive topic in the *Stratagems* and is widely attested elsewhere in ancient Chinese literature.[52]

Enthymeme of Comparison. A type of refutation: citing an instance in which a proposal failed even though its probability of success was much greater than that of the argument presently being considered. This topic generally takes the form: "If even X, then certainly Y, given that X is less likely to occur than Y." Examples: (1) Even the mother of Zeng Can 曾參,[53] a leading disciple of Confucius, finally believed that her son was a murderer after hearing such a rumor three times. How much more precarious now is the position of Gan Mao 甘茂, since the king has less faith in him than Zeng Can's mother had in her son, and Gan Mao's enemies number far more than three?[54] (2) If even Zou Ji is duped by flatterers, the mighty king can expect no less.[55] (3) If the King of Wei can be moved to believe the preposterous idea that there is a tiger in the market after only three reports to that effect, then he can hardly avoid being swayed by false accusations of Pang Cong, who has more than three detractors.[56]

Tiger and Fox. Showing that the root cause of a phenomenon lies hidden behind the ostensible cause. Or vice versa: obscuring the root cause by pointing to the ostensible one. Examples: (1) Zou Ji is praised not because of his beauty but because of his influence.[57] (2) King Xiang of Qi 齊襄王 can take all the credit for extraordinary acts of charity undertaken by Tian Dan 田單 by ordering grandly that everyone protect the needy. Then people will assume that Tian Dan is merely carrying out the king's beneficent instructions.[58] (3) A tiger is about to eat a fox, when the fox declares that he is the most powerful creature in the world, challenging the tiger to follow him around and see for himself. The tiger does so and is convinced when he sees all the other animals flee; he does not realize that they are afraid of him, not of the fox.[59]

Adding Feet to the Snake. Showing that too much of a good thing can be ruinous. Examples: (1) The archer Yang Youji 養由基 should stop after a hundred consecutive bull's-eyes, lest he miss once and nullify his achievement.[60] (2) A group of associates agree on a novel way of drawing lots for a single cup of wine: they should each draw a snake, and the drink will go to whoever finishes first. One of them claims victory, takes hold of the cup, and proudly adds feet to the snake with his spare hand. But then another contestant finishes his own snake and snatches the goblet away: for a snake with feet is no longer a snake at all.[61]

Dueling Tigers. Showing that contending enemies weaken each other and that the best policy is therefore to bide one's time and strike when they are both exhausted. Examples: (1) Guan Zhuangzi 管莊子 comes upon two tigers fighting over carrion. He is about to slay them, but Guan Yu 管與 persuades him to wait until one is dead and the other wounded. Then he can win fame for killing two tigers with less effort than it would take to defeat a single healthy one.[62] (2) A mussel has caught a predatory heron by the beak. Neither animal is willing to give way, so they are both caught by a passing fisherman.[63]

Bad Faith. Obtaining a valuable concession (such as property or territory) from an opponent in exchange for a reciprocal favor that is supposed to be granted later, but then reneging when circumstances are such that the opponent does not find it expedient to complain or seek redress. Agents who negotiate in bad faith never have any intention of honoring their agreements in the first place. Examples: (1) Yan Shuai 顏率, Zhou's ambassador, secures an alliance with Qi by promising to hand over the Nine Cauldrons. But Yan Shuai never transports the cauldrons, claiming that there is no safe route from Zhou to Qi. Qi does not dare have them sent.[64] (2) Zhang Yi, Qin's ambassador, offers the King of Chu 600 square *li* 里 of land as enticement to break with Qi, Chu's most powerful ally. Although the minister Chen Zhen is suspicious, the king ignores him. Just as Chen Zhen surmised, Zhang Yi later refuses to cede the land when he is sure that Chu has indeed ended its alliance with Qi. The King of Chu is incensed and attacks Qin—again despite the protestations of the loyal Chen Zhen—but is defeated by the combined might of Qin and Qi, Chu's former ally.[65]

Subreption. The use of mendacious testimony, forged documents, or the procured loyalty of venal officials. Usually, the purpose is to destroy a rival in front of the king, but sometimes the ruler himself is the victim. Examples: (1) Gan Mao, the Prime Minister of Qin, has learned of the king's secret plan to replace him with Gongsun Yan 公孫衍. Gan proceeds, with great fanfare, to compliment the king on his excellent choice and, when interrogated, explains falsely that Gongsun Yan himself told him the news. Gongsun Yan is banished.[66] (2) Zou Ji's minion plants an agent in the marketplace who pretends to be an assistant of Zou Ji's enemy, Tian Ji. The spy loudly announces that his supposed master, Tian Ji, is plotting to usurp the throne and calls for a fortune-teller to divine the likelihood of success. The upright fortune-teller promptly informs the king, and Tian Ji is forced to flee.[67] (3) The King of Zhao seizes the sacrificial precinct of Zhou but is cozened into abandoning it when he falls ill and is told by his Grand Diviner, who has been suborned, that the precinct is the cause of his affliction.[68] (4) Naïveté costs a delightful young concubine her nose. (This piece will be discussed further below.)[69]

These examples are by no means exhaustive. Other topics include executing disloyal henchmen, warning the king of slander, and more methods of dealing with underhandedness. *Stratagems of the Warring States* also displays the familiar Warring States concern that names fit reality. Kings are encouraged to identify their favorite wife through a gift of distinctive jewelry,[70] or to grant a large fief or lofty title to an especially meritorious minister, so that all may know who is in favor—and who is not. Such anecdotes can be seen as variations on the theme of distinguishing reality from misleading appearances, or Tiger and Fox.

Several of the topics in the *Stratagems* appear, at least in some form, in Greco-Roman rhetoric as well. Historical Allusion, Literary Allusion, and Apophthegm are arguments from authority and correspond to what Aristotle calls "from a previous judgement" (*ek kriseōs*),[71] while Enthymeme of Comparison is similar to Aristotle's topic "from the more and less" (*ek tou mallon kai hētton*).[72] Cicero lists several commonplaces in his *De inventione*—a work that he later repudiated but that can still serve as a reliable source of devices that were fashionable in his day—including *inductio* (induction), precisely the same strategy exploited by the persuaders of the *Stratagems*.[73] Such general techniques of rhetoric may be common to several disparate cultures, if not all humanity.

However, other topics in the *Stratagems* raise deeper problems about the place of rhetoric in the work as a whole. What do these strategies accomplish? In Historical Allusion, Literary Allusion, and Apophthegm, the speaker merely finds a proper quotation from the font of received wisdom. Of themselves, such sayings are ineffectual, because any audience will certainly have heard them before (and some of them, such as "Look before you leap" and "He who hesitates is lost," may be mutually contradictory). The persuader's challenge is to fit them into the oration as appropriate and not to exhaust their efficacy by overusing them.

Induction, Dilemma, and Enthymeme of Comparison are entirely different: these are topics with a limitless range of possible applications. They are blueprints of argumentation that can be used repeatedly and with undiminished power, because they can appear in a variety of contexts. Tiger and Fox, Adding Feet to the Snake, and Dueling Tigers lie somewhere in between the arguments from authority and the broader topics like Induction and Dilemma. They are not simply recitations of proverbs, but they are not universally applicable, either. They are, rather, illustrative clichés: they can be used only in certain situations but can be varied with different parables and examples.

But how do Bad Faith and Subreption relate to any of these topics? These two are not rhetorical topics at all, because they do not use language as their only tool—or even their primary tool. Indeed, they demonstrate the general inadequacy of classifying the *Stratagems* as exercises in rhetoric: such an interpretation only diminishes the book's worth and fails to account for the nonrhetorical pieces that make up so much of the anthology. Consider, for example, the following anecdote:

魏王遺楚王美人，楚王說之。夫人鄭袖知王之說新人也，甚愛新人。衣服玩好，擇其所喜而為之；宮室臥具，擇其所善而為之。愛之甚於王。王曰：婦人所以事夫者，色也；而妒者，其情也。今鄭袖知寡人之說新人也，其愛之甚於寡人，此孝子之所以事親，忠臣之所以事君也。鄭袖知王以己不妒也，因謂新人曰：王愛子美矣。雖然，惡子之鼻。子為見王，則必掩子鼻。新人見王，因掩其鼻。王謂鄭袖曰：夫新人見寡人，則掩其鼻，何也？鄭袖曰：妾知也。王曰：雖惡必言之。鄭袖曰：其似惡聞君王之臭也。王曰：悍哉！令劓之，無使逆命。[74]

The King of Wei sent a beautiful woman to the King of Chu; the King of Chu was pleased by her. His wife, Zheng Xiu, knew that the king was pleased by the new woman and was very kind to her. Whatever clothing or baubles [the new woman] liked, [Zheng Xiu] gave her; whatever rooms and bed furnishings she liked, [Zheng Xiu] gave her. She was kinder to her than the king was.

The king said: "A wife serves her husband with sex, but she is disposed to jealousy. Now you, Zheng Xiu, know that I am pleased by the new woman, and you are kinder to her than I am. This is how a filial son would serve his parents, how a loyal minister would serve his lord."

Relying on her knowledge that the king did not consider her jealous, Zheng Xiu addressed the new woman, saying: "The king loves your beauty! Though this is so, he dislikes your nose. When you see the king, you must

> cover your nose." So the new woman would cover her nose whenever she went to see the king.
>
> The king addressed Zheng Xiu, saying: "Why does the new woman cover her nose when she sees me?"
>
> Zheng Xiu said: "I know why."
>
> The king said: "You must say it even if it is horrible."
>
> Zheng Xiu said: "It seems she hates to smell your odor."[75]
>
> The king said: "Shrew!" He ordered [the new woman's] nose cut off and would not allow anyone to disobey the command.

This trick is memorable, but it is not rhetoric. Yet no one would argue that it is out of place in the text. But then what kind of a text is it?

Stratagems of the Warring States is a document from turbulent times, an imaginative record of the devious means that clever people might have used to obtain their desired objects: position, fame, revenge, glory, and so on. Since the advisors in the *Stratagems* often find the best resource to be the king, they naturally focus their attention on motivating him with candied speeches to undertake some action—action that is sometimes beneficial to the king and his state but often more advantageous to the counselors themselves. These are the pieces that have established the book's reputation as a repository of brilliant rhetoric. The cynicism of much of this material, moreover, explains why figures who were famed for their rhetoric in ancient China were generally considered eristic and unprincipled.[76] (This antipathy discloses yet another contrast with ancient Rome, where the greatest orators were immortalized as titans of their culture.) But there are other kinds of stories in the collection as well: often, the characters dispense with rhetoric altogether and resort to such methods as conspiracy, espionage, or false incrimination.

The text as a whole, then, is primarily about intrigue. The lively and disjointed narratives present a coherent and irreverent picture of Warring States politics. Cunning advisors live by their wits, rising and falling according to their ingenuity, while kings are continually hoodwinked by their own ministers. Some, like Lord Mengchang 孟嘗君,[77] tolerate the chicanery of their retainers and even encourage it, on a manageable scale, rather than oppose it fruitlessly. But most lords do not have such an enlightened attitude and are deceived throughout. The milieu of the persuaders is the court, the cockpit where diverse interests collide and where shrewd ministers can accumulate fortunes with self-serving counsel and cajolery. This is the same treacherous world in which the great rhetorician Han Fei thrived—that is, until he too was ensnared by a scheming adversary.

It is worth remembering in this connection that *Stratagems of the Warring States* was not traditionally understood as a handbook of rhetoric or a chrestomathy of school exercises, but as a collection of anecdotes that illustrates the dangerous arts of machination and dissimulation, and thus implicitly espouses a world view antithetical to orthodox Confucianism.[78] And precisely therein, for ancient readers, lay the book's value.[79] To conclude with the words of the redactor himself:

> 戰國之時，君德淺薄，為之謀策者，不得不因勢而為資，據時而為。故其謀，扶急持傾，為一切之權，雖不可以臨國教化，兵革救急之勢也。皆高才秀士，度時君之所能行，出奇策異智，轉危為安，運亡為存，亦可喜。皆可觀。[80]

> In the age of the Warring States, the virtue of lords was shallow and meager; those who made schemes and stratagems for them could not but rely on strategic advantage when rendering assistance [to their lords] and make [plans][81] in accordance with the times. Thus their schemes, which provided stability during emergencies and shored up precarious situations, were methods of expedience; although they cannot be compared to instructing and transforming the nation,[82] they [exemplify] strategic advantage, which involves warfare and rescuing [the state] from emergencies. These were all outstanding men-of-service of lofty talent; they gauged what the lords of the time were able to do and produced extraordinary stratagems and uncommon bits of wisdom. They turned danger into security and converted doom into preservation—indeed, in a manner that can be entertaining. All these things are worth reading.[83]

—6—

Insidious Syncretism in the Political Philosophy of *Huainanzi*

> A government might be established on the principle of benevolence towards the people, like that of a father towards his children. Under such a *paternal government* (*imperium paternale*), the subjects, as immature children who cannot distinguish what is truly useful or harmful to themselves, would be obliged to behave purely passively and to rely upon the judgement of the head of state as to how they *ought* to be happy, and upon his kindness in willing their happiness at all. Such a government is the greatest conceivable *despotism*.
>
> Immanuel Kant (1724–1804)

Current scholarly opinion endorses two complementary observations concerning "Zhushu" 主術 (The techniques of the ruler), the ninth chapter of the *Huainanzi* 淮南子. First, the chapter is said to advocate a novel and practicable ethic centered on the beneficent ideal of *limin* 利民, "bringing profit to the people"; and second, by combining elements of pre-imperial Confucianism, Daoism, and Legalism, "Zhushu" displays the syncretism so characteristic of the *Huainanzi* compendium.[1]

The former assessment goes back at least to the noted critic Hu Shi (1891–1962), who was so impressed with the text's concern for the populace that he was prompted to announce: "These theories have a very democratic spirit."[2] Contemporary views, if more circumspect, echo Hu's statement. Kanaya Osamu describes the essence of "Zhushu" as "a political theory that held *wuwei* [nonaction] and *ziran* 自然 [self-so] to be central" and "government for the people."[3] Xu Fuguan, similarly, contends that Western Han thinkers like Liu An 劉安 (d. 122 B.C.) and his clients[4] inherited the concept of *tianxia wei gong* 天下為公 (All under Heaven is for the people) common to the pre-imperial schools of Confucianism, Daoism, and Mohism, and constructed out of this legacy a more advanced political theory.[5] And, most recently, Roger T. Ames, who has published a complete translation of the text, asserts that "the notion of government *for* the people constitutes the unifying spirit of its entire political philosophy" (emphasis in original).[6]

I believe the notion of *limin* in the "Zhushu" chapter, far from implying an ancient form of democracy or "government for the people," represents a consciously articulated ideology of autistic paternalism. The basic assumption—and hence the epithet "autistic"—is that the ruler's subjects are not possessed of minds in any philosophical sense.[7] Generations of commentators, moreover, have missed this theme in the text because of certain stultifying traditions of Chinese intellectual historiography. Scholars have been led astray by the interrelated assumptions that the dominant intellectual viewpoints in the first decades of the Han dynasty were Confucianism, Daoism, and Legalism, and that the *Huainanzi* is a syncretic text marking the confluence of all three streams.

First, the terminology is obsolete; of the names "Confucianism," "Daoism," and "Legalism," the latter two do not refer to a discernible philosophy with adherents who identified themselves as such.[8] What "Legalism" denotes is never clear,[9] and to speak of "Daoism," as though this is what Sima Tan 司馬談 (d. ca. 110 B.C.) meant by *daojia* 道家, is simply anachronistic.[10] But the more pressing problem lies elsewhere: there is more to the study of Chinese philosophy than merely identifying and classifying phrases like *wuwei* and *renyi* 仁義 (humanity and righteousness) as "Daoist" or "Confucian." Scholars have hastened to point out which terms and ideas correspond to which of the august Six Houses of ancient Chinese thought, as though this kind of mapping represented an end in itself. But the real task of a modern critic is to consider the arguments themselves and the ways in which thinkers presented new ideas and responded to old ones. "Zhushu" is an excellent case in point. The mere cataloging of its sources can lead only to the confining pronouncement that the essay represents an amalgam of various philosophical schools.[11] The more eye-opening, indeed the more sinister, interpretation of "Zhushu" is apparent only if we take seriously the ramifications of the text's claims.

"Zhushu" opens with a description, in grave and austere language, of the proper techniques of rulership:

> 人主之術，處無為之事，而行不言之教。清靜不動，一度[12]而不搖，因循而任下，責成而不勞。(L 9.269; *S* 9.1a)[13]

> The techniques of the ruler of men are "located in affairs [undertaken] without action and practiced in unspoken teachings."[14] Clear and tranquil,

> he does not move. He rules with unity and is not agitated. He follows and complies [with things] and delegates responsibilities to his subordinates. His duties are completed yet he does not toil.

Readers of the second century B.C. would have easily recognized this idiom. "Nonaction" was, by this time, a clear political concept: it means to rule with the Way and not to interfere by means of any purposive action that might prove inimical to the cosmic order.[15]

The text continues: the primary element of rulership lies in *renxia* 任下, "delegating responsibilities to inferiors."

> 心知規而師傅諭導，口能言而行人稱辭，足能行而相者先導，耳能聽而執正進諫[＝謀][16]。(L 9.269; *S* 9.1a)

> His mind knows its schemes, but his instructors and teachers issue the edicts of guidance. His mouth can speak, but his envoys make the laudatory speeches. His legs can walk, but those who assist him lead the way. His ears can listen, but those who grasp government [i.e., his ministers][17] decide which plans to put forward.[18]

Classical readers would still have found themselves on familiar ground. It was a cardinal principle of *wuwei* thought that the ruler must assign duties to his subjects and reward or punish them according to their performance, rather than undertake the onerous task of administration personally.[19] A famous illustration of this idea appears in the writings on Han Fei:

> 鄭子產晨出，過東匠[＝巷][20]之閭，聞婦人之哭，撫其御之手而聽之。有閒，遣吏執而問之，則手絞其夫者也。異日，其御問曰：夫子何以知之？子產曰：其聲懼。凡人於其親愛也，始病而憂，臨死而懼，已死而哀。今哭已死不哀而懼，是以知其有姦也。或曰：子產之治，不亦多事乎？姦必待耳目之所及而後知之，則鄭國之得姦者寡矣。不任典成之吏，不察參伍之政，不明度量，恃盡聰明，勞智慮，而以知姦，不亦無術乎？且夫物眾而智寡，寡不勝眾，智不足以知物，故因物以治物。下眾而上寡，寡不勝眾，者言君不足以遍知臣也，故因人以治人。是以形體不勞而事治，智慮不用而姦得。[21]

> Zichan of Zheng went out one morning and, passing the gate of the Eastern Ward [of the capital], heard a woman crying. He stilled his driver's hand and listened. When he had time, he sent a deputy to arrest and interrogate

her; [he discovered that] she had strangled her husband with her own hands. Another day, his driver asked, "How did you know it?"

Zichan said, "Her sound was fearful. People always relate to their loved ones [as follows]: at the beginning of illness, they are worried; at the approach of death, they are fearful; after death, they are in grief. Now she was crying for one who was already dead and was not in grief but was fearful; from this I knew her crime."

Someone [i.e., Han Fei] said: "Did Zichan's rulership not [require] many things? One could know of crime only after it had reached one's ears and eyes, and the state of Zheng apprehended but few criminals. Not enlisting officials of laws and punishments,[22] not observing the 'government of threes and fives' [a method of dividing the populace into manageable groups], not clarifying rules and measures, but depending entirely on shrewdness and working one's wisdom and deliberation in order to know of crime—is this not a lack of technique? Now objects are many and wisdom is rare. What is rare does not vanquish what is manifold, and wisdom is not sufficient to know all things. Therefore one follows things in order to rule things. Inferiors are many and superiors are few. The few do not vanquish the many,[23] that is to say, the lord [alone] is not sufficient to know all his subjects. Therefore one follows people in order to rule people. In this [way], one does not cause one's form and body to toil, but affairs are ordered; one does not employ one's wisdom and deliberation, and criminals are apprehended."

Zichan's method of rulership requires "many things," Han Fei says, because it depends entirely on "shrewdness"—not to mention circumstances. Zichan had to pass by the woman's residence on precisely the right morning, and had to possess, moreover, an uncanny ability to detect dissimulation, for her crime to be discovered. Han Fei pays Zichan a backhanded compliment: he is so talented and so wise that a typical minister cannot be expected to discern what he can. Zichan's rulership lacks *shu*, "technique," because it requires a genius like himself to catch all the villains in the state. With his sensitive ear, Zichan elevates criminology to an art form, but Han Fei is hardly interested in art. Han Fei is interested in technique, in procedures that can be reproduced by common ministers without extraordinary skills.[24]

The father of *shu* is Shen Buhai, who is famous for the dictum "The sage ruler relies on standards and does not rely on wisdom; he relies on technique, not on persuasions" 聖君任法而不任智，任數而不任說.[25] An argument very much like Han Fei's is attributed to Shen Buhai in the *Springs and Autumns of Mr. Lü:*

> 韓昭釐侯視所以祠廟之牲，其豕小。昭釐侯令官更之，官以是豕來也。昭釐侯曰：是非嚮者之豕邪？官無以對，命吏罪之。從者曰：君王何以知之？君曰：吾以其耳也。申不害聞之，曰：何以知其聾？以其耳之聰也。何以知其盲？以其目之明也。何以知其狂？以其言之當也。故曰：去聽無以聞則聰，去視無以見則明，去智無以知則公，去三者不任則治，三者任則亂。以此言耳目心智之不足恃也。耳目心智，其所以知識甚闕，其所以聞見甚淺，以淺闕博居天下，安殊俗，治萬民，其說固不行。十理之間，而耳不能聞，帷牆之外，而目不能見，三畝之宮，而心不能知。[26]
>
> Marquis Zhaoxi of Han [r. 362–333 B.C.?][27] saw a sacrifice [about] to be offered in the temple; the pig was small. Marquis Zhaoxi ordered an official to replace it, [but] the official returned with the [same] pig. Marquis Zhaoxi said, "Is this not the pig that was to be sacrificed?"[28] The official had no response, [so the marquis] commanded a deputy to punish him.
>
> His followers said, "How did my Lord King know it?"
>
> The lord said, "I used my ears."
>
> Shen Buhai heard of this and said, "How does one know that someone is deaf? By the keenness of his ears. How does one know that he is blind? By the clarity of his eyes. How does one know that he is mad? By the appropriateness of his words. Therefore I say, if you discard listening and do not use it to hear, you will be keen; if you discard looking and do not use it to see, you will be clear; if you discard wisdom and do not use it to know, you will be all-encompassing. If you discard [these] three things and do not rely [on them], there will be order; if you rely on [these] three things, there will be chaos. This is to say that the ears, eyes, mind, and wisdom are not sufficient to depend on. That which can be known and recognized by the ears, eyes, mind, and wisdom is very incomplete; that which they can hear and see is very superficial. Using what is superficial and incomplete to dwell [i.e., rule] broadly under Heaven, pacify divergent practices, and rule the myriad people—this proposition will certainly not succeed. The ears cannot hear [from a] space of ten *li;* the eyes cannot see [from] outside a curtain or wall; and the mind cannot know every house of three *mu.*"[29]

What the ruler needs, then, is not keen eyes and ears but *shu.*

There are many ways in which the "Zhushu" chapter invites the reader to consider Shen Buhai's philosophy. First, and most obviously, the chapter is titled "Zhushu," which can mean not only "The Techniques of the Ruler," as it is generally taken, but also (with *zhu* as a putative verb), "Taking *Shu* as One's Ruler," that is to say, "Esteeming Technique." The author may even intend to allude to the famous chapter of the *Han Feizi* known as "Zhudao," or the "The Way of the Ruler," which can, similarly, also mean "Esteeming the Way."[30]

Second, "Zhushu" alludes in subtle ways to Shen Buhai's writings. For example, the very first sentence in the text, quoted above, contains the phrase *yinxun er renxia* 因循而任下: "to follow and comply, and delegate responsibilities to one's subordinates." *Yinxun* was a term intimately associated with Shen Buhai in classical times.[31] In the *Xinxu* 新序 (Newly arranged [anecdotes]), for example, Liu Xiang wrote: "Master Shen's writings say that the lord of men should grasp *shu* and do away with punishments, and *yinxun* in order to supervise and hold responsible his vassals and subordinates" 申子之書言人君當執術無刑，因循以督責臣下.[32]

Finally, the administrative recommendations made in the "Zhushu" chapter square with Shen Buhai's naturalistic philosophy. In order to rectify names and settle affairs, the "Zhushu" claims, one must not interfere with the natural tendency of names and affairs to manage themselves. "Each name names itself, each category categorizes itself. Things are so of themselves; [the ruler] lets nothing emerge from himself" 名各自名，類各自類，事猶自然，莫出於己 (L 9.270; *S* 9.1a). This idea was also expressed, we remember, by Shen Buhai in "The Great Body": "Names rectify themselves; affairs settle themselves. Thus he who has the Way grants names their autonomy but still rectifies them; he follows affairs but still settles them."[33] Because of this axiomatic naturalism—what is so ought to be so—Shen Buhai's ideal ruler merely rests within the palace and allows the world around him to rule itself naturally.

Crucially, "Zhushu" agrees with Shen Buhai that the ruler must not use his own abilities, but should co-opt those of his subjects instead.

> 得用人之道，而不任己之才者也。故假[=駕][34]輿馬者，足不勞而致千里，乘舟楫者，不能游而絕江海。(L 9.294; *S* 9.12a f.)
>
> Whoever obtains the Way of Using People does not rely on his own ability. Thus, one who rides a carriage or horse makes his feet go one thousand *li* without making them toil; one who takes advantage of a boat and oars traverses rivers and oceans even if he cannot swim.

"Using people" (or "using the populace" 用眾) is one of the text's favorite themes.[35] "The ruler of men looks with the eyes of all under Heaven, listens with the ears of all under Heaven, deliberates with the wisdom of all under Heaven, and fights with the power of all under Heaven" 人主者，以天下之目視，以天下之耳聽，以天下之智慮，以天下之力爭 (L 9.293; *S* 9.12a).[36] Echoing Shen Buhai yet again, "Zhushu" asserts: "The flock of ministers are like spokes of a wheel coming together at the hub" 群臣輻湊 (L 9.293; *S* 9.12a).[37] And further:

> 勇力不足以持天下矣。智不足以為治，勇不足以為強，則人材不足任，明也。而君人者不下廟堂之上，而知四海之外者，因物以識物，因人以知人也。故積力之所舉，則無不勝也，眾智之所為，則無不成也。(L 9.279; *S* 9.5a f.)
>
> Courage and energy are not sufficient to maintain all under Heaven. Wisdom is not sufficient for government; courage is not sufficient for strength. Thus it is clear that one's [own] abilities are not sufficient to rely on. But the lord does not descend from the ancestral hall yet still knows what is beyond the Four Seas. He complies with things to understand things; he complies with man to understand man. Thus what is established through accumulated energies is not overcome by anything; what is created through the wisdom of the populace is not left incomplete in any respect.

As long as he harnesses the energies of his populace, the ruler can dwell in his ancestral hall, completely unmoving, and yet retain control over all the earth.[38] He achieves this mastery by recognizing the particular talents of each of his subjects. For each person has a native specialty, which the lord must discover. By assigning duties commensurate with his vassals' talents, the ruler can ensure the efficient running of the machinery of state.

> 鹿之上山，獐不能跂也，及其下，牧豎能追之。才有所修短也。是故有大略者，不可責以捷巧，有小智者，不可任以大功。人有其才，物有其形，有任一而太重，或任百而尚輕。(L 9.292; *S* 9.11b)
>
> When a deer goes up a mountain, the roebuck cannot tiptoe [there]; when it reaches the bottom, [even] a herd boy can chase it. Abilities have their advantages and disadvantages. For this reason, someone who possesses the great outline [i.e., someone of broad vision] cannot be charged with duties that [require] cleverness and agility; someone who possesses little wisdom cannot be placed in charge of large projects. Men have their abilities; things

have their forms. There are those who, delegated one responsibility, think it a magnificent burden; others, delegated a hundred, still find it easy.

However, it is not enough merely to entrust affairs of state to one's ministers and then retire; the ruler must take care to establish his bureaucracy in accordance with the principles of the universe. His methods must be in line with the Way. "States may have vanquished rulers, but the Way never decays in the world. Men may have poverty and hardship, but principles are all-pervading" 國有亡主，而世無廢道，人有困窮，而理無不通 (L 9.277; *S* 9.5a). And more explicitly:

古之置有司也，所以禁民，使不得自恣也，其立君也，所以剬有司，使無專行也，法籍禮義者，所以禁君，使無擅斷也。人莫得自恣，則道勝，道勝而理達矣。故反於無為，無為者，非謂凝滯而不動也，以其言莫從己而出也。(L 9.295; *S* 9.13a)

The ancients established officials in order to restrain the people—to make sure that they did not do as they pleased. They raised lords in order to goad the officials—to make sure that they did not act of their own accord.[39] They standardized and recorded rituals and protocols in order to restrain the lords—to make sure that they did not adjudicate freely. When people do not do as they please, then the Way prevails. When the Way prevails, principles arrive. Thus they returned to nonaction. "Nonaction" does not refer to congealing oneself and not moving; it means that nothing emerges from the self.

"Nothing emerges from the self" because names and affairs simply regulate themselves if the Way is allowed to flourish. The ruler must let all things be so of themselves; he must not force his private motives onto the delicate system.[40]

法者，天下之度量而人主之準繩也。縣法者，法不法也，設賞者，賞當賞也。法定之後，中程者賞，缺繩者誅，尊貴者不輕其罰，而卑賤者不重其刑，犯法者雖賢必誅，中度者雖不肖必無罪。是故公道通而私道塞矣。(L 9.295; *S* 9.13a)

Standards are the measure of all under Heaven and the level and marking line of the ruler of men. Standards are assembled in order to make standard those who are not standard. Rewards are established in order to reward those who should be rewarded. After standards are settled, those who conform to the regulations are rewarded; those who fail to reach the

> marking line are punished. Punishments are not lessened for the honorable and noble or increased for the lowly and base. Those who violate the standards, even if they are virtuous, must be punished. Those who conform to the measures, even if they are ignoble, must not be judged guilty. In this manner, the all-encompassing Way passes through [everywhere] and private ways are stopped.

And similarly:

> 夫民之好善樂正，不待禁誅而自中法度者，萬無一也。下必行之令，從之者利，逆之者凶，日陰未移而海內莫不被繩矣。(L 9.304; *S* 9.16b)

> There is not one in ten thousand among the people who loves goodness and delights in rectitude, conforming to the standards and measures without having to be restrained or punished. There are commands that inferiors must carry out. Who follows them benefits; who opposes them encounters disaster. Before the shadow of the sun has moved [i.e., immediately], there is no one within the seas who is not brought in line with the mark.

But what about the claim that names name themselves and affairs regulate themselves? Is this harsh and rigorously prescriptive theory of government not wholly incongruous with the quietist inaction of Shen Buhai? Not according to "Zhushu." We have already seen that "non-action" is not pacifism or know-nothingism; it refers in this text to the conscious suppression of private action. Indeed, *wuwei* may have had this connotation from its very beginnings,[41] even in Shen Buhai, but "Zhushu" raises the element of forcible repression to a new and perhaps unimagined level. "Standards are assembled in order to make standard those who are not standard." In creating its ideal kingdom, Liu An's text severs influential keywords from their original philosophical contexts and reveals its utter disdain for the independent virtue of agents not beholden to the state.

Moreover, the text takes pains to point out that "standards" and "marking lines" are not unnatural. On the contrary, the Way prevails, we remember, only after people "do not do as they please." Implementing strict measures is as natural as yoking an ox and using its natural strength to one's own advantage. It is pointless to try to pull an ox if it is standing still, but "if one directs it with a length of mulberry strung through its nose, then a small boy can pull it around the four seas, because he is following [the nature of things]" 若指之桑條以貫其鼻，則五尺童子牽而

周四海者，順也 (L 9.305; *S* 9.16b).[42] Activism—if it is the right kind of activism—is natural.

> 夫防民之所害，開民之所利，威行也，若發城決唐[=塘][43]。故循流而下易至，背風而馳易遠。(L 9.305; *S* 9.17a)
>
> If [the ruler] prevents what harms the people and makes blossom what benefits the people, the progression of his authority will be like [water] swelling over the dikes and flowing over the embankments. Thus by complying with the current, it is easy to arrive downstream; with the wind at one's back, it is easy to gallop far.

The benefits of harnessing the resources of the world were known to the legendary charioteer Zaofu 造父.[44] This hero took the image of piercing the bull's nose to its logical conclusion:[45]

> 聖王之治也，其猶造父之御，齊輯之于轡銜之際，而急緩之于唇吻之和，正度于胸臆之中，而執節[=策][46]于掌握之間，內得於心中，外合於馬志，是故能進退履繩，而旋曲中規，取道致遠，而氣力有餘，誠得其術也。(L 9.297; *S* 9.13b)
>
> The rule of the sage king is like the charioteering of Zaofu. He unites and harmonizes [the horses] through the edge between the reins and the bit; he speeds them up and slows them down through the harmony of the corners of their lips. He regulates the measures within his breast and grasps the whip in his palm. What he attains inside his mind accords on the outside with the will of the horses. For this reason they can move along a marking line in advancing and retreating, and [can] trace a compass as they turn. He makes use of the Way and brings [the horses] far; they have *qi* and energy to spare, because he has perfectly attained such technique.[47]

The express purpose of government, however—the reason why such awesome "techniques" are justified—is not to maximize the power of the ruler but to confer benefit on the people, as many commentators have pointed out.[48] "Standards are born of righteousness; righteousness is born of what is appropriate to the populace; what is appropriate to the populace accords with the hearts of men. This is what is essential in government" 法生於義，義生於眾適，眾適合於人心。此治之要也 (L 9.296; *S* 9.13a).[49] The commentary of Gao You ("'Essential' means covenant" 要約也) suggests that the phrase "essentials of government" implies a social covenant:[50] the ruler is granted the power to determine his terrible "standards," but these must in turn conform to the "hearts of men." Be that as it may—nowhere does the text assert this explicitly—it is clear that the ruler, according to "Zhushu," ought not to indulge his senses to the extent that his populace is impoverished.

> 高臺層榭，接屋連閣，非不麗也，然民有掘穴狹廬所以託身者，明主非樂也。(L 9.305 f.; *S* 9.17a)
>
> It is not that lofty terraces, storied kiosks, connecting chambers, and linked pavilions are not beautiful; but when the people have hollowed caves and narrow huts in which to dwell, the enlightened ruler does not enjoy them.[51]

The great Sage King Yao 堯 exemplified the correct attitude of the ruler:

> 堯之有天下也，非貪萬民之富而安人主之位也，以為百姓力征，強凌弱，眾暴寡，於是堯乃身服節儉之行，而明相愛之仁，以和輯之。是故茅茨不翦，采椽不斷[=斲][52]，大路不畫，越席不緣，大羹不和，粢食不鑿，巡狩行教，勤勞天下，周流五嶽。豈其奉養不足樂哉？舉天下而以為社稷，非有利焉。(L 9.290; *S* 9.10b)
>
> When Yao possessed all under Heaven, he did not covet the wealth of the myriad people or remain at peace in the ruler's position. He considered the common people to be aggressive in their energies: the strong mistreat the weak and the many violate the few. Therefore Yao personally submitted to moderate and frugal behavior, and made clear the humanity of mutual love, in order to harmonize [the populace]. For this reason, his grass thatch was not trimmed, his patterned[53] rafters not hewn, his royal chariot not adorned, his knotted[54] mat not hemmed, his Great Soup not seasoned,[55] and his millet meal not refined. On his inspection tours he disseminated his teachings, diligently laboring for all under Heaven, meandering to the Five Peaks. How could his virtuous way of life[56] not be joyous enough? He took up all under Heaven and treated it like the Altars of Soil and Millet; he did not profit from it.

Yao "diligently labored for all under Heaven," while himself leading a humble existence, because he knew that a virtuous ruler must use the advantages of his station in order to profit the people. Yao's conduct, however, is praiseworthy for another reason as well: by furnishing a model of correct behavior, he influenced his people. For the ability to change popular customs is a natural consequence of the ruler's exalted position.

> 靈王好細要［＝腰］，而民有殺食自飢也；越王好勇，而民皆處危爭死。由此觀之，權勢之柄，其以移風易俗矣。(L 9.287; *S* 9.8b)
>
> King Ling [of Chu, r. 540–529 B.C.] was fond of slim waists, and the people reduced their food and starved themselves; the King of Yue [i.e., Goujian 句踐, r. 496–465 B.C.] was fond of courage, and the people all placed themselves in danger and contended [with one another] for death.[57] From this we see that the handle of power and authority is that by which [the ruler] changes customs.

The consequence of this view is that the ruler must act in the manner that he wishes his people to act, for they will inevitably look to his example and modify their own conduct accordingly. Yao drinks unseasoned soup and eats unrefined millet in order to encourage frugality in his own people. The classical philosophy with which this particular point of view is most compatible is that attributed to the so-called *nongjia* 農家, or "School of the Tillers."[58] This school of thought saw its cultural hero in Shennong 神農, the Divine Farmer, whose teachings include the tenet that the ruler must share in the labors of his subjects. One "practitioner of the words of Shennong" 為神農之言者, named Xu Xing 許行, appears in *Mencius* 3A.4, saying, "The worthy [ruler] plows and eats together with his people; he governs while he prepares his morning and evening meals" 賢者與民並耕而食，饔飧而治.[59]

The authors of "Zhushu" know of this tradition and ostensibly display their approval of it in the form of a paean to Shennong (L 9.271; *S* 9.1b). But we should not interpret references to Shennong as an indication that "Zhushu" necessarily espouses the Tiller ideal as articulated by Xu Xing. The ruler of the "Zhushu," after all, far from tilling in the fields, is encouraged to remain screened off in his palace, aloof from the world, governing it through the peculiar brand of "nonaction" that we have examined above. The text alludes to Shennong when it is rhetorically convenient, immediately disposing of him when his egalitarianism proves incompatible with the other theories that the authors wish to put forward.[60]

This rhetorical opportunism is apparent in the golden eulogy of Confucius toward the end of the chapter.

> 孔子之通，智過於萇弘，勇服於孟賁，足躡郊菟［＝兔］，力招城關，能亦多矣。然而勇力不聞，伎巧不知，專行教道，以成素王，事亦鮮矣‥‥‥‥圍

> 於匡，顏色不變，絃歌不輟，臨死亡之地，犯患難之危，據義行理而志不懾，分亦明矣。然為魯司寇，聽獄必為斷，作為春秋，不道鬼神，不敢專己。(L 9.312 f.; *S* 9.20b)
>
> The insight of Confucius—his wisdom exceeded that of Chang Hong [d. 492 B.C.], his courage that of Meng Ben.[61] His feet stepped like a wild hare's; his strength could raise the portcullis of a fort. His abilities were many. But his courage and strength are not heard of, his skill and agility not known. Solely through his practice of teaching the Way, he became the Uncrowned King. His activities were few.... When he was surrounded in Kuang,[62] his color did not change; his strumming and singing did not cease. When he approached the land of death and destruction, meeting with worrisome and difficult perils, he relied on righteousness and practiced the pattern [of the Way]; his will was not cowed. His lot was clear. And when he heard litigation as minister of justice[63] in Lu, he always came to [the correct] decision; in compiling the *Springs and Autumns,* he did not speak of ghosts and spirits and did not dare focus on himself.

Elsewhere too, the authors have peppered the text with phrases that can only have been intended as allusions to Confucius and Confucianism: "The ruler of men prizes uprightness and esteems integrity" 人主貴正而尚忠 (L 9.286; *S* 9.8a). In particular, the latter sections contain so many references to "humanity" and "righteousness" that a number of scholars are inclined to see in "Zhushu" the acceptance of basic Confucian ideals.[64]

Some passages even refer directly to the Confucian classics. "What one has in oneself one does not oppose in others; what is not present in oneself one does not require in others" 有諸己不非諸人，無諸己不求諸人 (L 9.296; *S* 9.13b). This sentence appears, almost verbatim, in the commentary to the *Great Learning* attributed to Zeng Can: "The gentleman requires it of others only after he has it in himself; he opposes it in others only after it is no longer present in himself" 君子有諸己而后求諸人，無諸己而后非諸人.[65] That is to say, the gentleman cannot be a hypocrite, demanding a higher level of virtue in others than he has attained himself. In the context of the *Analects,* this principle is understood as an element of *shu* 恕, "reciprocity"; "not treating others as one would not want others to treat oneself" is one of the most important concepts in Confucius' philosophy.[66]

But how seriously are we to take this phraseology? Is the ruler of "Zhushu" expected to practice the Confucian virtues of loyalty and reciprocity even as he harmonizes all under Heaven with his "techniques" and "standards"? There are several reasons why this is unlikely to be the message that the authors wish to convey. The first indication appears in the repeated juxtaposition of Confucius and Mozi as ancient paragons of wisdom.[67] I am not aware of any text of Confucian origin that praises both Confucius and Mozi in the same sentence;[68] on the contrary, well into the third century, the Confucian and Mohist lineages saw in each other their most sophisticated intellectual opposition. Certainly the term *ru-Mo* 儒墨 (Confucians and Mohists) existed long before the *Huainanzi*, but it was typically used by thinkers who did not consider themselves members of either group in passages ridiculing both.[69] Zhuang Zhou, for example, speaks of the "Confucians and Mohists" in his "Discourse on Making Things Equal" (Qiwu lun 齊物論) as hairsplitters who are blind to his own great insight, namely, that all argumentation is useless, because both participants in a philosophical discussion are equally right from their own point of view—and hence equally wrong from the impartial perspective of the Way.[70]

More important, the context in which "Confucius and Mozi" appear in "Zhushu" reveals a distinct attitude toward traditional scholarship and its place in the proper world order.

> 湯武聖主也，而不能與越人乘幹舟而浮於江湖，伊尹賢相也，而不能與胡人騎騵馬而服騊駼，孔墨博通，而不能與山居者入榛薄險阻。(L 9.278; *S* 9.5a)
>
> Tang and Wu were sage rulers, but they could not compete with the men of Yue in navigating little boats and sailing on the rivers and lakes. Yi Yin was a worthy minister, but he could not compete with the Hu people [i.e., steppe nomads] in riding horses from Yuan[71] and breaking wild steeds.[72] Confucius and Mozi had broad understanding, but they could not compete with mountain dwellers in entering overgrown thickets and hazardous defiles.

Despite their broad expertise, the value of Confucius and Mozi is not limitless. Like all other subjects, they have their talents. They may be good at whatever it is they are good at (and the text prefers not to elaborate on this issue), but they are not good at tracking and mountain climbing, and to employ them in such tasks would be foolish. Confucius and Mozi, then, are just two more of the ruler's many tools, which he must learn to use appropriately.[73] Their philosophical interests are politically irrelevant and their teachings valuable only insofar as they facilitate the ruler's rulership; their legacy must remain subordinate to the interests of state.

Confucius and Mozi are important, then, not because of their profound ethical teachings, but because their knowledge might prove useful to a ruler. In a sense, this claim should not be surprising, for the authors of "Zhushu" have already made it plain that they regard moral excellence with sheer ambivalence. Virtuous men are, if anything, a threat to the undisputed sovereignty of the ruler in his palace. The only way to judge someone, as we have seen, is by his or her performance with regard to the "standards": "Those who violate the standards, even if they are virtuous, must be punished." Of course, no orthodox Confucian could ever make such an argument, as this manner of thinking is, at root, irreconcilably anti-Confucian, as well as anti-Mohist. But "Zhushu" is not a Confucian or Mohist text—nor a syncretism of the two.

On the contrary, one of the fundamental premises of the text is that the ruler must make the best use of his resources by taking advantage of their particular strengths and weaknesses. Confucius and Mozi are resources too, and the ruler who uses them improperly—for example, by thoughtlessly adopting their teachings in government—is using the wrong tool for the wrong task. Assigning duties to people with inappropriate talents is "like using an axe to split a hair or using a knife to chop wood: in both cases, you fail to use what is appropriate" 猶以斧僃毛，以刀抵[=伐][74]木也，皆失其宜矣 (L 9.293; *S* 9.12a).

But if even Confucius and Mozi deserve no special consideration, how much less do the ruler's typical subjects? These passages depict philosophy, ethics, and scholarship as material to be exploited by the ruler, placing the concept of "bringing benefit to the people" in an entirely new light. *Limin* may entail shepherding the people (as in the phrase *mumin* 牧民), but only in the sense that one shepherds sheep. The ruler must treat the people kindly and instruct them in the ways of agriculture and animal husbandry, but only because these occupations bring prosperity to the state. Specifically, what is absent is any concern whatsoever for the life of the mind. Man lives by bread alone.[75]

> 食者民之本也，民者國之本也，國者君之本也，是故君者，上因天時，下盡地材，中用人力。(L 9.308; *S* 9.18b)
>
> Food is the basis of the people; the people are the basis of the state; the state is the basis of the lord. For this reason, the lord follows the Heavenly seasons above and makes the most of the Earth's riches below; he employs the energies of the people in the middle.

We remember the following apophthegm: "Standards are born of righteousness; righteousness is born of what is appropriate to the populace; what is appropriate to the populace accords with the hearts of men." But what "accords with the hearts of men" is merely a beneficent ruler who provides regular food and shelter. Indeed, we must retain the translation "*hearts* of men" for *renxin* 人心—that is, rather than "minds of men"—because it is clear that "Zhushu" does not recognize the existence of "minds" in the sense to which readers are accustomed through the writings of Mencius and other classical thinkers.

And why not? Because human beings are made of matter (which the text calls *qi* 氣), and all matter obeys certain physical rules. It is an argument that anticipates, in its way, a strikingly modern idea. For "Zhushu," moreover—as for the rest of the *Huainanzi*—the primary physical rule is that of "stimulus and response" (*ganying* 感應): if *qi* is stimulated in one place, the *qi* elsewhere responds sympathetically.[76] The idea is especially well illustrated in music:

> 今夫調弦[77]者，叩宮宮應，彈角角動，此同聲相和者也。(L 6.200)
>
> Now when the string tuner strikes the note *gong,* the *gong* [string on other instruments] responds; if he plucks *jue,* the *jue* is set in motion. This is because of the mutual harmony of the same sound.[78]

Sound represents excited *qi,* and when the vibrations are heard by a human being, they inevitably stimulate his or her own *qi* in like manner. Therefore, in the presence of music, the listener's mood necessarily conforms to the emotions expressed by the performer.

> 甯戚商歌車下，桓公喟然而寤，至精入人深矣！故曰：樂聽其音則知其俗，見其俗則知其化。(L 9.275; *S* 9.3b f.)
>
> When Ning Qi[79] played a song in the key of *shang*[80] beneath his cart, Lord Huan [of Qi, r. 685–643 B.C.] was aroused with a sigh: the utmost essence [of music] enters man deeply! Therefore it is said: In music, when one listens to the sound, one can know the [people's] customs; when one sees their customs, one can know their transformation.

Sincere music affects the emotions of the listener for the same reason that it reflects the genuine internal state of the performer: everyone is made of *qi.*

古之為金石管絃者，所以宣樂也，兵革斧鉞者，所以飾怒也，觴酌俎豆，酬酢之禮，所以效善也，衰絰菅屨，辟踊哭泣，所以諭哀也。此皆有充於內，而成像於外。(L 9.306 f.; *S* 9.17b)

The ancients used bells, chimes, pipes, and strings in order to proclaim their joy; weapons, cuirasses, axes, and halberds in order to adorn their rage; [ceremonial] goblets, beakers, stands, platters, and the rituals of pledging with wine in order to make their goodness effective; hempen mourning dress, grass sandals, beating the breast, leaping about, and wailing, in order to indicate their grief. In all these [cases], there is a fullness on the inside that is given a manifestation on the outside.[81]

Music, in other words—like weeping and offering sacrifice—is the external manifestation of a person's internal emotional state; in the words of the text, it is the "manifestation on the outside" of the "fullness on the inside." This view builds on the classical conception of music examined in connection with Xunzi in chapter 2.[82] The authors of "Zhushu" even allude to Xunzi's essay directly. The passage above, about the ancients who proclaimed their joy and adorned their anger, is itself an adornment of a remark along the same lines by Xunzi.[83]

A similar theme, articulated in similar language, is taken up in the *Springs and Autumns of Mr. Lü,* another text that the authors of "Zhushu" would have expected their readers to know.

凡音者產乎人心者也，感於心則蕩乎音，音成於外而化於內。是故聞其聲而知其風，察其風而知其志，觀其志而知其德。盛衰賢不肖，君子小人，皆形於樂。[84]

Since all tones are produced in the hearts of men, a stimulus in the heart causes agitation in a tone; when tones are completed outside, they transform [the hearer] inside.[85] For this reason, when one hears [someone's] sounds, one knows his habits; if one inspects his habits, one knows his will; if one observes his will, one knows his virtue. The prosperous and the fallen, the worthy and the ignoble, the gentleman and the lesser man are all formed by music.[86]

The several essays on music in the *Springs and Autumns of Mr. Lü,* however, add a dimension that Xunzi had only hinted at.[87]

音樂之所由來者遠矣。生於度量，本於太一，太一出兩儀，兩儀出陰陽，陰陽變化，一上一下，合而成章，渾渾沌沌，離則復合，合而復離，是謂天常。天地車輪，終則復始，極則復反，莫不咸當，日月星辰，或疾或徐，日月不同，以盡其行，四時代興，或暑或寒，或短或長，或柔或剛，萬物所出，造於太一，化於陰陽。萌芽始震，凝寒以形，形體有處，莫不有聲，聲出於和，和出於適，先[88]王定樂，由此生。[89]

The source of tones and music is distant. They are born in measures and based on the Magnificent Unity. The Magnificent Unity emits the two attitudes [i.e., Heaven and Earth];[90] the two attitudes emit *yin* and *yang*. *Yin* and *yang* change and transform: one rises; one sinks. They unite and create transformations. In primordial chaos, they separate and then unite again; they unite and then separate again. This is called Heaven's Constancy. Heaven and Earth [turn like] the wheel of a chariot: the end is again the beginning; [having reached] the highest point, it returns again. Everything is as it should be. The sun, moon, stars, and constellations—some are fast and some are slow. The sun and moon are dissimilar in their orbital period.[91] The four seasons arise one after the other. Some are hot and some are cold; some are short and some are long; some are soft and some are hard. As for the origin of the Myriad Things: they are created by the Magnificent Unity and transformed by *yin* and *yang*. Once the germs are excited, they congeal into a form; the form is embodied in a place, and nothing is without sound. The sound comes from harmony; harmony comes from accord. When the Former Kings established music, it was born of this.[92]

The significance of this argument is spelled out at the very end: "Nothing is without sound." At the time of the creation, the movements of *yin* and *yang* and the rotations of Heaven and Earth were all accompanied by sounds that marked the harmony and accord of the world and the Way. The consequence is that when we make music today, we are recreating the patterns of the universe. This is why so much space is devoted in the *Springs and Autumns of Mr. Lü* to the task of distinguishing proper music from perverse music. Music is a representation of the universe, and an improper rendition can only have inauspicious consequences.[93]

These "links between numerology, measures, cosmogony, and astronomy"[94] clearly appealed to the authors of the *Huainanzi*, who produced a similar genealogy of the cosmos in chapter 3 of their collection:

道始於一，一而不生，故分而為陰陽，陰陽合和而萬物生。故曰：一生二，二生三，三生萬物。天地三月而為一時，故祭祀三飯以為禮，喪紀三踊以為節，兵重三罕以為制。以三參物，三三如九，故黃鐘之律九寸而宮音調。因而九之，九九八十一，故黃鐘之數立焉。黃者，土德之色，鐘者，氣之所種也，日冬至德氣為土，土色黃，故曰黃鐘。律之數六，分為雌雄，故曰十二鐘，以副十二月，十二各以三成。故置一而十一，三之，為積分十七萬七千一百四十七，黃鐘大數立焉。(L 3.112 f.)

The Way begins[95] with the One, but the One does not give birth. Thus it divides into *yin* and *yang; yin* and *yang* unite in harmony, and the Myriad Things are born. Thus it is said: "The One bore the Two; the Two bore the Three; the Three bore the Myriad Things."[96] In Heaven and Earth, three months make one season. Thus in a sacrifice, the ritual calls for a threefold presentation of food; the mourning period is measured by three years; armies are controlled by emphasizing the three flags. If we use threes to make things three, three threes is nine; thus when the pitch pipe of the Yellow Bell is nine inches long, the tone *gong* is tuned. If we continue to make things nine, nine nines is eighty-one; thus the number of the Yellow Bell is established by this. Yellow is the color of the virtue of Earth; a bell is where *qi* is sown.[97] At the instant of the winter solstice, the *qi* is in its Earth Phase;[98] since the color of Earth is yellow, it is called the Yellow Bell. The number of the pitch pipes is six, subdivided into male and female; thus we say that the Twelve Bells are the assistants of the twelve months. Each twelve is made up of threes. Thus if one takes one and triples it eleven times [i.e., 3^{11}], one accumulates 177,147 parts; the great number of the Yellow Bell is established by this.[99]

The text continues in this vein for several tedious sections.[100] The most important claim is made only in passing: the dimensions of the Yellow Bell correspond to the Earth Phase of *qi*. Each of the five notes in the pentatonic scale corresponds to one particular aspect of *qi*. The consequence is essential: since everything—including humanity—is made of *qi*, music can be used to regulate the entire cosmos.[101]

This is the background of the use of music in "Zhushu." With skillful tuning and performance, one can make the audience experience any emotion one wants it to:

君人者，其猶射者乎！於此豪末，於彼尋常矣。故慎所以感之也。夫榮啟期一彈，而孔子三日樂，感于和，鄒忌一徽，而威王終夕悲，感于憂。動諸琴瑟，形諸音聲，而能使人為之哀樂。

The lord—oh how he is like an archer! A minute [error] here [counts] for feet and yards[102] there. Therefore [the lord] is cautious about how he stimulates [the people]. When Rong Qiqi plucked [his instrument] once, Confucius was joyous for three days; he was stimulated by harmony. When

> Zou Ji strummed once wildly, King Wei [of Qi, r. 357–320 B.C.] was sorrowful all night; he was stimulated by melancholy.[103] If one moves them with the lute and cithern, and forms them with tones and sounds, one can make the people grieve or be joyous. (L 9.275; *S* 9.3b)

As the *Huainanzi* puts it elsewhere: "Everything is an image of its *qi:* everything responds to its kind" 皆象其氣，皆應其類 (L 4.141).

Like so much else in "Zhushu," the passages on music employ language from classical sources that would have been well known to contemporary readers. We should be on our guard, however, lest we be misled into thinking that, by borrowing such familiar terminology, "Zhushu" intends to invoke the same argument as its source texts.[104] The chapter transfigures Xunzi, for example, into an apologist for a kind of materialistic determinism. But that thinker has a very clear concept of mind and could never accept, despite the frequent allusions in "Zhushu" to his work, the idea that human beings are simply containers of *qi.* In one of the very rare instances where he even uses the term, Xunzi takes care to emphasize that the mind can always function, regardless of the physical state of one's *qi.* This occurs in the middle of a discussion about abdication:

> 曰：老衰而擅。是又不然。血氣筋力，則有衰，若夫智慮取舍，則無衰。[105]
>
> They say: "When [the king] is old and decrepit, he should abdicate."[106] This is also not so. In his blood, *qi,* sinews, and energy, there may be decay; but in his wisdom, deliberations, choices, and rejections, there is no decay.[107]

Xunzi's world view may not be any less problematic, philosophically speaking, than that of the *Huainanzi;* for he has introduced at this point something that comes very close to the arch-vexation of Western philosophy, the "mind-body problem." In Xunzi's system, the *qi* and the mind appear to flourish and decay independently of each other. He does not address the evident difficulty: what material, then, is the mind made of?

Nevertheless, to struggle with a terrific problem must count as more noble than to ignore it. Failing to engage the concept of mind is, ultimately, the *Huainanzi*'s greatest defect. According to Xunzi, two of the human abilities that endure until the very end are the power to "choose and reject." These are precisely the qualities that are denied by the *Huainanzi*'s conception of human nature. In that blissfully regulated world, the sovereign simply strikes the appropriate chord, and his subjects assume perforce the intended attitude. These claims are all presented without any consideration of the people's ability or even their will to resist this form of control. The text grants only that the people may be disaffected and cause trouble if they are maltreated. "Zhushu" refuses to accept the notion that people may have any kind of spiritual life, that they may have likes and dislikes that are not motivated solely by their five senses, that they have the capability and obligation of moral development.

Moreover, if human beings are no more than conglomerations of *qi* that respond to stimuli in predictable ways, why is the ruler himself any different? There must be something about the lord that distinguishes him from the rest of humanity; otherwise, the text would have to take into account the possibility that the people might start to control the ruler by playing influential music of their own!

The solution to this paradox is found in an argument borrowed from Shen Buhai, who said:

> 上明見，人備之，其不明見，人惑之，其知見，人惑之，不知見，人匿之，其無欲見，人司[＝伺][108]之，其有欲見，人餌之。故曰：吾無從知之，惟無為可以規之。[109]
>
> If the superior's enlightenment is apparent, the people will prepare for it; if his lack of enlightenment is apparent, the people will delude him. If his knowledge is apparent, the people will delude him; if his lack of knowledge is apparent, the people will keep [affairs] hidden from him. If his lack of desires is apparent, the people will spy on him [i.e., to find out what his desires are];[110] if his desires are apparent, the people will entice him. Therefore he says: There is nothing I can follow in order to know them; only through nonaction can I regulate them.

The point is by now familiar: the ruler must not reveal himself, because his ministers can take advantage of his weaknesses. "Zhushu" brings this argument into line with its own manipulative ontology by combining it with the concept of *qi*. "The rarefied essence of the ancient sage kings was formed on the inside, but their likes and dislikes were not shown on the outside" 古聖王至精形於內，而好憎忘於外.[111] And most explicitly:

> 昔者，齊桓公好味，而易牙烹其首子而餌之，虞君好寶，而晉獻以璧馬釣之，胡王好音，而秦穆公以女樂誘之。是皆以利見制於人也，故善建者不拔。夫火熱而水滅之，金剛而火銷之，木強而斧伐之，水流而土遏之，惟造化者，物莫能勝也。(L 9.300; *S* 9.15b)

> In former times, Lord Huan of Qi was fond of flavors, so Yiya boiled his firstborn son and enticed him. The Lord of Yu was fond of treasures, so [Lord] Xian of Jin [r. 676–651 B.C.] hooked him with jade and horses. The King of Hu was fond of tones, so Lord Mu of Qin [r. 659–621 B.C.] seduced him with women and music.[112] These [men] were all controlled by others, because the profit was apparent. Thus: "What is well constructed cannot be uprooted."[113] Fire is hot, but Water extinguishes it; Metal is hard, but Fire melts it; Wood is strong, but [metal] axes chop it; Water flows, but Earth stops it. Only the Creator and Transformer cannot be overcome by things.

The passage concludes by enumerating each of the Five Phases of *qi*. Each overcomes one phase but is itself overcome by another. By the "Creator and Transformer" we are meant to understand the Sage, who removes himself from the eternal cycle of matter by stopping his own emanations of *qi*. That godlike state is the goal of the ruler. How it is to be achieved is not explained in "Zhushu," but the text returns to the issue in other chapters.[114]

To revisit, in closing, the question that opened this study: to which school does the "Zhushu" chapter belong? This is a text that intends to subvert all of them.[115] Some of the motivations and strategies encountered in "Zhushu" also appear in Sima Tan's summary of the House of the Way:

> 其為術也，因陰陽之大順，采儒墨之善，撮名法之要，與時遷移，應物變化，立俗施事，無所不宜。[116]

> In their techniques, they follow the great flow of *yin* and *yang;* they pick what is good among the Confucians and Mohists; they grasp the essentials of the Names and Methods [schools]. They shift and move with the seasons, responding to the transformations of things; they establish customs so that they reflect affairs. There is nothing that is not appropriate.

Sima Tan might well have had the *Huainanzi* in mind when he drafted this account.[117] In "picking what is good" and "grasping the essentials" of the other houses, the House of the Way insidiously repudiates all its predecessors. Its syncretism does not simply take ideas from every conceivable corner. It takes ideas that sound as though they come from every conceivable corner but melds them into the justification of a body politic that subdues all philosophical disputation. The *Huainanzi* is a "school" all to itself: it is the autistic-paternalistic anti-intellectual school.

—7—

Ban Zhao in Her Time and in Ours

Over the past decade, Ban Zhao 班昭 (d. A.D. 116?), author of the controversial *Admonitions for Women* (*Nüjie* 女誡, also translated as *Lessons for Women*), has been the subject of several publications in English alone. Two of these are reissues of earlier works: Nancy Lee Swann's *Pan Chao: Foremost Woman Scholar of China* (first published in 1932) and R. H. van Gulik's *Sexual Life in Ancient China* (1961). The eagerness of publishers to bring these works back into print testifies to the interest that they detect in Chinese gender studies in general and in Ban Zhao in particular. It is worth asking why Ban Zhao has been the focus of so much renewed attention, and I shall suggest below that the answer involves the emergence of gender studies as a legitimate branch of academic inquiry. But I also aim to show that researchers engaged in these topics have overestimated the usefulness of Ban Zhao's work as a historical source.

Throughout most of the twentieth century, scholarly discussions of Ban Zhao fit into one of three general camps. There were those who praised her as a pioneer for women's education, a paragon to be emulated by women in modern times. Swann is only the most famous of such exponents. In the late Qing, Chinese critics honored Ban Zhao as a brilliant example with an important message for Chinese women on the threshold of modernity: "To be a woman you must have an education!"[1] Swann also influenced many Western minds, most notably that of Florence Ayscough (1878–1942), who, in her popular *Chinese Women: Yesterday and To-Day,* placed Ban Zhao at the head of the rubric "The Educators," concluding, "her example has shone, a light, to succeeding ages."[2] Tien-chi Martin-Liao concurs: "Ban Zhao did indeed earn glory as a champion of women's education."[3]

The second commonplace point of view is completely opposed to the first. Writers such as Chen Dongyuan 陳東原 and Van Gulik decried

Ban Zhao as a mighty enemy of the cause of women. Chen went so far as to say that she "poisoned" women and that she is responsible for the fact that Chinese marriages are devoid of love.[4] Van Gulik called her manual of uxorial behavior "one of the most bigotted books in Chinese literature."[5] Siegfried Englert espouses a similar view: Ban Zhao's ideas "meant...a powerful burden for women."[6] To these critics, Ban Zhao may have been an outstanding teacher, but she taught women all the wrong things.

Finally, there are writers for whom Ban Zhao is neither heroine nor villain, but simply a child of her times. According to Kazuo Enoki, for example, the manual "tell[s] us the status of [a] wife in her husband's family at the time of Pan Chao, that is to say in the first century A.D."[7] Joanna F. Handlin, similarly: "While at the first glance oppressive, [Ban Zhao's manual] should be understood in the broader context of *li,* norms of proper behavior, to which boys no less than girls were expected to conform."[8] Scholars in this third category take Ban Zhao as a faithful recorder of conventional views regarding relations between the sexes and appropriate behavior for women.

The most recent opinion surveyed above dates to 1984 (Martin-Liao), and none would be accepted unconditionally today. The third view, as plausible as it may seem, is now probably the least defensible, for if contemporary studies of Ban Zhao agree on one point, it is that her prescriptions were exceptional even in her own day. Lily Lee has demonstrated this convincingly in a three-part argument: (1) Ban Zhao "does not encourage [women] to excel in any area, but counsels them to mediocrity," whereas Empress Dowager Deng 鄧太后 (d. A.D. 121), Ban Zhao's own pupil, "could hardly be said to have been the exemplification of a self-effacing woman"; (2) Lee finds no earlier references "which stipulate that women were not allowed to speak their minds, especially when they were wronged"; moreover, "the interdiction on socializing between men and women did not seem to exist or be enforced very strictly in pre-Qin times"; and (3) relying heavily on the pathbreaking work of Jack L. Dull, Lee reminds us that "remarriage of women was not an uncommon phenomenon in ancient China" and that it was possible for women to divorce their husbands or even leave them without officially divorcing them.[9] I have recently submitted similar observations: the values that Ban Zhao advanced in the name of tradition were really her own moralizing invention.[10]

One of the most frequently cited studies is by Yu-shih Chen: "The Historical Template of Pan Chao's *Nü Chieh.*" Two recent publications refer to it in glowing terms. In her preface to the Swann reprint, Susan Mann declares that "Chen's radical rereading of the Taoist language in Pan Chao's work brings the *Lessons for Women* into an utterly new perspective."[11] And Bret Hinsch has called Chen's essay "an exciting alternative reading of *Admonitions for Women*," adding, "close analysis of this work's language has revealed remarkable similarities with texts on Huanglao and military strategy that were also in vogue during the Han."[12]

"The Historical Template of Pan Chao's *Nü Chieh*" includes more than a study of Ban Zhao's language; the first two-thirds of the essay are devoted to recounting the fortunes of the Ban family and to presenting various episodes from Han history designed to show that accommodation rather than overt confrontation was often viewed as a politically expedient manner of dealing with powerful superiors. But the core of the essay indeed consists of the radical reinterpretation of "key concepts used in the *Nü chieh*," in comparison with such works as *Laozi* and *Sunzi* 孫子.

Chen's thesis rests on the claim that *Admonitions for Women* "was not a work of the Confucian persuasion." She endeavors to show that Ban Zhao was not "a Confucian moralist" but that, like her celebrated brother Ban Gu 班固 (A.D. 32–92), she maintained attitudes close to "that of the Taoist school."[13] This is a strange appropriation of the terms "Confucian" and "Taoist." In effect, Chen means that Ban Zhao regarded "self-preservation and survival as man's first order of business." But Daoism—whatever it means—is surely not the same thing as "self-preservation and survival." (That would make Thomas Hobbes a Daoist!) Chen writes as though there were two organized and accredited schools of thought in Han China, dubbed "Confucianism" and "Daoism," and that allegiance to one precluded inspiration from the other. That is an antiquated and simplistic model.

Chen's most notable suggestion is that Ban Zhao crafted her manual in suggestive language: that her prescriptions were intended as subtle references to *Laozi* and *Sunzi,* and that her unspoken design was to provide young wives with a set of skills necessary for survival in the hostile world of the in-laws' house.[14] Obeying mother-in-law thus becomes a matter of life and death, not moral rectitude: "The advice here seems to be: 'Always keep yourself at a safe distance.' . . . Pan Chao does not seem at all to be advising the girls to submit themselves, either in thinking or in action, to the dictate of others. But she considers it foolhardy and perilous to dash oneself against superior forces."[15] Then Chen cites *Laozi* 22 ("Those that bend remain intact" 曲則全, which she renders jarringly as "bowed down then preserved") and opines: "If we look again at the text... we will see that Pan Chao there is not suggesting that when practicing 'bow down and follow' a daughter-in-law no longer has her own judgment of right and wrong. What is suggested is that, even though the daughter-in-law may sometimes know that her mother-in-law is not in the right, for the sake of her own preservation, she nevertheless should 'bow down' and follow her mother-in-law."[16]

In other words, what Chen calls "bow down and follow" is a calculated strategy, inspired by *Laozi,* to avoid disastrous conflicts with the ineluctable mother-in-law. Ban Zhao herself, it should be noted, says nothing of the kind. Her only explicit fear is that her untutored daughters may humiliate their ancestors and clan if they do not learn proper conduct,[17] not that they must learn to dissimulate in order to appease potential enemies.

More important, it is doubtful that Ban Zhao's audience would have had the schooling necessary to discern such allusions. *Admonitions for Women* is not written in a learned style. Often it resorts to language that can only be considered colloquial. A good example is in chapter 5:

> 若夫動靜輕脫，視聽陝輸，入則亂髮壞形，出則窈窕作態，說所不當道，觀所不當視，此謂不能專心正色矣。[18]
>
> If her actions are frivolous and untrammeled, if she sees and hears *shanshu,* if she has disheveled hair and an unkempt body when at home, if she is *yaotiao* and puts on airs when abroad, if she speaks of what ought not be said, if she watches what ought not be seen—then she cannot be single-minded or correct in her bearing.

Published translations of *Admonitions for Women* regularly mangle *shanshu,* an obscure word, variously written and glossed, in the semantic range of "inconstant" and "wanton," usually in reference to an alluring woman. (*Shan* may be related to *shan* 閃, as in the inconstant twinkling of a star.) This term has a long history in the vernacular.

Knowledgeable Han readers would have recognized *yaotiao* immediately as the attribute of the lovely lady described in "The *Guan*-ing Ospreys" (Guanju 關雎), the first poem in the *Odes.* In that context, *yaotiao* is traditionally taken to mean something like "retiring, modest"; modern readers may object to the inherent moralism in that gloss, yet it is clear that, however one chooses to interpret the phrase, *yaotiao* is understood as a laudable characteristic. Ban Zhao, however, can mean it only in a pejorative sense, and commentators typically pounce on the term, explaining it as something more or less like "sluttish." How does the term designating the noble lady in "Guanju" come to mean "sluttish"? *Yaotiao* is an old and versatile disyllabic word with a basic meaning of "elegantly feminine"; in the *Odes,* it is used as a compliment, but by Ban Zhao's time, it seems to have acquired a more vulgar meaning. As early as the *Lyrics of Chu* (*Chuci* 楚辭), *yaotiao* has racy connotations—not "sluttish," but not "modest" either.[19] (Dictionaries sometimes attempt to distinguish between the senses of "retiring" and "seductive"; while there may be some lexicographical merit in keeping definitions orderly, it is misleading to present these nuances as anything other than artifacts of usage.)[20]

At any rate, what concerns us here is that Ban Zhao is manifestly not alluding to the *Odes* and is unconcerned that her audience might be waylaid by thinking otherwise. An audience that is not expected to recognize a reference to a piece as famous as "The *Guan*-ing Ospreys" would hardly be prepared for the abstruse allusions that Chen postulates. In any case, Ban Zhao is not in the habit of vague citation: when she does cite earlier texts, she labels them prominently, and the list is hardly Daoist: *Analects, Rites, Odes, Changes,* and a lost source, presumably in the genre of domestic guidebooks, called *Regulations for Women* (*Nüxian* 女憲).

One final difficulty: Chen does not take Ban Zhao's other writings into account. Mann laments that "to this day, little attention has been paid to [the] other fragments of Pan Chao's work,"[21] but let us be fair: if all that survived of Ban Zhao's oeuvre were those other pieces, and not "Admonitions for Women," she would be known today as a pedestrian author who wrote monitory little poems about industry and modesty. Still, in this instance the fragments are worth consulting, because they shed light on her habits of composition. They consist of (1) two memorials, formulaic and hence not very informative; (2) odes to the cicada, to needle and thread, and to some foreign bird that her brother brought back from Parthia; and (3) a medium-sized rhapsody, brimming with erudite allusions, titled "An Eastward Journey" (Dongzheng fu 東征賦). The last item is the most useful, because one can test whether its allusions corroborate Chen's theory that Ban Zhao wrote according to a Daoist "template."

They do not. David R. Knechtges has carefully translated and annotated "An Eastern Journey." (In her complaint, Mann does not acknowledge Knechtges—or, for that matter, the older translation by Erwin von Zach.)[22] From Knechtges' work we can see that Ban Zhao cites virtually the same sources in "An Eastward Journey" as in *Admonitions for Women:*

Analects, Odes, Application of Equilibrium, Zuo Commentary. (The only text that she cites from outside the Confucian canon is *Lyrics of Chu,* unexceptional in a stylized rhapsody about travel.) Furthermore, the conspicuous moral of "An Eastward Journey" is irreconcilable with the view that "self-preservation and survival [are] man's first order of business":

知性命之在天	We know that life and fate rest with Heaven;
由力行而近仁	But through vigorous effort, one may approach benevolence.
勉仰高而蹈景	Strive to gaze on high and tread in greatness;
盡忠恕而與人	Be fully devout and altruistic—associate with good men.
好正直而不回兮	Love the straight and upright, do not waver,
精誠通於明神	And your pure devotion shall affect even the gods.
庶靈祇之鑒照兮	May the blessed spirits shine upon you;
祐貞良而輔信	For they bless the upright, assist the faithful.[23]

Man's first order of business is the cultivation of virtue. Life and death are left to Heaven.

Admonitions for Women may use language reminiscent of the *Laozi,* but not because the author wishes to impart a Daoist message. Rather, Ban Zhao adopts keywords traditionally associated with femininity, such as "weakness," "softness," "inferiority," and "malleability." The *Laozi* transformed this familiar lexicon into a coherent philosophy of rulership that involved presenting an exterior manifestation of weakness and softness in order to attune oneself to the irresistible *dao* and thereby dominate all the brittle beings that defy the natural order. Exalting attributes conventionally associated with inferiority and femininity was a powerful rhetorical device: *Laozi* redefined "weakness" and "softness" as profound philosophical concepts. When Ban Zhao, in contrast, says "weak and soft," she means "weak and soft." Not every discussion of femininity can be interpreted as a veiled reference to the *Laozi.*

In the name of traditional morality, *Admonitions for Women* reduced the complex gender discourse of the venerable canons to a rigid and inhibiting set of protocols that has long been an embarrassment to traditional Chinese ethics. Why, then, has so much been written about her lately—and why has Chen's attempt to rehabilitate her image met with so much scholarly sympathy?

Susan Mann has touched on the essential point: "Pan Chao and her *Lessons for Women* have once again returned to historical visibility, among

Chinese as well as Euro–North American feminist historians eager to revisit China's classics and history, and Confucian ideologies, using gender as a category of analysis."[24]

The unexamined assumption here is that a feminist historian ought to begin the project of "revisiting China's classics" with Ban Zhao. Her role in furthering the cause of women's education has been grossly overrated—it is evident from the fine article by Beatrice Spade, for example, that women's education in the Southern Dynasties bore little resemblance to Ban Zhao's narrow program[25]—as has her influence on familial relations both in her own day and in subsequent dynasties. Historians interested in gender will discover more fertile territory in the real classics: *Zuo Commentary, Discourses of the States,* and especially the *Canon of Odes.* Even the demotic *Romance of the Three Kingdoms* (*Sanguo yanyi* 三國演義), amid all the swashbuckling, discloses a richer vision of women's place in society. It is also more fun to read.

—8—

Those Who Don't Know Speak

Translations of *Laozi* by People Who Do Not Know Chinese

Nowhere are the vices of thin description more apparent than in American expropriations of Daoism. It has often been said that *Laozi* (or *Daode jing*) is the most frequently translated work next to the Bible.[1] But that exception may no longer hold: a typical bookstore in the United States today will have several different versions of the *Daode jing* on its shelves, and Americans purchase more copies of that Chinese classic than of Goethe, Molière, and possibly Aristotle.[2] This trend is not surprising: the recent proliferation of *Daode jing* translations is simply a consequence of the increasing general interest in Asian thought. What is disturbing, however, is that alongside the many competent works, marketed at reasonable prices by a large assortment of publishers, there are now several offerings by people who declare without embarrassment that they have no knowledge of the Chinese language, let alone the ancient idiom of the *Daode jing*.[3]

It is hard to imagine how anyone can get the idea that it is possible to translate a Chinese text without knowing Chinese.[4] The requisite hubris is astounding. Chinese people do not attempt to translate Shakespeare without knowing English. In certain cases, such as when a rare text has been translated only into some other language, it may be defensible, as a stopgap, to publish an indirect English translation that relies on another translation, rather than on the original text. (For instance, the Ming novel *Rou putuan* 肉蒲團 was unavailable in English for many years, so Grove Press published an English translation of the German translation by Franz Kuhn.)[5] But those are special circumstances that do not apply to the *Daode jing*. There are plenty of serviceable English translations as it is.

The standard modus operandi of these pseudotranslators is to imbibe a broad selection of scholarly translations, digest their import, and expectorate a new rendition of their own. This is an objectionable procedure: rummaging through the corpus of received translations merely circumscribes oneself within the range of interpretations that they offer and can result only in the repackaging of the same old ideas in a novel and usually gimcrack integument.[6]

To illustrate the problems, four such renditions are considered below: *The Way of Life According to Lao Tzu,* by Witter Bynner (1881–1968);[7] *Tao Te Ching: A New English Version,* by Stephen Mitchell; *Tao Te Ching: About the Way of Nature and Its Powers,* by Thomas H. Miles; and *Lao Tzu Tao Te Ching: A Book about the Way and the Power of the Way,* by Ursula K. Le Guin (daughter of the anthropologist A. L. Kroeber).[8] All four writers freely admit that they do not command Chinese. Only Le Guin was aided by a genuine authority (J. P. Seaton, a specialist in Chinese literature at the University of North Carolina), and her book, as might be expected, is by far the best of the lot, although it too has major weaknesses. Bynner had consulted earlier with a redoubtable Chinese scholar named Kiang Kang-hu 江亢虎 (1883–1954?),[9] but *The Way of Life According to Lao Tzu* was entirely his own work. Miles asked some unnamed Chinese students at West Virginia University to walk him through the text character by character.

Before considering these books in detail, it is worth observing that the authors justify their publications with apologies that are revealing in themselves.[10] Mitchell, for example, announces that "the most essential preparation for my work was a fourteen-year-long course of Zen training, which brought me face to face with Lao-tzu and his true disciples and heirs, the early Chinese Zen Masters."[11] This devotion may be admirable, but a course of Zen training, however rigorous, does not in itself qualify one to translate the *Daode jing.*[12] The *Daode jing* is not a Buddhist text. In any case, it is only in an unclarified metaphorical sense that Mitchell's Zen experience could have brought him "face to face with Lao-tzu and his true disciples and heirs." Who are the "false" heirs? Who, for that matter, is Lao-tzu? (Mitchell seems to believe that there was a man named Lao-tzu who lived long ago and wrote a great book.) Far from allaying concerns, the exposition of his credentials only raises further questions about his peculiar conception of the text's history.[13]

Bynner, for his part, writes: "Though I cannot read Chinese, two years spent in China and eleven years of work with Dr. Kiang in translating *The Jade Mountain* have given me a fair sense of the 'spirit of the

Chinese people' and an assiduity in finding English equivalents for idiom which literal translation fails to convey."[14] It is striking that Bynner felt obliged to put the phrase "spirit of the Chinese people" in quotation marks; his own conscience seems to have balked at such a self-serving platitude. To suggest, moreover, that two years spent in China in the twentieth century should provide an adequate understanding of the Chinese world over two thousand years earlier belittles one of the most vibrant civilizations on the planet. No one would propose in earnest that a sojourn in Italy would constitute sufficient training for an American to discourse on Ovid and Livy. If Mitchell's and Bynner's claims seem less than outrageous, it is only because they manipulate Americans' general unfamiliarity with the cultures of East Asia.

To Miles belongs the most ludicrous pronouncement of all. In his acknowledgments, he thanks "several Chinese students, whom I cannot name because reprisals might be taken against their families on the mainland if their work with me became known. Communist Chinese bureaucrats have, at least since the days of the Red Guards, forbidden the Chinese people to possess or read the Confucian and Taoist classics, as well as most ancient Chinese literature."[15]

This he writes in 1992, long after "the days of the Red Guards," at a time when state-sponsored presses in the People's Republic of China have published thousands of books and articles on "ancient Chinese literature," including every Confucian and Daoist classic, and representing an array of diverse approaches. A writer who contends that helping a foreigner read the *Daode jing* would make Chinese citizens vulnerable to reprisals is either uninformed or disingenuous.

To proceed now to the first of the faults shared by all of these pseudotranslations: they cull from earlier publications, but in a desultory manner; usually, they take someone else's idea and make it worse.[16]

For example, the end of chapter 2 of the received text reads:

> 是以聖人處無為之事，行不言之教。萬物作而不辭，生而不有，為而不恃，成功而弗居，夫唯弗居，是以不去。[17]

This is rendered by Miles as follows:

> Therefore wherever the sage is,
> he dwells among affairs by not-doing.
> He teaches without words.
> The ten-thousand things arise, but he doesn't impel them.

He gives birth, but he doesn't possess.
He acts, but he doesn't rely on what he has done.
He has successes, but he doesn't claim credit.
So, by not claiming credit, he is never left empty.[18]

The interesting phrase here is "to claim credit," which Miles uses for *ju* 居. The normal sense of *ju* is simply "to dwell, to reside," which works well in several of the most recent translations. Consider that of Victor H. Mair: "He completes his work but does not dwell on it. Now, simply because he does not dwell on them, his accomplishments never leave him."[19] Or Robert G. Henricks: "He accomplishes his tasks, but he doesn't dwell on them; it is only because he doesn't dwell on them that they therefore do not leave him."[20] Taking *ju* in this sense also explains a textual variant that has the synonym *chu* 處 (to reside in, to be located in) for *ju*.[21]

How, then, does Miles arrive at "claim credit"? The extended meanings of *ju* include "to occupy" and hence possibly "to claim," as in "to claim territory." The phrase "claim credit" must go back to the famous translation by Wing-tsit Chan: "He accomplishes his task but does not claim credit for it. It is precisely because he does not claim credit that his accomplishment remains with him."[22] (Chan did not comment further on this idiosyncratic translation.) Miles could not have known to render *ju* in this manner without consulting Chan. Unequipped to resolve the philological issues, Miles simply browsed through the available translations and selected the rendering of this phrase that appealed to him most.

The same clause (with *chu* instead of *ju*) appears at the end of chapter 77, and Mitchell, who avoids the idea of "claiming credit" in chapter 2, freely appropriates it here: "[she] succeeds without taking credit."[23] Miles renders *chu* in chapter 77 dubiously as "to take advantage,"[24] not observing the parallel with chapter 2. It is evident that both Miles and Mitchell have read Wing-tsit Chan and help themselves to his phrasing as it suits them.[25] But neither one acknowledges his debt or reflects on the larger hermeneutic consequences of following an authority in one chapter and not in another.

Le Guin also sifts through earlier translations for help, but she uses them with more care and integrity. In her notes, she explains chapter by chapter her grounds for following various interpretations. Moreover, she usually tries to rework each passage in her own words, rather than simply copying convenient phrases from those who have preceded her. Still, there are times when she falls short of her own sources. In her note to chapter 69, for example, she says: "Waley is my guide to the interpretation of the second verse, but I make very free with the last two lines of it."[26] The passage in question reads:

> 是謂行無行，攘無臂，仍無敵，執無兵。禍莫大於輕敵，輕敵幾喪吾寶。[27]

Arthur Waley (1889–1966) translated this as follows:

> This latter is what we call to march without moving,
> To roll the sleeve, but present no bare arm,
> The hand that seems to hold, yet has no weapon in it.
> A host that can confront, yet presents no battle-front.
> Now the greatest of all calamities is to attack and find no enemy.
> I can have no enemy only at the price of losing my treasure.[28]

Waley's interpretation happens to be a very good one to follow today. For the phrase *qingdi* 輕敵, "to take the enemy lightly," Waley, working in 1958, took a risk and followed the scantly attested variant *wudi* 無敵, "there is no enemy." In 1973, a few years after Waley's death, this reading was confirmed in both of the Mawangdui recensions. Despite his providential textual instincts, however, Waley's translation of the final line is somewhat opaque,[29] and it is understandable that Le Guin wished to alter it. What she writes, however, is indefensible:

> It's called marching without marching,
> rolling up your sleeves without flexing your muscles,
> being armed without weapons,
> giving the attacker no opponent.
> Nothing's worse than attacking what yields.
> To attack what yields is to throw away the prize.[30]

"To throw away the prize" is loose, but creative, for *sang wu bao* 喪吾寶. "To attack what yields," in contrast, is simply wrong. The original says: "There is no greater calamity than not to have an enemy"—or, in the so-called putative construction, "There is no greater calamity than thinking that one has no enemy." Yielding is a characteristic theme of the *Daode jing,* so Le Guin may have felt safe to insert it here. But that is a mistake. As long as she stays close to Waley, Le Guin is on firm ground; once she leaves him and sets out on her own, she stumbles.

This raises point 2: All of these pseudotranslations are inaccurate. Their handling of chapter 10, which contains some valuable references to meditation and other macrobiotic techniques, is telling:

> 載營魄抱一，能無離乎？專氣致柔，能嬰兒乎？滌除玄覽，能無疵乎？愛人治國，能無知乎？天門開闔，能為雌乎？明白四達，能無為乎？[31]

This is Chan's translation:[32]

> Can you keep the spirit and embrace the One without departing from them?
> Can you concentrate your vital force and achieve the highest degree of weakness like an infant?
> Can you clean and purify your profound insight so it will be spotless?
> Can you love the people and govern the state without knowledge?
> Can you play the role of the female in the opening and closing of the gates of Heaven?
> Can you understand all and penetrate all without taking any action?[33]

Not one of the translations considered here manages to render these lines without tripping. Miles does best; his only errors occur in the first sentence: "While enabling your body and soul to embrace oneness—are you able to do it without needing to be secluded?"[34] "While enabling your body and soul to embrace oneness" is impossible for *zai ying po bao yi* 載營魄抱一, since there is no word in the original that could be construed as "to enable." We are asked to embrace oneness ourselves, not to enable our bodies and souls to do so. "Without needing to be secluded" is also questionable for *neng wu li* 能無離. Literally that phrase means "can you be without parting?"; Chan interprets it as "without departing from them," and it might also mean "can you cause them not to part from you?" Miles' image of seclusion is distracting and imprecise. Le Guin also misses the sense of *neng wu li:* "Can you keep your soul in its body, hold fast to the one, and so learn to be whole?"[35] "And so learn to be whole" may follow plausibly from "hold fast to the one," but it simplifies the original (and groundlessly inserts the notion of learning). Her rendition of the third sentence is tenuous, if vivid: "Can you keep the deep water still and clear, so it reflects without blurring?" Presumably, "deep water" is supposed to translate *xuanlan* 玄覽, the difficult compound that Chan renders as "profound insight." But *lan* can hardly mean "water."

Mitchell's translation is substantially freer:

Can you coax your mind from its wandering
and keep to the original oneness?
Can you let your body become
supple as a newborn child's?
Can you cleanse your inner vision
until you see nothing but the light?
Can you love people and lead them
without imposing your will?
Can you deal with the most vital matters
by letting events take their course?
Can you step back from your own mind
and thus understand all things?

Where Miles and Le Guin struggle with *neng wu li,* Mitchell simply ignores the phrase. Then he proceeds to rob the passage of its most distinctive image—playing the part of the female in the opening and closing of the gates of Heaven—replacing it with the New Age cliché "letting events take their course." In the final line, Mitchell employs another vapid locution, "step back from your own mind," and defuses all the tension in the original between understanding and not acting.

Bynner's translation is one of a kind:

Can you hold the door of your tent
Wide to the firmament?
Can you, with the simple stature
Of a child, breathing nature,
Become, notwithstanding,
A man?
Can you continue befriending
With no prejudice, no ban?
Can you, mating with heaven,
Serve as the female part?
Can your learned head take leaven
From the wisdom of your heart?[36]

This is a species of poetry all its own, so distantly removed from the Chinese text that it would be senseless to point out all the "errors." The translations by Mitchell and Bynner take such liberties that they might be considered original works in their own right. The most relevant criterion, in that case, is not how faithfully Mitchell or Bynner reproduces the sense of the Chinese, but how the character of their work, taken as a whole, compares to that of the *Daode jing*.[37]

Third, the pseudotranslations distort and simplify the philosophy of the *Daode jing*. This is the gravest defect of all.

The late A. C. Graham published an incisive review of Bynner's translation in 1991, and his specific points need not be rehearsed here.[38] Graham's general criticism is that Bynner systematically disburdens the original of its complexity. A typical example is found in the first couplet of chapter 5:

> 天地不仁，以萬物為芻狗；聖人不仁，以百姓為芻狗。[39]

These lines are straightforward: "Heaven and Earth are inhumane; they treat the Myriad Things as straw dogs. The Sage is inhumane; he treats the Hundred Clans as straw dogs." Here is Bynner's version:

> Nature, immune as to the sacrifice of straw dogs,
> Faces the decay of its fruits.
> A sound man, immune as to the sacrifice of straw dogs,
> Faces the passing of human generations.[40]

As Graham notes, this is not so much incorrect as overdetermined. The "straw dogs" 芻狗 are accouterments at a sacrifice; thus they are accorded a crucial function at a certain time and place but are summarily discarded thereafter. The Sage, like Heaven and Earth, treats all things as straw dogs: he recognizes their momentary value but does not cling to them after their time has passed.[41] To quote Graham:

> The difference here is that Bynner, accustomed to mean only one thing at a time, cannot bear to risk being misunderstood, while Lao-tzu never apologises and never explains. The "Straw dogs" passage is naked vision defined with perfect economy . . . ; Lao-tzu does not qualify it, he leaves you to go in your own direction when you notice its collisions and interactions with other parts of the book. Bynner on the other hand is anxious to make it quite plain that Lao-tzu is recommending indifference, not to the welfare of other people, but to our common mortality. It is as though a translator of Blake's "Sooner murder an infant in its cradle than nurse unacted desires" were to adapt his phrasing to avoid the impression that he condones infanticide.[42]

Graham might have pursued the matter even further, for the *Daode jing* may very well have recommended indifference to the welfare of other people after all. The statement that "Heaven and Earth are inhumane" was as mordant in the fourth century B.C. as it is today. Ancient readers would have been well acquainted with nature's capacity for cruelty. If we aspiring sages are to model ourselves after the Way of nature, then we too must be prepared to be inhumane when circumstances warrant. In Chinese, the implications of this little couplet are ferocious. Bynner, in trying to clarify them, makes them comfortable, if not banal.

Similar complaints were registered soon after the publication of Mitchell's book in 1988. From a philosophical point of view, the most serious problem is that Mitchell "has completely eliminated *te* from the text."[43] Mitchell's unease with the *de* in *Daode jing* is apparent on the very first page: "*Tao Te Ching* (pronounced, more or less, *Dow Deh Jing*) can be translated as *The Book of the Immanence of the Way* or *The Book of the Way and How It Manifests Itself in the World* or, simply, *The Book of the Way*."[44]

The Book of the Way would be *Dao jing*, not *Daode jing*. To be sure, elucidating *de* is not easy; it is one of the most difficult concepts in the text.[45] But that is precisely why a modern translator must make a sustained effort to come to grips with it. Mitchell declines this task and rewrites the text so as to eliminate the problem. Wherever the original contrasts *dao* and *de*, Mitchell removes the more difficult term. Consider chapter 51:

> 故道生之，德畜之、長之、育之、亭之、毒之、養之、覆之。[46]

Wing-tsit Chan translates this as follows:

> Therefore the Tao produces them and virtue fosters them.
> They rear them and develop them.
> They give them security and give them peace.
> They nurture them and protect them.[47]

As the referent of "them" 之 is left entirely unspecified, commentators have proposed dozens of different interpretations. What is critical, however one chooses to construe the sentence, is to recognize that *dao* and *de* are separate entities. Mitchell does not:

> The Tao gives birth to all beings,
> nourishes them, maintains them,

cares for them, comforts them, protects them,
takes them back to itself.

Where the original has two protean subjects, Mitchell allows only one. A reader of the original has more to ponder.

Mitchell does not hesitate to rewrite the text as he pleases (in his words: "I have also paraphrased, expanded, contracted, worked with the text, played with it, until it became embodied in a language that felt genuine to me"),[48] and his changes always have the effect of making the text easier. Chapter 39 discusses "the One" 一 (another concept that Mitchell conflates with *dao*), the mysterious vital force that permeates all provinces of the cosmos:

> 昔之得一者：天得一以清，地得一以寧，神得一以靈，谷得一以盈，萬物得一以生，侯王得一以為天下貞。其致之，天無以清將恐裂，地無以寧將恐發，神無以靈，將恐歇；谷無以盈將恐竭，萬物無以生將恐滅，侯王無以貴高，恐將蹷。[49]

The translation of Chan:

Of old those that obtained the One:
Heaven obtained the One and became clear.
Earth obtained the One and became tranquil.
The spiritual beings obtained the One and became divine.
The valley obtained the One and became full.
The myriad things obtained the One and lived and grew.
King and barons obtained the One and became rulers of the empire.
What made them so is the One.
If heaven had not thus become clear,
It would soon crack.
If the earth had not thus become tranquil,
It would soon be shaken.
If the spiritual beings had not thus become divine,
They would soon wither away.
If the valley had not thus become full,
It would soon become exhausted.
If the myriad things had not thus lived and grown,
They would soon become extinct.
If kings and barons had not thus become honorable and high in position,
They would soon fall.[50]

Mitchell then seizes upon Chan's word "extinct"[51] and revises the entire passage accordingly:

In harmony with the Tao,
the sky is clear and spacious,
the earth is solid and full,
all creatures flourish together,
content with the way they are,
endlessly repeating themselves,
endlessly renewed.

When man interferes with the Tao,
the sky becomes filthy,
the earth becomes depleted,
the equilibrium crumbles,
creatures become extinct.

By turning this into a homily for environmentalism,[52] Mitchell once again simplifies the original. The great cosmic axes of "Heaven and Earth" are reduced to "the sky" and "the earth," and all the other diverse elements of the universe, from "the spiritual beings" down to "the kings and barons," are compressed into the anodyne categories of "equilibrium" and "creatures." Where the *Daode jing* works on a canvas as large as the cosmos itself, Mitchell confines the text within a stereotyped post-industrial setting.

He also fails to confront the stark and troubling revelation that "kings and barons" are as essential to the mechanics of nature as Heaven and Earth themselves. This might have been an occasion to ask why the *Daode jing* seems to consider it natural for some men to rule others. Instead, Mitchell consistently mollifies the notoriously sinister political pronouncements in the text.[53] Take the famous saying in chapter 3:

聖人治，虛其心，實其腹，弱其志，強其骨。[54]

The rule of the Sage: empty their minds, fill their bellies, weaken their wills, strengthen their bones.

Mitchell writes:

The Master leads
by emptying people's minds

and filling their cores,
by weakening their ambition
and toughening their resolve.

"By emptying people's minds" is fine; the rest is benign and sentimental. The original is frightening.[55]

Even Le Guin, who is more concerned than Bynner and Mitchell about staying true to the original, occasionally prunes untidy passages that do not resonate with what she calls her "spiritual sense."[56] Often these too involve politics, as in chapter 25:

有物混成，先天地生寂漠！獨立不改，周行不殆，可以為天下母。吾不知其名，字之曰道，吾強為之名曰大，大曰逝，逝曰遠，遠曰反。故道大，天大，地大，王亦大。域中有四大，而王居其一焉。人法地，地法天，天法道，道法自然。[57]

Wing-tsit Chan's translation:

There was something undifferentiated and yet complete,
Which existed before heaven and earth.
Soundless and formless, it depends on nothing and does not change.
It operates everywhere and is free from danger.
It may be considered the mother of the universe.
I do not know its name; I call it Tao.
If forced to give it a name, I shall call it Great.
Now being great means functioning everywhere.
Functioning everywhere means far-reaching.
Being far-reaching means returning to the original point.

Therefore Tao is great.
Heaven is great.
Earth is great.
And the king is also great.
There are four great things in the universe, and the king is one of them.
Man models himself after Earth.
Earth models itself after Heaven.
Heaven models itself after Tao.
And Tao models itself after Nature.[58]

The prominent reference to the king, though in line with the depiction of the universe in chapter 39, appears to displease Le Guin. She truncates the chapter after the first section:

> There is something
> that contains everything.
> Before heaven and earth
> it is.
> Oh, it is still, unbodied,
> all on its own, unchanging,
>
> all-pervading,
> ever-moving.
> So it can act as the mother
> of all things.
> Not knowing its real name,
> we only call it the Way.
>
> If it must be named,
> let its name be Great.
> Greatness means going on,
> going on means going far,
> and going far means turning back.[59]

In a supplementary note, Le Guin explains why she has deleted the final stanza: "I think a Confucian copyist slipped the king in. The king garbles the sense of the poem and goes against the spirit of the book. I dethroned him."[60] Re-editing an ancient text by eliminating anything that clashes with one's chimeras about "the spirit of the book"—rather than enduring the agony of reconsidering one's assumptions—is anesthetized text criticism. Once again, the original Chinese discloses a vision that is vastly more difficult to comprehend than the translator's attenuated surrogate.[61]

Why do reputable presses continue to publish translations that borrow phrases uncritically from previous work, fail any basic test of accuracy, and diminish the philosophy of the original? One obvious answer is that they are profitable. Precise data concerning book sales are hard to come by, but the Internet bookseller Amazon.com indicates sales rankings for all its products and allows the public to share this information. The numbers, while probably unsuitable for a rigorous empirical study, paint a clear enough picture to be useful for my purpose.[62]

Three of the four works considered here have rankings in the top 100,000. (To put this into perspective: Amazon sells over two million different titles.) The only exception is Miles' book, which was released by a tiny press and cannot be expected to compete (although its suggestive illustrations of women squatting in various bushy landscapes may indicate that Avery also hoped to market the title to a wide audience). Mitchell enjoys the highest ranking: 3,489, extraordinary for a work of literature. Here are, for the sake of comparison, the rankings of a few Western classics: *The Selected Verse of Goethe* (Penguin), 419,893; Aristotle, *Nicomachean Ethics* (Penguin), 195,613; Molière, *The Miser and Other Plays* (Penguin), 174,379; Dickens, *Bleak House* (Everyman), 55,116; Dante, *The Divine Comedy* (Everyman), 2,323. These figures leave little doubt that Mitchell's six-digit advance[63] has long been earned back. Moreover, sales seem to be only increasing, and the many available translations have not come close to saturating the market. In 2001, Signet (an imprint of Penguin Putnam, Inc.) reissued the antique version by R. B. Blakney, undeterred by its obsolete introduction and discredited principles of translation;[64] one year later, the book's ranking has already soared to 77,864.

With so much money to be made, the central question is not why presses are publishing them but why people are buying them. Here too Amazon is helpful. The company posts ratings and reviews voluntarily submitted by registered customers, and although these voices represent only a minuscule fraction of Amazon's clientele, they are instructive.[65] The respondents like the pseudotranslations, because, of the available choices, these are the most easily adaptable to their own experience. Scholarly translations seem pedantic to them: "As a poet, Bynner sees through the 'scholarly poo poo' of some translations and gives us what appears to be an effortlessly simple adaptation"; "Bynner avoids the lecture trap and captures the spirit of the original in a gentle way that speaks subtly to the reader and lingers in the heart." They explicitly prefer the simplicity of the pseudotranslations: "The bare, simple beauty of her language [seems] to me very much an expression of the Tao" (speaking of Le Guin); "There is nothing complicated, nothing intricate about Taoist wisdom. . . . I was very lucky to read her version, which has helped me see the beauty, the magic, the simplicity, the Tao"; "With non-sexist language and beautifully illustrating examples, [Mitchell] shows the modern westerner how to truly comprehend and embrace this wise and simple philosophy. Mitchell sometimes strays from the literal translation, but always for the better."

Above all, these reviewers applaud language that is readily understandable: "It is the duty of the translator to attempt to restate a classic for his or her generation, in a language that they can best understand"; "Le Guin's 'rendition' startled me with its everyday language and showed me the Tao in a new light." Just what is so desirable about "everyday language"? We do not go to the theater in order to hear Othello speak as though he were born in our generation. Americans make statements about the *Daode jing* that they would think twice before saying with regard to any other classic.

The *Daode jing* is old; it is alien; it is Chinese; and it is difficult. These are the recalcitrant facts that too many readers seem disinclined to accept. Instead, they seek out the most facile translations and consume insipid approximations of the original. This phenomenon must be attributable at least in part to intellectual laziness. The public is not obliged to restrict itself to academic monographs, but readers still have a responsibility to investigate the merit of a translation before adopting it. Not much research is necessary to discover that there is more to Daoism than "letting events take their course" and that the scary political overtones cannot be disregarded as the detritus of imaginary interpolators. Like any profound work of philosophy, the *Daode jing* is dangerous. We do it no justice by pretending that it is easy to swallow. Chinese philosophy made simple is no longer Chinese philosophy.

Appendix

References to the *Odes* in Pre-Imperial Texts, Arranged by Mao Number

Where not self-explanatory, references follow section divisions as they appear in the following sources: *Zuozhuan: Chunqiu Zuozhuan zhu; Xunzi:* Knoblock; *Lüshi chunqiu:* Knoblock and Riegel; *Zhanguo ce:* Crump, *Chan-kuo Ts'e. Ẓiyi* is cited according to the sequence in the Guodian recension, which differs from that of the *Liji.* References to *Wuxing* follow the edition of Ikeda, and only the sections identified as *jing* 經 (Canon) are considered here, since the *shuo* 說 (Explication) probably dates from the Han. Finally, references to the ancient commentary to the *Daxue* (attributed to Zengzi) are listed in brackets, since the authenticity of that text has been questioned. References to the *Odes* in *Han-Shi waizhuan* are included (also in brackets) for the reader's convenience, even though it is unquestionably a Han text.

1
Analects 3.20
Analects 8.15
Ziyi 21
[*Han-Shi waizhuan* 1.16]
[*Han-Shi waizhuan* 5.1]

2
Ziyi 19

3
Zuozhuan, Xiang 15.3
Xunzi 21.6

5
[*Han-Shi waizhuan* 9.1]
[*Han-Shi waizhuan* 9.2]

6
[*Daxue,* commentary § 9]

7
Zuozhuan, Cheng 12.4
Lüshi chunqiu 15/4.2

9
[*Han-Shi waizhuan* 1.3]

10
[*Han-Shi waizhuan* 1.17]
[*Han-Shi waizhuan* 9.4]

12
Zuozhuan, Zhao 1.4

13
Zuozhuan, Yin 3.3
Zuozhuan, Wen 3.4
Zuozhuan, Zhao 1.4

14
Wuxing 5
[*Han-Shi waizhuan* 1.18]

15
Zuozhuan, Yin 3.3
Zuozhuan, Xiang 28.12

16
Zuozhuan, Xiang 14.3
Zuozhuan, Ding 9.2
[*Han-Shi waizhuan* 1.28]

17
Zuozhuan, Xi 20.4
Zuozhuan, Xiang 7.6
[*Han-Shi waizhuan* 1.2]

18
Zuozhuan, Xiang 7.7

20
Zuozhuan, Xiang 8.8

21
[*Han-Shih waizhuan* 1.1]

23
Zuozhuan, Zhao 1.4

24
Zuozhuan, Xiang 27.5

25
Mozi 7

26
Zuozhuan, Xiang 31.31
Mencius 7B.19
Xunzi 28.2
[*Han-Shi waizhuan* 1.8]
[*Han-Shi waizhuan* 1.9]
[*Han-Shi waizhuan* 1.10]
[*Han-Shi waizhuan* 1.11]
[*Han-Shi waizhuan* 1.12]
[*Han-Shi waizhuan* 9.6]

27
Zuozhuan, Cheng 9.5

28
Wuxing 7
Lüshi chunqiu 6/3.4

29
[*Han-Shi waizhuan* 1.19]
[*Han-Shi waizhuan* 9.14]

32
Mencius 6B.3

33
Analects 9.27
Zuozhuan, Xuan 2.3
Xunzi 28.4
[*Han-Shi waizhuan* 1.13]
[*Han-Shi waizhuan* 1.14]

[*Han-Shi waizhuan* 1.15]
[*Han-Shi waizhuan* 1.20]

34
Analects 14.39
Zuozhuan, Xiang 14.3
[*Han-Shi waizhuan* 1.21]

35
Zuozhuan, Xi 33.6
[*Han-Shi waizhuan* 1.22]
[*Han-Shi waizhuan* 5.2]
[*Han-Shi waizhuan* 9.17]

36
Zuozhuan, Xiang 29.4

37
Lüshi chunqiu 18/2.3
[*Han-Shi waizhuan* 1.23]
[*Han-Shi waizhuan* 1.24]
[*Han-Shi waizhuan* 9.19]

38
Zuozhuan, Xiang 10.2
Lüshi chunqiu 3/3.4

39
Zuozhuan, Wen 2.5

40
[*Han-Shi waizhuan* 1.25]
[*Han-Shi waizhuan* 1.26]
[*Han-Shi waizhuan* 1.27]

42
Zuozhuan, Ding 9.2
[*Han-Shi waizhuan* 1.20]

48
Zuozhuan, Cheng 2.6

49
Zuozhuan, Xiang 27.5
[*Han-Shi waizhuan* 9.7]

51
[*Han-Shi waizhuan* 1.20]

52
Zuozhuan, Zhao 3.4
Zuozhuan, Ding 10.4
Yanzi chunqiu 1.2
Yanzi chunqiu 7.1
[*Han-Shi waizhuan* 1.4]
[*Han-Shi waizhuan* 1.5]
[*Han-Shi waizhuan* 1.6]
[*Han-Shi waizhuan* 1.7]
[*Han-Shi waizhuan* 3.22]
[*Han-Shi waizhuan* 5.3]
[*Han-Shi waizhuan* 6.20]
[*Han-Shi waizhuan* 9.8]

53
Zuozhuan, Ding 9.2
[*Han-Shi waizhuan* 2.1]

54
Zuozhuan, Wen 13.5
Zuozhuan, Xiang 19.12
Zuozhuan, Min 2.5
[*Han-Shi waizhuan* 2.2]
[*Han-Shi waizhuan* 2.3]
[*Han-Shi waizhuan* 2.4]

55
Analects 1.15
Zuozhuan, Zhao 2.1
Xunzi 17.7

Xunzi 27.84
[*Daxue,* commentary § 3]
[*Han-Shi waizhuan* 2.5]
[*Han-Shi waizhuan* 2.6]
[*Han-Shi waizhuan* 9.9]

57
Analects 3.8
Zuozhuan, Yin 3.7
Zhongyong 33

58
Zuozhuan, Cheng 8.1
[*Han-Shi waizhuan* 2.7]

60
Xunzi 3.2

63
[*Han-Shi waizhuan* 3.38. Also Mao 121]

64
Zuozhuan, Zhao 2.1

69
[*Han-Shi waizhuan* 2.8]
[*Han-Shi waizhuan* 2.9]

71
Zuozhuan, Wen 7.3

73
Yanzi chunqiu 2.20

75
Zuozhuan, Xiang 26.7
Ziyi 1

76
Zuozhuan, Xiang 26.7
Guoyu, Jin 4.2

78
[*Han-Shi waizhuan* 2.10]
[*Han-Shi waizhuan* 2.11]
[*Han-Shi waizhuan* 2.12]

79
Zuozhuan, Min 2.6

80
Zuozhuan, Xiang 27.6
Yanzi chunqiu 5.3
?*Guanzi* 51.2
[*Han-Shi waizhuan* 1.13]
[*Han-Shi waizhuan* 1.14]
[*Han-Shi waizhuan* 1.15]
[*Han-Shi waizhuan* 9.10]
[*Han-Shi waizhuan* 9.11]
[*Han-Shi waizhuan* 9.12]

81
Zuozhuan, Zhao 16.3

83
Zuozhuan, Zhao 16.3

85
Zuozhuan, Zhao 16.3

87
Zuozhuan, Zhao 16.3
Lüshi chunqiu 22/5.5

90
Zuozhuan, Zhao 16.3

94
Zuozhuan, Xiang 27.5
Zuozhuan, Zhao 16.3
[*Han-Shi waizhuan* 2.16]

100
Xunzi 27.4

101
Mencius 5A.2

108
[*Han-Shi waizhuan* 2.17]
[*Han-Shi waizhuan* 2.18]

109
[*Han-Shi waizhuan* 9.20]

112
Mencius 7A.32
[*Han-Shi waizhuan* 2.19]
[*Han-Shi waizhuan* 2.20]

113
[*Han-Shi waizhuan* 2.21]
[*Han-Shi waizhuan* 2.22]
[*Han-Shi waizhuan* 2.23]

114
Zuozhuan, Xiang 27.5

115
[*Han-Shi waizhuan* 2.24]

116
Zuozhuan, Ding 10.5

117
[*Han-Shi waizhuan* 2.25]

121
[*Han-Shi waizhuan* 2.26]
[*Han-Shi waizhuan* 3.38. Also Mao 63]

128
Xunzi 30.4
[*Han-Shi waizhuan* 2.27]

130
[*Han-Shi waizhuan* 2.28]

131
Zuozhuan, Wen 6.3

133
Zuozhuan, Ding 4.3

138
[*Han-Shi waizhuan* 2.29]

139
[*Han-Shi waizhuan* 9.23]

149
[*Han-Shi waizhuan* 2.30]

151
Zuozhuan, Xi 24.3
Guoyu, Jin 4.8

152
Ziyi 3
Ziyi 18
Wuxing 7
Xunzi 1.6
Xunzi 10.14
Xunzi 15.2
Xunzi 24.5
Xiaojing 9

Lüshi chunqiu 3/3.2
Guanzi 59
[*Daxue,* commentary § 9]
[*Han-Shi waizhuan* 2.31]
[*Han-Shi waizhuan* 2.32]
[*Han-Shi waizhuan* 9.27]

154
Zuozhuan, Zhao 4.2
Mencius 3A.3
Xunzi 27.91
[*Han-Shi waizhuan* 8.24]

155
Mencius 2A.4

156
[*Han-Shi waizhuan* 2.33]

158
Guoyu, Yue B.7
Zhongyong 13
[*Han-Shi waizhuan* 2.34]

160
Zuozhuan, Zhao 20.8 = *Yanzi chunqiu* 7.5
Yanzi chunqiu 7.5 = *Zuozhuan,* Zhao 20.8

161
Zuozhuan, Xiang 4.3
Zuozhuan, Zhao 7.12
Zuozhuan, Zhao 10.3
Ziyi 20

162
Zuozhuan, Xiang 4.3
Zuozhuan, Xiang 8.7
Zuozhuan, Xiang 29.5
[*Han-Shi waizhuan* 7.1]
[*Han-Shi waizhuan* 8.35. Also Mao 167]

163
Zuozhuan, Xiang 4.3
Guoyu, Jin 4.2
Mozi 12
[*Han-Shi waizhuan* 7.2]

164
Zuozhuan, Xi 24.2 = *Guoyu,* Zhou B.1
Zuozhuan, Xiang 20.6
Zuozhuan, Zhao 1.4
Zuozhuan, Zhao 7.11
Guoyu, Zhou B.1 = *Zuozhuan,* Xi 24.2
Zhongyong 15
[*Han-Shi waizhuan* 8.24]

165
[*Han-Shi waizhuan* 9.25]

166
[*Han-Shi waizhuan* 6.16]

167
Zuozhuan, Wen 13.5
[*Han-Shi waizhuan* 8.35. Also Mao 162]

168
Zuozhuan, Min 1.2
Xunzi 27.4
[*Han-Shi waizhuan* 7.3]

170
Zuozhuan, Xiang 20.6
Xunzi 3.1
Xunzi 27.11

172
Zuozhuan, Xiang 20.6
Zuozhuan, Xiang 24.2
Zuozhuan, Zhao 13.3
[*Daxue,* commentary § 10]

173
Zuozhuan, Xiang 26.7
Zuozhuan, Zhao 12.3
[*Daxue,* commentary § 9]

174
Zuozhuan, Wen 4.7

175
Zuozhuan, Wen 4.7
Zuozhuan, Xiang 8.8

176
Zuozhuan, Wen 3.7
Zuozhuan, Zhao 17.1

177
Zuozhuan, Xi 23.6
Zuozhuan, Xuan 12.2
Zuozhuan, Xiang 19.3
Zuozhuan, Zhao 13.3
Guoyu, Jin 4.10

179
Ziyi 17
Mencius 3B.1

180
Zuozhuan, Zhao 3.12

181
Zuozhuan, Wen 13.5
Zuozhuan, Xiang 16.5

183
Zuozhuan, Xi 23.6
Guoyu, Jin 4.10
[*Han-Shi waizhuan* 7.5]

184
Xunzi 8.6
[*Han-Shi waizhuan* 7.6]

185
Zuozhuan, Xiang 16.5
[*Han-Shi waizhuan* 7.7]

188
Analects 12.10

191
Zuozhuan, Cheng 7.1
Zuozhuan, Xiang 7.6
Zuozhuan, Xiang 13.5
Zuozhuan, Zhao 2.1
Guoyu, Chu A.8
Ziyi 5
Ziyi 8
Xunzi 10.9
Xunzi 28.3
Xiaojing 7
Han Feizi 32.5 (with explanation)
[*Daxue,* commentary § 10]
[*Han-Shi waizhuan* 3.22]

192
Zuozhuan, Xi 22.6
Zuozhuan, Xiang 29.8
Zuozhuan, Zhao 1.3
Zuozhuan, Zhao 10.4. Also Mao 214
Ziyi 10
Mencius 1B.5
Zhongyong 33
[*Han-Shi waizhuan* 7.9]

193
Zuozhuan, Xi 15.4
Zuozhuan, Zhao 7.4
Zuozhuan, Zhao 32.4
Xunzi 18.6
Xunzi 24.4
[*Han-Shi waizhuan* 5.4]
[*Han-Shi waizhuan* 7.10]
[*Han-Shi waizhuan* 7.11]

194
Zuozhuan, Wen 15.11
Zuozhuan, Zhao 8.1
Zuozhuan, Zhao 16.2

195
Analects 7.11
Analects 8.3
Zuozhuan, Xi 22.7
Zuozhuan, Xuan 16.1
Zuozhuan, Xiang 8.7
Zuozhuan, Zhao 1.1
Ziyi 23
Xunzi 2.1
Xunzi 13.7
Xiaojing 3
Lüshi chunqiu 10/3.4
Lüshi chunqiu 15/1.1
[*Han-Shi waizhuan* 6.27]

196
Zuozhuan, Zhao 1.3
Guoyu, Jin 4.10
Xiaojing 5
[*Han-Shi waizhuan* 7.12]
[*Han-Shi waizhuan* 7.13]
[*Han-Shi waizhuan* 8.22]

197
Zuozhuan, Xiang 25.15
Mencius 6B.3
[*Han-Shi waizhuan* 5.33]
[*Han-Shi waizhuan* 7.14]

198
Zuozhuan, Huan 12.2
Zuozhuan, Wen 2.1
Zuozhuan, Xuan 17.2
Zuozhuan, Xiang 14.4
Zuozhuan, Xiang 29.17
Zuozhuan, Zhao 3.3 = *Yanzi chunqiu* 6.21
Ziyi 4
Yanzi chunqiu 6.21 = *Zuozhuan,* Zhao 3.3
Mencius 1A.7
Xunzi 27.80
[*Han-Shi waizhuan* 4.1]
[*Han-Shi waizhuan* 4.2]
[*Han-Shi waizhuan* 4.3]
[*Han-Shi waizhuan* 4.4]
[*Han-Shi waizhuan* 4.5]
[*Han-Shi waizhuan* 7.15]
[*Han-Shi waizhuan* 7.16]

199
Xunzi 8.4
Xunzi 22.4b

200
Ziyi 1
[*Han-Shi waizhuan* 3.37]

201
[*Han-Shi waizhuan* 7.17]

202
Zuozhuan, Zhao 24.6
[*Han-Shi waizhuan* 7.27]

203
Mozi 16
Mencius 5B.7
Xunzi 28.3
[*Han-Shi waizhuan* 3.22]
[*Han-Shi waizhuan* 4.6]
[*Han-Shi waizhuan* 4.7]
[*Han-Shi waizhuan* 7.18]

204
Zuozhuan, Wen 13.5
Zuozhuan, Xuan 12.3
[*Han-Shi waizhuan* 7.19]

205
Zuozhuan, Xiang 13.3
Zuozhuan, Zhao 7.2
Zuozhuan, Zhao 7.14
Mencius 5A.4
Xunzi 24.1
Lüshi chunqiu 14/6.2
Han Feizi 22 = *Zhanguo ce,* Zhou, 42
Han Feizi 51
Zhanguo ce, Zhou 42 = *Han Feizi* 22
[*Han-Shi waizhuan* 1.27]

206
Xunzi 27.98
[*Han-Shi waizhuan* 7.20]

207
Zuozhuan, Xi 24.3
Zuozhuan, Xiang 7.6
Mozi 27
Ziyi 2
Xunzi 1.2
[*Han-Shi waizhuan* 4.8]
[*Han-Shi waizhuan* 4.9]
[*Han-Shi waizhuan* 8.27]
[*Han-Shi waizhuan* 8.28]

209
Xunzi 2.2
Xunzi 19.3
[*Han-Shi waizhuan* 3.11–12]
[*Han-Shi waizhuan* 4.10]
[*Han-Shi waizhuan* 4.11]
[*Han-Shi waizhuan* 4.12]
[*Han-Shi waizhuan* 7.22]

210
Zuozhuan, Cheng 2.3
[*Han-Shi waizhuan* 4.13]

212
Mencius 3A.3
Lüshi chunqiu 13/6.1
[*Han-Shi waizhuan* 4.14]
[*Han-Shi waizhuan* 8.21]

214
Zuozhuan, Xiang 3.4
Zuozhuan, Zhao 10.4
Xunzi 3.5
[*Han-Shi waizhuan* 7.4]

215
Zuozhuan, Cheng 14.1
Zuozhuan, Xiang 27.5 (twice)

217
[*Han-Shi waizhuan* 4.15]

218
Zuozhuan, Zhao 25.1
Zuozhuan, Zhao 26.11 = *Yanzi chunqiu* 7.10, *Han Feizi* 34
Yanzi chunqiu 4.6
Yanzi chunqiu 7.10 = *Zuozhuan,* Zhao 26.11

Han Feizi 34.1 (explanation) = *Zuozhuan,* Zhao 26.11
[*Han-Shi waizhuan* 7.23]

219
Zuozhuan, Xiang 14.1
Xunzi 25.12

220
Yanzi chunqiu 5.15

222
Zuozhuan, Xiang 11.5
Zuozhuan, Zhao 17.1
Guoyu, Jin 4.10
Yanzi chunqiu 1.9
Xunzi 1.12
Xunzi 8.6
[*Han-Shi waizhuan* 4.16]
[*Han-Shi waizhuan* 4.17]
[*Han-Shi waizhuan* 8.26]

223
Zuozhuan, Xuan 2.1
Zuozhuan, Xiang 8.8
Zuozhuan, Zhao 2.1
Zuozhuan, Zhao 6.7
Xunzi 5.3
Xunzi 8.6
[*Han-Shi waizhuan* 4.18]
[*Han-Shi waizhuan* 4.19]
[*Han-Shi waizhuan* 4.20]
[*Han-Shi waizhuan* 4.21]
[*Han-Shi waizhuan* 4.22]
[*Han-Shi waizhuan* 4.23]
[*Han-Shi waizhuan* 4.24]
[*Han-Shi waizhuan* 7.25]

224
Zhanguo ce, Chu 222
[*Han-Shi waizhuan* 4.25]

225
Zuozhuan, Xiang 4.11
Ziyi 9

227
Zuozhuan, Xiang 19.3
Zuozhuan, Xiang 27.5
Guoyu, Jin 4.10
Xunzi 10.5

228
Zuozhuan, Xiang 27.5
Xiaojing 17
[*Han-Shi waizhuan* 4.26]
[*Han-Shi waizhuan* 4.27]
[*Han-Shi waizhuan* 4.28]

229
[*Han-Shi waizhuan* 4.29]
[*Han-Shi waizhuan* 4.30]
[*Han-Shi waizhuan* 4.31]
[*Han-Shi waizhuan* 4.32]
[*Han-Shi waizhuan* 7.26]

230
Xunzi 27.52
[*Daxue,* commentary § 3]
[*Han-Shi waizhuan* 4.33]

231
Zuozhuan, Zhao 1.4

235
Zuozhuan, Huan 6.4
Zuozhuan, Zhuang 6.1
Zuozhuan, Wen 2.1
Zuozhuan, Xuan 15.6
Zuozhuan, Cheng 2.8
Zuozhuan, Xiang 4.3
Zuozhuan, Xiang 13.3

Zuozhuan, Xiang 30.12
Zuozhuan, Zhao 6.3
Zuozhuan, Zhao 10.2
Zuozhuan, Zhao 23.9
Zuozhuan, Zhao 28.3
Guoyu, Zhou A.4
Mozi 31
Ziyi 1
Ziyi 16
Wuxing 18
Mencius 2A.4
Mencius 4A.3
Mencius 4A.7
Xunzi 12.10
Xiaojing 1
Lüshi chunqiu 5/5.12
Lüshi chunqiu 15/4.2
Guanzi 2
Zhongyong 33
[*Daxue,* commentary § 2]
[*Daxue,* commentary § 3]
[*Daxue,* commentary § 10]
[*Han-Shi waizhuan* 5.5]
[*Han-Shi waizhuan* 5.6]
[*Han-Shi waizhuan* 8.20]
[*Han-Shi waizhuan* 10.1]
[*Han-Shi waizhuan* 10.2]
[*Han-Shi waizhuan* 10.3]

236
Zuozhuan, Xiang 4.3
Zuozhuan, Xiang 24.2
Zuozhuan, Zhao 1.3
Zuozhuan, Zhao 26.10 = *Yanzi chunqiu* 7.6
Guoyu, Jin 4.2
Yanzi chunqiu 7.6 = *Zuozhuan,* Zhao 26.10
Wuxing 17
Wuxing 26
Xunzi 18.1
Xunzi 21.10
Lüshi chunqiu 13/6.3
Lüshi chunqiu 20/6.3
Guanzi 59
[*Han-Shi waizhuan* 3.13]
[*Han-Shi waizhuan* 5.8]
[*Han-Shi waizhuan* 10.4]

237
Zuozhuan, Xiang 4.3
Zuozhuan, Zhao 2.1
Zuozhuan, Ai 2.3
Mencius 1B.5
Mencius 7B.19

238
Yanzi chunqiu 4.13
Xunzi 10.4
[*Han-Shi waizhuan* 5.9]

239
Zuozhuan, Xi 12.4
Zuozhuan, Cheng 8.2
Guoyu, Zhou B.10
Guoyu, Zhou C.5
Yanzi chunqiu 5.3 = *Lüshi chunqiu* 20/3.4
Lüshi chunqiu 20/3.4 = *Yanzi chunqiu* 5.3, *Xinxu* 8.10, *Han-Shi waizhuan* 2.13
Zhongyong 12

240
Zuozhuan, Xi 19.5
Guoyu, Jin 4.24
Mencius 1A.7
Xunzi 27.91

241
Zuozhuan, Xi 9.6
Zuozhuan, Wen 2.1
Zuozhuan, Wen 4.6
Zuozhuan, Xiang 31.31
Zuozhuan, Zhao 28.3
Mozi 27
Mozi 28
Mencius 1B.3
Xunzi 2.11
Zhongyong 33
[*Han-Shi waizhuan* 5.10]
[*Han-Shi waizhuan* 10.5]

242
Zuozhuan, Zhao 9.7
Guoyu, Chu A.5
Mencius 1A.2

243
Ziyi 7
Mencius 5A.4
Xunzi 7.2
[*Han-Shi waizhuan* 5.11]
[*Han-Shi waizhuan* 5.12]

244
Zuozhuan, Wen 3.4
Yanzi chunqiu 2.19
Mencius 2A.3
Xunzi 8.2
Xunzi 11.6
Xunzi 15.1
Xiaojing 16
[*Han-Shi waizhuan* 4.10]
[*Han-Shi waizhuan* 4.15]
[*Han-Shi waizhuan* 5.2]

246
Zuozhuan, Yin 3.3

247
Zuozhuan, Yin 1.4
Zuozhuan, Cheng 2.3
Zuozhuan, Xiang 27.8
Zuozhuan, Xiang 31.31
Guoyu, Zhou C.4
Ziyi 22
Mencius 6A.17
Xunzi 27.91 (twice)
Xunzi 29.2
[*Han-Shi waizhuan* 8.24]

249
Zuozhuan, Wen 3.7
Zuozhuan, Cheng 2.8
Zuozhuan, Xiang 26.7
Zuozhuan, Zhao 21.2
Zuozhuan, Ai 5.4
Mencius 4A.1
Zhongyong 17
[*Han-Shi waizhuan* 5.27]
[*Han-Shi waizhuan* 6.15]

250
Mencius 1B.5
Mencius 3A.3

251
Zuozhuan, Yin 3.3
Xunzi 19.10
Xiaojing 13
Lüshi chunqiu 18/6.4
Guanzi 83.10
[*Han-Shi waizhuan* 6.22]
[*Han-Shi waizhuan* 8.10]
[*Han-Shi waizhuan* 8.11]

252
Xunzi 22.4a
[*Han-Shi waizhuan* 6.21]

[*Han-Shi waizhuan* 8.7]
[*Han-Shi waizhuan* 8.8]
[*Han-Shi waizhuan* 8.9]

253
Zuozhuan, Xi 28.6
Zuozhuan, Wen 10.5
Zuozhuan, Zhao 2.3
Zuozhuan, Zhao 20.9
Xunzi 14.2

254
Zuozhuan, Xi 5.2
Zuozhuan, Wen 7.4
Zuozhuan, Xuan 9.6
Zuozhuan, Cheng 8.1
Zuozhuan, Xiang 31.6
Zuozhuan, Zhao 6.5
Zuozhuan, Zhao 28.2
Zuozhuan, Zhao 32.3
Ziyi 4
Mencius 4A.1
Xunzi 12.5
Xunzi 16.4
Xunzi 27.54
[*Han-Shi waizhuan* 3.9]
[*Han-Shi waizhuan* 3.18]
[*Han-Shi waizhuan* 5.13]
[*Han-Shi waizhuan* 5.14]
[*Han-Shi waizhuan* 5.15]
[*Han-Shi waizhuan* 5.16]
[*Han-Shi waizhuan* 10.6]
[*Han-Shi waizhuan* 10.7]
[*Han-Shi waizhuan* 10.8]
[*Han-Shi waizhuan* 10.9]
[*Han-Shi waizhuan* 10.10]

255
Zuozhuan, Xuan 2.3
Zuozhuan, Xiang 31.13
Guoyu, Zhou C.3
Yanzi chunqiu 1.16
Mencius 4A.2
Xunzi 6.10
Zhanguo ce, Qin 75
Zhanguo ce, Qin 90
[*Han-Shi waizhuan* 5.17]
[*Han-Shi waizhuan* 5.18]
[*Han-Shi waizhuan* 5.19]
[*Han-Shi waizhuan* 5.20]
[*Han-Shi waizhuan* 8.23]
[*Han-Shi waizhuan* 8.36]
[*Han-Shi waizhuan* 10.13]
[*Han-Shi waizhuan* 10.14]
[*Han-Shi waizhuan* 10.15]

256
Analects 11.6
Zuozhuan, Xi 9.4
Zuozhuan, Xi 9.6
Zuozhuan, Xiang 2.3
Zuozhuan, Xiang 21.5
Zuozhuan, Xiang 22.4
Zuozhuan, Xiang 30.12
Zuozhuan, Xiang 31.13
Zuozhuan, Zhao 1.1
Zuozhuan, Zhao 5.1
Guoyu, Chu A.7
Mozi 16
Ziyi 6
Ziyi 14
Ziyi 15
Ziyi 17
Xunzi 3.4
Xunzi 6.12
Xunzi 10.6
Xunzi 12.7
Xunzi 13.7
Xunzi 14.8
Xiaojing 8

Lüshi chunqiu 22/5.5
Zhongyong 16
Zhongyong 33
[*Han-Shi waizhuan* 5.21]
[*Han-Shi waizhuan* 5.22]
[*Han-Shi waizhuan* 6.1]
[*Han-Shi waizhuan* 6.2]
[*Han-Shi waizhuan* 6.3]
[*Han-Shi waizhuan* 6.4]
[*Han-Shi waizhuan* 6.5]
[*Han-Shi waizhuan* 6.6]
[*Han-Shi waizhuan* 6.7]
[*Han-Shi waizhuan* 6.8]
[*Han-Shi waizhuan* 10.16]
[*Han-Shi waizhuan* 10.17]

257
Zuozhuan, Wen 1.9
Zuozhuan, Xiang 31.10
Zuozhuan, Zhao 24.9
Guoyu, Zhou C.3
Yanzi chunqiu 4.18
Mozi 9
Mencius 4A.7
Mencius 4A.9
Xunzi 8.11
[*Han-Shi waizhuan* 4.13]
[*Han-Shi waizhuan* 5.23]
[*Han-Shi waizhuan* 5.25]
[*Han-Shi waizhuan* 5.26]
[*Han-Shi waizhuan* 6.9]
[*Han-Shi waizhuan* 6.10]
[*Han-Shi waizhuan* 6.11]
[*Han-Shi waizhuan* 6.12]
[*Han-Shi waizhuan* 8.18]
[*Han-Shi waizhuan* 10.22]
[*Han-Shi waizhuan* 10.23]
[*Han-Shi waizhuan* 10.24]
[*Han-Shi waizhuan* 10.25]

258
Mencius 5A.4

259
[*Han-Shi waizhuan* 5.24]
[*Han-Shi waizhuan* 8.3]

260
Zuozhuan, Wen 3.4
Zuozhuan, Wen 10.5
Zuozhuan, Xuan 2.3
Zuozhuan, Cheng 9.5
Zuozhuan, Xiang 25.15
Zuozhuan, Zhao 1.13
Zuozhuan, Ding 4.3
Yanzi chunqiu 4.27
Mencius 6A.6
Xunzi 16.7
Xiaojing 4
Guanzi 59
Zhongyong 27
Zhongyong 33
[*Han-Shi waizhuan* 5.28]
[*Han-Shi waizhuan* 6.16]
[*Han-Shi waizhuan* 6.17]
[*Han-Shi waizhuan* 6.18]
[*Han-Shi waizhuan* 6.19]
[*Han-Shi waizhuan* 6.20]
[*Han-Shi waizhuan* 8.2]
[*Han-Shi waizhuan* 8.3]
[*Han-Shi waizhuan* 8.4]
[*Han-Shi waizhuan* 8.5]
[*Han-Shi waizhuan* 8.6]
[*Han-Shi waizhuan* 8.24]

262
[*Han-Shi waizhuan* 5.24]
[*Han-Shi waizhuan* 8.14]

263
Xunzi 5.7
Xunzi 12.2
Xunzi 15.5
[*Han-Shi waizhuan* 6.23]
[*Han-Shi waizhuan* 6.24]
[*Han-Shi waizhuan* 6.25]
[*Han-Shi waizhuan* 8.15]

264
Zuozhuan, Wen 6.3
Zuozhuan, Xiang 26.10
Zuozhuan, Zhao 25.2
Yanzi chunqiu 1.9
[*Han-Shi waizhuan* 6.13]
[*Han-Shi waizhuan* 6.14. Also Mao 192]

265
[*Han-Shi waizhuan* 5.29]
[*Han-Shi waizhuan* 6.26]
[*Han-Shi waizhuan* 8.16]

266
Xunzi 19.2b

267
Zuozhuan, Xiang 27.6
Zhongyong 26

269
Zuozhuan, Xiang 21.5
Zuozhuan, Zhao 1.11
Zuozhuan, Ai 27.3
Zhongyong 33
[*Daxue,* commentary § 3]

270
Guoyu, Jin 4.7
Xunzi 9.14
Xunzi 17.4
[*Han-Shi waizhuan* 3.1]

271
Guoyu, Zhou C.4

272
Zuozhuan, Wen 4.4
Zuozhuan, Wen 15.11
Zuozhuan, Zhao 6.3
Zuozhuan, Zhao 16.3
Mencius 1B.3
[*Han-Shi waizhuan* 3.2]
[*Han-Shi waizhuan* 3.3]
[*Han-Shi waizhuan* 8.18]

273
Zuozhuan, Xuan 12.2
Zuozhuan, Xiang 4.3
Guoyu, Zhou A.1
Xunzi 19.6
[*Han-Shi waizhuan* 3.4]
[*Han-Shi waizhuan* 3.5]
[*Han-Shi waizhuan* 3.6]
[*Han-Shi waizhuan* 8.19]
[*Han-Shi waizhuan* 8.20]

274
Zuozhuan, Xiang 4.3
Xunzi 10.9
[*Han-Shi waizhuan* 3.7]
[*Han-Shi waizhuan* 5.30]

275
Zuozhuan, Cheng 16.5
Zuozhuan, Xiang 4.3
Guoyu, Zhou A.4

276
[*Han-Shi waizhuan* 3.8]

278
Zhongyong 29

279
Zuozhuan, Xiang 2.3
[*Han-Shi waizhuan* 5.23. Also Mao 290]

280
[*Han-Shi waizhuan* 3.10]

281
[*Han-Shi waizhuan* 3.11–12. Also Mao 212, 239]

282
Analects 3.2
Xunzi 18.5c

283
Mozi 12

285
Zuozhuan, Xuan 12.2
Zuozhuan, Xuan 12.2
Xunzi 8.8
Xunzi 18.5c
Xunzi 19.11
Xunzi 20.3
Xunzi 27.42
[*Han-Shi waizhuan* 3.13]

288
Zuozhuan, Xi 22.7
Zuozhuan, Cheng 4.3
[*Han-Shi waizhuan* 3.14]
[*Han-Shi waizhuan* 3.15]
[*Han-Shi waizhuan* 3.16]
[*Han-Shi waizhuan* 3.17]
[*Han-Shi waizhuan* 3.22]
[*Han-Shi waizhuan* 8.24]
[*Han-Shi waizhuan* 8.25]

290
[*Han-Shi waizhuan* 5.23. Also Mao 279]

292
[*Han-Shi waizhuan* 3.18]

293
Zuozhuan, Xuan 12.2
[*Han-Shi waizhuan* 3.19]
[*Han-Shi waizhuan* 3.20]
[*Han-Shi waizhuan* 5.23]

294
Zuozhuan, Xuan 12.2, 744–745

295
Zuozhuan, Xuan 11.4
Zuozhuan, Xuan 12.2

297
Analects 2.2
[*Han-Shi waizhuan* 3.21]

299
[*Han-Shi waizhuan* 3.22]
[*Han-Shi waizhuan* 3.23]
[*Han-Shi waizhuan* 3.24]
[*Han-Shi waizhuan* 3.25]
[*Han-Shi waizhuan* 8.26]
[*Han-Shi waizhuan* 8.30]

300
Zuozhuan, Wen 2.5
Mencius 3A.4
Mencius 3B.9
?*Guanzi* 41
[*Han-Shi waizhuan* 3.26]

301
Guoyu, Lu B.20
Xunzi 27.91
Guanzi 59
[*Han-Shi waizhuan* 8.29]

302
Zuozhuan, Zhao 20.8 = *Yanzi chunqiu* 7.5
Yanzi chunqiu 7.5 = *Zuozhuan,* Zhao 20.8
Zhongyong 33

303
Zuozhuan, Yin 3.5
[*Daxue,* commentary § 3]

304
Zuozhuan, Cheng 2.3
Zuozhuan, Zhao 20.9
Guoyu, Jin 4.6
Wuxing 20
Xunzi 4.12
Xunzi 13.9
[*Han-Shi waizhuan* 3.27]
[*Han-Shi waizhuan* 3.28]
[*Han-Shi waizhuan* 3.29]
[*Han-Shi waizhuan* 3.30]
[*Han-Shi waizhuan* 3.31]
[*Han-Shi waizhuan* 3.32]
[*Han-Shi waizhuan* 3.33]
[*Han-Shi waizhuan* 3.34]
[*Han-Shi waizhuan* 3.35]
[*Han-Shi waizhuan* 3.36]
[*Han-Shi waizhuan* 5.31]
[*Han-Shi waizhuan* 5.32]
[*Han-Shi waizhuan* 8.31]
[*Han-Shi waizhuan* 8.32]
[*Han-Shi waizhuan* 8.33]
[*Han-Shi waizhuan* 8.34]

305
Zuozhuan, Xiang 26.10
Zuozhuan, Ai 5.4, 1631

Lost odes
?*Analects* 9.30
Zuozhuan, Zhuang 22.1
Zuozhuan, Cheng 9.10
Zuozhuan, Xiang 5.7
Zuozhuan, Xiang 8.7
Zuozhuan, Xiang 21.5
Zuozhuan, Xiang 26.7
Zuozhuan, Xiang 28.9
Zuozhuan, Zhao 4.6
Zuozhuan, Zhao 12.10
Zuozhuan, Zhao 12.11
Zuozhuan, Zhao 25.1
Zuozhuan, Zhao 26.10
Guoyu, Zhou C.9
Yanzi chunqiu 7.6 = *Zuozhuan,* Zhao 26.10
Ziyi 12
Xunzi 11.3
Xunzi 13.3
Xunzi 17.5
Xunzi 21.2
Xunzi 21.10
Xunzi 22.4
Xunzi 30.2
Lüshi chunqiu 8/5.2
Lüshi chunqiu 20/6.4
?*Lüshi chunqiu* 23/6.1
Guanzi 51.12
?*Zhanguo ce,* Qin 95, 96
?*Zhanguo ce,* Zhao 240

Notes

Introduction

1. Trans. Oakes, 109. The original text appears in Weber's *Gesammelte Aufsätze zur Wissenschaftslehre,* 331 f. See also *Basic Concepts in Sociology,* esp. 34–55; and "Über einige Kategorien der verstehenden Soziologie," *Gesammelte Aufsätze zur Wissenschaftslehre,* 427–474.

2. Ryle, 2, 480. See also ibid., 2, 474.

3. Geertz, *The Interpretation of Cultures,* 9. Geertz' best known case study in thick description is "Deep Play: Notes on the Balinese Cockfight," in *The Interpretation of Cultures,* 412–453; see also *Local Knowledge,* 55–70; and, most recently, *Available Light,* 133–140. The value of thick description to history and anthropology is discussed cogently in Biersack, 74 ff. See also Tongs, esp. 3 ff.

4. E.g., Li Jinglin; Defoort; Van Norden, "What Should Western Philosophy Learn from Chinese Philosophy?"; Thoraval; Laurence G. Thompson, 19 f.; Hatton; and Hall and Ames, e.g., 325. See also He Zhonghua et al.

5. As in the famous formulation by Whitehead, 63: "The safest general characterization of the European philosophical tradition is that it consists of a series of footnotes to Plato. . . . Thus in one sense by stating my belief that the train of thought in these lectures is Platonic, I am doing no more than expressing the hope that it falls within the European tradition."

6. E.g., Lloyd and Sivin, 16–81 (with a sustained investigation of the institutions of patronage); Lewis, *Writing and Authority in Early China,* 73–83; and idem, "Warring States: Political History," 641–645.

7. Duda; Soles; Vorenkamp; Ahern; Tseu, 130 ff. (who argues that Mozi was a "theist"—by which he means monotheist—and thus not a utilitarian). Similarly, Nivison, in *The Ways of Confucianism,* concerns himself repeatedly with the

question of whether Chinese philosophers offer consequentialist or deontological arguments (see, for example, 106–108, 210, and 274).

8. Joseph S. Wu, 1 and 7f., calls this "the fallacy of 'the misplaced hamburger'": like American customers who order hamburgers in a Chinese restaurant, some readers of Chinese philosophy vainly seek certain issues familiar from Western philosophy—such as causality and the analytic-synthetic distinction—in Chinese sources. "If we are tempted to write a research paper on 'The Syllogistic Theory in Confucius' or 'Lao Tzu's Theory of Causality,' this will be the same as asking for a hamburger in a Chinese restaurant" (7).

Wu's approach is not the same as the avowed methodology of Quentin Skinner, 1, 86f.: "The question we accordingly need to confront in studying... texts is what their authors—in writing at the time they wrote for the specific audience they had in mind—could in practice have intended to communicate by issuing their given utterances." The difference is that Skinner consciously assumes the task of gauging authors' intentions, a form of the intentional fallacy devastated by Keane, 205ff. I hope to avoid the specter of intentionalism in these essays by referring to the (often multifaceted) meanings that texts had in their culture, rather than to the authors' intended "illocutionary force," to use the phrase that Skinner has borrowed from J. L. Austin. On intentionalism, see also the classic essay by Wimsatt and Beardsley, "The Intentional Fallacy" (and Skinner's most recent response, 1, 90–102).

9. Some critics of thick description argue that it is naturally suited to the analysis of particular situations and phenomena rather than to synthetic accounts of culture or society as a whole. See, for example, Walters, 551f.

10. These are the so-called category 4 languages, judged to be the most difficult of those offered at the Defense Language Institute Foreign Language Center and Presidio of Monterey (private communication from Command Sergeant Major Eugene B. Patton III). See also Hadley, 26. To be sure, certain languages not taught at Monterey may be even harder.

11. A useful conspectus is Shaughnessy, *New Sources of Early Chinese History.* See also the extensive review by Giele. Qian Cunxun, 15–36, provides an overview of the field current to the mid-1980s; Scarpari, "Riscrivere la storia e la cultura della Cina antica," is more up to date.

12. The textual corpus from Mawangdui is published in the series *Mawangdui Hanmu boshu,* which has still not been completed.

13. See especially chapter 88, "Rulin zhuan" 儒林傳; for a representative example, see *Hanshu* 88.3597.

14. Thus, for example, Granet, *La pensée chinoise,* 345; see also Sivin, "Text and Experience in Classical Chinese Medicine," esp. 187f.

15. Compare the discussion in Wang Bo, *Jianbo sixiang wenxian lunji,* esp. 188.

16. Liu Xinfang, 403, speculates that some of these texts may have made their way to Chu from other regions. As Friedman, 35 ff., observes, "Chu culture" has become a hot topic of study in Mainland China, in part because it provides the newly wealthy and powerful southern region of the country with a patrimony to be proud of.

17. E.g., MacCormack, 3; Latourette, 1, 53 and 81; and Rosthorn, 36 f.; more circumspect is Duyvendak, e.g., 39. A representative Marxist view is offered in Yang K'uan, "Shang Yang's Reforms," esp. 88–99. See also Asano, 264–270; Bodde, "The State and Empire of Ch'in," 34–38; and Li Jing, 22–42. The scholarly preoccupation with Lord Shang is probably due to the existence of a book purporting to contain his doctrines (*Shangjun shu* 商君書, of questionable authenticity) and to the old Chinese historiographical trope of attributing social progress to the agency of heroic individuals.

18. Now published in *Shuihudi Qinmu zhujian.* The most thorough studies in English are by Hulsewé and Yates. A different cache of Qin laws was discovered at Longgang 龍崗, near Shuihudi, and has been published in *Longgang Qinjian.* Most recently (summer of 2002), a group of administrative documents from the Qin dynasty was found at Liye 里耶, Hunan province 湖南省; see Li Xueqin, "Chudu Liye Qinjian."

19. Cf. H. L. A. Hart, 132 f.

20. Li Jing, 112, argues that the Qin laws were inherently unfair (in that punishments varied according to the social class of the offender) but that, within these bounds, they were fairly applied. This conclusion contrasts starkly with the more old-fashioned view offered in Watson, *Records of the Grand Historian: Qin Dynasty,* xiv: "Qin's law are noted . . . for the equality with which they were applied to high and low alike, regardless of social rank." Cf. also Hulsewé, *Remnants of Ch'in Law,* 7 f.

21. See, for example, the comments of Gu Yanwu 顧炎武 (1612–1681) in *Shiki kaichū kōshō* 6.64, discussed in Goldin, *The Culture of Sex in Ancient China,* 164n.25.

22. This is one of the central arguments in Darnton (e.g., 4 f. and 77 f.), where Geertz' method is consciously applied to historiography.

23. Zhou Fagao contains literally hundreds of glosses on early Chinese personal names. See also Alleton, *Les Chinois et la passion des noms;* and Bauer.

24. Thus, for example, Creel, *The Origins of Statecraft in China,* 67 f. See also Schaberg, *A Patterned Past,* 63.

25. See, for example, Wang Shoukuan, 7 ff.; Yang Ximei, 274–281; and, for an opposing view, Peng Yushang, esp. 4 ff. The personal names of Wen and Wu were Chang 昌 and Fa 發, respectively.

It is not clear when the practice of granting posthumous names began in

China. See the references in Creel, *The Origins of Statecraft in China,* 68n.55; as well as the discussions in Wang Shoukuan, 1–16; and Tong Shuye, 382–386. Most scholars (e.g., Keightley, 33ff.) believe that the *gan* 干 names, also called "temple names" 廟號, of Shang kings were determined posthumously. In contrast, the late Zhang Guangzhi (K. C. Chang), in "Shangwang miaohao xinkao," presented an elaborate argument dividing the *gan* names, which are generally thought to have been posthumous, into two categories and linking these with two putative lineages within the ruling house; this scheme would suggest that the Shang kings must have had at least some idea of their posthumous designations. See also Chang's *"T'ien kan";* as well as *Early Chinese Civilization,* 72–114; and "Guanyu 'Shangwang miaohao xinkao' yiwen de buchong yijian." More recently, Nivison, "The Key to the Chronology of the Three Dynasties," 13ff., has suggested that a king's *gan* name indicates the first official day of his rule in the ten-day week (called *xun* 旬).

26. The discussion below considers only names that were acquired in adulthood, for it was common practice to bestow names on babies and children on the basis of their appearance. Cf. Bauer, 311–313. For example, Tong 同, the son of Lord Huan of Lu 魯桓公 (r. 711–694 B.C.) and the future Lord Zhuang of Lu 魯莊公 (r. 693–662), was so dubbed because there was speculation that he may have been a bastard and "resembled" (*tong*) another man: *Chunqiu Guliang zhuan zhushu* 3.2375a (Huan 桓 6 = 706 B.C.). See also Goldin, *The Culture of Sex in Ancient China,* 141n.99. The birth of this same lad prompts a general discussion of naming in *Chunqiu Zuozhuan zhu,* 1, 115f., discussed in Li Xueqin, *Li Xueqin juan,* 674ff.; Emmrich, 15f.; Grafflin, 384f.; Xiao Yaotian, 26–30; and Bauer, 255.

27. "Minggui xia" 明鬼下, *Mozi jiaozhu* 8.31.338.

28. Following the commentary of Lu Wenchao 盧文弨 (1717–1796).

29. Following the commentary of Sun Yirang 孫詒讓 (1848–1908).

30. Compare the translation in Mei, 163f. Cf. also Maspero, *China in Antiquity,* 116f.

31. *Lunheng jiaoshi* 25.76.1051ff.

32. Incidentally, it has been suggested that Mozi itself is also not a proper name but means simply "Tattooed Master," implying that Mo Di and his followers were convicts or slaves. See, for example, Fung, 1, 79; and Qian Mu, *Mozi,* 1ff. In contrast, Xu Xiyan, 67, points out that no contemporary document confirms this suggestion; consequently, Mo may well have been a genuine surname. See also Chow, "A New Theory on the Origins of Mohism," 126f.; and Gu Jiegang and Tong Shuye. In the early twentieth century some scholars speculated that Mozi may have been a foreigner, but there is no concrete evidence for this assertion either. See the review by Zhang Jiewen.

33. "Guji liezhuan" 滑稽列傳, *Shiji* 126.3197–3199. A man by the same name appears in various contexts (most notably *Mencius* 4A.17) as a renowned philoso-

pher or rhetorician; it is impossible to know whether the same person is intended. See Sato, 78 f.; and Goldin, *Culture of Sex,* 174n.94.

34. Jia Yi 賈誼 (201–169 B.C.) explains the term in *Hanshu* 48.2244. Cf. Hinsch, "Women, Kinship, and Property," 5 ff.; Sheng Yi, 254 ff.; Hellmut Wilhelm, 265n.25; Ch'ü, 252n.8; Chen Guyuan, 70; and Niida, 2, 483 ff. One of the oldest uses of the term is in a statute of the state of Wei, dated 252 B.C., in "Wei li zhi dao" 為吏之道, *Shuihudi Qinmu zhujian,* 175; trans. (as "debt slaves") in Hulsewé, *Remnants of Ch'in Law,* § F1.

35. The surname Chunyu was taken from the name of the capital of the ancient state of Zhou 州; see *Chunqiu Zuozhuan zhu,* 1, 108 (Huan 5 = 707 B.C.). See also the comments by Ying Shao in "Xingshi" 姓氏 (as reconstructed from surviving fragments), *Fengsu tongyi jiaozhu,* 509. Cf. Zhu Hongbin, 481. So *Chunyu kun* might just mean "the shaved man from Chunyu." Granet, *Danses et légendes de la Chine ancienne,* 17n.1, misconstrues the name totally and reads it as though it were "Shun Yukun."

36. Sheng Yi, 258 f.; Knechtges, "Riddles as Poetry: The '*Fu*-Chapter' of the *Hsün-tzu,*" 22n.98; and idem, "Wit, Humor, and Satire in Early Chinese Literature (to A.D. 220)," 83. On *kun* as a form of corporal punishment, see Xu Fuchang, *Shuihudi Qinjian yanjiu,* 266–271; and Liu Hainian, 192.

37. *Lunyu jishi* 27.922–924. For later elaborations, see "Dangwu" 當務, *Lüshi chunqiu jiaoshi* 11.596; and "Wudu" 五蠹, *Han Feizi xin jiaozhu* 49.1104. This passage is discussed further in chapter 2, below.

38. "Changgong" 長攻, *Lüshi chunqiu jiaoshi* 14.792. The same text discusses a man named Dunqia Choumi 敦洽讎糜; Chen Qiyou points out that this too is a meaningful epithet: "Cordial, Decorous, and Without Foe." See "Yuhe" 遇合, *Lüshi chunqiu jiaoshi* 14.816 and 824n.40.

39. Following the commentary in *Lüshi chunqiu jiaoshi* 14.800n.45.

40. "Sunzi Wu Qi liezhuan" 孫子吳起列傳, *Shiji* 65.2162.

41. Průšek, *Chinese History and Literature,* 66.

42. "What's in a Name?" 29. Cf. also Hsu, 72: "Sun the Cripple." Incidentally, Sun Bin's writings have recently been discovered and reconstructed; see *Sun Bin Bingfa.* For translations, see Sawyer; and Lau and Ames.

43. Petersen, "What's in a Name?" 28 f.

44. See *Chunqiu Zuozhuan zhu,* 1, 407 (Xi 僖 23 = 637 B.C.) for *pianxie.* Petersen has pointed out in a private correspondence that two of Chonger's famous half-brothers also have meaningful names: the foolhardy Yiwu 夷吾 (Destroy Me) and the revenant Shensheng 申生 (Born Again). The latter name might also be explained as Born in Shen; see Emmrich, 19.

45. See especially the example of Lao Ai 嫪毐 (Lustful Misdeed) discussed in Goldin, *Culture of Sex,* 82 ff. One might also be suspicious of the name Han Fei 韓非

(Han the Refuter), since Han Fei is one of the most elenctic writers in the history of Chinese philosophy. Like Sun Wu, the name Han Fei may be what Průšek calls *trop typique.* (The ancient name Fei is elsewhere interpreted as *fei* 飛, "to fly": see Zhou Fagao, 26; and Bauer, 313n.1.) Han Fei himself attributes the famous paradox "A white horse is not a horse" 白馬非馬也 to a man named 兒說; this name is usually pronounced Ni Yue, but might also be read as Ni Shui, meaning Ni the Persuader (or perhaps even Wa Shui 晲說, Babbling Persuader). Text in "Wai chushuo zuo shang" 外儲說左上, *Han Feizi xin jiaozhu* 11.32.674.

It is sometimes suggested that Ke 軻, the personal name of Mencius, might be interpreted as an abbreviation for *kanke* 轗軻 / 坎坷 (hard times), which would refer to his indigence; see Zhou Fagao, 203 f. And for the various explanations of Confucius' personal name (Qiu 丘, Hillock), see the commentary of Duan Yucai 段玉裁 (1735–1815) in *Shuowen jiezi Duan zhu fu liushu yinyun biao* 8A.31a (under the character *ni* 屔), reproduced in Zhou Fagao, 218. Cf. also Jensen, 196; Emmrich, 16n.75; Xiao Yaotian, 27; and Granet, *Danses et légendes,* 432 f.

Zhai Hao 翟灝 (1736–1788) explained the name Jieyu 接輿 (see *Analects* 18.5) as Receiving the Chariot (namely, of Confucius), but other exegetes disagree. See the commentary in *Lunyu jishi* 36.1261 ff. There is another possibility: in a later tale Jieyu is said to have been courted by a royal emissary whose chariots left deep grooves in front of his gate. (This visitation prompted Jieyu and his wife to change their names and flee the land.) See *Han-Shi waizhuan jianshu* 2.183; and *Lienü zhuan buzhu* 2.37 f. ("Xianming" 賢明).

Finally, the name of Gongshu Ban 公輸般, the famous engineer whose siege machinery Mozi confounds in "Gongshu" 公輸, *Mozi jiaozhu* 13.50.764–765, may belong to the same category. In his commentary to "Ailei" 愛類, *Lüshi chunqiu jiaoshi* 21.1465n.10, Gao You asserted that Gongshu is the appellation of Lu Ban 魯般, which appears to be an ordinary name. But *Lu ban* might also mean "a carpenter from Lu," since *ban* 般 (or *pan* 槃) can bear the sense of "to construct," as in the *Shijing* (Mao 56, "Kaopan" 考槃); see *Shijing zhuxi,* 1, 160. On the basis of similar evidence, Chen Guangyu suggests that the Shang king known as Pangeng may have earned that name in honor of his role in constructing a new capital for the dynasty.

46. I borrow both these renderings from Mair, *Wandering on the Way,* 46 f. and 126 f., respectively.

47. Wang Shoukuan, 220–229, places this text in the fourth century B.C. *Analects* 5.15 also discusses the rationale behind the choice of a certain posthumous name.

48. *Yi Zhoushu jixun jiaoshi* 6.54.92.

49. See Bauer, 8–15, for the various categories of names in traditional China.

50. Cf. Chenyang Li, 94: "The Confucians would say that a person's name becomes meaningful when it bears some description of the person."

51. For some general studies of Xi Wangmu, see Lü Simian, *Lü Simian shuo shi,* 1–5; Frühauf; James; Cahill; Birrell, 171–175; Major, *Heaven and Earth in Early Han Thought,* 200 ff.; Rainey; Fracasso; Wu Hung; Loewe, *Ways to Paradise,* 86–126; Mathieu, 44n.109 and 180–185; Münke, 301–306; Ying-shih Yü, "Life and Immortality in the Mind of Han China," 96 ff.; and Dubs.

There are well-known references to a spirit named Ximu 西母 in the oracle bone literature; for a concise review, see Rao Zongyi, *Zhongguo zongjiao sixiang shi xinye,* 109–114. Schipper, "Taoism: The Story of the Way," 54n.12, writes that Xi Wangmu "is not mentioned in the Confucian Classics . . . which in fact do not mention a single female deity, as they are profoundly misogynistic." But the statement in "Dalüe" 大略, *Xunzi jijie* 19.27.489, that the sage Yu 禹 studied at Xi Wang Guo 西王國 must be an allusion to the legend that Yu visited Xi Wangmu. For other references, see esp. "Wuxing" 無形, *Lunheng jiaoshi* 2.7.67; as well as *Han-Shi waizhuan jianshu* 5.500; and *Xinxu xiangzhu* 5.142. However, Karlgren, "Legends and Cults in Ancient China," 271, assuming that Yu "would not have had a female teacher," takes Xiwang mu as 西王畝, "acres of the Western King"; for the name can also refer to a place, as in, for example, *Mu tianzi zhuan* 2.5b; and "Shidi" 釋地, *Erya zhushu* 7.2616b.

52. "Shiqin" 釋親, *Erya zhushu* 4.2592b. Frühauf, 50, is aware of this passage, but denies its significance.

53. "Shiqin," *Erya yishu* A4.1b.

54. The most famous occurrence is probably in Hexagram 35 of the *Yijing,* "Jin" 晉, *Zhou-Yi zhengyi* 4.49b: "One receives these boon blessings from one's *wangmu*" 受茲介福于其王母. Even the most accomplished translators sometimes render this mistakenly as "royal mother": e.g., Shaughnessy, *I Ching,* 139. Most other published translations have "grandmother," "departed grandmother," "ancestress," and so forth. Compare the commentary in *Du Yi huitong* 5.423. Wang Fanzhi, 67, suggests a connection between this *wangmu* and Xi Wangmu. *Wangfu* as "deceased paternal grandfather" is attested also in "Quli shang" 曲禮上, *Liji zhengyi* 3.1248b.

55. "Bing" 病, *Rishu jiazhong* 日書甲種, strips 七〇正貳 to 七三正貳, in *Shuihudi Qinmu zhujian,* 193. For the characters presented here as *zuo* 作, the editors of *Shuihudi Qinmu zhujian* have *zuo* 酢; and for *gui* 劌, the editors have *sui* 歲. For the readings presented here, see Liu Lexian, 117nn.2, 5. One might not expect *gui zai xi fang* 劌在西方 at the end of the second section, because the offerings and infirmities discussed there all clearly pertain to the color yellow, and the west is naturally associated with white (as in the next section of the text, not cited here). Cf. Kudō, 35. The types of animals offered in sacrifice also do not conform

to later Five Phase systems. For example, according to the chart in Sterckx, 79, red corresponds to feathered beasts and yellow to hairless ones. In Warring States sources, such details vary.

For similar passages from Shuihudi, see "Youji" 有疾, *Rishu yizhong* 日書乙種, *Shuihudi Qinmu zhujian,* 246. *Wangfu* appears to be associated with disease in materials from Baoshan as well: see "Bushi jidao jilu" 卜筮祭禱記錄, strip 222, in *Baoshan Chujian,* 34. Cf. Chen Wei, *Baoshan Chujian chutan,* 154 f.

56. On the basis of similar usage in other early medical texts, Kudō, 39, explains the phrase *de zhi* 得之 as an indication that eating the food of the sacrifice is the cause of the illness in question. See also Liu Lexian, 118–119. For a different interpretation, see Wu Xiaoqiang, 75 f. See also Xu Fuchang, "Shuihudi Qinjian *Rishu* zhong de guishen xinyang," 923–924.

57. The three characters *wu kan xing* 巫堪行 are not easy to understand; perhaps the meaning is that a shaman named Kan carries out the worship of *wangmu.* Wu Xiaoqiang, 71, identifies Kan with the spirit Kanpi 堪坏, who is mentioned in "Da zongshi" 大宗師, *Zhuangzi jishi* 3A.6.247. But Wu presents no evidence to support this conjecture. Kanpi probably refers to the same spirit elsewhere called Qinpi 欽駓. (In Old Chinese, the name would have been *khəm-phrə.) See, for example, "Xishan jing" 西山經, *Shanhai jing jiaozhu* 2.50; and "Zhang Heng liezhuan" 張衡列傳, *Hou-Han shu* 49.1931. The commentary of Lu Deming 陸德明, *Zhuangzi jishi* 3A.6.249n.11, asserts that the name appears as Qinfu 欽負 in the *Huainanzi,* but no such form is found in the received text (the nearest equivalent being Qianju 鉗且). See the well-documented discussion in *Zhuangzi jiaoquan,* 6.233n.10. See also Sterckx, 172 and 299n.26.

For the name Kan, Wolfgang Behr (private communication) has suggested a possible connection with the Old Turkic word *qam,* meaning "sorcerer, shaman."

58. "Lilun" 禮論, *Xunzi jijie* 13.19.375.

59. Yang goes on to propose that *wang* is actually an error for *shen,* but this is not likely: the two characters are not easily confused, and in any case, it is *wang* that must be considered *lectio difficilior.* (On the concept of *lectio difficilior,* the more difficult reading, see, for example, Maas, § 16a et passim.)

60. See the commentary in *Xunzi jianshi,* 278. The passage is in "Liyun" 禮運, *Liji zhengyi* 22.1426a: "Thus the rite is carried out in the suburbs, and the many spirits receive their offices from it" 故禮行於郊，而百神受職焉.

61. Titles conventionally applied to females, similarly, can be used by male gods: consider *hou* 后, literally "queen," the title of such deities as Houji 后稷 (Millet God) and Houtu 后土 (Soil God), even though the former is normally conceived as male. (The sex of the latter is ambiguous.) Karlgren, "Some Fecundity Symbols in Ancient China," 16, interprets *hou* in this context as a verb, "to rule over," because "a title in Chinese is put *after,* not *before* its principal word"

(emphasis in original). But there are many counterexamples (e.g., King Ji 王季, the father of King Wen of Zhou; and Marquis Yi of Zeng 曾侯乙).

Miller, 199 et passim, discusses references to a certain Jinwang 晉王, which may be a designation of a local riverine goddess with whom the Jin shrines 晉祠 have long been associated. See, for example, *Weishu* 106A.2466. Jinwang can hardly mean "King of Jin," because the ancient state of Jin was a marquisate, not a kingdom. (I have been unable to find a single instance in which the ruler of Jin is called Jinwang.) Thus Jinwang probably means "spirit of the Jin [waters]" and could refer either to this goddess or to Tang Shuyu 唐叔虞, the progenitor of the House of Jin.

62. Taking *wang* in this sense, incidentally, explains the name of the antipodal deity Dong Wanggong 東王公 (or Dong Wangfu 東王父), usually rendered as "King Father of the East" (no doubt on the model of "Queen Mother of the West"). But the phrase *wanggong*, which normally means "kings *and* dukes," makes little sense as a royal title; rather, the name Dong Wanggong probably means something like "Spirit Lord of the East."

63. For *wang* 往, "past," compare the words attributed to Jieyu in *Analects* 18.5: "One cannot remonstrate with the past" 往者不可諫.

64. See Mao 254, "Ban" 板: "August Heaven is shining and bright; it is with you wherever you go" 昊天日明，及爾出王. Tjan, 1, 300n.87, lists several ancient texts that attempt to forge a quasi-etymological link between *wang* 王, "king," and *wang* 往, "to go."

65. Schafer, "Ritual Exposure in Ancient China," 161. Qiu Xigui, 253, explains, however, that the phonetic component of *kuang* 匡 and *kuang* 狂 was not *wang* 王 in archaic script; rather, it was a protoform of the character now written *wang* 往 (presumably in the sense of "going across" to the spirit world). In addition to Qiu's other examples, *wang* 迋, "to go," should probably be added to this group; cf. Wang Li, 352 f.

66. "Yangsheng zhu" 養生主, *Zhuangzi jishi* 2A.3.126.

67. See Wang Shumin's discussion in *Zhuangzi jiaoquan* 111n.8.

68. The *Shiming* 釋名 of Liu Xi 劉熙 (fl. ca. A.D. 200) glosses the *wang* of *wangfu* and *wangmu* as *wang* 暀: *wangfu* is "he who returns and *wang*s in the household" 家中所歸暀也. See "Shi qinshu" 釋親屬, *Shiming shuzheng bu* 3.11.150. The commentaries of Bi Yuan 畢沅 (1730–1797) and Ye Dejiong 葉德炯 both emend this *wang* to *wang* 往, yielding "he who comes and goes in the household."

69. Many examples are cataloged in Coblin, 145–310, but the numerous abbreviations and unkeyed citations make those tables unnecessarily difficult to use. See also Ames, "Thinking through Comparisons," 107; and Unger, 70–71.

70. "Zhongyong," *Liji zhengyi* 52.1629b. For more on the *Application of Equilibrium*, see Tu Wei-ming, *Centrality and Commonality*. The gloss appears to be lifted

from *Mencius* 7B.16, which is probably an older text; I cite from the *Application of Equilibrium* because the occurrence of the gloss there is better known.

71. See, for example, *Analects* 4.5. For more on the place of *ren* in Confucius' philosophy, see, for example, Lau, *Confucius: The Analects,* 14–22.

72. See, for example, *Analects* 6.20, 6.28, 12.1, 12.2, 12.22, 13.19, 17.6. Cf. Wing-tsit Chan, "Chinese and Western Interpretations of *Jen* (Humanity)," 109.

73. This is known as *shu* 恕, reciprocity. See, for example, Fingarette; Van Norden, "Unweaving the 'One Thread' of *Analects* 4:15"; Ivanhoe, "Reweaving the 'One Thread' in the *Analects*"; Creel, "Discussion of Professor Fingarette on Confucius"; S. Y. Chan; and Nivison, *Ways of Confucianism,* 59–76.

74. *Ren* 人 may have originally denoted a nobleman (as opposed to *min* 民, used for the people at large). See, for example, Graham, *Disputers of the Tao,* 19. But by Confucius' day, the word could freely be extended to any (morally noble) person.

75. Old Chinese reconstructions are taken from Baxter, with modifications corresponding to Baxter's unpublished "Old Chinese, Version 1.1," which is briefly described in Baxter and Sagart, 72n.19.

76. Cf. Boodberg, 37.

77. "Zongzu" 宗族, *Baihu tong shuzheng* 8.398.

78. A quotation from "Yaodian" 堯典, *Shangshu zhengyi* 2.119a f.

79. *Jiu* 究 has two Old Chinese readings, *kuw: and *kus.

80. Compare the translation in Tjan, 2, 576.

81. Cf. Anthony C. Yu, 239: "Without the conventions of the alphabet as stable phonetic anchors, determining in Chinese whether an appeal to identical or approximate vocalization for semantic elucidation indicates a real cognate or merely sporting with sounds is difficult." For a similar example involving the characters *gong* 公 and *si* 私 (which both contain the element 厶), see chapter 3, below.

82. *Mencius* 7A.46, *Mengzi zhengyi* 27.948–950.

83. Baxter reconstructs *tshin for *qin,* but the initial cluster almost certainly reflects an older *sn-. (Compare his own discussion in Baxter, 223 f.) It is clear that many of the words for which he reconstructs an initial *tsh- must have had a consonant cluster involving *s-. For example, for *qing* 青, "green, the color of life," he reconstructs *srēng, but for *qing* 清, "pure," which belongs to the same phonetic series, he has *tsheng. More plausible would be an initial cluster *sr- for both words.

84. See, for example, *Mencius* 1A.1, *Mengzi zhengyi* 2.43, for a similar usage: "There has never been someone who was *ren* and yet neglected those who were *qin* to him" 未有仁而遺其親者也.

85. *Mencius* 7B.12, *Mengzi zhengyi* 28.972.

86. *Xunzi jijie* 16.22.420.

87. Jakobson, 411.

88. See, for example, Long Yuchun, 107–126; and Goldin, *Rituals of the Way,* 145n.35.

89. For a similar emphasis on annotation, see Nienhauser, "The Implied Reader and Translation," 19.

90. See, for example, Quine, *Theories and Things,* 1–23; *Ontological Relativity and Other Essays,* 1–25; and, generally, *Word and Object.* See also Gibson.

1. The Reception of the *Odes* in the Warring States Era

1. *A History of Chinese Literature,* 13. For the phrase "exegetical debris," see Zhang Longxi, 213.

Around the same time as Giles, scholars in China were voicing similar criticisms of the commentarial tradition to the *Odes;* for typical examples, see Gu Jiegang, "Ye you si jun"; and Hu Shi, "Tantan *Shijing.*" A representative sample of comparable opinions can be found in Pauline Yu, 45f. See also Lin Qingzhang, 107–112; Li Jiashu, 91–94; Wong and Lee; and Zhao Peilin, 273f. Gu Jiegang's views of the *Odes* are also discussed at length in Zhao Zhiyang, 267–295.

2. See, for example, Riegel, "Eros, Introversion, and the Beginnings of *Shijing* Commentary," 147n.14; Su Xuelin, 19–24; Van Zoeren, 92ff.; and Zhao Peilin, 251–269. For dissenting opinions, see Wang Chenglüe; and Lü Simian, *Lü Simian dushi zhaji,* 692ff.

3. Compare the opinion of Wu Wanzhong, 87: "We consider the tendency to explain the *Odes* in this manner to be more or less related to the ideology of Confucian scholars at the beginning of the Han who regarded the rituals as the bonds of an established social order." See also Rouzer, 15–26; and Watson, *Early Chinese Literature,* 202–230.

For more on the notion that the *Odes* were originally folksongs, see Luo Qikun, 37–73; Lu Hongsheng; and esp. Qu Wanli.

4. For a recent overview of ancient citations of the *Odes,* see Lewis, *Writing and Authority,* 155–176. Wang Zhongjiang, "Jingdian de tiaojian," 52, briefly refers to the phenomenon.

5. The fragmentary remains of the three competing schools of exegesis (known as Qi, Lu, and Han), similarly, do not always agree with the interpretations found in the Prefaces and the Mao commentary. See, for example, Lin Yaolin; and the classic studies in Pi Xirui, 2.12–25 and 41–44. The three lost traditions of the *Odes* are described in Hightower, 251ff.

Among the recently discovered "Shanghai Museum manuscripts," which surfaced on the Hong Kong antiquities market in 1994 and were quickly purchased by the Shanghai Museum, is a discussion of the *Odes* ascribed to Confucius and titled *Kongzi shilun* 孔子詩論. This text offers pithy interpretations of several odes, differing substantially from those of the received Prefaces. But as the provenance of the Shanghai Museum manuscripts is still unknown, they are considered here only in the notes. The first two volumes of these manuscripts have been published under the general editorship of Ma Chengyuan. Although the manuscripts may well be genuine, their authenticity is not established by Ma Chengyuan's publication.

6. Cf. Lin Qingzhang, 96 ff.; Shaughnessy, *Before Confucius,* 221; Dai Junren, 2, 1214 ff., and 3, 1832–1834.

7. Both texts date to the fourth century at the latest. *Wuxing* was discovered at both Mawangdui and Guodian; *Ziyi* has been transmitted as a chapter of the *Liji* and was found in an alternate recension at Guodian. (Both texts are discussed in chapter 2, below.) The Mawangdui *Wuxing* includes an "Explication" 說 of the text that probably dates to the Han dynasty. The Shanghai Museum manuscripts (including *Kongzi shilun* and another version of *Ziyi*) are not included in this catalog. References to the *Odes* in *Kongzi shilun* are listed in Zhou Fengwu, "*Kongzi shilun* xin shiwen ji zhujie," 166–172.

8. See the Appendix. This total does not include roughly thirty alleged references (some of them questionable) to lost odes and perhaps another thirty-five general references to the entire collection or one of its three sections. If one were to add such references to the total, the sum would approach six hundred.

Dong Zhi'an, *Xian-Qin wenxian yu xian-Qin wenxue,* 35–45 and 64–88; and Schmölz, 155–163, both contain useful (but incomplete) charts that can be consulted in conjunction with the appendix here. For references to the *Odes* in the *Zuozhuan,* see Zeng Qinliang, 13–29; Zhang Suqing, 261–288; Yang Xiangshi; and Kamata Tadashi, 346 f. and 362–378. For references in the *Xunzi,* see Pei Puyan, 152–169. For the *Lüshi chunqiu,* see Tian Fengtai, 357–359. For the *Zhanguo ce,* see He Jin, 180–182.

9. "Dalüe," *Xunzi jijie* 19.27.486.

10. Ibid. See also *Mencius* 2B.2.

11. *Mencius* 3A.3, *Mengzi zhengyi* 10.332; and "Dalüe," *Xunzi jijie* 19.27.510. Lewis, *Writing and Authority in Early China,* 165, calls this ode "the earliest surviving account of the activities and moral nature of the common people." Such opinions are considered and criticized in Luo Qikun, 42 ff.

12. *Mencius* 3B.1, *Mengzi zhengyi* 12.414.

13. For *ru* 如 as *er* 而, see Karlgren, *Glosses on the Book of Odes,* § 471. But in "Loan Characters in Pre-Han Texts II," §§ 529 and 532, Karlgren rejects similar proposals in other contexts.

14. *Chunqiu Zuozhuan zhu,* 4, 1288 (Zhao 昭 7 = 535 B.C.). Cf. Zeng Qinliang, 366–367. On the use of the *Odes* in the *Zuozhuan,* see (in addition to the items

listed in note 8 above) Tsuda Sōkichi, *Saden no shisōshiteki kenkyū* 左傳の思想史的研究, in *Tsuda Sōkichi zenshū,* 15, 315 ff.

15. *Chunqiu Zuozhuan zhu,* 1, 365 (Xi 15 = 645 B.C.). Cf. Zeng Qinliang, 76–77.

16. "Zhenglun" 正論, *Xunzi jijie* 12.18.338. For my view of Xunzi's concept of Heaven, see *Rituals of the Way,* 39–54. See also Kodama, *Junshi no shisō,* 114; and Itano, 31–66.

17. *Chunqiu Zuozhuan zhu,* 1, 134 (Huan 12 = 700 B.C.). See also *Chunqiu Zuozhuan zhu,* 3, 1168 (Xiang 襄 29 = 544 B.C.). Cf. Zeng Qinliang, 48–50 and 306.

18. *Mencius* 3A.3, *Mengzi zhengyi* 10.342.

19. "Minggui xia," *Mozi jiaozhu* 8.31.340. This quotation is effective, insofar as evidence from canonical texts is considered to be decisive in Mohist epistemology. See, for example, Graham, *Disputers of the Tao,* 52 f. On Mozi's general view of the *Odes,* see Wang Changhua, 67–77; and Luo Genze, esp. 147–150.

Karlgren, *Glosses on the Book of Odes,* § 751, points out that Mao seems to have understood this line as a description of King Wen's activities while still alive. The same is implied in "Guyue" 古樂, *Lüshi chunqiu jiaoshi* 5.286. Cf. Dong Zhi'an, "*Lüshi chunqiu* zhi lun Shi yin Shi yu Zhanguo moqi Shixue de fazhan," 40.

20. "Zhifen" 知分, *Lüshi chunqiu jiaoshi* 20.1347. For the *Yanzi chunqiu,* see "Cui Qing jie Qi jiangjun dafu meng Yanzi bu yu" 崔慶劫齊將軍大夫盟晏子不與, *Yanzi chunqiu jishi* 5.298.

21. See the commentary in *Shijing yidu,* 355 f.

22. See *Chunqiu Zuozhuan zhu,* 4, 1313 (Zhao 9 = 533 B.C.); *Mencius* 1A.2, *Mengzi zhengyi* 2.45–47; and "Wu Ju lun tai mei er Chu dai" 伍舉論臺美而楚殆, *Guoyu* 17.545. Cf. Sterckx, 113; Chun-chieh Huang, 91; Schaberg, "Social Pleasures in Early Chinese Historiography and Philosophy," 20; Schmölz, 131; and Zeng Qinliang, 374–375.

23. See "Taizi Jin jian Lingwang yong Gushui" 太子晉諫靈王壅穀水, *Guoyu* 3.112; and *Mencius* 4A.2, *Mengzi zhengyi* 14.491.

24. See the commentary of Zheng Xuan 鄭玄 (A.D. 127–200) in *Mao-Shi zhengyi* 16C.516b.

25. Cf. Dong Zhi'an, "*Lüshi chunqiu* zhi lun Shi yin Shi," 42.

26. See "Junzi" 君子, *Xunzi jijie* 17.24.450; "Shenren" 慎人, *Lüshi chunqiu jiaoshi* 14.802; "Shuolin shang" 說林上, *Han Feizi xin jiaozhu* 7.22.471; "Wenren zhi Zhou" 溫人之周, *Zhanguo ce* 1.16. Cf. Wu Wanzhong, 36–41. Waley, *The Book of Songs,* 189, tentatively annotated these lines as "A proverbial saying?"

27. *Mencius* 5A.4, *Mengzi zhengyi* 18.637. Cf. Wu Wanzhong, 38–40; Cook, "Cong lijiao yu xingfa zhi bian kan xian-Qin zhuzi de quanshi chuantong," 19; Yuan Changjiang, 114 f., 137 f., and 158 f.; and Schmölz, 126 ff. Mencius'

interpretation, incidentally, is in line with that of the Minor Preface (*Mao-Shi zhengyi* 13A.463b).

28. This practice of indiscriminate quotation—called *duanzhang quyi* 斷章取義, "taking meaning by breaking stanzas," after *Chunqiu Zuozhuan zhu,* 3, 1145 (Xiang 28 = 545 B.C.)—is a productive theme in the critical literature. For a brief and elegant discussion, see Qian Zhongshu, *Guanzhui bian,* 1, 224–226; trans. in *Limited Views,* 221–223.

29. Cf. Dong Zhi'an, *Xian-Qin wenxian,* 31 f.; Schmölz, 99; and Pei Puyan, 172. The names of these sections, incidentally, appear as *xia* 夏, *song* 訟, and *bangfeng* 邦風, respectively, in the Shanghai Museum manuscripts. See, for example, *Kongzi shilun,* strips 2–3; Ma Chengyuan, 1, 127–129. The "Hymns" are also sometimes called *rong* 容, as in *Xing zi ming chu* 性自命出, strips 21 and 66; *Guodian Chumu zhujian,* 179 and 181. Cf. Kern, "*Shi jing* Songs as Performance Texts," 50n.6.

30. All ten instances, furthermore, involve either of the following lines: "The good man, the noble man—his deportment is unified" 淑人君子，其儀一也 and "The good man, the noble man—his deportment is not faulty" 淑人君子，其儀不忒. Apparently these were popular formulae and were commonly quoted into the Han dynasty. Cf. Wu Wanzhong, 19–30.

31. E.g., Schmölz, 115 and 119; and esp. Shih-Hsiang Chen, 31 and 35. Schaberg, *A Patterned Past,* 74 ff., suggests that odes involving the figure of King Wen, which dominate the "Greater Elegantiae" and "Hymns," were especially popular because that monarch was conceived as the embodiment of *wen* itself.

32. See Qian Zhongshu, *Guanzhui bian,* 1, 104–105 for a discussion of this poem as an *alba.*

33. The sexual content of the poems might even be conveyed by the title of the section to which they belong. *Feng* 風 (literally "wind") is usually understood in this context as the equivalent of *feng* 諷, "to satirize," and in rendering the term into English, many writers exploit the multivalence of the word "air." But *feng* can also denote the mating songs of animals; this sense informs the well-known saying *feng ma niu bu xiang ji* 風馬牛不相及, "The lowing horses and cattle do not attract each other," used in *Chunqiu Zuozhuan zhu,* 1, 289 (Xi 4 = 656 B.C.), to describe two states so distant from one another that their herd animals do not interbreed. So it is not far-fetched to read *Guofeng* as "The Mating Songs of the States." This suggestion goes back to Lu Kanru and Feng Yuanjun, 15. (The idea seems to have been proposed independently by Chen Mengjia, 5.) See also Geaney, *On the Epistemology of the Senses in Early Chinese Thought,* 22–30; Sterckx, 170; Zhu Bingxiang, 1080 f.; Yuan Changjiang, 225; Lévi, "Langue, rite et écriture," 167; Su Xuelin, 119 et passim; Ye Shuxian, 550–559; Lewis, *Sanctioned Violence in Early China,* 215; and Gibbs, 287. Kuriyama, *The Expressiveness of the Body and the Divergence of Greek and*

Chinese Medicine, 238 ff., refers to many of the same texts as Lewis but does not cite him. See also Kuriyama's earlier article, "The Imagination of Winds."

Conventional glosses of *feng* are reviewed succinctly in Su Xuelin, 113–114; and Qian Zhongshu, *Guanzhui bian,* 1, 58–59. See also Fan Shuyun.

34. A possible exception may be found in Confucius' famous statements about the "sounds of Zheng" 鄭聲, which he decries in *Analects* 15.11 and 17.18. Scholars disagree as to whether Confucius was referring to the subsection of the "Airs" called "Airs of Zheng" 鄭風 or to other songs popular in that state. It may be significant that none of the "Airs of Zheng" appears in the *Analects,* although Confucius is said to have cited them in other texts (such as *Ziyi*). For a judicious discussion of the issue, see Diény, 17–40. Some scholars have tried to explain Confucius' statements by considering the content and rhythmic peculiarities of the "Airs of Zheng": e.g., Luo Qikun, 216–219; Harbsmeier, "Eroticism in Early Chinese Poetry," 335 ff.; DeWoskin, *A Song for One or Two,* 92 ff.; Kurihara, 135 ff. and 415 f.; and esp. Picken, 103. Such arguments hang on the assumption that Confucius was indeed referring to those poems.

Elsewhere, the probity of the "Airs of Zheng" is indeed impugned. When Noble Son Zha of Wu 吳公子札 hears them performed, his prescient comment is: "Beautiful—but it is too trifling, and the people will not be able to bear it. This is why [Zheng] will be among the first to perish" 美哉！其細已甚，民弗能堪也。是其先亡乎！; *Chunqiu Zuozhuan zhu,* 3, 1162 (Xiang 29 = 544 B.C.). Cf. Nylan, *The Five "Confucian" Classics,* 91; Van Zoeren, 266n.39; and DeWoskin, *A Song for One or Two,* 22 ff. On Noble Son Zha generally, see Cai, 40 ff.; Schaberg, *A Patterned Past,* 86–95; Schmölz, 168–171; and Zhang Suqing, 109–115.

35. "Dalüe," *Xunzi jijie* 19.27.511. Xunzi continues: "Their perfection can be compared to that of bells and chimes; their sounds are permitted within the ancestral temple" 其誠可比於金石，其聲可內於宗廟. According to the commentary of Yang Liang, this proverb means that the *Odes* teach us to rein in our desires even when they are about to overflow. Cf. Goldin, *Culture of Sex,* 156n.71; Wu Wanzhong, 72; Yuan Changjiang, 150 f. and 166; Du Yongming et al., 1, 332; and Su Xuelin, 122. Compare also "Ruxiao" 儒效, *Xunzi jijie* 4.8.133: "The 'Airs' are not lubricious because they restrain themselves by adopting [the Way]" 故風之所以不逐者，取是以節之也. Cf. Schmölz, 53. *Kongzi shilun* contains several illuminating statements on this issue. See, for example, strip 3, Ma Chengyuan, 1, 129: "In the 'Airs of the States' are included affairs. The people's customs are encyclopedically observed in them, their fruits greatly collected in them. The words are refined, the sounds good" 邦風其納物也，溥觀人俗焉，大斂材焉。其言文，其聲善; and strip 10, Ma Chengyuan, 1, 139: "'The *Guan*-ing Ospreys' [i.e., the first poem in the 'Airs'] uses sex as an allegory for ritual" 關雎以色喻禮. On the last statement, cf. Rao Zongyi, "Zhushu *Shixu* xiaojian," 229 f.

There are similar statements in the *Analects,* e.g., 3.20 and 8.15. For Confucius' response to eroticism in the *Odes,* see Goldin, *Culture of Sex,* 11–13; Harbsmeier, "Eroticism in Early Chinese Poetry," 333–339; Yau-woon Ma, 24f.; and Tsuda, *Rongo to Kōshi no shisō* 論語と孔子の思想, in *Tsuda Sōkichi zenshū,* 16, 200.

36. For an analysis of several linguistic and prosodic features contributing to the ambiguity of the *Shijing* in general, see Xiang Xi. See also Qian Zhongshu, *Guanzhui bian,* 1, 151f.; *Limited Views,* 228f.

37. "Qiuren" 求人, *Lüshi chunqiu jiaoshi* 22.1515.

38. See the commentary in *Lüshi chunqiu zhushu* 22.2773.

39. Compare the translation in Knoblock and Riegel, 581. The careers of Zichan and Shuxiang are studied in Yasumoto. See also Martin, "Le cas Zichan"; Rubin; and Bodde and Morris, 16f.

40. The most accessible overview of the philosophical orientation of this text is Knoblock and Riegel, 27–55. See also my review of that work in *Early Medieval China* 7 (2001), 109–139; and Cook, "The *Lüshi chunqiu* and the Resolution of Philosophical Dissonance."

41. Cf. Dong Zhi'an, *"Lüshi chunqiu,"* 42. One could continue in this vein: since the speaker in Mao 87 is female, Zichan may be acknowledging Jin's superior force by assuming a feminine voice, if a defiant one. The same ode is used, to the same effect, in an exchange between representatives of Jin and Zheng in *Chunqiu Zuozhuan zhu,* 4, 1381 (Zhao 16 = 526 B.C.). Cf. Martin, "La parole poétique," 64; idem, "Le *Shijing,* de la citation à l'allusion," 15; and Zeng Qinliang, 389–390. Granet, *Études sociologiques sur la Chine,* 76, berates traditional commentators for finding in Mao 87 "je ne sais quel incident de politique seigneuriale," making no mention of its versatile usage in diplomatic discourse.

42. Lü Simian, *Lü Simian dushi zhaji,* 697, notes that the Minor Prefaces frequently explain specific odes in the same manner as Warring States texts. There is one important difference: the Han commentaries aim systematically to associate each poem with specific historical circumstances—a tendency not displayed in the pre-imperial literature. See Zhang Haiyan, 352–358; Wang Shuomin; James J. Y. Liu, 96; and Pauline Yu, 401ff. See also Schmölz, 129.

43. *Mao-Shi zhengyi* 4C.342b.

44. For more on the relation between a man and a woman as a metaphor for that between a ruler and his subjects, see Goldin, *Culture of Sex,* 18ff.

45. *Chunqiu Zuozhuan zhu,* 2, 837 (Cheng 成 8 = 583 B.C.). Cf. Zeng Qinliang, 188–191.

46. For this interpretation of *ji* 極, see Karlgren, *Glosses on the Book of Odes,* § 182.

47. Compare the translation in Legge, 5, 366f.

48. Once again, the representative of the weaker state identifies himself with the female voice in the poem.

49. For a similar example, see Martin, "L'entrevue de 525 A.C."

50. Cf. Schaberg, *A Patterned Past*, 346n.58 (and, more generally, 72 ff. and 234 ff.); Lin Qingzhang, 94–95; Martin, "Le *Shijing*, de la citation à l'allusion," 15; Su Xuelin, 45; Schmölz, 89 ff.; and esp. Van Zoeren, 41. Luo Qikun, 50, interprets such examples rather implausibly as indications of the general decline of aristocratic education during the Springs and Autumns period.

51. "Xianji," *Lüshi chunqiu jiaoshi* 3.145.

52. Following the commentary of Gao You 高誘 (ca. A.D. 168–212). In *Lüshi chunqiu zhushu* 3.334, Wang Liqi points out that Hong Xingzu 洪興祖 (1090–1155) once cited a variant of this story from *Lienü zhuan* 列女傳, in which Confucius says *keyi zhi tianxia* 可以治天下 (one can rule the world) where the *Lüshi chunqiu* has *keyi wei tianxia*. (This remark reveals considerable erudition on Wang Liqi's part, as the passage is no longer found in the extant *Lienü zhuan*.) See Hong Xingzu's commentary to "Fengfen" 逢紛, "Jiutan" 九歎, *Chuci zhangju buzhu* 16.176 (under the verse *zhizu zhe buneng zhi xi* 執組者不能制兮).

53. Compare the translation in Knoblock and Riegel, 105.

54. Cf. Dong Zhi'an, "*Lüshi chunqiu*," 41.

55. *Lunyu jishi* 30.1031–1035.

56. Compare the translation in Lau, *Analects*, 130.

57. Notably in the phrase *si ji er yi yi* 斯己而已矣, which is sometimes taken as an error for *si yi* 已 *er yi yi* ("then just stop").

58. It is impossible to tell whether Confucius' final comment is intended sincerely or sarcastically. For further exegesis on Mao 34 and its use in this passage from the *Analects*, see Van Zoeren, 27 and 36; and Riegel, "Poetry and the Legend of Confucius's Exile," 15 f. Cf. Goldin, *Culture of Sex*, 106 f.

For general studies of Confucius' understanding of the *Odes*, see, in addition to the works cited in note 35 above: Lévi, *Confucius*, 63–69; Yuan Changjiang, 59–104; Holzman; Zau; and Gu Jiegang, "*Shijing* zai Chunqiu Zhanguo jian de diwei."

59. *Lunyu jishi* 5.157–159.

60. Cf. Karlgren, *Glosses on the Book of Odes*, § 167; the translation above contradicts Karlgren's § 166.

61. The third line is not found in Mao 57. This problem prompted Zhu Xi 朱熹 (1130–1200) to assert that the poem in question is not Mao 57 but a lost ode; various other commentators disagree.

62. Compare the translation in Lau, *Analects*, 68.

63. Cf. Lévi, *Confucius*, 66 f.; Nylan, *Five "Confucian" Classics*, 97 f.; Zou Ran, 337; Martin, "Le *Shijing*, de la citation à l'allusion," 19 f.; Schmölz, 57 f.; Zhao Zhiyang, 18; and Zhu Ziqing, *Jingdian changtan*, 25.

64. Cf. Yau-woon Ma, 22.

65. "Bugou" 不苟, *Xunzi jijie* 2.3.39. The example of "Eggs have hair" is cited also in "Tianxia" 天下, *Zhuangzi jishi* 10B.33.1105.

66. Compare the translation in Knoblock, 1, 174. Cf. Yuan Changjiang, 133 and 160 f.

67. Elsewhere, he affirms that certain lines from Mao 191 ("Jie Nanshan" 節南山) "refer to" the evil consequences of following Mohism: "Fuguo" 富國, *Xunzi jijie* 6.10.187 f. We should be accusing Xunzi of gross anachronism if we were to judge him strictly by the letter. Cf. Harbsmeier, "Eroticism in Early Chinese Poetry," 337 f.

68. It is not certain whether *jiugao* 九皋 means "nine marshes" or "ninth marsh." Cf. Karlgren, *Glosses on the Book of Odes,* § 484.

69. "Ruxiao," *Xunzi jijie* 4.8.128. Cf. Yuan Changjiang, 130. Hexagram 61 ("Zhongfu" 中孚) of the *Yijing* contains a similar image—"A squalling crane is present in the shade" 鳴鶴在陰—with a strikingly similar traditional explanation. To quote Wang Bi 王弼 (A.D. 226–249): "If your stand is sincere and your dedication perfect, then even if you are located in darkness and obscurity, things will surely respond to you" 立誠篤至，雖在闇昧，物亦應焉. Text in *Zhou-Yi zhengyi* 6.71b. Likewise the *Xici* 繫辭 commentary, *Zhou-Yi zhengyi* 7.79b f., focuses on the noble man's ability to transform the world from within his closet. Lloyd and Sivin, 74, ridicule such interpretations.

70. Compare Karlgren, *The Book of Odes,* 127: "The metaphorical sense of this [poem] is doubtful. . . . Probably it expresses somebody's desire in living in retreat, enjoying the pleasures of nature, and refusing to come forth and engage in official work." The Mao commentary reads it in the same spirit as Xunzi: the line "speaks of someone whose person is hidden but whose reputation is manifest" 言身隱而名著; *Mao-Shi zhengyi* 11A.433a. Cf. Saussy, *The Problem of a Chinese Aesthetic,* 143.

71. For a fine recent study of the text, see Cook, "Consummate Artistry and Moral Virtuosity."

72. Ikeda, 187; see also Ikeda's translation on p. 188 and discussion in 192n.25. Other scholars interpret the passage differently; e.g., Pang Pu, *Zhubo* Wuxing *pian jiaozhu ji yanjiu,* 34; and Wei Qipeng, *Jianbo* Wuxing *jianshi,* 15–17.

73. Cf. Liao Mingchun, "Guodian Chujian yin *Shi* lun *Shi* kao," 172 ff.; and Liu Xinfang, 33. On the use of the *Odes* in *Wuxing* generally, see Wang Bo, *Jianbo sixiang wenxian lunji,* 39–42.

74. For the various possible meanings of this line, see Karlgren, *Glosses on the Book of Odes,* § 40.

75. The sexual nuances of the word *gou* 覯 (translated here as "to join") are discussed in the commentary by Zheng Xuan and the subcommentary by Kong

Yingda 孔穎達 (574–648), *Mao-Shi zhengyi* 1D.286ab. Cf. Granet, *Fêtes et chansons anciennes de la Chine,* 118. Liao Mingchun, "Guodian Chujian yin *Shi* lun *Shi* kao," 174, takes *gou* more innocently as a synonym of *jian* ("to see") in the previous line.

76. *Mengzi zhengyi* 18.638.

77. Compare the translation in Lau, *Mencius,* 142.

78. On the intentional fallacy, see the Introduction, note 8, above. Geaney, "Mencius's Hermeneutics," discusses the differences between Mencius' position and ordinary intentionalism. See also James J. Y. Liu, 95 ff.

79. This passage is much discussed in the secondary literature. See Wu Wanzhong, 39; Lewis, *Writing and Authority in Early China,* 165; Yuan Changjiang, 116 f.; Zhang Xiaokang and Liu Sanfu, 43; Schmölz, 52; Wang Changhua, 109 ff.; Zhao Zhiyang, 19 and 273 f.; Guo Shaoyu, 31; Zhu Ziqing, *Jingdian changtan,* 26; and esp. Zhu Ziqing, *Shi yan zhi bian* 詩言志辨, in *Zhu Ziqing shuo shi,* 25 f.

80. Cf. Cai, 122 ff.; and Eno, 56 ff.

2. Xunzi in the Light of the Guodian Manuscripts

1. For the first official report of this excavation, see Hubei Sheng Jingmen Shi Bowuguan. On the date of the tomb, see Li Boqian, 18–19; Liu Zuxin, 31; Wang Bo, "Meiguo Damusi Daxue Guodian *Laozi* guoji xueshu taolunhui jiyao," 2; Peng Hao, "Guodian yihao mu de niandai ji xiangguan de wenti"; idem, "Guodian yihao mu de niandai yu jianben *Laozi* de jiegou," 13–15; Wang Baoxuan; Luo Yunhuan; and Cui Renyi. The identity of the deceased is unclear; the earlier suggestion that he may have been a tutor to the crown prince of the state of Chu has recently been challenged. See, for example, Xing Wen, 246; and Li Ling, "Guodian Chujian yanjiu zhong de liangge wenti—Meiguo Damusi Xueyuan Guodian Chujian *Laozi* guoji xueshu taolunhui ganxiang," 47–49. Peng Hao, "Guodian yihao mu de niandai yu jianben *Laozi* de jiegou," 16, concludes that "the tomb occupant may have been born into a prominent aristocratic family and, not having attained rank and status, pursued the theories of Daoism and Confucianism."

2. Since the publication of *Guodian Chumu zhujian,* scholars dissatisfied with the editorial group's choice of the title *Cheng zhi wen zhi* (the meaning of which was never clear) have begun to refer to this manuscript by various other names. The most common such alternate title is *Tian jiang dachang* 天降大常 (*Heaven Lays Down Its Great Constancy*)—or simply *Dachang*—which is the most important phrase in the text (and is discussed further below). See, for example, Guo Yi, 208–229. In order to avoid confusion, the text is cited here by the name *Cheng zhi wen zhi.* Guo also presents a new arrangement of this text that is vastly more successful than the version in *Guodian Chumu zhujian,* but as his work

may not be available to all readers, I quote the text as it appears in *Guodian Chumu zhujian.*

3. The first four titles in this list, incidentally, may belong together as a single text. They are written on bamboo strips of the same dimensions and expound remarkably similar ideas, as will be demonstrated below. Cf. Ding Sixin, 358; and Wang Bo, *Jianbo sixiang wenxian lunji,* 249 f.

4. Tang and Yu are the sage kings Yao 堯 and Shun 舜, respectively.

5. Two of the few publications to make this point are Ning Chen, "The Ideological Background of the Mencian Discussion of Human Nature," 36; and Li Zehou, 420–421.

6. The seminal manifesto of this view is Li Xueqin, "Jingmen Guodian Chujian zhong de *Zisizi.*" See also idem, "The Confucian Texts from Guodian Tomb Number One," 109–110; "Xian-Qin rujia zhuzuo de zhongda faxian"; and "Cong jianbo yiji *Wuxing* tandao 'Daxue,'" esp. 50–51. Jiang Guanghui, "Guodian Chujian yu *Zisizi*—Jian tan Guodian Chujian de sixiangshi yiyi," 88, concludes that the following texts were all written by Zisi: *Tang Yu zhi dao, Ziyi, Wuxing, Xing zi ming chu, Qiongda yi shi, Cheng zhi wen zhi* (which he calls *Qiuji* 求己), *Lu Mugong wen Zisi* 魯穆公問子思, and *Liude.* But we do not know nearly enough about the figure of Zisi, let alone his teachings, to make such specific attributions.

One philological argument in favor of an association with the *Zisizi* is made by Liao Mingchun in two separate articles: "Jingmen Guodian Chujian yu xian-Qin ruxue," 42; and "Guodian Chujian rujia zhuzuo kao," 71. In his commentary to the *Wenxuan* 文選, Li Shan 李善 (d. A.D. 689) cited a number of lines from *Ziyi* and attributed them to the *Zisizi.* See "Sizi jiangde lun" 四子講德論, *Liuchen zhu Wenxuan* 51.14b; and "Da He Shao" 荅何劭, *Liuchen zhu Wenxuan* 24.15b. Since the *Zisizi* still existed in Li Shan's day, Liao Mingchun surmises that it must have included at least part of *Ziyi.* And it is well known that Shen Yue 沈約 (A.D. 441–513) listed *Ziyi,* among other texts, as part of the *Zisizi* in a memorial recorded in "Yinyue shang" 音樂上, *Suishu* 13.288. However, these points do not convince Cheng Yuanmin, 30–32, who argues that Shen Yue was mistaken and that the ostensible parallels between *Ziyi* and *Zisizi* are merely repetitions of common Confucian aphorisms.

Other Mainland scholars associate the Guodian manuscripts with Mencian Confucianism; see, for example, Pang Pu, "Chudu Guodian Chujian," 6. For an overview of Guodian studies in Mainland China, see Jiang Guanghui, "Guodian Chujian yu yuandian ruxue" and idem, "Guodian Chujian yu zaoqi daojia."

7. To date, the most comprehensive study of the graphs used in the manuscripts is Cheung Kwong-yue.

8. Private communication from Professor Xu Shaohua, Wuhan University.

9. "Zhengming," *Xunzi jijie* 16.22.412.

10. Graham, *Studies in Chinese Philosophy and Philosophical Literature,* 7–66. See also Goldin, *Rituals of the Way,* 11 f.

11. "Xing" 性, *Mengzi ziyi shuzheng* B.25; cf. Goldin, *Rituals of the Way,* 12 f.

Incidentally, the great Neo-Confucian Cheng Yi 程頤 (1033–1107) also observed that Mencius' use of the term *xing* was different from that of Gaozi. See Zhu Xi, 18.229. Cheng Yi was referring to a peculiar Neo-Confucian dichotomy between the "fundamental *xing*" 性之本, which corresponds to the principle of the universe, and the "physical *xing*" 性質之性, which is the imperfect human form made up of *qi*. But since neither Mencius nor Gaozi (nor Xunzi, for that matter) makes such a distinction, Cheng Yi cannot be said to have identified the salient difference in usage.

12. Cf. Ning Chen, "Ideological Background," 22 f.

13. *Xing zi ming chu,* strip 9; *Guodian Chumu zhujian,* 179. Compare "Quanxue" 勸學, *Xunzi jijie* 1.1.2: "The children of Gan, Yue, Yi, and Mo all make the same sounds when born but grow up to have different customs; teaching makes this so" 干、越、夷、貉之子，生而同聲，長而異俗，教使之然也. This idea is echoed in *Analects* 17.2, *Lunyu jishi* 34.1177: "[People's] *xing* are close to one another; practice makes them distant from one another" 性相近也，習相遠也.

14. For the reading of this character as *tian* 天, see Chen Ning, "*Guodian Chumu zhujian* zhong de rujia renxing yanlun chutan," 39; and idem, "Ideological Background," 38n.33. But scholars disagree as to the interpretation of the entire phrase. See, for example, Zhou Fengwu, "Guodian Chujian shizi zhaji," 357 f.; Li Ling, *Guodian Chujian jiaodu ji,* 122 and 124; and Guo Yi, 218.

15. *Cheng zhi wen zhi,* strips 26–28; *Guodian Chumu zhujian,* 168. Compare "Xing'e" 性惡, *Xunzi jijie* 17.23.438: "That by which the Sage is the same as the populace and is not different from the populace is his *xing*" 故聖人之所以同於眾，其不異於眾者，性也. Cf. Cook, "Cong lijiao yu xingfa zhi bian kan xian-Qin zhuzi de quanshi chuantong," 15.

16. Qiu Xigui 裘錫圭, in *Guodian Chumu zhujian,* 170n.28, suspects that the character *mo* 莫 should be read as *mu* 慕, thus: "the Sage cannot be venerated [on account of his *xing*]." Guo Yi, 221, interprets this to mean that common people cannot match the Sage's level of cultivation.

17. *Xing zi ming chu,* strips 3–4; *Guodian Chumu zhujian,* 179.

18. For this translation of *qing,* see Hansen, *A Daoist Theory of Chinese Thought,* esp. 405n.14. The meaning of *qing* (which is also commonly understood either as "essence" or "emotion") is the subject of much scholarly controversy. I earlier supported a translation along the lines of "essence" (Goldin, *Rituals of the Way,* 112n.2) but am now persuaded that Hansen's "reality response" works far better for texts such as *Xing zi ming chu.* See also Hansen's "Qing (Emotions) 情 in Pre-Buddhist Chinese Thought."

19. *Yucong* 1, strips 22–23; *Guodian Chumu zhujian,* 194. The preceding section appears to be missing a strip, but it is clear that the subject of discussion is the same: "Of the Way of Humanity, some [components] emerge from inside, some enter from outside. What emerges from inside is humanity, integrity, and trustworthiness; from..." 人之道也，或由中出，或由外入。由中出者，仁、忠、信。由—and here the text breaks off.

20. *Liude,* strip 26; *Guodian Chumu zhujian,* 188.

21. Cf. Wang Zhongjiang, "Chuanjing yu hongdao," esp. 255–264 (Wang, surprisingly, does not refer to the Guodian manuscripts in this article).

22. "Quanxue," *Xunzi jijie* 1.1.12.

23. Compare the translation in Knoblock, 1, 139f. See also "Ruxiao," *Xunzi jijie* 4.8.133, and the discussion in Puett, *To Become a God,* 187.

24. "Quanxue," *Xunzi jijie* 1.1.12.

25. *Xing zi ming chu,* strips 12–18; *Guodian Chumu zhujian,* 179. Cf. Cook, "Cong lijiao yu xingfa," 14f.

26. For this reading, see Ning Chen, "Ideological Background," 24. Guo Yi, 237, and Li Ling, *Guodian Chujian jiaodu ji,* 108, both suggest *ni* 逆 (which might mean "lead astray" in this context).

27. This confusing sentence is variously interpreted; see the discussion in Ding Sixin, 252. Most recently, the editors of the Shanghai Museum manuscripts have suggested (dubiously) that the "four techniques" refer to the canonical *Odes, Documents, Rites,* and *Music.* See Ma Chengyuan, 1, 230f.; and Chen Ligui, "*Xingqing lun* shuo 'dao,'" 146–150. More plausible is a connection with Xunzi's statement that "the Way is not the Way of Heaven or the Way of Earth, but what people take as the Way and what the noble man is guided by" 道者，非天之道，非地之道，人之所以道也，君子之所道也; "Ruxiao," *Xunzi jijie* 4.8.122. Yang Liang's explanation: "This is to emphasize that the Way of the Former Kings is not a matter of *yin* and *yang,* mountains and streams, or prodigies and anomalies, but the Way as it is practiced by human beings" 重說先王之道非陰陽、山川、怪異之事，是人所行之道也. Cf. Tang Yijie, 272.

28. *Liude,* strips 24–25; *Guodian Chumu zhujian,* 188.

29. For the reading *zhi* 志, see Liao Mingchun, *Zhou-Yi jingzhuan yu Yixue shi xinlun,* 231. Cf. Kern, "*Shi jing* Songs as Performance Texts," 69f. Consider also *Kongzi shilun,* strip 1; Ma Chengyuan, 1, 123: "The *Odes* do not depart from the will" 詩亡離志.

30. *Yucong* 1, strips 37–41; *Guodian Chumu zhujian,* 194–195. The text goes on to include the *Rites, Music,* and *Documents* in the canonical group. (Li Ling, *Guodian Chujian jiaodu ji,* 163, argues that the editors of *Guodian Chumu zhujian* have jumbled the original order of the classics in this passage.) Cf. Wang Bo, *Jianbo sixiang wenxian lunji,* 37f.

For similar statements in received texts, compare "Tianxia," *Zhuangzi jishi* 10B.33.1067: "The *Odes* speak of aspirations; the *Documents* speak of affairs; the *Rites* speak of actions; the *Music* speaks of harmony; the *Changes* speak of *yin* and *yang;* and the *Springs and Autumns* speak of titles and allotments" 詩以道志，書以道事，禮以道行，樂以道和，易以道陰陽，春秋以道名分. Also *Shenzi* 慎子: "The *Odes* are bygone aspirations; the *Documents* are bygone announcements; the *Springs and Autumns* are bygone affairs" 詩往志也，書往誥也，春秋往事也, in P. M. Thompson, § 97; the source text is *Yilin* 2.14b.

31. Cf. Wang Zhongjiang, "Jingdian de tiaojian," 51 f. Incidentally, some recent unpublished conference papers have suggested that the Guodian manuscripts refer here to prototexual traditions, rather than actual canonical texts, but the two references to the *Springs and Autumns* constitute good evidence that these are indeed to be understood as texts largely as we have received them. Pines, "Intellectual Change in the Chunqiu Period," 82 ff., for example, has suggested provocatively that the received *Springs and Autumns* derives from ritualistic reports to ancestral spirits inscribed on *ce* 策 (large bamboo strips)—in other words, that the *Chunqiu* was a written text from the time of its inception. See further Pines, *Foundations of Confucian Thought,* 17 f. Cf. also Kern, "*Shi jing* Songs as Performance Texts," 70; Guo Qiyong, "Guodian Rujia jian de yiyi yu jiazhi," 6; and Liao Mingchun, *Zhou-Yi jingzhuan,* 229 ff. Li Ling, "Cong jianbo faxian kan gushu de tili he fenlei," 36, remarks that titles such as *Odes* and *Springs and Autumns* might refer generally to bibliographic categories rather than to specific texts.

32. "Lilun," *Xunzi jijie* 13.19.346.

33. Compare the translation in Knoblock, 3, 55. Compare also *Yucong* 2, strips 10–12, *Guodian Chumu zhujian,* 203: "Desires are born of human nature; deliberation is born of desires; rebelliousness is born of deliberation; contention is born of rebelliousness; partisanship is born of contention" 欲生於性，慮生於欲，倍生於慮，爭生於倍，黨生於爭.

34. "Xing'e," *Xunzi jijie* 17.23.441.

35. Compare the translation in Knoblock, 3, 157.

36. Knoblock, 1, 296n.53, cites this proposed emendation by Yu Xingwu 于省吾 (b. 1896). The traditional commentators are baffled by the phrase.

37. "Feixiang" 非相, *Xunzi jijie* 3.5.78–79.

38. The *xingxing* (also written 猩猩) is described in "Nanshan jing" 南山經 and "Hainei nan jing" 海內南經, *Shanhai jing jiaozhu* 1.1 and 10.325, respectively. See also Yuan Ke's notes (especially 325n.2); and Strassberg, §§ 2 and 263.

39. Others (e.g., Knoblock, 1, 206; and Ivanhoe, "A Happy Symmetry," 313) construe this sentence to mean that the noble man eats stews and steaks made of *xingxing* meat.

40. Compare the translation in Knoblock, 1, 206.

41. This was the philosophical position that I deduced from Xunzi's writings in *Rituals of the Way,* 72 ff. and 103 ff.; at the time, I considered it quite revolutionary within the Confucian school.

42. *Yucong* 1, strip 31; *Guodian Chumu zhujian,* 194.

43. *Yucong* 2, strip 1; *Guodian Chumu zhujian,* 203.

44. For the reading *jiang* 降, see Guo Yi, 210; and Chen Wei, "Guodian Chujian bieshi," 70.

45. For the reading *zuo* 作, see Li Ling, *Guodian Chujian jiaodu ji,* 123.

46. *Cheng zhi wen zhi,* strips 31–33; *Guodian Chumu zhujian,* 168. Guo Yi, 211, and Ding Sixin, 304, both assert that similar notions are present in the "Da Yu mo" 大禹謨 chapter of the *Shangshu,* but I can find no obvious parallel. Compare here *Zun deyi,* strips 5–6; *Guodian Chumu zhujian,* 173: "Yu ordered his people in accordance with the Way of Humanity; Jie disordered his people in accordance with the Way of Humanity. Jie did not change Yu's people before he could disorder them; Tang did not change Jie's people before he could order them. The Sage orders the people by means of the Way of the people" 禹以人道治其民，桀以人道亂其民。桀不易禹民而後亂之，湯不易桀民而後治之。聖人之治民，民之道也.

47. Cf. Li Zehou, 412 f.

48. E.g., Sato, 302–314; Hu Jiacong; Yu Mingguang; Li Deyong; Ivanhoe, "A Happy Symmetry," 316 f.; and Du Guoxiang, 97–125. The most sophisticated discussion to date is Stalnaker.

49. For a fuller account, see Goldin, *Rituals of the Way,* 14–17. See also Uchiyama, 83 ff.; Yearley; and Tang Junyi, 57 f.

50. "Zhongni" 仲尼, *Xunzi jijie* 3.7.109; and "Fuguo," *Xunzi jijie* 6.10.196.

51. Following the commentary of Hao Yixing. For *xing* 刑 as "mold," see Makeham, "The Legalist Concept of *hsing-ming,*" 100–106.

52. I insert the character *you* 有 on the basis of the pattern in the next clause.

53. "Qiangguo" 彊國, *Xunzi jijie* 11.16.291.

54. Compare the translation in Knoblock, 2, 238–239.

55. "Jundao" 君道, *Xunzi jijie* 8.12.234.

56. Compare the translation in Knoblock, 2, 180.

57. *Ziyi,* strips 8–9; *Guodian Chumu zhujian,* 129. For the received version of this passage, which differs slightly from the Guodian version, see "Ziyi," *Liji zhengyi* 55.1650a–b. Compare *Mencius* 4B.3, in *Mengzi zhengyi* 16.546: "If the lord regards his subjects as his hands and feet, the subjects will regard their lord as their belly and heart" 君之視臣如手足，則臣視君如腹心.

58. *Ziyi,* strips 10–11; *Guodian Chumu zhujian,* 129. The received version appears in *Liji zhengyi* 55.1648a. Compare *Analects* 13.4, *Lunyu jishi* 26.897 f.: "If the

superiors are fond of ritual, none among the people will dare not be reverent; if the superiors are fond of righteousness, none among the people will dare not be submissive; if the superiors are fond of trustworthiness, none among the people will dare not apply their [genuine] disposition" 上好禮，則民莫敢不敬；上好義，則民莫敢不服；上好信，則民莫敢不用情.

59. *Ziyi,* strips 14–15; *Guodian Chumu zhujian,* 129. The received version appears in *Liji zhengyi* 55.1647c–48a. Compare also *Mencius* 3A.2, *Mengzi zhengyi* 10.330: "If the superiors are fond of something, there must be those among their inferiors who outdo them in that regard" 上有好者，下必有甚焉者矣. Cf. Cook, "Cong lijiao yu xingfa," 16.

60. *Zun deyi,* strips 36–37; *Guodian Chumu zhujian,* 174. Wang Bo, *Jianbo sixiang wenxian lunji,* 259, suggests that *Zun deyi* is intended as an explication of *Ziyi.*

61. *Cheng zhi wen zhi,* strips 1–3; *Guodian Chumu zhujian,* 167.

62. Perhaps most famous are the examples in the "Jian'ai zhong" 兼愛中 and "Jian'ai xia" 下 chapters of the *Mozi.* Thus "Jian'ai zhong," *Mozi jiaozhu* 4.15.159: "In the past, King Ling of Chu [r. 540–529 B.C.] was fond of slight waists in his warriors; thus King Ling's subjects would all restrain themselves and eat once [a day]" 昔楚靈王好士細要[＝腰]，故靈王之臣，皆以一飯為節. See also Geaney, *On the Epistemology of the Senses,* 67–80 and 137 f.

63. See, for example, "Jiebi" 解蔽, *Xunzi jijie* 15.21.397: "The mind is the lord of the body and the patron of 'spiritual illumination' [i.e., deliberation]. It issues commands but does not receive commands" 心者，形之君也，而神明之主也，出令而無所受令. Cf. Geaney, *On the Epistemology of the Senses,* 95; and Goldin, *Rituals of the Way,* 20 f. and 31 f. A similar idea appears in *Wuxing,* strips 45–46, *Guodian Chumu zhujian,* 151: "The six [organs]—the ears, the eyes, the nose, the mouth, the hands, and the feet—are the mind's servants. If the mind says 'yes,' none of them dares say 'no'; [if it] assents, none of them dares not assent" 耳目鼻口手足六者，心之役也。心曰唯，莫敢不唯；諾，莫敢不諾. Compare the text in *Mawangdui Hanmu boshu,* 1, 18–19; and Ikeda, 485. For the reading *yi* 役, see Guo Yi, 201; and Yan Shixuan, 399–400.

64. *Xing zi ming chu,* strip 23; *Guodian Chumu zhujian,* 180.

65. *Xing zi ming chu,* strips 36–37; *Guodian Chumu zhujian,* 180.

66. There seems to be a character missing here.

67. "Yuelun" 樂論, *Xunzi jijie* 14.20.382. This pejorative sense of *wei* 偽 can be confusing, since Xunzi normally employs the term to denote the good "artifice" that transforms one's evil *xing.*

68. "Yuelun," *Xunzi jijie* 14.20.379.

69. This statement is difficult to construe, and there is a conspicuous lack of commentary about it. Perhaps Xunzi means to say that music ("sounds and tones,

movement and quietude") is a technique for improving the *xing* and thus fulfilling the Way of Humanity; this would be in line with his general views.

70. Unlike most commentators, I prefer not to emend *xi* 諰. See the commentary of Hao Yixing. Coincidentally, *cong* 謥, which is another possible reading (*xi* and *cong* are easily confused because of their graphic similarity), has a comparable meaning.

71. Compare the translation in Knoblock, 3, 80.

72. See Goldin, *Rituals of the Way,* 78–81 and 137n.64; idem, "Reflections on Irrationalism in Chinese Aesthetics," 176–178; DeWoskin, *A Song for One or Two,* 89–98; Kurihara, 214–221; and Chow Tse-tsung, "Early History of the Chinese Word *Shih,*" 155.

73. See "Feiyue shang" 非樂上, *Mozi jiaozhu* 8.32.379–399. Cf. Scott Cook, "Xun Zi on Ritual and Music," 21 ff.; and Kurihara, 170 ff. and 190 f.

74. "Yuelun," *Xunzi jijie* 14.20.380. Cf. also *Mencius* 7A.14, *Mengzi zhengyi* 26.897; and "Yueji," *Liji zhengyi* 37.1527b, 1529b, et passim.

75. Compare the translation in Knoblock, 3, 82.

76. *Xing zi ming chu,* strips 23–26; *Guodian Chumu zhujian,* 180.

77. For the readings *tao* 陶 and *ji* 悸, see Guo Yi, 244; and Li Ling, *Guodian Chujian jiaodu ji,* 109. On the basis of the faint parallel in "Tangong xia" 檀弓下, *Liji zhengyi* 9.1304b f., Chen Lai, 313, suggests the reading *qi* 戚, "sorrowful," for *ji*. See also Peng Lin.

78. Following the editors' suggestion of *zuo* 作. Perhaps *zuo* 祚 ("blessed") might fit the context better.

79. For a description of the "Wu" and "Xia" dances, see, for example, Shaughnessy, *Before Confucius,* 166–169; and Maspero, *China in Antiquity,* 154–157. "Lai" is the title of Mao 295, an ode that was sung as part of the Wu dance (which takes its own name from Mao 285). The "Shao" is supposedly the music of the sage king Shun; see, for example, *Analects* 3.25, 7.14, and 15.11.

80. "Fei shier zi" 非十二子, *Xunzi jijie* 3.12.94. This *xíng* 行, of course, is not to be confused with *xìng* 性, the term discussed above. The passage is discussed in Chun-chieh Huang, 106. The authenticity of this reference to Zisi and Mencius, incidentally, is sometimes questioned; see the careful study by Zheng Liangshu, *Zhuzi zhuzuo niandai kao,* 228–238, who concludes that it is in fact genuine. See also Liang Tao, "Si-Meng xuepai kaoshu," 28 f.

81. The term "Five Constancies" apparently derives from the Han dynasty. See, for example, *Hanshu* 56.2505, where the term is explained in a memorial by Dong Zhongshu 董仲舒 (179–104 B.C.); and "Wen Kong" 問孔, *Lunheng jiaoshi* 9.28.408. Cf. Svarverud, 287.

82. E.g., Guo Moruo, *Qingtong shidai,* 53 ff.; and Gu Jiegang, "Wude zhongshi shuo xia de zhengzhi he lishi," 407 ff. See also Akatsuka, *Chūgoku kodai shisōshi ken-*

kyū, 388 f. Knoblock, 1, 215–219 (and 300n.5), is aware of the Mawangdui *Wuxing* text but nevertheless prefers to take Xunzi's use of the phrase as a reference to the Five Phases. Wang Bo, *Jianbo sixiang wenxian lunji*, 59–71, discusses the possible connections between the "Five *Xing*" of *Wuxing* and the Five Phases.

83. The pathbreaking article to make this point was Pang Pu, "Mawangdui boshu jiekaile Si-Meng wuxing shuo zhi mi" 馬王堆帛書解開了思孟五行說之謎 (*Wenwu* 1977.10, 63–69), reprinted in *Zhubo* Wuxing *pian jiaozhu ji yanjiu*, 121–132. See also Asano, 607 f.; and Wei Qipeng, "Si-Meng wuxing shuo de zai sikao."

It has been assumed until recently that the oldest mention of the famous phrase *shen qi du* 慎其獨 ("cautious when alone"—an attribute of the moral *junzi*) was in "Bugou," *Xunzi jijie* 2.3.46, and that its appearance in such texts as *Wuxing* and "Zhongyong" could be traced back to this usage; e.g., Riegel, "Eros, Introversion, and the Beginnings of *Shijing* Commentary," 165 f.; Dai Junren, 2, 845 ff.; and Hughes, 171, who considers *shen qi du* a "suspiciously late" term in "Zhongyong." (For less widely cited appearances of the phrase, see "Liqi" 禮器, *Liji zhengyi* 23.1434b; and the ancient commentary to "Daxue" 大學, attributed to Zengzi, *Liji zhengyi* 60.1673a.) With the discovery of the Guodian "Wuxing" and the appearance of the phrase in two places in that text (strips 16–18; *Guodian Chumu zhujian*, 149–150), it is clear now that if one text was borrowing from another, it was Xunzi who took from *Wuxing*, and not vice versa. Cf. Liu Xinfang, 344 ff. The language of the relevant passage from "Bugou" (with its emphasis on *xing* 形, or giving the proper internal form to one's *de* 德) is reminiscent of *Wuxing* (as well as "Zhongyong") and may represent Xunzi's attempts to come to grips with this earlier Confucian tradition. Cf. Sato, 286–295; Akatsuka, *Juka shisō kenkyū*, 479 ff.; and the inadequate discussion in Goldin, *Rituals of the Way*, 19 f.

84. The story appears in "Youzuo" 宥坐, *Xunzi jijie* 20.28.526–528. Cf. Li Yinghua. Doubts about the authenticity of the "Youzuo" chapter go back to Yang Liang, who attributed it to Xunzi's disciples; see his comment to "Youzuo," *Xunzi jijie* 20.28.520. Knoblock, 3, 237 f., presents the attractive argument that "Youzuo" is part of a corpus of traditional materials that Xunzi selected as a "proper curriculum" for Confucians. The implication in "Youzuo" that Heaven can be fickle and that an individual's talent and virtue do not by themselves guarantee success is hard to reconcile with Xunzi's philosophy as it is presented in the more reliable chapters of the book. See further Liang Tao, "Zhujian *Qiongda yi shi* yu zaoqi rujia tianrenguan," 68–69; and Ning Chen, "The Problem of Theodicy in Ancient China," 65 f.

85. "Between Chen and Cai," 79–81. See also Watanabe, 107–159.

86. *Lunyu jishi* 31.1050.

87. Compare the translation in Lau, *Analects*, 132.

88. *Qiongda yi shi*, strip 11; *Guodian Chumu zhujian*, 145.

89. "Youzuo," *Xunzi jijie* 20.28.527.

90. *Qiongda yi shi,* strips 1–2; *Guodian Chumu zhujian,* 145.

91. "Youzuo," *Xunzi jijie* 20.28.527.

92. Compare the translation in Knoblock, 3, 249.

93. For a different account of the relationship between "Youzuo" and *Qiongda yi shi,* see Liao Mingchun, "Jingmen Guodian Chujian yu xian-Qin ruxue," 43–45; and idem, "Guodian Chujian rujia zhuzuo kao," 72. Other close parallels to *Qiongda yi shi* appear in *Han-Shi waizhuan jianshu* 7.599–601; and "Zayan" 雜言, *Shuoyuan jiaozheng* 17.422 ff. The lines of transmission among these several texts are blurry; many of the historical examples in *Qiongda yi shi* do not appear in Xunzi's account but are included in the *Han-Shi waizhuan* and *Shuoyuan,* although the latter two are probably later than Xunzi. Presumably all four texts were making use of a common set of sources or fund of commonplaces.

94. *Guodian Chumu zhujian,* 164n.16.

95. *Zhongxin zhi dao,* strips 6–7; *Guodian Chumu zhujian,* 163.

96. "Wangba" 王霸, *Xunzi jijie* 7.11.228.

97. Compare the translation in Knoblock, 2, 169.

98. Li Zehou, 421, suggests another possible parallel: *Qiongda yi shi,* strip 1 (*Guodian Chumu zhujian,* 145), says: "There is Heaven and there is man; there is a division between Heaven and man" 有天有人，天人有分; this is reminiscent of Xunzi's concept of the distinction between Heaven and man. See, for example, his reference in "Tianlun," *Xunzi jijie* 11.17.308, to "those who are enlightened with respect to the division between Heaven and man" 明於天人之分. Wang Bo, *Jianbo sixiang wenxian lunji,* 82–84, argues that the discussion of abdication in "Zhenglun," *Xunzi jijie* 12.18.331–336, may have been written in response to views like those expressed in *Tang Yu zhi dao.*

99. For a survey of Xunzi's insights into linguistics, see William S.-Y. Wang; and Djamouri.

100. "Bugou," *Xunzi jijie* 2.3.38.

101. See, for example, Goldin, *Rituals of the Way,* 83–95. Xunzi's argument, essentially, is that such paradoxes commit the fallacy of equivocation, as defined in Copi, 92–93. Cf. Wang Guowei, 123 ff.

102. On "falsidical paradoxes," see Quine, *The Ways of Paradox and Other Essays,* 3 ff.

103. "Tianlun," *Xunzi jijie* 11.17.313–314. Cf. Goldin, *Rituals of the Way,* 47 ff.; and Kodama, *Junshi no shisō,* 96–97.

104. However, even this aspect of Xunzi's philosophy appears to be anticipated by the recently excavated text *Lubang dahan* 魯邦大旱 (*There Was a Great Drought in the State of Lu*), one of the Shanghai Museum manuscripts, a corpus that many scholars suspect may be related to Guodian. In *Lubang dahan,* Confu-

cius states that the best way of dealing with a drought is not to make offerings to natural spirits but to emphasize good government (for which he uses the interesting term *xingde* 刑德). See Ma Chengyuan, 2, 201–210. (For *xingde* in other contexts, see Major, "The Meaning of *hsing-te*.") A similar idea appears also in "Shenda" 慎大, *Lüshi chunqiu jiaoshi* 15.845; trans. Knoblock and Riegel, 341. And cf. *Mencius* 1A.3.

105. Following the commentary of Hao Yixing.

106. Following the commentary of Lu Wenchao 盧文弨 (1717–1796).

107. "Yibing," *Xunzi jijie* 10.15.283–284.

108. Following the commentary of Wang Niansun 王念孫 (1744–1832).

109. Compare the translation in Knoblock, 2, 230.

110. See Goldin, *Rituals of the Way*, 66–67; and Xu Junru, 151.

111. Berlin, 436–498.

112. It is important to reiterate that the philosophical positions outlined above are not exemplified by all of the Guodian manuscripts; therefore, the following discussion does not consider the three *Laozi* texts, *The Magnificent One Produced Water* (*Taiyi sheng shui* 太一生水), or *The Five Forms of Conduct*. The last text is sufficiently vague to allow for several different interpretations, but I believe that its conception of the five virtues as "formed internally" 形於內 (strips 1–4; *Guodian Chumu zhujian*, 149) is incompatible with *Liude*, for example, which affirms that humanity is internal and morality external. We are probably still correct in taking *Wuxing* as a document closest to the Mencian school of Confucianism. Cf. Asano, 608 ff. It can be no coincidence, for example, that the five virtues are listed in *Mencius* 7B.24, *Mengzi zhengyi* 28.991. Nevertheless, it is apparent from the above discussion that Xunzi was aware of the *Wuxing* tradition and referred to it in his works. Guo Lihua suggests that Xunzi intended to criticize *Wuxing* for its understanding of ritual and music, with which his own views were incompatible.

Yucong 4, which has been shown to differ in important respects from *Yucong* 1–3 (Ding Sixin, 214–222), is also not considered here.

113. *Guanzi jiaozheng* 10.26.156: "Humanity emerges from inside; morality is constructed from outside" 仁從中出，義從外作. Luo Xinhui, 28, mentions also the passage in "Jing xia" 經下, *Mozi jiaozhu* 10B.41.543, without indicating that this is an intended *refutation* of the "humanity is internal, morality is external" maxim. Cf. Graham, *Later Mohist Logic, Ethics and Science*, 450–451; and Guo Moruo, *Shi pipan shu*, 273. For similarities between "Jie" and *Tang Yu zhi dao*, see Wang Bo, *Jianbo sixiang wenxian lunji*, 80–82.

114. Graham, *Studies in Chinese Philosophy and Philosophical Literature*, 22.

115. Cf. Chen Guying, 404; Li Zehou, 420; Chen Lai, 304; and Pang Pu, "Kong Meng zhi jian," 32. The various extant references to Gaozi are conveniently assembled in Zhang Bingnan, 76–80. For an opposing view, see Ding Sixin, 357 f.

116. *Liude,* strips 15–23; *Guodian Chumu zhujian,* 187–188. Cf. Luo Xinhui, 28f. Such lists of virtues appropriate to various social roles were not uncommon in ancient China. See the examples cited in Liao Mingchun, "Jingmen Guodian Chujian yu xian-Qin ruxue," 63–65; cf. also idem, "Guodian Chujian rujia zhuzuo kao," 81. To Liao's examples one can add the "six forms of compliance" 六順 in *Chunqiu Zuozhuan zhu,* 1, 32 (Yin 隱 3 = 720 B.C.): "The lord is righteous; the subject carries out [the lord's commands]; the father is kind; the son is filial; the elder brother is loving; the younger brother is respectful" 君義，臣行，父慈，子孝，兄愛，弟敬; as well as *Mencius* 7B.24, *Mengzi zhengyi* 28.991: "the relation of humanity to father and son, the relation of righteousness to lord and subject, the relations of ritual to guest and host" 仁之於父子也，義之於君臣也，禮之於賓主也.

117. *Liude,* strips 26–30; *Guodian Chumu zhujian,* 188.

118. These ritual prescriptions seem to square with those found in "Sangfu" 喪服, *Yili zhushu* 30.1103b–5c and 34.1123b.

119. Probably read *shài,* "to reduce." A similar sense is found in the phrase *qinqin zhi shai* 親親之殺, "decreasing [categories of] intimacy with relatives," in "Zhongyong," *Liji zhengyi* 52.1629b. Liu Guosheng, 43, reads this character as *pan* 叛, "to rebel against." See also Ding Sixin, 347.

120. Pang Pu, "Chudu Guodian Chujian," 8, compares the argument in *Liude* with *Mencius* 7A.35. Cf. also Pines, "Friends or Foes," 40; and Li Weiwu, 66.

121. Compare the translation in Lau, *Analects,* 121. See the Introduction for the Chinese text of this passage. A similar dilemma is explored in "Gaoyi" 高義, *Lüshi chunqiu jiaoshi* 19.1247; Knoblock and Riegel, 483.

122. *Mencius* 6A.4, *Mengzi zhengyi* 22.743–744. Cf. Goldin, *Rituals of the Way,* 35f.; and Shun, 94–112. Chong, in his chapter, shows no awareness of the Guodian manuscripts.

123. *Mencius* 6A.3, *Mengzi zhengyi* 22.738–739.

124. Compare the translation in Lau, *Mencius,* 160–161.

125. Graham, *Later Mohist Logic,* 171, in what is still the most lucid account of this technique of disputation.

126. Dai Junren, 2, 1341, suggested this many years before the discovery of the tomb at Guodian. (See also 2, 1345–1348, and 3, 1848ff.)

127. *Mencius* 6A.6, *Mengzi zhengyi* 22.748.

128. Compare the translation in Lau, *Mencius,* 162.

129. *Zun deyi,* strips 22–23; *Guodian Chumu zhujian,* 174.

130. *Zun deyi,* strips 36–37; *Guodian Chumu zhujian,* 174. This is apparently a quotation from "Ziyi," strips 14–15; *Guodian Chumu zhujian,* 129.

131. Thus Liu Huan 劉瓛 (A.D. 433–489), cited by Lu Deming 陸德明 (556–627) in his commentary to "Ziyi," *Liji zhengyi* 55.1647b. See also Cook, "Cong li-

jiao yu xingfa," 9; and Cheng Yuanmin, 34. As we have seen (note 6, above), *Ziyi* is also frequently attributed to Zisi rather than to Gongsun Nizi.

132. *Hanshu* 30.1725. Cf. Kodama, "Junshi jinseiron no shūhen," 198.

133. For the meager information available on Gongsun Nizi, see Cheng Yuanmin, 32–34; Ruan Tingzhuo, *Xian-Qin zhuzi kaoyi,* 33–45; Guo Moruo, *Qingtong shidai,* 182–201; and Forke, *Geschichte der alten chinesischen Philosophie,* 188. According to *Hanshu* 30.1725, he was a disciple of one of Confucius' seventy disciples; this would place him in the mid–fifth century B.C. However, Cheng Yuanmin, 32–33, suggests that this notice is incorrect and that Gongsun Nizi was in actuality a disciple of Confucius himself. Some scholars (such as Guo Moruo, *Qingtong shidai,* 186) suspect that the name Gongsun Long 公孫龍, which appears in the list of Confucius' disciples in *Shiji* 67.2219, is an error for "Gongsun Ni." Finally, Couvreur, 2, 514, says that Gongsun Nizi "vivait, dit-on, deux ou trois siècles avant notre ère." Unfortunately, Couvreur does not specify the source of his information, and I can find no source that corroborates it.

134. Thus Zhang Shoujie 張守節 (fl. A.D. 737), in his commentary to *Shiji* 24.1234n.11. See Cook, *"Yue Ji,"* 3–7, on Gongsun Nizi and his possible connection to the "Yueji." See also Zhu Ziqing, *Jingdian changtan,* 33; and Guo Moruo, *Qingtong shidai,* 185. The extant "Yueji" is heavily indebted to Xunzi, and Gongsun Nizi (whatever his exact dates) must have lived long before Xunzi.

135. Cf. Li Rui, 24 f.; Guo Qiyong, "Chutu jianbo yu jingxue quanshi de fanshi wenti," 24 f.; Ding Sixin, 201–213; Li Xueqin, "Arrangement of Bamboo Slips in *Cheng Zhi Wen Zhi* and *Xing Zi Ming Chu,*" 240; and idem, "Guodian jian yu *Yueji,*" 26.

136. "Benxing" 本性, *Lunheng jiaoshi* 3.13.132–133 and 141–142.

137. Cf. Ding Sixin, 178 f.; Chen Ning, "*Guodian Chumu zhujian* zhong de rujia renxing yanlun chutan," 44; and Chen Lai, 309. (Chen Lai, 305, also speculates briefly on the possible influence of *Xing zi ming chu* on Xunzi.) For a contrary view, see Liao Mingchun, "Jingmen Guodian Chujian yu xian-Qin ruxue," 60–62; and idem, "Guodian Chujian rujia zhuzuo kao," 78–79.

138. Igai Hikohiro, *Junshi hoi,* 14b, glossed the "Master Gongsun" 公孫子 in "Qiangguo," *Xunzi jijie* 11.16.293, as a reference to Gongsun Ni. Few other commentators follow this suggestion, however, as there is no firm evidence for it.

139. The evidence of the Guodian manuscripts should also put to rest the long-standing debate over whether Gaozi was a Confucian, a Mohist, or a "Daoist." For the particulars of this controversy, see Liao Qifa, 160–164; Kodama, "Junshi jinseiron no shūhen," 204 f.; Shun, 119–126; Nivison, *The Ways of Confucianism,* 130–132; Scarpari, *Studi sul Mengzi,* 38 ff.; and Scarpari, "Gaozi, Xunzi e i capitoli 6A1–5 del *Mengzi.*" It is well known that a figure named Gaozi appears in "Gongmeng" 公孟, *Mozi jiaozhu* 12.48.708–709. One cannot say for sure that this is the

same Gaozi, but I suspect it is—in part because this Gaozi also emphasizes the virtues *ren* and *yi*. The passage thus implies that Gaozi was Mozi's junior and Mencius' senior (and was born not long before 410 B.C.). See the commentary of Cao Yaoxiang 曹耀湘 (fl. 1906) in *Mozi jiaozhu* 12.48.730n.155. See also Qian Mu, *Xian-Qin zhuzi xinian,* § 62; and Mei, 241n.1.

140. Cf. Chen Ning, "*Guodian Chumu zhujian* zhong de Rujia renxing yanlun chutan," 44–46, with which this précis is largely in agreement.

141. As recently as 1997, when *Wuxing* was known only from Mawangdui, it was possible for Riegel, "Eros, Introversion, and the Beginnings of *Shijing* Commentary," 145n.5, to suppose that "the *Wu-hsing p'ien* version of early Confucian *Innerlichkeit* clearly owes a conceptual debt to Xunzi." Now it is obvious that the debt is the other way around. This is just one example of the many respects in which our understanding of early Confucianism will have to be revised in light of the Guodian manuscripts.

3. Han Fei's Doctrine of Self-Interest

1. E.g., Sahleen, 328; Lévi, *Han-Fei-tse ou Le Tao du Prince,* 520; Watson, *Han Fei Tzu,* 106; and W. K. Liao, 2, 286. Similarly, the translator F. W. Mote obfuscates the discussion in Hsiao, *A History of Chinese Political Thought,* 388, with his choice of the renderings "public" and "private."

Thiel, 249, suggests, more defensibly, *gemeinnützig* and *eigensüchtig*. Knoblock and Riegel, 70–75, have "impartiality" and "selfish partiality"—renderings that might not be satisfactory for the *Han Feizi* but are appropriate for these passages in the *Lüshi chunqiu*. See "Guigong" 貴公 and "Qusi" 去私, *Lüshi chunqiu jiaoshi* 1.44–62. Cf. also Sellmann, 37–43; and Cook, "The *Lüshi chunqiu* and the Resolution of Philosophical Dissonance," 318 ff. ("community" and "self-interest"). Another early discussion of *gong* and *si* appears in the *Shenzi* 慎子, in P. M. Thompson, §§ 73 ff.

Finally, "Jian'ai xia," *Mozi jiaozhu* 4.16.175 ff., draws a similar distinction between *jian* 兼 (universality), or acting in the best interests of the community at large, and *bie* 別 (separatism), or acting in one's private—and ultimately self-destructive—interests.

2. *Han Feizi xin jiaozhu* 19.49.1105.

3. Following the commentary of Wang Xianshen 王先慎 (1859–1922).

4. Cf. Miao Fenglin, 53; Mizoguchi, 3 f. and 42; Sawada, "Sen-Shin ni okeru kōshi no kannen," 1 f.; Kurita, 371 f.; Kanaya, *Shin-Kan shisōshi kenkyū,* 41 and 44; and Itano, 197. Han Fei's argument is cited by Xu Shen 許慎 (ca. A.D. 55–ca. 149) in the entry for *gong* in *Shuowen jiezi jizhu* 2A.218. Of course, this explanation of the graph is epigraphically untenable.

5. Cf. Oliver, 230. The *Shenzi* fragments (P. M. Thompson, §§ 29 ff.) espouse a

similar point of view: rulers must bear in mind that their underlings act out of self-interest.

6. Cf. Hsiao, *History of Chinese Political Thought,* 388; Chen Qitian, 177 ff.; Kanaya, *Kanaya Osamu Chūgoku shisō ronshū,* 1, 441; and, more generally, Hsu, 152. Compare also "Gufen" 孤憤, *Han Feizi xin jiaozhu* 4.11.251.

Gong in this sense probably referred originally to the lord of a state, as in such terms as *gongjia* 公家 (the Duke's family) and *gongshi* 公室 (the Duke's household); later, as an abstract noun, it came to denote anything that benefits the lord. Cf. Chun-chieh Huang, 61 and 72; Huang Junjie, *Mengxue sixiangshi lun,* 1, 147 ff. (with copious primary sources); Ochi, 1, 52–55; Liu Jiyao, 179; Sawada, "Sen-Shin ni okeru kōshi no kannen," 3 f.; Tay, 551; Kurita, 377; Wu Ch'i-ch'ang, 67 f.; and Gu Jiegang, *Gu Jiegang gushi lunwenji,* 2, 328.

7. On these alliances, see, for example, Lewis, "Warring States: Political History," 632 ff.; Yang Kuan, *Zhanguo shi,* 341–421.

8. "Wudu," *Han Feizi xin jiaozhu* 19.49.1114.

9. Following the commentary of Chen Qiyou. On *mingshi* (names and realities), see, for example, Makeham, "The Legalist Concept of *hsing-ming,*" 93 and 112–114. The phrase is similar to *xingming* (see below) and probably means what the ministers say and what they do. Consider "Shenying" 審應, *Lüshi chunqiu jiaoshi* 18.1141: "Take their statements as their 'names,' and grasp their 'realities' in order to hold them responsible for their 'names'" 以其言為之名，取其實以責其名. For possible connections between *Han Feizi* and *Lüshi chunqiu,* see Hu Shi, *Hu Shi wencun,* 3, 253 f.

10. This line is difficult to construe. Probably the meaning is that courtiers will put forward all manner of hit-and-miss schemes, hoping for a stroke of luck, because they know that they will not be punished if their proposals fail. Compare the translation in Lévi, *Han-Fei-tse,* 524 f.: "[Comme les souverains] omettent de les châtier si elles échouent, les sophistes et les rhéteurs ont toutes les raisons de tenter leur chance en hasardant des suggestions qui pourraient leur apporter—sait-on jamais?—gloire et fortune."

11. For representative examples, see "Zhushu" 主術, *Huainan Honglie jijie* 9.295, which laid the groundwork for the Han imperial ideology; and the "Tongzhi" 通志 chapter of the lost *Fuzi* 傅子 of Fu Xuan (A.D. 217–278), reconstructed from fragments in Yan Kejun, *Quan Shanggu Sandai Qin Han Sanguo Liuchao wen* 48.4a–5b. The former source is discussed in chapter 6 below; the latter in Holcombe, 36, and Paper, 25 and 46–51.

For more general studies of *gong* and *si* in Chinese thought, see Jiang Rongchang; and Mizoguchi, 3–89. The famous saying "All under Heaven is *gong*" 天下為公 is found in "Liyun," *Liji zhengyi* 21.1414a.

12. "Wudu," *Han Feizi xin jiaozhu* 19.49.1122, following the commentary of

Gu Guangqi 顧廣圻 (1776–1835). Some commentators also suggest that *weishe* 為設 should be read *weishe* 偽設 (thus *weishe zhacheng:* "plan falsely and flatter deceitfully"), but Chen Qiyou disagrees. The "Altars of Soil and Millet" are a common synecdoche for the state.

13. "Shuinan," *Han Feizi xin jiaozhu* 4.12.261.

14. Following the commentary of Chen Qiyou, *Han Feizi xin jiaozhu* 4.12.263n.8.

15. Following the commentary of Wang Xianshen.

16. "Shuinan," *Han Feizi xin jiaozhu* 4.12.254. Compare "Yuhe," *Lüshi chunqiu jiaoshi* 14.815: "There was once a client who played the oboe in order to obtain an audience with the King of Yue. He played the *yu, jue, gong, zhi,* and *shang* notes without error, but the King of Yue did not approve; when he produced rustic tones, in contrast, [the king] did approve. In the Way of persuasion there are also cases like this" 客有以吹籟見越王者，羽角宮徵商不繆，越王不善，為野音而反善之。說之道亦有如此者也. Cf. Lloyd, 77 ff.; and Oliver, 221 ff.

17. See esp. Rong Zhaozu, 31a–33a. Similarly, Brooks opines that the "doctrinal reversals (on transcendency and Confucianism)" of the *Han Feizi* imply a long "internal timespan." This sort of theorizing always assumes that a writer must maintain a consistent world view. See Lundahl, esp. 92–113, for a succinct overview of scholarship on this issue and some thoughts on using "inconsistencies" as a criterion in determining the authenticity of the collection. To date, the most rigorous investigation of the issue is Zheng Liangshu, *Han Fei zhi zhushu ji sixiang.*

18. Graham, *Disputers of the Tao,* 267 ff. Saussy, *Great Walls of Discourse and Other Adventures in Cultural China,* 149, aptly cites *Han Feizi* as an example of a Chinese philosophical book that cannot be forced "into a systematic unity."

19. See Chen Qiyou, "Han Fei yu Laozi," 183–191; Wang Changhua, 273–281; Lau, "Taoist Metaphysics in the *Chieh Lao* 解老 and Plato's Theory of Forms," 101 f.; Hsiao-po Wang and Leo S. Chang, 93 ff.; Li Jing, 103 ff.; and Chen Anren, 125 f.

This idea is doubtless influenced by Sima Qian's decision to place his biography of Han Fei together with that of Laozi and by Sima's own opinion: "[Han Fei] liked the doctrines of 'forms and names' and 'standards and techniques,' but his roots were in Huang-Lao" 喜刑名法術之學，而其歸本於黃老; "Laozi Han Fei liezhuan" 老子韓非列傳, *Shiji* 63.2146. Cf. Anne Cheng, 233 f.

20. "Zhudao," *Han Feizi xin jiaozhu* 1.5.66. Compare "Yangquan" 揚權, *Han Feizi xin jiaozhu* 2.8.145.

21. *Boshu Laozi jiaozhu,* 74. Compare also *Laozi* 42: "The Way engendered the One; the One engendered the Two; the Two engendered the Three; the Three

engendered the Myriad Things" 道生一，一生二，二生三，三生萬物; *Boshu Laozi jiaozhu,* 29.

22. The seminal work on Shen Buhai is Creel, *Shen Pu-hai.* See also Asano, 231–239; and Vandermeersch, 41 ff. et passim. Shen Buhai is still often overlooked and misunderstood. For example, in a serious and otherwise well-informed work, Lin Congshun, 128 ff., continually compares the "Zhushu" chapter to Han Fei—rather than to Shen Buhai, whom he almost never cites—even though Shen Buhai would bear out Lin's points more clearly.

23. See esp. "Dingfa" 定法, *Han Feizi xin jiaozhu* 17.43.957–964, wherein Han Fei offers a critical assessment of Shen Buhai and his famous contemporary Gongsun Yang. Cf. Itano, 211 and 221; Kanaya, *Kanaya Osamu Chūgoku shisō ronshū,* 1, 437 ff.; Gao Boyuan, 37 f. and 137 ff.; Graham, *Disputers of the Tao,* 278 ff.; Hsiao, *A History of Chinese Political Thought,* 381 ff.; Wang Yunwu, 312 f.; Du Guoxiang, 143 ff.; and Guo Moruo, *Shi pipan shu,* 360 ff.

24. Creel, *Shen Pu-hai,* 349, fragment 1 (6), with a slightly different translation. The source text is *Qunshu zhiyao* 36.630. See also chapter 6, below. (Shen Buhai's "Dati" is to be distinguished from the chapter 29 of the *Han Feizi,* which bears the same title.)

25. Cf. Wang Yunwu, 309 f.

26. See, for example, Makeham, "The Legalist Concept of *hsing-ming,*" 88–92; and Creel, *Shen Pu-hai,* 119 f.

27. Cf. Lévi, "Quelques aspects de la rectification des noms dans la pensée et la pratique politiques de la Chine ancienne," 33–38; Dai Junren, 2, 912; and Creel, *What Is Taoism? and Other Studies in Chinese Cultural History,* 79–91. Similar ideas appear in the *Shenzi* fragments: "Duties are received according to one's abilities; lucre is received according to [one's performance of] one's duties" 以能受事，以事受利 (P. M. Thompson, § 27; the source text is *Qunshu zhiyao* 37.636).

Makeham, "The Legalist Concept of *hsing-ming,*" 97, objects that *ming* in *xingming* refers not to the minister's title but to his "claim to possess a certain ability and competence." But this distinction is not one that Han Fei himself makes; on the contrary, it is clear from the passage above that the minister's title is to be bestowed on him precisely according to the claims that he makes ("One who speaks spontaneously makes a 'name'"). Therefore *ming* refers either to the minister's title or to his claims.

28. Creel, *Shen Pu-hai,* fragment 1 (4); the source text is *Qunshu zhiyao* 36.630.

29. See, for example, Lewis, "Warring States," 609; and, more generally, Zhang Chuanxi, 140–208; as well as Lao Kan. The function of the tally is well illustrated in an anecdote in "Shangde" 上德, *Lüshi chunqiu jiaoshi* 19.1257; Knoblock

and Riegel, 487. See also the fragment from *Shenzi* in P. M. Thompson, § 70; the source texts are *Taiping yulan* 430.5a; and *Beitang shuchao* 104.10a.

30. Han Fei is fond of this image and repeats it in "Zhudao," *Han Feizi xin jiaozhu* 1.5.81; and "Erbing" 二柄, *Han Feizi xin jiaozhu* 2.7.126. Cf. Lévi, "Quelques aspects de la rectification des noms," 35 f.; Makeham, "The Legalist Concept of *hsing-ming*," 107 ff.; and Hsu, 153. The idea that words and actions must correspond like two halves of a tally appears also in "Jian'ai xia," *Mozi jiaozhu* 4.16.177. See also Geaney, *On the Epistemology of the Senses in Early Chinese Thought,* 79 f. and 93 f.; and Lewis, *Writing and Authority in Early China,* 31.

31. "Zhudao," *Han Feizi xin jiaozhu* 1.5.66. Compare "Youdu" 有度, *Han Feizi xin jiaozhu,* 2.6.107; and "Yangquan," *Han Feizi xin jiaozhu* 2.8.157.

32. E.g., *Laozi* 37: "If one is tranquil and without desires, the world will rectify itself" 不欲以靜，天下將自正, *Boshu Laozi jiaozhu,* 427; and *Laozi* 19: "Abrogate sagehood, abandon wisdom, and the people will benefit a hundredfold" 絕聖棄智，民利百倍, *Boshu Laozi jiaozhu,* 311 f. Han Fei uses similar language in "Erbing," *Han Feizi xin jiaozhu* 2.7.131.

33. Creel, *Shen Pu-hai,* fragment 1 (5); the source text is again *Qunshu zhiyao* 36.630. Han Fei attributes a similar argument to Shen Buhai in "Wai chushuo you shang" 外儲說右上, *Han Feizi xin jiaozhu* 13.34.775; see Creel, *Shen Pu-hai,* 364 f., fragment 16.

34. Following Creel, *Shen Pu-hai,* 349n.6.

35. Cf. Lévi, *Han-Fei-tse,* 48–52. Similar ideas appear in military manuals of the same era. Consider *Sunzi:* "Subtle! Subtle! He arrives at shapelessness. Divine! Divine! He arrives at soundlessness. Thus he can be a Director of Destiny to his enemy" 微乎！微乎！至於無形。神乎！神乎！至於無聲。故能為敵之司命, and "Thus the acme in shaping the army is to arrive at shapelessness; if you are shapeless, then those who are deep in your midst cannot spy, and the wise cannot scheme" 故形兵之極，至於無形；無形，則深間不能窺，智者不能謀 ("Xushi" 虛實, *Shiyi jia zhu Sunzi jiaoli* B.6.112 and 122). The "Director of Destiny" is the god of death.

36. These are (1) when a minister is able to shut the ruler's access to the outside world, (2) when a minister attains control of the state's wealth, (3) when a minister usurps the power to issue commands, (4) when a minister is able to carry out enterprises that earn a reputation for righteousness, and (5) when a minister is able to ensconce his own partisans in the government. See "Zhudao," *Han Feizi xin jiaozhu* 1.5.74 f. *Quot servi tot hostes*—or, as Han Fei puts it, "Superiors and inferiors fight a hundred battles a day" 上下一日百戰; "Yangquan," *Han Feizi xin jiaozhu* 2.8.170.

37. Cf. Gu Fang, esp. 216–218.

4. Li Si, Chancellor of the Universe

1. There are four complete English translations of the biography: Nienhauser, *The Grand Scribe's Records,* 7, 335–359; Dawson, 25–53; Watson, *Records of the Grand Historian: Qin Dynasty,* 179–206; and Bodde, *China's First Unifier,* 12–55.

China's First Unifier is still the only book-length study of Li Si in English. Other useful studies include Meng Xiangcai, 229–238; Bodde, "The State and Empire of Ch'in"; Machida, 111–131; Ma Feibai, 1, 216–228; Hsiao, *A History of Chinese Political Thought,* 434–446; Miyazaki, 5, 230–266; and Hu Shi, *Zhongguo zhonggu sixiangshi changbian,* 75–82. Durrant, "Ssu-ma Ch'ien's Portrayal of the First Emperor," is an incisive study of Sima Qian's treatment of the First Emperor and Qin imperial institutions with passing references to Li Si.

2. For a rarely cited but insightful study of this problem see Lévi, "Sima Qian, Han Wudi et l'éternité."

3. "Li Si liezhuan" 李斯列傳, *Shiji* 87.2539.

4. "Yibing," *Xunzi jijie* 10.15.280, contains a fragment in which Li Si disagrees with his teacher about the reasons for Qin's success. Cf. Sato, 270 ff.; Lévi, *Les fonctionnaires divins,* 187; and Oliver, 208 f.

5. "Li Si liezhuan," *Shiji* 87.2539.

6. Ibid., 87.2544.

7. Cf. Yu Kunqi, 55 ff.

8. "Qin shihuang benji" 秦始皇本紀, *Shiji* 6.232.

9. "Han shijia" 韓世家, *Shiji* 45.1878, records the date as 234; this is possible if we assume that Han Fei departed from Han late in 234 and arrived in Qin early the next year. The matter is discussed further in Bodde, *China's First Unifier,* 62–77. For an overview of Li Si's relations with Han Fei, with somewhat different conclusions, see Ma Feibai, 1, 454–456.

10. "Cun Han" 存韓, *Han Feizi xin jiaozhu* 1.2.29–37.

11. Ibid., 1.2.37–42.

12. Ibid., 1.2.42–47.

13. "Chu jian Qin" 初見秦, *Han Feizi xin jiaozhu* 1.1.1–28.

14. "Qin shihuang benji," *Shiji* 6.239. Cf. Puett, *The Ambivalence of Creation,* 145 ff.

15. The discussion of Li Si's influence on the First Emperor in Yu Kunqi, 257 ff., is brief and inconclusive.

16. This we can deduce from the fact that he is still mentioned in 219 B.C. as a "chamberlain" 卿; the same Wang Wan and one Wei Lin 隗林 (sometimes called Wei Zhuang 隗狀) are listed as chancellors in that year. But the sources are clear that Li Si was chancellor by 213. It is commonly, but erroneously, supposed that Li Si was appointed chancellor immediately after the unification in

221; even as eminent a scholar as Loewe, in *A Biographical Dictionary of the Qin, Former Han and Xin Periods,* 228, makes this mistake. The source of the confusion is probably "Li Si liezhuan," *Shiji* 87.2546, which implies that he was already Chancellor when he objected to Wang Wan's feudalistic proposals, though it is clear from "Qin shihuang benji," *Shiji* 6.239, that he was then still Commandant of Justice. Cf. Ma Feibai, 2, 869.

17. "Qin shihuang benji," *Shiji* 6.255; and "Li Si liezhuan," *Shiji* 87.2546. On this memorial, see Petersen, "Which Books *Did* the First Emperor of Ch'in Burn?" See also Puett, *Ambivalence of Creation,* 148; Kern, *The Stele Inscriptions of Ch'in Shih-huang,* 183–196; Kanaya, *Shin-Kan shisōshi kenkyū,* 233 ff.; and Ma Feibai, 2, 893–898.

18. Cf. Qian Cunxun, 9.

19. Cf. Li Jing, 54.

20. "Li Si liezhuan," *Shiji* 87.2547.

21. "Qin shihuang benji," *Shiji* 6.258. On Meng Tian's military campaigns, see Di Cosmo, 174 f. Meng Tian's biography is translated in Bodde, *Statesman, Patriot, and General in Ancient China,* 53–62.

22. Cf. Yu Kunqi, 101 ff. It is perhaps not a coincidence that Sand Hill was also the name of a legendary pleasure park erected by the apolaustic King Zhòu 紂 of Shang; see "Yin benji" 殷本紀, *Shiji* 3.105. Cf. Sterckx, 112. Although geography at the time of King Zhòu is largely a matter of speculation, traditional commentators are convinced that the two Sand Hills refer to the same place; see, for example, *Shiji* 3.107n.7 and 6.264n.3.

23. An ancient bronze model of such a chariot was recently excavated and is currently on display in the Museum of the First Emperor's Mausoleum, Shaanxi province. See Wang Xueli; as well as Peng Wei and Yang Zhenhong, 265 ff.

24. "Qin shihuang benji," *Shiji* 6.264; and "Li Si liezhuan," *Shiji* 87.2548.

25. "Li Si liezhuan," *Shiji* 87.2550.

26. For insightful discussions of Sima Qian's view of history, see Puett, *Ambivalence of Creation,* 177–212; and Durrant, *The Cloudy Mirror,* 123–143. Another character who stares up at Heaven when he recognizes his imminent doom is the refugee General Fan Wuqi 樊於期: "Cike liezhuan" 刺客列傳, *Shiji* 86.2532; compare the parallel account in "Yan taizi Dan zhi yu Qin wanggui" 燕太子丹質於秦亡歸, *Zhanguo ce* 31.1134. In similar scenes, two other Qin generals who have lost their sovereigns' favor, namely, Bai Qi 白起 and the aforementioned Meng Tian, ask what crime they have committed against Heaven before committing suicide ("Bai Qi Wang Jian liezhuan" 白起王翦列傳, *Shiji* 73.2337; and "Meng Tian liezhuan," *Shiji* 88.2570). Cf. Bodde, *Statesman, Patriot, and General,* 63 f. The thrust of these commonplaces is to suggest that the rise and fall of the Qin dynasty followed some predetermined and mysterious plan. The tragicomic climax occurs in

the story of Jing Ke 荊軻 (d. 227 B.C.), the master swordsman whose attempt to assassinate the future First Emperor is foiled at the last instant. With no armed guards standing in his way, Jing Ke is confounded by the unlikeliest of foes: an attendant physician, who hurls a medicine bag at Jing Ke, impeding him just long enough for the monarch to ready his own weapon. For a moment, the future of the world depended on this frail doctor and his sack of nostrums. See "Cike liezhuan," *Shiji* 86.2535; and "Yan taizi Dan zhi yu Qin wanggui," *Zhanguo ce* 31.1139. Cf. Fields.

27. "Qin shihuang benji," *Shiji* 6.268; "Li Si liezhuan," *Shiji* 87.2551.

28. "Li Si liezhuan," *Shiji* 87.2560.

29. Ibid., 87.2555 ff.

30. Ibid., 87.2559.

31. Ibid., 87.2562.

32. E.g., Balazs.

5. Rhetoric and Machination in *Stratagems of the Warring States*

1. "Le roman de Sou Ts'in"; and *Mélanges posthumes sur les religions et l'histoire de la Chine,* 3, 52–62. The general observation that *Zhanguo ce* cannot be reckoned as history goes back at least to the time of Chao Gongwu 晁公武 (d. 1171). See He Jin, 133.

2. See the classic study by Zheng Liangshu, *Zhanguo ce yanjiu,* esp. 177–212; as well as He Jin, 24–59 (with He's study of the historicity of the text, 132–154); and Durrant, *Cloudy Mirror,* 101 ff. Pokora, "Pre-Han Literature," 28, remarks that "much information given *en passant*" in *Zhanguo ce* can be corroborated from other sources. See also Vasil'ev, 20 ff. and 90 ff. (cited by Pokora).

3. Thus Watson, *Early Chinese Literature,* 75. See also Reding, 341, who calls the work "une vaste collection de pièces rhétoriques, des exercises d'école sans doute."

4. Cf. Lloyd, 77.

5. The last work has long been attributed to Cicero. See, for example, Grube, 165–167 (as well as 92–102 for the *Rhetoric,* and 168–192 for *De oratore*).

6. *Intrigues: Studies of the Chan-kuo Ts'e;* and "The *Chan-kuo Ts'e* and Its Fiction." Crump's complete translation, *Chan-kuo Ts'e,* has gone through several editions, and he has gathered some selections for a more general readership in *Legends of the Warring States.*

7. Crump, *Intrigues,* 103 f. Cf. He Jin, 59–82, who emphasizes that such rhetorical exercises represent only a portion of the materials in *Zhanguo ce.*

8. Hawkes, 63. This suggestion is refuted by Liu Xiang's own explanation of the title: he meant *ce* in the sense of *cemou* 策謀, "stratagems and schemes." See "Liu Xiang shulu" 劉向書錄, *Zhanguo ce,* 1195. Cf. He Jin, 12 ff.

9. "A New Exegesis of Chan-kuo-ts'e," 590.

10. Clark, 219.

11. See Kennedy, *A New History of Classical Rhetoric,* 166–172; and Grube, 257–261.

12. Juvenal I.16, Persius III.45, both in *Juvenal and Persius,* trans. Ramsay. Cf. further Bonner, 22 ff.

13. Cf. Xu Zhongshu, 134.

14. Cf. Russell, 117–119.

15. Cf. Lloyd and Sivin, 249; Nylan, "Textual Authority in Pre-Han and Han," 220; Kennedy, *Comparative Rhetoric,* 143; and Garrett, 22 f.

16. Cf. Russell, 4 and 29 f.; and Kennedy, *A New History of Classical Rhetoric,* 59.

17. The most comprehensive discussion appears in chapter 12 of the *Han Feizi,* "Shuinan." Cf. Xing Lu, 275–277; and Lloyd, 77 ff. See also chapter 3 above.

18. *Institutio Oratoria* III.8.34; trans. Butler, 497, slightly modified. *Ad Herennium* III.2 makes a similar point: "Deliberative speeches are either of the kind in which the question concerns a choice between two courses of action, or of the kind in which a choice among several is considered"; trans. Caplan, 157. Cf. Bonner, 53.

19. *Zhanguo ce* 3.117 f.; Crump, *Chan-kuo Ts'e,* § 57. (For the reader's convenience, the corresponding section numbers in Crump's translation will be provided for all references to the *Zhanguo ce,* although the translation offered here will sometimes differ substantially.)

20. "Taishi gong zixu" 太史公自序, *Shiji* 130.3286. See also "Sima Qian zhuan," *Hanshu* 62.2708. Cf. Durrant, "Creating Tradition," 287; and Dzo, 168.

21. Cf. Meng Xiangcai, 240 f.; and Sage, 113 ff. and 199–201.

22. Trans. Winterbottom, 2, 591.

23. But see the description of the hunt in Mao 154, "Qiyue," *Mao-Shi zhengyi* 8A.391a, for an example of chiasmus in the *Odes:* "For private [consumption] are the yearling boars, but we present the three-year-old boars to the lord" 言私其豵，獻豜于公. Cf. Unger, 101.

24. For some possible cases of hypallage in classical Chinese, see Unger, 105–107. (The major weakness of this otherwise useful reference book is that it is organized according to standard categories of Greco-Roman rhetoric and thus cannot take into account those characteristic Chinese devices for which there are no conventional Western equivalents.) Yang Bojun, 104, also discusses instances in which an attribute is placed before a nominal phrase other than the one it is intended to modify. See also Unger, 42–65, for some examples of anaphora and related figures in classical Chinese.

25. *Intrigues,* 100.

26. E.g., Genesis 1:9–10: "And God said, 'Let the waters [A] under the heaven be gathered together unto one place, and let dry land [B] appear.' And it was so. And God called the dry land [B′] earth, and the gathering together of waters [A′] called He seas; and God saw that it was good." Unger, 118, calls this chiasmus *als Gedankenfigur* (as opposed to *als Wortfigur*).

27. For example: "You must not be alone in knowing [the worth of a possession]" 必無獨知, in "Sikou Bu wei Zhou Zui wei Zhoujun" 司寇布為周最謂周君, *Zhanguo ce* 2.60 (Crump, §4). Unger, 119–120, uses the term *brachylogia* for this device.

28. Unger, 34–35.

29. See, for example, Curtius, 79ff. See also Blinn and Garrett; Cole, 88f.; and Bonner, 60ff.

30. Schaberg, *A Patterned Past,* 43ff., finds a number of similar devices in the speeches of the *Zuozhuan.*

31. "Su Qin shi jiang lianheng" 蘇秦始將連橫, *Zhanguo ce* 3.81; Crump, §47.

32. "Zhang Yi you wu Chen Zhen yu Qinwang" 張儀又惡陳軫於秦王, *Zhanguo ce* 3.127; Crump, §54.

33. "Zhang Yi shui Qinwang" 張儀說秦王, *Zhanguo ce* 3.99; Crump, §107.

34. Bentham, 43–53.

35. E.g., "Wei Qinwang" 謂秦王, *Zhanguo ce* 5.266; Crump, §75.

36. E.g., "Qin keqing Zao wei Ranghou" 秦客卿造謂穰侯, *Zhanguo ce* 5.172; Crump, §89.

37. E.g., "Qi Xuanwang jian Yan Chu" 齊宣王見顏斶, *Zhanguo ce* 11.409; Crump, §130.

38. Ibid., 11.410.

39. "Su Qin shi jiang lianheng," *Zhanguo ce* 3.80; Crump, §47.

40. "Qin gong Handan" 秦攻邯鄲, *Zhanguo ce* 5.209; Crump, §105. See also "Pang Cong yu taizi zhi yu Handan" 龐蔥與太子質於邯鄲, *Zhanguo ce* 23.845–846; Crump, §302. Cf. Harbsmeier, *Language and Logic,* 246f.; idem, "Conceptions of Knowledge in Ancient China," 13; and Oliver, 226.

41. "Su Qin shui Qi Minwang" 蘇秦說齊閔王, *Zhanguo ce* 12.433; Crump, §158. On Meng Ben, see chapter 6, note 61, below.

42. "Su Qin wei Qiwang" 蘇秦謂齊王, *Zhanguo ce* 11.424–445; Crump, §157.

43. "Su Dai wei Tian Xu shui Weiwang" 蘇代為田需說魏王, *Zhanguo ce* 23.819–820; Crump, §325.

44. "Chu jiang fa Qi" 楚將伐齊, *Zhanguo ce* 8.330–331; Crump, §117.

45. "Qin Xuan taihou ai Wei Choufu" 秦宣太后愛魏醜夫, *Zhanguo ce* 4.167; Crump, §98. This item is illustrative of the typically pragmatic Chinese attitude toward the question of life after death. Compare *Chunqiu Zuozhuan zhu,* 3, 1013 (Xiang 14 = 559 B.C.): a duke intends to lie to his ancestral spirits but is dissuaded

by a noblewoman, who observes that if such spirits do not exist, there is no reason to converse with them, whereas if they do exist, they cannot be deceived 無神，何告？若有，不可誣也. Cf. Pines, *Foundations of Confucian Thought,* 86; and Schaberg, *A Patterned Past,* 129.

46. See Qian Mu, *Xian-Qin zhuzi xinian,* 617, for Zou Ji's dates.

47. "Chenghou Zou Ji wei Qi xiang" 成侯鄒忌為齊相, *Zhanguo ce* 8.318; Crump, § 118.

48. "Han Gongshu you Qi Wei" 韓公叔有齊魏, *Zhanguo ce* 14.496; Crump, § 207. Crump, *Chan-kuo Ts'e,* 42 ff., cites further examples of this topic (which he calls "doubled persuasion"). See also Lloyd, 76; Raphals, 120; and Kroll, 125.

49. "Zhang Yi zhu Hui Shi yu Wei" 張儀逐惠施於魏, *Zhanguo ce* 16.543–544; Crump, § 198.

50. "Su Dai wei Yan Zhaowang" 蘇代謂燕昭王, *Zhanguo ce* 29.1073 f.; Crump, § 459.

51. "Yanwang wei Su Dai" 燕王謂蘇代, *Zhanguo ce* 29.1075; Crump, § 460.

52. Consider, for example, the well-known tale at the beginning of the *Zuozhuan* in which a penitent son and his mother are reconciled despite his headstrong vow not to see her until they have arrived in the Yellow Springs 黃泉, the mythic home of the dead: he meets his mother in a tunnel by a subterranean waterway: *Chunqiu Zuozhuan zhu,* 1, 14 f. (Yin 1 = 722 B.C.). Cf. Schaberg, *A Patterned Past,* 184 f., and idem, "Social Pleasures," 5 ff. *Mencius* 4B.24 contains another piece with this theme: the archer Yugong Si 庾公之斯 is sent by his lord to kill Zizhuo Ruzi 子濯孺子. But Yugong Si's teacher happens to have been Zizhuo Ruzi's student. Yugong Si cannot disobey his ruler, but he cannot kill his master's master, either. His solution is to remove the tips from his arrows before shooting Zizhuo Ruzi. See also *Chunqiu Zuozhuan zhu,* 3, 1012 f. (Xiang 14 = 559 B.C.). Finally, a much later example from a different kind of literature: a beautiful girl is importuned by an ardent suitor but has vowed to save her virginity for marriage; so she satisfies her lover and still preserves her maidenhead by allowing him to sodomize her. See Li Yu, *The Carnal Prayer Mat,* trans. Hanan, 197 f. (I cite Hanan's translation because reliable and unabridged Chinese editions of *Rou putuan* are notoriously difficult to find. This passage appears just after the midway point of chapter 17.)

53. The controversy over the correct pronunciation of Zengzi's given name is centuries old. Fang Yizhi 方以智 (1611–1671) and Wang Yinzhi 王引之 (1766–1834) both contend that it should be read Can (rather than the more usual Shen); see *Shiki kaichū kōshō* 67.32. Hong Enbo 洪恩波 (fl. 1897), ibid., points out that Xu Shen evidently followed the other reading in *Shuowen jiezi jizhu* 6A.1275, for he says that the character *shen* 森 "is read like the *shen* in Zeng Shen" 讀若曾參之參 (the modern Mandarin pronunciation *sen* 森 is irregular; one would expect

shen). Cf. also Creel, *Confucius and the Chinese Way,* 305n.8. For Zengzi's dates, see Qian Mu, *Xian-Qin zhuzi xinian,* §§ 29 and 48.

54. "Qin Wuwang wei Gan Mao" 秦武王謂甘茂, *Zhanguo ce* 4.150; Crump, § 66.

55. "Zou Ji xiu bachi youyu" 鄒忌脩八尺有餘, *Zhanguo ce* 8.324–326; Crump, § 119.

56. "Pang Cong yu taizi zhi yu Handan," *Zhanguo ce* 23.845–846; Crump, § 302. As we have seen under the rubric of Apophthegm, "three men make a tiger" apparently went on to become a maxim.

57. "Zou Ji xiu bachi youyu," *Zhanguo ce* 8.324–325; Crump, § 119.

58. "Yan gong Qi Qi po" 燕攻齊齊破, *Zhanguo ce* 13.460–462; Crump, § 162.

59. "Jing Xuanwang wen qunchen" 荊宣王問群臣, *Zhanguo ce* 14.482; Crump, § 176. As in the example of the tiger and the fox, King Xuan mistakenly assumes that neighboring states fear his general, Zhao Xixu 昭奚恤, when they are really afraid of the king's army.

60. "Su Li wei Zhoujun" 蘇厲謂周君, *Zhanguo ce* 2.56; Crump, § 13.

61. "Zhaoyang wei Chu fa Wei" 昭陽為楚伐魏, *Zhanguo ce* 9.356; Crump, § 134.

62. "Chu jue Qi Qi jubing fa Chu" 楚絕齊齊舉兵伐楚, *Zhanguo ce* 4.140; Crump, § 59.

63. "Zhao qie fa Yan" 趙且伐燕, *Zhanguo ce* 30.1115; Crump, § 468.

64. "Qin xing shi lin Zhou er qiu jiuding" 秦興師臨周而求九鼎, *Zhanguo ce* 1.1–3; Crump, § 20.

65. "Qi zhu Chu gong Qin" 齊助楚攻秦, *Zhanguo ce* 4.133–138; Crump, § 58. Chen Zhen proposes a way out of this quagmire, a Type C Dilemma. The King of Chu should gain Qin's friendship by offering a city to that state. Chu and Qin can then attack the isolated Qi, and Chu will obtain in battle a city to match what was given to Qin. The King of Chu does not heed this counsel.

66. "Gan Mao xiang Qin" 甘茂相秦, *Zhanguo ce* 4.161; Crump, § 73.

67. "Chenghou Zou Ji wei Qi xiang," *Zhanguo ce* 8.318; Crump, § 118.

68. "Zhao qu Zhou zhi jidi" 趙取周之祭地, *Zhanguo ce* 1.32; Crump, § 32.

69. "Weiwang yi Chuwang meiren" 魏王遺楚王美人, *Zhanguo ce* 17.553–554; Crump, § 200.

70. Compare the episode in *Chunqiu Zuozhuan zhu,* 1, 269 f. (Min 閔 2 = 660 B.C.), in which a crown prince is outfitted with abnormal clothing, signifying his father's disfavor. "The clothes display the person" 衣身之章也, observes a member of the prince's retinue. See Schaberg, *A Patterned Past,* 63 and 225.

71. *Rhetoric* II.xxiii.12; trans. John Henry Freese, 309. See Bonner, 61 f., for Roman examples. As variants of *argumentum ad verecundiam,* these are all informal fallacies. Cf. Copi, 80–81.

72. *Rhetoric* I.ii.21 and II.xxiii.4; trans. Freese, 31 and 301. Similarly, some of the examples that Aristotle uses to illustrate "stating the reason for the false impression" (*to legein tēn aitian tou paradoxou: Rhetoric* II.xxiii.24; trans. Freese, 319) could be classified under Tiger and Fox.

73. *De inventione* I.xxxi–xxxiii. Elsewhere, Cicero discusses the merits of *complexio,* or dilemma (I.xxix): "A dilemma is a form of argument in which you are refuted, whichever alternative you grant, after this fashion: 'If he is a scoundrel, why are you intimate with him? If he is an honest man, why accuse him?'"; trans. Hubbell, 85. The general idea of being lost in all possible cases is present in both the Roman and Chinese versions of dilemma. On dilemma generally, see Copi, 237–241.

74. "Weiwang yi Chuwang meiren," *Zhanguo ce* 17.553–554; Crump, § 200. There are two variants of this story in "Nei chushuo xia," *Han Feizi xin jiaozhu* 10.31.634 f. See also Knechtges, "Wit, Humor, and Satire in Early Chinese Literature (to A.D. 220)," 89 f.

75. The commentator Bao Biao 鮑彪 (1106–1149) opines that the king must have suffered from some illness that produced a foul smell.

76. Even Mencius (*Mencius* 3B.9, *Mengzi zhengyi* 13.446) felt compelled to respond to the potentially damning criticism that he was "fond of disputation" 好辯, an insinuation that he distorted the truth. Cf. Lloyd and Sivin, 63 f.; and Zhenhua Zhang, 35. Compare also the Wang Bi version of *Laozi* 81, *Boshu Laozi jiaozhu,* 155: "Those who are good do not debate; those who debate are not good" 善者不辯，辯者不善.

77. See "Mengchang jun chu xingguo zhi Chu" 孟嘗君出行國至楚, *Zhanguo ce* 385–387; Crump, § 153.

78. Crump discusses the early reception of the text in *Chan-kuo Ts'e,* 28 ff.

79. This idea is expressed perspicuously in the preface to the work by Zeng Gong 曾鞏 (1019–1083, misidentified in Durrant, *Cloudy Mirror,* 102, as "Zeng Gu"), "Zeng Zigu xu" 曾子固序, *Zhanguo ce,* 1200.

80. "Liu Xiang shulu," *Zhanguo ce,* 1198.

81. There may be a character missing here; Miao Wenyuan, 13, inserts *hua* 畫 on the basis of an unspecified edition.

82. As Liu Xiang has explained earlier, moral instruction was the august policy of the preceding Zhou dynasty.

83. Compare the language in Sima Qian's comment (*Shiji* 71.2321) after the biography of Gan Luo 甘羅, the grandson of the aforementioned Gan Mao: "Gan Luo was young, but he produced one extraordinary plan, and the rumor of it redounded in subsequent ages. Though not a noble man of scrupulous conduct, he was indeed a strategist of the Warring States. That was the moment when Qin was mighty, and the world was especially inclined to plots and schemes!"

甘羅年少，然出一奇計，聲稱後世。雖非篤行之君子，然亦戰國之策士也。方秦之彊時，天下尤趨謀詐哉.

6. Insidious Syncretism in the Political Philosophy of *Huainanzi*

Epigraph. "Über den Gemeinspruch: Das mag in der Theorie richtig sein, taugt aber nicht für die Praxis" (1793), *Gesammelte Schriften,* 8, 290 f.; *Political Writings,* trans. Nisbet, 74. Cf. Fleischacker, 4 f. See also Kant's "Muthmaßlicher Anfang der Menschengeschichte" (1786), *Gesammelte Schriften,* 8, 121: "We need only look at *China,* whose position may expose it to occasional unforeseen incursions but not to attack by a powerful enemy, and we shall find that, for this very reason, it has been stripped of every vestige of freedom" (trans. Nisbet, 232).

1. See, in addition to the sources cited below, Jin Chunfeng, 244–245; Chen Qitian, 70 f.; Miyamoto, 9 et passim; Honda, 182–186; and Lü Simian, *Jingzi jieti,* 196. Miyamoto, 16 ff., suggests that "Zhushu" should be read as an indictment of the Han state.

2. *Zhongguo zhonggu sixiangshi changbian,* 155.

3. *Rō-Sō teki sekai,* 215.

4. The *Huainanzi* was commissioned by Liu An, Prince of Huainan. See Vankeerberghen, *The* Huainanzi *and Liu An's Claim to Moral Authority;* Kandel, "Der Versuch einer politischen Restauration"; and Wallacker. For the history of the text, see Roth, *The Textual History of the* Huai-nan-tzu; Yu Dacheng, 1–56; as well as the three appendixes to Zheng Liangshu, *Huainanzi jiaoli,* 322–408.

5. Xu Fuguan, 2, 136. For the phrase *tianxia weigong,* see chapter 3, note 11, above.

6. *The Art of Rulership,* 164. See also Ames, "'The Art of Rulership' Chapter of the Huai Nan Tzu," 239: "It would seem that the author of this chapter ... attempts to concede the minimum amount of political structure necessary to guarantee the maximum degree of individual freedom." It will become clearer in the course of this chapter why "art" is a problematic rendering of the term *shu.*

7. My choice of the word "autism" is inspired by the recent clinical observation that the inability to attribute mental states to other human beings is an essential feature of the horrible psychiatric disorder of the same name. See, for example, Baron-Cohen et al.; and Astington, 145–149. Naturally, I do not mean to suggest that the authors of "Zhushu" were really "autists" as the term is used in contemporary medicine—only that their avowed conception of the mind is stunted.

8. Despite Li Ling, "Cong jianbo faxian kan gushu de tili he fenlei," 31, who includes Daoism (together with Confucianism and Mohism) in his list of genuine ancient schools.

9. See Creel, *What Is Taoism? and Other Studies,* 92–120.

10. Cf. Smith, esp. 145–150; Csikszentmihalyi, 88; Queen, 5–11; and Ames, "Putting the *Te* back into Taoism," 123. Sima Tan's famous essay ("Liujia zhi yaozhi" 六家之要指) dividing all antique thought into six categories, called *jia* 家, is preserved in "Taishi gong zixu," *Shji* 130.2288–2293. The meaning of the term *jia* in such contexts is disputed; Petersen, "Which Books *Did* the First Emperor of Ch'in Burn?" 34 ff., argues that in classical times it would have referred to "specialists" or "experts." Some writers (e.g., Lloyd and Sivin, 53) mistakenly assert that "Liujia zhi yao zhi" is the first text to use *jia* in this sense. But see the much earlier usage in "Jiebi," *Xunzi jijie* 15.21.393. As Petersen demonstrates (38 f.), this sense is common in Xunzi. Cf. also Dai Junren, 2, 885.

There is some disagreement as to whether Sima Tan, and not his son Sima Qian, wrote "Liujia zhi yaozhi" as it has survived. See, for example, Wang Quchang, *Zhuzi xuepai yaojuan,* 159n.1.; however, Fu Wuguang, 111, speculates that the text was written by Sima Tan early in life.

11. This is Xu Fuguan's description in 2, 146 ff.

12. A parallel passage in *Qunshu zhiyao* 41.714 has *dong* 動 for *du* 度, thus: "Once he has moved..."

13. Quotations from chapter 9 of the *Huainanzi* are cited according to two editions. "L" refers to Liu Wendian, *Huainan Honglie jijie;* "S" refers to the more widely circulated *Sibu congkan* edition. Readers can also follow Ames' translation, since he indicates the *S* page numbers in his margins; however, the translations here often differ significantly from those of Ames. Quotations from other chapters are cited in Liu Wendian's edition.

14. An allusion to *Laozi* 2, *Boshu Laozi jiaozhu,* 231 f. In accordance with the aims of this study, I attempt to cite all important parallels in older traditions that Liu An's clients can be expected to have known. Later parallels are presented only when they shed light on the *Huainanzi* itself and are not regularly considered. The frequent parallels furnished by the received *Wenzi* 文子 are not cited, as that text was almost certainly compiled after the *Huainanzi.* This was first demonstrated by Gu Guanguang 顧觀光 (1799–1862) in his *Wenzi jiaokan ji,* 1a; see also Ding Yuanzhi, esp. 145–202; and Kandel, *Wen Tzu,* 6 ff., and 323–332 for a useful list of parallels between the two texts. The recent discovery of an ancient version of the *Wenzi* at Dingxian 定縣, Hebei province, has fueled speculation that the *Wenzi* might actually antedate the *Huainanzi.* For the most recent discussions, see Le Blanc, *Le Wen zi à la lumière de l'histoire et de l'archéologie,* 1–10; Chen Ligui, "Shi jiu jinben *Wenzi* yu *Huainanzi* de bu chongxi neirong tuice guben *Wenzi* de jige sixiang lunti"; Zeng Dahui; and Zhang Fengqian.

15. Cf. Aihe Wang, 194. See also chapter 3 above.

16. Following the commentary of Gao You, who notes that some editions

read *mou* 謀 for *jian* 諫; Ames, *The Art of Rulership,* 239n.2, observes that *mou* fits the rhyme scheme. Moreover, *jinjian* 進諫 is a frequent classical compound, so *jinmou* qualifies as *lectio difficilior.*

17. Following the commentary of Sun Yirang 孫詒讓 (1848–1908).

18. This passage is virtually lifted from Shen Dao (P. M. Thompson, § 111): "His feet could walk, but his attendants led him forward; his mouth could speak, but his envoys made the laudatory speeches" 足能行而相者導進，口能言而行人稱辭; the source text is *Taiping yulan* 76.9a. Wang Yinglin 王應麟 (1223–1296) also cites the passage a number of times, e.g., *Han Yiwen zhi kaozheng* 漢藝文志考證 6.15b, in *Yuhai.* Cf. further Ames, *Art of Rulership,* 239n.2; and Ruan Tingzhuo, "Lun *Huainanzi* yu xian-Qin zhuzi yishu zhi guanxi," 73. (The last study, however, misses more allusions than it catches.)

19. See, for example, Creel, *What Is Taoism?* 79–91. Surprisingly, Slingerland's new book-length study of *wuwei* deliberately removes Han Fei from consideration (see, for example, 288n.9); this decision severely limits the book's usefulness for the study of later texts, such as *Huainanzi,* that derived their concept of *wuwei* directly from such antecedents.

20. Following the suggestion of Chen Qiyou in *Han Feizi xin jiaozhu* 16.38.913n.1; most commentators agree that "Dongjiang" (or "Dongxiang") refers to a place. A parallel passage in the *Lunheng,* however, reads *Dongjiang zhi gong* 東匠之宮 (the house of Dongjiang); Dongjiang is sometimes taken to be the name of the murdered husband. See "Fei Han" 非韓, *Lunheng jiaoshi* 10.29.444; cf. the translation in Forke, *Lun-heng,* 1, 443.

21. "Nan san" 難三, *Han Feizi xin jiaozhu* 16.38.913 f.

22. Following the commentary of Ōta Masashi 太田方 (d. 1829).

23. Compare the *Shenzi* (P. M. Thompson, § 92): "It is certain that the many will vanquish the few" 眾之勝寡，必也; the source text is the commentary of Li Shan in *Liuchen zhu Wenxuan* 57.3b (cited erroneously as 57.2b in Thompson).

24. Cf. Itano, 226 ff.; and Lévi, *Les fonctionnaires divins,* 57—and 38, where he erroneously refers to Zichan as a disciple of Confucius, though the latter was a generation younger. The same mistake, curiously, appears also in Kamenarović, *Xun Zi (Siun Tseu) introduit et traduit du chinois,* 235; and idem, *Wang Fu,* 286. (Cf. Martin, "Le cas Zichan," 69n.1.) There is a similar criticism of Zichan in *Mencius* 4B.2: Zichan may be magnanimous in using his own vehicles to help people ford rivers, but it would be more effective and would require less personal labor simply to build bridges.

Elsewhere, however, Han Fei admires Zichan: see "Xianxue" 顯學, *Han Feizi xin jiaozhu* 19.50.1147; and cf. Hsiao, *A History of Chinese Political Thought,* 390. In fact, in the *Zuozhuan,* the figure of Zichan is famous for charging officials with tasks that accord with their skills, as the doctrine of *shu* warrants; see, for example,

Chunqiu Zuozhuan zhu, 3, 1191 (Xiang 31 = 542 B.C.). Watson, *The Tso chuan,* 154–163, translates several passages in the *Zuozhuan* dealing with Zichan.

25. Creel, *Shen Pu-hai,* 356 f., fragment 6; the source texts are *Yiwen leiju* 54.967; and *Taiping yulan* 638.4b. Compare the reference to "relying on standards" 任法 in the *Shenzi* (P. M. Thompson, § 64); *Qunshu zhiyao* 37.639. There is also a parallel passage in "Renfa" 任法, *Guanzi jiaozheng* 15.45.255.

26. Creel, *Shen Pu-hai,* 370 ff., fragments 17 (2) and 17 (3). The source text is "Renshu" 任數, *Lüshi chunqiu jiaoshi* 17.1065.

27. See Creel, *Shen Pu-hai,* 370n.4, for a discussion of Marquis Zhaoxi's dates.

28. Despite ibid., 371n.6. I take *xiang* 嚮 in the permissible sense of *xiang* 饗.

29. Compare the translations in Vandermeersch, 227 f.; and Richard Wilhelm, *Frühling und Herbst des Lü Bu We,* 270 f. See also Asano, 233; and Numajiri, 273.

30. Cf. Lévi, *Les fonctionnaires divins,* 180 f.; and Zhang Shunhui, 11. Compare also the usage in *Analects* 9.25, *Lunyu jishi* 18.618: "Make integrity and trustworthiness your ruler; do not befriend anyone unequal to yourself; and do not be ashamed to correct your mistakes" 主忠信，毋友不如己者，過則不憚改.

31. Kanaya overlooks this point in his study of the term, "Mui to injun" 無為と因循, *Kanaya Osamu Chūgoku shisō ronshū,* 2, 353–365. "Yinxun" was also the title of a chapter of the *Shen* 慎 *zi;* see *Qunshu zhiyao* 37.636. Cf. Dai Junren, 2, 859.

32. Creel, *Shen Pu-hai,* 391 f., fragment 27; the source text is the *Shiji jijie* 集解 by Pei Yin 裴駰 (fl. A.D. fifth century), *Shiji* 63.2146n.2. See also Makeham, "The Legalist Concept of *hsing-ming,*" 90 f. The passage does not appear in extant editions of the *Xinxu;* cf. *Xinxu xiangzhu,* 384. For the term *duze* 督責, see Creel, *Shen Pu-hai,* 391n.6; as well as Bodde, *China's First Unifier,* 205 f. It should be added that *duze* was an unpopular phrase after the Qin dynasty since the Second Emperor, inspired by a memorial of Li Si, used it as a euphemism for raising taxes and executing rivals (*Shiji* 87.2557). Cf. Machida, 117; and Hsiao, "Legalism and Autocracy in Traditional China," 126 f.

33. Creel, *Shen Pu-hai,* 349, fragment 1 (6), with a slightly different translation. The source text is *Qunshu zhiyao* 36.630. See chapter 3 above. Ames, *The Art of Rulership,* 239n.6, notes several classical antecedents to this passage, but both he and Ruan Tingzhuo overlook the oldest source, namely, Shen Buhai. See Svarverud, 161n.28.

34. Following the commentary of Gao You.

35. Cf. Xu Fuguan, 2, 142 f. Hu Shi, "Du *Lüshi chunqiu*" 讀呂氏春秋 (1930), in *Hu Shi wencun,* 3, 240 ff., demonstrates that this conception of statecraft had been mapped out carefully in the *Lüshi chunqiu,* an important source for the *Huainanzi.* Cf. also Sellmann, 103–115; and Tian Fengtai, 139 ff. and 244 ff.

For a general comparison of *Lüshi chunqiu* and *Huainanzi,* see Akatsuka, *Shoshi shisō kenkyū,* 613 ff. and 630 ff.

36. Compare *Laozi* 49; *Boshu Laozi jiaozhu,* 63: "The Hundred Clans all entrust their eyes and ears to him; the Sage treats them all as children" 百姓皆注其耳目焉，聖人皆孩子.

37. The same expression, *fucou* 輻湊, is attributed to Shen Buhai in *Qunshu zhiyao* 36.629; Creel, *Shen Pu-hai,* 343 f., fragment 1 (1). Cf. Asano, 235. Wang Niansun, in his commentary (L 9.293), points out that the phrase also appears both in "Renfa," *Guanzi jiaozheng* 15.45.256 (= *Guanzi jijiao* 45.759) and in "Nan yi" 難一, *Han Feizi xin jiaozhu* 15.36.852. Ames, *The Art of Rulership,* 249n.158, claims that a similar passage appears in the *Shen* 慎 *zi* but does not cite an edition in his bibliography, and I have been unable to locate the phrase in the extant fragments of that work. However, the concept of using people with different talents as resources is well attested: "The abilities of inferiors are not the same, but all are of use to the sovereign. Therefore the great lord relies on the people's abilities as his resource" 下之所能不同而皆上之用也。是以大君因民之能為資 (P. M. Thompson, § 34 f.; *Qunshu zhiyao* 37.637). Cf. Wang Yongxiang et al., 93 ff. (which contains one of the few recent studies of Shen Dao in any language).

38. Cf. Howard, 123 f.

39. Contrast the scheme laid out in *Chunqiu Zuozhuan zhu,* 3, 1016 (Xiang 14 = 559 B.C.): "Lords are established over the people to act as their superintendents and shepherds; helpmates are then assigned to the lords to act as their teachers and protectors, and to prevent the lords from transcending due measure" 有君而為之貳，使師保之，勿使過度. Cf. Schaberg, *A Patterned Past,* 150. The *Huainanzi* does not countenance this degree of moral autonomy on the part of ministers.

40. Cf. Liu Xiaogan, "Wuwei (Non-action): From *Laozi* to *Huainanzi,*" 54 ff.; Uno, 154; and Hu Shi, *Zhongguo zhonggu sixiangshi changbian,* 70 f.

41. Slingerland, 109 ff., argues against what he calls a "Legalistic interpretation" of *wuwei* in such texts as *Laozi,* denying that the concept can be taken as an "authoritarian technique" of the all-powerful ruler.

42. This example is drawn from "Zhongji" 重己, *Lüshi chunqiu jiaoshi* 1.34 (cf. Ames, *The Art of Rulership,* 252n.231), but the inspiration for the image appears to go back to "Qiushui" 秋水, *Zhuangzi jishi* 6B.17.590 f.: "An ox or horse has four legs; that is Heaven. Haltering the horse's head and running a string through the ox's nose is man. Thus it is said: Do not destroy Heaven by means of man" 牛馬四足，是謂天，落[=絡]馬首，穿牛鼻，是謂人。故曰：無以人滅天. For the reading of *luo* 落 as *luo* 絡, I follow the commentary of Cheng Xuanying 成玄英 (fl. 631–652).

Needless to say, in this formulation, running a string through an ox's nose is the opposite of "following the nature of things." Therefore, despite the recent suggestions that the *Zhuangzi* text may have been redacted at the court of Liu An, we must keep in mind that the authors of the *Huainanzi* still felt free to allude to passages in the *Zhuangzi* in the course of formulating arguments that were entirely incompatible with that source. (For an allusion closer to the original spirit of "Qiushui," see L 1.20.) For connections between the *Zhuangzi* and *Huainanzi,* see Roth, "Who Compiled the *Chuang-tzu?*" esp. 118 ff.; Le Blanc, "From Ontology to Cosmogony; Rand, 7 f.; Dai Junren, 2, 898 ff.; Kusuyama; Wang Shumin, "*Huainanzi* yu *Zhuangzi*"; and Zhou Junfu. Le Blanc, *Huai-nan Tzu,* 83, shows that the text to which *Huainanzi* alludes most often is *Zhuangzi.*

43. Following the commentary of Zhuang Kuiji 莊逵吉 (1760–1813).

44. Zaofu was the charioteer of King Mu of Zhou. See, for example, *Shiji* 5.175; and *Mu tianzi zhuan* 1.4a. See also Mathieu, 185–186; and Granet, *Danses et légendes,* 1, 363 ff.

45. Cf. Le Blanc, *Huai-nan Tzu,* 36 and 90 ff.

46. Following the commentary of Gao You.

47. This passage may be inspired by "Shiwei" 適威, *Lüshi chunqiu jiaoshi* 19.1280: "The Former Kings employed their people as they drove fine horses: they kept their responsibilities light and their restrictions fresh" 先王之使民，若御良馬，輕任新節. Compare also the anecdote in "Dasheng" 達生, *Zhuangzi jishi* 7A.19.660 ff., with parallels in many texts, including the "Aigong" 哀公, *Xunzi jijie* 20.31.545 ff.

48. Cf. Kanaya, *Rō-Sō teki sekai,* 213 f.; idem, *Shin-Kan shisōshi kenkyū,* 519; and Miyamoto, 7 ff.

49. Cf. Uno, 155; Xu Fuguan, 2, 140 f.; and Hu Shi, *Zhongguo zhonggu sixiang-shi changbian,* 82.

50. For more on political "covenants" (or "bonds") in ancient China, see Lewis, *Sanctioned Violence in Early China,* 68 ff.

51. The text continues with two more examples to the same effect. There is considerable textual disagreement concerning the phrase *juexue* 掘穴, which is addressed in the commentaries of Wang Niansun and Tao Fangqi 陶方琦 (1845–1884).

52. Following the commentary of Wang Niansun.

53. Following the commentary of Gao You.

54. Following the commentary of Gao You.

55. See Laloy, 507 ff., for the "grand bouillon," or *dageng* 大羹, a symbol of Yao's frugal living. Gao You's gloss on *buhe* 不和, "not harmonized," is *buzhi wuwei* 不致五味: "one does not bring the Five Flavors." Yu Yue 俞樾 (1821–1907) also points out that the parallel passage in the *Zuozhuan* reads *dageng buzhi* 大羹不致,

with a similar meaning ("[into] the Great Soup one does not bring [seasoning]"); *Chunqiu Zuozhuan zhu,* 1, 86 (Huan 2 = 710 B.C.). *Chunqiu Zuozhuan zhu,* 4, 1419 (Zhao 20 = 522 B.C.), similarly, uses the example of seasoned soup as part of a philosophical argument about the difference between *he* 和 and *tong* 同; and see the parallel in *Yanzi chunqiu jishi* 7.442 f. Cf. Knechtges, "A Literary Feast: Food in Early Chinese Literature," in *Court Culture and Literature in Early China,* 51.

56. This is an approximation of what the context seems to demand. *Fengyang* 奉養 (lit. "presenting nourishment") usually implies filial conduct but can also mean simply "way of life."

57. The examples of King Ling and King Goujian are commonplace in philosophical literature. See chapter 2, note 62, above.

58. For this name and the seminal study on the subject, see Graham, *Studies in Chinese Philosophy and Philosophical Literature,* 67–110. See also Graham, *Disputers of the Tao,* 64–74; as well as Lewis, *Sanctioned Violence in Early China,* 176 ff.; and Ōshima.

59. *Mengzi zhengyi* 11.367. See the commentary of Zhao Qi 趙崎 (d. A.D. 201) for the terms *yong* 饔 and *sun* 飧. Mencius' refutation, which follows, is famous; see also *Mencius* 7A.32, *Mengzi zhengyi* 27.925–926. For more on Xu Xing, see, in addition to Graham's article, Forke, *Geschichte der alten chinesischen Philosophie,* 559 f.; and Fung, 1, 144 f. Qian Mu, *Xian-Qin zhuzi xinian,* § 113, identified him with one Xu Fan 許犯, who is said in "Dangran" 當染, *Lüshi chunqiu jiaoshi* 2.96, to have studied with the Mohist Qin Guli 禽滑釐; see also Qian Mu, *Mozi,* 56 f.; and, more recently, Wang Liqi in *Lüshi chunqiu zhushu* 2.236. This idea has been refuted several times. See esp. Fang Shouchu, 143 f.; as well as Hsiao, *A History of Chinese Political Thought,* 61n.86 and 220n.21; and Yang Junguang, 304 f.

60. Despite Lévi, *Les fonctionnaires divins,* 188 et passim.

61. See the commentary of Tao Fangqi for information on Chang Hong and Meng Ben. Chang Hong appears in *Chunqiu Zuozhuan zhu,* 4, 1622 f. (Ai 2 = 492 B.C.) and is the central figure in an account in *Guoyu* 3.144 ff.; see also the sources cited in Yang Bojun, as well as Ames, *The Art of Rulership,* 253n.267. Tao Fangqi presents a fragment of Xu Shen's commentary to the *Huainanzi* (preserved in *Qunshu zhiyao*), asserting that Meng Ben came from the state of Wei 衛; Ying Shao agrees in his commentary to *Hanshu* 44.2139n.6. Cf. also Wang Quchang, *Qinshi,* 181. Ames, *The Art of Rulership,* 253n.268, says he is a hero from Qi.

62. See *Analects* 9.5, *Lunyu jishi* 17.576 ff.

63. Thus Hucker, 5671.

64. E.g., Vankeerberghen, *The* Huainanzi *and Liu An's Claim to Moral Authority,* 89; Kanaya, *Rō-Sō teki sekai,* 148; Xu Fuguan, 2, 146 ff.; and Lin Congshun, 122. Xu Fuguan, 2, 150, goes so far as to suggest that the Confucianism evident in "Zhushu" can be traced back to the school of Zisi and Mencius.

65. *Liji zhengyi* 60.1674c. I know of no commentator who has made note of this parallel. Forke, *Geschichte der mittelalterlichen chinesischen Philosophie,* 44n.3, points out the similarity with the opening line of "Shu" 恕, *Shizi* A.370c. The authenticity of the *Shizi,* however, is doubtful (despite Graham's treatment in *Disputers of the Tao,* 495). See Zhang Xitang; and especially Jin Dejian, who presents considerable evidence that much of the *Shizi* was "restored" in the third century A.D. and even later.

66. See the Introduction, note 73, above.

67. See, in addition to the example below, L 9.302f., *S* 9.16a; and L 9.313, *S* 9.21a.

68. In "Gongmeng," *Mozi jiaozhu* 12.48.707, Mo Di is said to have cited Confucius. Cf. Graham, *Disputers of the Tao,* 37.

69. One of the most famous examples is "Xianxue," *Han Feizi xin jiaozhu* 19.50.1124ff. See also "Wudu," *Han Feizi xin jiaozhu* 19.49.1096; and *Shiji* 87.2550 (discussed in chapter 4 above), where Zhao Gao persuades Li Si to anoint Huhai as Second Emperor of Qin—rather than his eldest brother, Fusu, whom the First Emperor had designated just before dying—by telling Li Si that he might thereby demonstrate "the wisdom of Confucius and Mozi" 孔墨之智. Cf. Bodde, *China's First Unifier,* 32, who also interprets the reference to Confucius as evidence that the *Shiji* account cannot be contemporaneous with the facts it narrates, since "references like these . . . fit in very well with the spirit of the Han dynasty, when Confucianism became orthodox, and when Confucius was regarded as the ultimate arbiter for all conduct" (93). On the contrary, it is evident that Zhao Gao, by mentioning Mozi in the same breath, does *not* view Confucius as "the ultimate arbiter." Zhao Gao's genuine contempt of Confucius' teachings is revealed by his repeated cajoling of Huhai for clinging to such outmoded notions as righteousness and filial piety (despite Dawson, 158). His rhetorical purpose is to refer to Confucius as one of any number of wiseacres whose fame extends to generations after their death and whom Li Si can emulate by backing the right horse.

The earliest such casual references to Confucius and Mozi seem to appear in the *Lüshi chunqiu;* see, for example, "Buqin" 不侵, *Lüshi chunqiu jiaoshi* 12.640: "Confucius and Mozi were scholars of plain garments, but rulers of ten thousand chariots and lords of one thousand chariots could not compete with them for the scholars [that they attracted]" 孔墨布衣之士也，萬乘之主、千乘之君，不能與之爭士也. Cf. also "Siwu" 思務, *Xinyu jiaozhu* B.12.173: "Among Mozi's disciples, there were many brave scholars; among Confucius' disciples there was much *dao* and *de*" 墨子之門多勇士，仲尼之門多道德 (a fascinating statement in its own right).

70. *Zhuangzi jishi* 1B.2.63: "The Way is darkened by 'small achievements'; words are darkened by 'glory and flowers.' Thus we have the 'right and wrong' of

the Confucians and Mohists, by which they affirm what the other denies and deny what the other affirms" 道隱於小成，言隱於榮華。故有儒墨之是非，以是其所非而非其所是. The commentary of Cheng Xuanying explains *xiaocheng* 小成 (small achievements) as constructed virtues that do not encompass the Way and *ronghua* 榮華 (glory and flowers) as euphuistic, and hence unreliable, speech.

71. A land famed for its fine horses, according to the commentary of Xu Shen, cited by Tao Fangqi.

72. Gao You writes that a *taotu* 騊駼 is a wild horse (*yema* 野馬), echoing the definition in "Shichu" 釋畜, *Erya zhushu* 10.2652b. In common Han usage, the term denotes a horse from the steppe (e.g., *Shiji* 110.2789); this is clearly the sense intended here. However, *taotu* also appears as the name of a mythical (blue) creature akin to a horse in the "Haiwai beijing" 海外北經, *Shanhai jing jiaozhu* 8.294. Cf. Strassberg, § 250.

73. This rhetorical strategy can be traced back to the *Lüshi chunqiu;* see Cook, "The *Lüshi chunqiu* and the Resolution of Philosophical Dissonance," 316 and 322n.39.

74. Following the commentary of Wang Niansun.

75. Compare the insightful discussion of anti-intellectualism in Yu Yingshi, *Lishi yu sixiang,* esp. 10 ff.

76. Cf. Le Blanc, *Huai-nan Tzu,* 191–206.

77. Some commentators suggest that *xian* 弦 should be read as *se* 瑟, "cithern"; see Le Blanc, *Huai-nan Tzu,* 138n.86.

78. Compare the translation in ibid., 138. This manner of thinking, including the specific example, is borrowed from "Zhaolei" 召類, *Lüshi chunqiu jiaoshi* 20.1360. *Gong* 宮 and *jue* 角 are the first and third note in the pentatonic scale, respectively. Such observations led to the practice known as *houqi* 候氣 (waiting for the *qi*), whereby the movements of *qi* were monitored with the aid of twelve specially tuned pitch pipes. See Hulsewé, "Watching the Vapors"; and Bodde, *Essays on Chinese Civilization,* 351–372.

79. See Ames, *The Art of Rulership,* 242n.43, for the sources of the story of Ning Qi, who gained the attention of Lord Huan by singing as the latter passed by his cart. Sometimes it is said that Ning Qi made his music by beating on the horn of an ox, a detail presumably related to the tradition that he was a master at physiognomizing cattle. There is a later treatise on that subject bearing his name; see Sterckx, 26. But the oxcart is more plausibly understood in Ning Qi's case as an emblem of poverty: a wealthier man would have had a horse (Sterckx, 49).

80. *Shang* 商 is the second note of the pentatonic scale. Xu Shen's opaque gloss on *shang,* adduced by Tao Fangqi ("The sound of metal is clear" 金聲清), must have been intended as an explanation of its cosmological significance.

Elsewhere Xu Shen is quoted as saying that *shang* refers to "autumnal sounds" 秋聲, as Tao notes. Cf. also Laloy, 422. Metal 金 and Autumn 秋 go together according to the *Huainanzi*'s famous cosmography. In a fragment of his lost *Xinlun* 新論, Huan Tan 桓譚 (43 B.C.–A.D. 28) confirms that each of the five notes corresponds to one of the Five Phases and four seasons (*gong* remains in the center); *shang* corresponds to autumn. See Pokora, *Hsin-lun (New Treatise) and Other Writings by Huan T'an,* fragment 124; the source texts are *Taiping yulan* 701.3b f. and *Beitang shuchao* 132.10b. Similarly, *Liutao* 3.24a asserts that *shang* is the note pertaining to metal; cf. DeWoskin, *A Song for One or Two,* 76. Xu Shen appears to be saying that Ning Qi's song was plaintive.

However, commentators have missed the significance of *shang* in this context. *Shang* is the note of the vassal (*gong* corresponds to the lord), and Ning Qi is doing his best to enter Lord Huan's service. See "Yueji," *Liji zhengyi* 37.1528a. Compare also the remarks on *shang* in *Fengsu tongyi jiaozhu* 6.275. Cf. Major, "Celestial Cycles and Mathematical Harmonics in the *Huainanzi,*" 122.

Finally, in the account in chapter 12 of the *Huainanzi* (L 12.389), Ning Qi travels to Qi with a group of merchants 商派 (cf. "Ju'nan" 舉難, *Lüshi chunqiu jiaoshi* 19.1311) and wishes to sell 商 his cart to Lord Huan; perhaps some connection is intended.

81. A similar idea is articulated more fully in the "Benjing" 本經 chapter (L 8.265 f.). For the various traditional instruments, see, for example, Kurihara, 542–584.

An ancient fragment, variously attributed, claims in the same spirit that musical instruments respond to the emotions of a performer. Thus human beings must be even more receptive to such stimulation: "Bells and drums, if struck in anger, will sound martial; if struck in sorrow, they will sound doleful; if struck in happiness, they will sound joyous. As one's sentiments change, so do their sounds. The genuine perception of sentiments extends even to bells and chimes—how much more so to human beings!" 鐘鼓之聲，怒而擊之，則武；憂而擊之，則悲；喜而擊之，則樂。其意變，其聲亦變。意誠感之達於金石，而況人乎！ This passage is preserved in two collectanea: *Taiping yulan* 575.4b (which cites *Shizi* as the source), and *Beitang shuchao* 108.2a (ascribed to *Yinwenzi* 尹文子). See also *Shizi* B.380b. "Xiuwen" 修文, *Shuoyuan jiaozheng* 19.497, places a near parallel in the mouth of Confucius. Cf. Lewis, *Sanctioned Violence in Early China,* 220.

82. Cf. Zhu Qianzhi, 16 f.

83. "Yuelun," *Xunzi jijie* 14.20.380: "Music is what the Former Kings used to adorn their happiness; armies, brigades, hatchets, and halberds are what the Former Kings used to adorn their anger" 且樂者，先王之所以飾喜也，軍旅鈇鉞者，先王之所以飾怒也.

84. "Yinchu" 音初, *Lüshi chunqiu jiaoshi* 6.335.

85. Following the commentary of Gao You, with the emendation proposed by Chen Changqi 陳昌齊 (1743–1820).

86. Compare the translations in Cook, "The *Lüshi chunqiu* and the Resolution of Philosophical Dissonance," 338; DeWoskin, *A Song for One or Two,* 87 f.; and Richard Wilhelm, *Frühling und Herbst des Lü Bu We,* 73.

87. Similarities between the conception of music in *Lüshi chunqiu* and that in Xunzi are observed in Numajiri, 61–73.

88. Following the commentary of Bi Yuan 畢沅 (1730–1797) and others.

89. "Dayue" 大樂, *Lüshi chunqiu jiaoshi* 5.255.

90. Following the commentary of Gao You.

91. Following the commentary of Gao You.

92. Compare the translations in Cook, "The *Lüshi chunqiu* and the Resolution of Philosophical Dissonance," 324 ff.; Yimin Jiang, 169 f.; DeWoskin, *A Song for One or Two,* 55 f.; and Richard Wilhelm, *Frühling und Herbst des Lü Bu We,* 56.

93. Cf. Puett, *To Become a God,* 174–175. See also "Mingli" 明理, *Lüshi chunqiu jiaoshi* 6.357–359. Such ideas are adumbrated in the *Guoyu* (e.g., "Shan Mugong jian Jingwang zhu dazhong" 單穆公諫景王鑄大鍾, 3.128), which also reserves a central role for music in the regular order of nature, though without subscribing to a rigidly materialistic system. Cf. Schaberg, *A Patterned Past,* 113 ff.; and James Hart.

94. Major, *Heaven and Earth in Early Han Thought,* 112.

95. Following the commentary of Wang Niansun.

96. A quote from *Laozi* 42; *Boshu Laozi jiaozhu,* 29.

97. There is an element of paronomasia here: except for the difference in tone, the words *zhong* 鐘 (bell) and *zhong* 種 (sow) would have been virtual homophones in Old Chinese, as they are today.

98. On the Five Phases generally, see Sivin, *Traditional Medicine in Contemporary China,* 70 ff.; and Major, "Substance, Process, Phase."

99. Compare the translation in Major, *Heaven and Earth in Early Han Thought,* 108–110. See also idem, "Celestial Cycles and Mathematical Harmonics," 125 f.

100. For more on the "Tianwen" 天文 chapter, see esp. Major, *Heaven and Earth in Early Han Thought,* 55–139, which provides a translation and commentary of the entire text. Cf. also Taki, 17–54; Fung, 1, 396 f.; Yang Molei; and Laloy, 514 f.

101. Cf. Major, *Heaven and Earth in Early Han Thought,* 27; DeWoskin, "Early Chinese Music and the Origins of Aesthetic Terminology," 194 f.; and idem, *A Song for One or Two,* 37 f.

102. *Xun* 尋 and *chang* 常 are measures of distance (one *chang* is equivalent to two *xun*); both are to be understood as terrible misses for an archer. Cf. Vankeerberghen, *The* Huainanzi *and Liu An's Claim to Moral Authority,* 190n.4.

103. See Ames, *The Art of Rulership,* 242n.40 f., for classical sources of these two anecdotes. See also Yimin Jiang, 45 ff.

104. See especially Lévi, "Quelques examples de détournement subversif de la citation dans la littérature classique chinoise," 44–50.

105. "Zhenglun," *Xunzi jijie* 12.18.333. See the discussion in Goldin, "A Mind-Body Problem in the *Zhuangzi?*" Lewis, *Sanctioned Violence in Early China,* 224; and Sawada, "*Junshi* to *Ryoshi Shunjū* ni okeru ki," 85 f., both discuss this passage but without considering its relevance to the mind-body problem.

106. Following the commentary of Yang Liang after the first appearance of the term *shan* 擅, *Xunzi jijie* 12.18.331.

107. Compare the translation in Knoblock, 3, 41.

108. Following the commentary of Chen Qiyou.

109. Creel, *Shen Pu-hai,* 364 f., fragment 16; the source text is "Wai chushuo you shang," *Han Feizi xin jiaozhu* 13.34.775. Cf. Asano, 235.

110. Following the suggestion of Creel, *Shen Pu-hai,* 365.

111. There is a similar passage later in the chapter: "When happiness and anger are formed in the heart and wishes and desires are apparent on the outside, then those who hold offices will depart from rectitude and flatter their superiors" 喜怒形於心，者[=耆]欲見於外，則守職者離正而阿上 (L 9.299 f.; *S* 9.15a). For the emendation of *zhe* 者 to *zhi* 耆, see the commentary of Wang Niansun.

112. See Ames, *The Art of Rulership,* for classical sources of these legends.

113. A quotation from *Laozi* 54; *Boshu Laozi jiaozhu,* 85.

114. See the perceptive article by Griet Vankeerberghen, "Emotions and Actions of the Sage"; and idem, *The* Huainanzi *and Liu An's Claim to Moral Authority,* 105 ff. See further Roth, "Evidence for Stages of Meditation in Early Taoism," 308 f.

115. Cf. especially Queen, 20 f., with whose conclusions this chapter is fundamentally in agreement.

116. *Shiji* 130.3289.

117. Cf. Roth, "Who Compiled the *Chuang-tzu?*" 83 ff.; Zhang Shunhui, 5 ff. and 302 f.; and Dai Junren, 2, 892 ff. For an opposing view, see Queen, 10 f.

7. Ban Zhao in Her Time and in Ours

1. See Xia Xiaohong, "Gudian xinyi: Wan-Qing ren dui jingdian de jieshuo —Yi Ban Zhao yü *Nüjie* wei zhongxin," *Zhongguo xueshu* 1.2 (2000), 87–89, as cited by Susan Mann in Swann, xi.

2. Ayscough, 263.

3. Martin-Liao, *Frauenerziehung im alten China,* 50 ("Ban Zhao [hat] mit ihrem *Nüjie* tatsächlich als Vorkämpfer der Frauenerziehung Ruhm verdient"). See also idem, "Traditional Handbooks of Women's Education," 171.

4. Chen Dongyuan, 49 f.

5. Van Gulik, 97.

6. Englert, 52 ("bedeuteten . . . eine gewaltige Last für die Frauen").

7. Enoki, 11. He also holds the tenuous line that *Lienü zhuan* "is a description of actual behavior of Confucian women" (5).

8. Handlin, 13.

9. Lee, 13 ff., relying on Dull. See also Lü Simian, *Lü Simian dushi zhaji,* 549–555.

10. Goldin, *Culture of Sex,* 99 ff. Ban Zhao's invention of tradition seems to be in line with the general observation of the phenomenon in Hobsbawm, 4: "we should expect [the invention of tradition] to occur more frequently when a rapid transformation of society weakens or destroys the social patterns for which 'old' traditions had been designed, producing new ones to which they were not applicable, or when such old traditions and their institutional carriers and promulgators no longer prove sufficiently adaptable and flexible."

11. In Swann, xiv, n. 12.

12. Hinsch, *Women in Early Imperial China,* 123.

13. Yu-shih Chen, 233 and 243 f.

14. The originality of this idea has been overstated by scholars such as Mann and Hinsch; a similar argument was presented some years ago in a German publication that Chen does not cite: Fricker, 190 ff. and 273 f.

15. Yu-shih Chen, 246.

16. Ibid., 254.

17. *Hou-Han shu* 84.2796.

18. Ibid., 84.2790.

19. As in "You adore me, attractive and *yaotiao*" 子慕予兮善窈窕, in "Shangui" 山鬼, *Jiuge* 九歌, *Chuci zhangju buzhu* 2.46. This line may be intended to recall "Guanju."

20. Cf. Martin, "Le *Shijing,* de la citation à l'allusion," 33.

21. In Swann, x. Swann describes and translates these fragments in toto (74–81 and 100–130).

22. Von Zach, 1, 133–135.

23. *Liuchen zhu Wenxuan* 9.28a; trans. Knechtges, *Wen xuan or Selections of Refined Literature,* 2, 177 (whose diction here is perhaps too Christian). See also idem, "Poetic Travelogue in the Han *fu,*" in *Court Culture and Literature in Early China,* 142 ff.

24. In Swann, xii.

25. Spade, "The Education of Women in China during the Southern Dynasties."

8. Those Who Don't Know Speak

1. E.g., Alan K. L. Chan, 1; and Mair, *Tao Te Ching,* xi.

2. More on this subject below. Ronald Reagan quoted the *Daode jing* in his State of the Union Address in 1988. He is not known for quoting Molière.

3. This phenomenon is observed also in Clarke, 53.

4. Part of the problem may be the lingering misconception that the Chinese language is uniquely free of grammar and thus open to immediate and intuitive comprehension. For example, Northrop, 316, writes: "Sentences, furthermore, in Chinese are constructed by setting such purely individual symbols the one after the other in columns in the order in which the items which they denote in immediate experience are associated." This statement is untrue—sentences in Chinese are constructed according to rules of syntax—and pernicious, insofar as it implies that as long as a reader is in tune with the appropriate "associations," he or she can understand Chinese writing without bothering to learn the grammar. (Some of Northrop's other assertions are even more absurd and call into question his familiarity with Chinese—as on p. 319, where he says that because the language is tonal, "if a person speaking Chinese becomes emotionally excited, thereby throwing his voice into a higher key than that required for the meaning which he desires to convey, he automatically says something having nothing to do with what he intended.") Likewise such luminaries as Schweitzer, 177; Granet, *Études sociologiques sur la Chine,* 124–136; and Rosemont, "On Representing Abstractions in Archaic Chinese." For a corrective discussion, see Saussy, *Great Walls of Discourse and Other Adventures in Cultural China,* 75–90; and cf. Harbsmeier, *Language and Logic,* 85 ff. Rosemont's position is criticized pungently in Cikoski, 18 ff. According to Mair, "Ma Jianzhong and the Invention of Chinese Grammar," 6, the notion that Chinese has no grammar may be traced in part to a faulty paradigm that considers only morphology, and not syntax, as "grammar."

5. Li Yu, *Jou Pu Tuan* (trans. Richard Martin from the German version by Franz Kuhn). This has now been superseded by the masterful direct translation by Patrick Hanan.

6. It should be borne in mind that the same method informed a *Laozi* translation by no less a figure than Leo Tolstoy (1828–1910). Two standard works on the subject are Shifman, 41–50; and Bodde, *Tolstoy and China,* 20 ff. (See also the stringent review of the latter work by Boodberg, *Selected Works of Peter A. Boodberg,* 481–493.)

The first American writer to popularize the practice of attacking Chinese poetry with no knowledge of the language was Ezra Pound (1885–1972); see Durrant, "Packaging the *Tao,*" 77. There is a vast bibliography on this issue; some basic works are Spence, 168 ff.; Kenner, esp. 192–231 and 445–459; Yip; Kennedy, *Selected Works of George A. Kennedy,* 443–462; and Achilles Fang. Pound's eminence has prompted as fine a scholar as Saussy to concede that this poet has taught English speakers "what to look for, what to value, what to avoid" in Chinese poetry (*Great Walls of Discourse,* 62).

7. Bynner, *The Chinese Translations,* 329–388.

8. On Le Guin's lifelong involvement with Daoism, see Herman, "Daoist Environmentalism in the West."

9. Kiang, the author of several books in Chinese and English, was a former secretary of Yuan Shikai 袁世凱 (1859–1916) who was forced to flee China after denouncing his usurpatory employer. Bynner met Kiang in 1918, when they were both on the faculty at the University of California at Berkeley. Kiang later returned to China and accepted the position of Minister of Education in the puppet state of Manchukuo. He was imprisoned afterward and is thought to have died in jail on December 6 or 7, 1954. See Bynner, *Chinese Translations,* 3–12.

10. Cf. Bradbury, 35 ff.

11. Mitchell, x. After the introduction, Mitchell's book ceases to be paginated, so it will be cited below by chapter number.

12. Compare the review by Eoyang, 492; and further LaFargue, 256 f. and 273n.3. The notion that Eastern philosophies—Daoism and Buddhism in particular—are essentially interchangeable seems to be widespread in popular writing; e.g., Capra, 19: "Although [Hinduism, Buddhism, and Taoism] comprise a vast number of subtly interwoven spiritual disciplines and philosophical systems, the basic features of their worldview are the same."

13. The archaeological discovery of the Guodian *Laozi* in 1993 has only complicated what was already a knotty problem. See Allan and Williams; and Henricks, *Lao Tzu's Tao Te Ching.*

14. *Chinese Translations,* 340.

15. Miles, vii.

16. For the case of Bynner, who relied on at least fourteen different published translations, see Lattimore, 311 ff.; also Bynner, *Selected Letters,* 178 f.

17. *Boshu Laozi jiaozhu,* 232 ff.

18. Miles, 26.

19. *Tao Te Ching,* 60.

20. *Lao-tzu Te-Tao Ching,* 54. Also Carus and Suzuki, 75: "Merit he accomplishes, but he does not dwell on it. Since he does not dwell on it, it will never leave him"; and John C. H. Wu, 5: "He accomplishes his task, but does not dwell upon it. And yet it is just because he does not dwell on it that nobody can ever take it away from him."

21. See the notes in *Boshu Laozi jiaozhu,* 233.

22. Wing-tsit Chan, *The Way of Lao Tzu (Tao-te ching),* 101. Chan may have been influenced by Blakney, 54: "As he succeeds, he takes no credit. And just

because he does not take it, credit never leaves him." (Chan knew Blakney's translation and referred to it throughout his notes.) Lau, *Lao Tzu,* 58, is similar: "It accomplishes its task yet lays claim to no merit. It is because it lays claim to no merit that its merit never deserts it."

23. Mitchell renders the relevant passage in chapter 2 as "When her work is done, she forgets it. That is why it lasts forever."

24. Miles, 123.

25. Cf. Eoyang, 492 f.

26. Le Guin, 124.

27. *Boshu Laozi jiaozhu,* 169 ff.

28. Waley, *The Way and Its Power,* 228. He alters the sequence of the third and fourth clauses of the first section.

29. Henricks, *Lao-tzu Te-Tao Ching,* 40, renders it more clearly: "To think you have no rival is to come close to losing my treasures." "My treasures," on this interpretation, are compassion 慈, frugality 儉, and not presuming to be the leader of the world 不敢為天下先, enumerated in chapter 67, *Boshu Laozi jiaozhu,* 160.

30. Le Guin, 89.

31. *Boshu Laozi jiaozhu,* 262 ff.

32. Here and following, Chan's translation is used as a baseline for two reasons: it is the most literal, and Mitchell, Miles, and Le Guin all reveal their indebtedness to it. My reliance on Chan for this purpose in no way implies that his is the only acceptable translation.

33. Chan, *The Way of Lao Tzu,* 116. He notes that *wei* 為 and *zhi* 知 are inverted in several editions, so the phrases that he has translated as "without knowledge" and "without taking any action" could be transposed.

34. Miles, 36.

35. Le Guin, 13.

36. *Chinese Translations,* 353.

37. Cf. LaFargue and Pas, 284. Some scholars, such as Hardy, 181–185, grant that popular interpretations of Daoism, though they may represent "bad scholarship," may still be valuable as "good religion" in their own right.

38. "Two Notes on the Translation of Taoist Classics," 119–130. See also Bradbury, 31 ff.

39. *Boshu Laozi jiaozhu,* 243.

40. *Chinese Translations,* 351.

41. Cf. Schipper, "Chiens de paille et tigres en papier," esp. 91.

42. Graham, "Two Notes on the Translation of Taoist Classics," 127.

43. Thus Hinton, 894. My example from chapter 51, below, is also taken from this review. Ames, "Putting the *Te* back into Taoism," 121–131, contends that even

specialists have neglected to account for *de* in studies of Daoist philosophy. There is even a translation by a native speaker of Chinese that deletes *de* from the title of the book: Wang Keping, *The Classic of the Dao.*

44. Mitchell, vii.

45. For a judicious discussion, see Ivanhoe, "The Concept of *de* ('Virtue') in the *Laozi.*"

46. *Boshu Laozi jiaozhu,* 72.

47. Chan, *The Way of Lao Tzu,* 190.

48. Mitchell, x.

49. *Boshu Laozi jiaozhu,* 8 ff.

50. Chan, *The Way of Lao Tzu,* 170.

51. Waley, *The Way,* 191, might also have been Mitchell's inspiration: "Were it not that the ten thousand creatures can bear their kind, they would soon become extinct." Cf. also John C. H. Wu, 79: "If the ten thousand creatures were not reproductive, they would be likely to come to extinction"; and, most recently, Ivanhoe, *The Daodejing of Laozi,* 42: "If the myriad creatures lacked what made them flourish they might become extinct." The Chinese term *mie* 滅, "to annihilate, to exterminate," can have the sense of extinguishing a clan or nation but not normally that of making a species extinct—an idea that is probably anachronistic.

52. Mitchell's translation evinces a pronounced fondness for green causes, and at times such allusions are forced into the text in purposefully jarring language. E.g., chapter 46: "When a country is in harmony with the Tao, the factories make trucks and tractors. When a country goes counter to the Tao, warheads are stockpiled outside the cities."

53. Cf. Bradbury, 37.

54. *Boshu Laozi jiaozhu,* 237.

55. Compare the review by Ann-Ping Chin, 38.

56. Le Guin, 111.

57. *Boshu Laozi jiaozhu,* 248–254.

58. Chan, *The Way of Lao Tzu,* 144.

59. Le Guin, 34.

60. Ibid., 114 f. Compare the review by Herman, 687; and idem, "Daoist Environmentalism in the West," 398.

61. Van Norden, "Method in the Madness of the *Laozi,*" 203, remarks that we can appreciate the value of the *Daode jing* while still recognizing that it "expresses a synoptic vision which we would be ill-advised to adopt."

62. All rankings cited below were obtained on March 7, 2002.

63. See, for example, McDowell.

64. With this addition, Penguin Putnam now offers four competing translations under different imprints: Blakney; Lau; Richard Wilhelm, *Tao Te Ching;*

and, with the most presumptuous title, Jonathan Star, *Tao Te Ching: The Definitive Edition.*

Blakney's qualifications are also dubious; he was a missionary in Fuzhou 福州 in the 1920s but does not seem to have had any specialized training in classical Chinese. His avowed methodology yields speciously fluid prose: "It is my belief that a finished translation should be free of all traces of the original language, especially when they mar English diction. If parts of the original are obdurately obscure, it is better, it seems to me, to omit them rather than to carry the obscurity over into English" (x). Blakney's understanding of *ziran* is criticized in Liu Xiaogan, "Naturalness (*Tzu-jan*), the Core Value in Taoism," 212.

65. All the reviews can be found on the appropriate pages of Amazon's website.

Bibliography

Classical Chinese Texts

The first entry under each title is the edition regularly cited in the text and notes; other listed works have been consulted for variants and commentary. Documents from after the Tang dynasty as well as archaeologically excavated texts are listed in Other Works, below.

Baihu tong 白虎通. Attributed to Ban Gu 班固 (A.D. 32–92) and others, but probably from the second century A.D. at the earliest.
Chen Li 陳立 (1809–1869). *Baihu tong shuzheng* 白虎通疏證. Ed. Wu Zeyu 吳則虞. 2 vols. Xinbian Zhuzi jicheng. Beijing: Zhonghua, 1994.

Beitang shuchao 北堂書抄. Miscellany compiled by Yu Shinan 虞世南 (558–638).
Beitang shuchao. Edition of 1888.

Chuci 楚辭. Attributed to Qu Yuan 屈原 (4th century B.C.?) and others.
Hong Xingzu 洪興祖 (1090–1155). *Chuci zhangju buzhu* 楚辭章句補注. In *Chuci zhu bazhong* 楚辭注八種. 5th edition. Taipei: Shijie, 1989.

Erya 爾雅.
Erya zhushu 爾雅注疏. *Shisan jing zhushu fu jiaokan ji* 十三經注疏附校勘記. 1817; rpt., Beijing: Zhonghua, 1980.
Hao Yixing 郝懿行 (1757–1825). *Erya yishu* 爾雅義疏. *Sibu beiyao* 四部備要.

Fengsu tongyi 風俗通義. By Ying Shao 應劭 (d. before A.D. 204).
Wang Liqi 王利器. *Fengsu tongyi jiaozhu* 風俗通義校注. 2d edition. Beijing: Zhonghua, 1981; rpt., Taipei: Mingwen, 1988.

Guliang zhuan 穀梁傳.
Chunqiu Guliang zhuan zhushu 春秋穀梁傳注疏. *Shisan jing zhushu.*

Guanzi 管子. Attributed proleptically to Guan Zhong 管仲 (d. 645 B.C.).
Dai Wang 戴望 (1783–1863). *Guanzi jiaozheng* 管子校正. *Zhuzi jicheng* 諸子集成.
Guo Moruo 郭沫若 et al. *Guanzi jijiao* 管子集校. 2 vols. Beijing: Kexue, 1956.

Guoyu 國語.
Guoyu. Shanghai: Guji, 1978.

Han Feizi 韓非子. By Han Fei 韓非 (d. 233 B.C.).
Chen Qiyou 陳奇猷. *Han Feizi xin jiaozhu* 韓非子新校注. 2 vols. Shanghai: Guji, 2000.

Han-Shi waizhuan 韓詩外傳. Attributed to Han Ying 韓嬰 (ca. 200–120 B.C.).
Qu Shouyuan 屈守元. *Han-Shi waizhuan jianshu* 韓詩外傳箋疏. Chengdu: Ba-Shu, 1996.

Hanshu 漢書. By Ban Gu and others.
Hanshu. 12 vols. Beijing: Zhonghua, 1962.

Hou-Han shu 後漢書. By Fan Ye 范曄 (398–446) and others.
Hou-Han shu. 12 vols. Beijing: Zhonghua, 1965.

Huainanzi 淮南子. Commissioned by Liu An 劉安 (d. 122 B.C.).
Liu Wendian 劉文典. *Huainan Honglie jijie* 淮南鴻烈集解. Ed. Feng Yi 馮逸 and Qiao Hua 喬華. 2 vols. Xinbian Zhuzi jicheng. Beijing: Zhonghua, 1989.
Huainanzi. Sibu congkan 四部叢刊.

Laozi 老子. Otherwise known as *Daode jing* 道德經.
Gao Ming 高明. *Boshu Laozi jiaozhu* 帛書老子校注. Xinbian Zhuzi jicheng. Beijing: Zhonghua, 1996.

Liji 禮記.
Liji zhengyi 禮記正義. *Shisan jing zhushu.*

Lienü zhuan 列女傳. Redacted by Liu Xiang 劉向 (79–8 B.C.); some sections may be spurious.
Wang Zhaoyuan 王照圓 (fl. 1879–1884). *Lienü zhuan buzhu* 列女傳補注. *Guoxue jiben congshu* 國學基本叢書.

Liutao 六韜.
Liutao. Sibu congkan.

Lunheng 論衡. By Wang Chong 王充 (A.D. 27–ca. 100).
Huang Hui 黃暉. *Lunheng jiaoshi (fu Liu Pansui jijie)* 論衡校釋(附劉盼遂集解). Xinbian Zhuzi jicheng. Beijing: Zhonghua, 1990.

Lunyu 論語 (i.e., *Analects*). Sayings attributed to Kong Qiu 孔丘 (i.e., Confucius, 551–479 B.C.).
Cheng Shude 程樹德 (1877–1944). *Lunyu jishi* 論語集釋. Ed. Cheng Junying 程俊英 and Jiang Jianyuan 蔣見元. Xinbian Zhuzi jicheng. Beijing: Zhonghua, 1990.

Lüshi chunqiu 呂氏春秋. Commissioned by Lü Buwei 呂不韋 (d. 235 B.C.).
Chen Qiyou. *Lüshi chunqiu jiaoshi* 呂氏春秋校釋. 2 vols. Shanghai: Xuelin, 1984.
Wang Liqi. *Lüshi chunqiu zhushu* 呂氏春秋注疏. 4 vols. Chengdu: Ba-Shu, 2002.

Mengzi 孟子 [i.e., *Mencius*]. Sayings attributed to Meng Ke 孟軻 (371–289 B.C.).
Jiao Xun 焦循 (1763–1820). *Mengzi zhengyi* 孟子正義. Ed. Shen Wenzhuo 沈文倬. 2 vols. Xinbian zhuzi jicheng. Beijing: Zhonghua, 1987.

Mozi 墨子. Attributed to Mo Di 墨翟 (d. ca. 390 B.C.) and his followers.
Wu Yujiang 吳毓江. *Mozi jiaozhu* 墨子校注. Ed. Sun Qizhi 孫啟治. 2 vols. Xinbian Zhuzi jicheng. Beijing: Zhonghua, 1993.

Mu tianzi zhuan 穆天子傳.
Mu tianzi zhuan. Sibu beiyao.

Qunshu zhiyao 群書治要. Excerpts from primary texts collected by Wei Zheng 魏徵 (580–643).
Qunshu zhiyao. Guoxue jiben congshu.

Shanhai jing 山海經.
Yuan Ke 袁珂. *Shanhai jing jiaozhu* 山海經校注. 2d edition. Chengdu: Ba-Shu, 1996.

Shiji 史記. By Sima Qian 司馬遷 (145?–86? B.C.) and others.
Shiji. 10 vols. Beijing: Zhonghua, 1959.
Takigawa Kametarō 瀧川龜太郎 (b. 1865). *Shiki kaichū kōshō* 史記會注考證. Tokyo: Tōhō Bunka Gakuin, 1932–1934; rpt., Taipei: Hongshi, 1986.
Chen Zhi 陳直. *Shiji xinzheng* 史記新證. Tianjin: Renmin, 1979.

Shijing 詩經.

Mao-Shi zhengyi 毛詩正義. *Shisan jing zhushu.*

Cheng Junying and Jiang Jianyuan. *Shijing zhuxi* 詩經注析. Zhongguo gudian wenxue jiben congshu. 2 vols. Beijing: Zhonghua, 1991.

Zhao Fansheng 趙帆聲. *Shijing yidu* 詩經異讀. Kaifeng: Henan Daxue, 2002.

Shiming 釋名. By Liu Xi 劉熙 (fl. ca. A.D. 200).

Wang Xianqian 王先謙 (1842–1917). *Shiming shuzheng bu* 釋名疏證補. *Guoxue jiben congshu.*

Shizi 尸子. Attributed to Shi Jiao 尸佼 (4th century B.C.), but many sections are spurious.

Wang Jipei 王繼培 (b. 1775). *Shizi. Ershi'er zi* 二十二子. Shanghai: Guji, 1985.

Shuowen jiezi 說文解字. By Xu Shen 許慎 (ca. A.D. 55–ca. 149).

Jiang Renjie 蔣人傑. *Shuowen jiezi jizhu* 說文解字集注. Ed. Liu Rui 劉銳. Shanghai: Guji, 1996.

Duan Yucai 段玉裁 (1735–1815). *Shuowen jiezi Duan zhu fu liushu yinyun biao* 說文解字段注附六書音韻表. *Sibu beiyao.*

Shuoyuan 說苑. Redacted by Liu Xiang.

Xiang Zonglu 向宗魯. *Shuoyuan jiaozheng* 說苑校證. Zhongguo gudian wenxue jiben congshu. Beijing: Zhonghua, 1987.

Suishu 隋書. By Wei Zheng and others.

Suishu. 6 vols. Beijing: Zhonghua, 1973.

Sunzi 孫子. Attributed to Sun Wu 孫武 (6th century B.C.).

Yang Bing'an 楊丙安, ed. *Shiyi jia zhu Sunzi jiaoli* 十一家注孫子校理. Xinbian Zhuzi jicheng. Beijing: Zhonghua, 1999.

Weishu 魏書. By Wei Shou 魏收 (A.D. 506–572).

Weishu. 5 vols. Beijing: Zhonghua, 1974.

Wenxuan 文選.

Liuchen zhu Wenxuan 六臣注文選. *Sibu congkan.*

Wenzi 文子.

Gu Guanguang 顧觀光 (1799–1862). *Wenzi jiaokan ji* 文子校勘記. *Sibu beiyao.*

Xinxu 新序. Redacted by Liu Xiang.
Zhao Zhongyi 趙仲邑. *Xinxu xiangzhu* 新序詳注. Beijing: Zhonghua, 1997.

Xinyu 新語. Attributed to Lu Jia 陸賈 (d. 178 B.C.).
Wang Liqi. *Xinyu jiaozhu* 新語校注. Xinbian Zhuzi jicheng. Beijing: Zhonghua, 1986.

Xunzi 荀子. By Xun Kuang 荀況 (3rd century B.C.).
Wang Xianqian. *Xunzi jijie* 荀子集解. Ed. Shen Xiaohuan 沈嘯寰 and Wang Xingxian 王星賢. Xinbian Zhuzi jicheng. Beijing: Zhonghua, 1988.
Igai Hikohiro 豬飼彥博 (1761–1845). *Junshi hoi* 荀子補遺. Edition of 1801 in *Wuqiubei zhai Xunzi jicheng* 無求備齋荀子集成 (where it is cited as *Junshi zōchū* 增注 *hoi*).
Liang Qixiong 梁啟雄. *Xunzi jianshi* 荀子柬釋. Taibei: Shangwu, 1965.

Yanzi chunqiu 晏子春秋. Narratives pertaining to Yan Ying 晏嬰 (d. 500 B.C.).
Wu Zeyu 吳則虞. *Yanzi chunqiu jishi* 晏子春秋集釋. 2 vols. Beijing: Zhonghua, 1962..

Yijing 易經.
Zhou-Yi zhushu 周易注疏. *Shisan jing zhushu.*
Ding Shouchang 丁壽昌 (1818–1865). *Du Yi huitong* 讀易會通. *Guoxue jiben congshu.*

Yiwen leiju 藝文類聚. Excerpts from primary texts compiled by Ouyang Xun 歐陽詢 (557–641) and others.
Yiwen leiju. Ed. Wang Shaoying 王紹楹. 2 vols. Beijing: Zhonghua, 1965.

Yi Zhoushu 逸周書.
Zhu Youzeng 朱右曾 (fl. 1846). *Yi Zhoushu jixun jiaoshi* 逸周書集訓校釋. *Guoxue jiben congshu.*

Yili 儀禮.
Yili zhushu 儀禮注疏. *Shisan jing zhushu.*

Yilin 意林. Miscellany compiled by Ma Zong 馬總 (d. 823).
Yilin. Sibu congkan.

Zhanguo ce 戰國策. Redacted by Liu Xiang.
Zhanguo ce. 2 vols. Shanghai: Guji, 1978; rpt., Taipei: Liren, 1990.

Miao Wenyuan 繆文遠. *Zhanguo ce xin jiaozhu* 戰國策新校注. 3d edition. Chengdu: Ba-Shu, 1998.

Zhuangzi 莊子. Attributed to Zhuang Zhou 莊周 (4th century B.C.) and his followers.

Guo Qingfan 郭慶藩 (1844–1896). *Zhuangzi jishi* 莊子集釋. Ed. Wang Xiaoyu 王孝魚. 4 vols. Xinbian Zhuzi jicheng. Beijing: Zhonghua, 1961.

Wang Shumin 王叔岷. *Zhuangzi jiaoquan* 莊子校詮. 2d edition. 2 vols. Zhongyang Yanjiuyuan Lishi Yuyan Yanjiusuo zhuankan 88. Taibei, 1994.

Zuozhuan 左傳.

Yang Bojun 楊伯峻. *Chunqiu Zuozhuan zhu* 春秋左傳注. 2d edition. Zhongguo gudian mingzhu yizhu congshu. Beijing: Zhonghua, 1990.

Other Works

Ad C. Herennium de ratione dicendi (Rhetorica ad Herennium). Trans. Harry Caplan. Loeb Classical Library 403. Cambridge, Mass.: Harvard University Press, 1954.

Ahern, Dennis M. "Is Mo Tzu a Utilitarian?" *Journal of Chinese Philosophy* 3.2 (1976): 185–193.

Akatsuka Kiyoshi 赤塚忠. *Juka shisō kenkyū* 儒家思想研究. Akatsuka Kiyoshi chosakushū 3. Tokyo: Kembunsha, 1986.

———. *Chūgoku kodai shisōshi kenkyū* 中國古代思想史研究. Akatsuka Kiyoshi chosakushū 2. Tokyo: Kembunsha, 1987.

———. *Shoshi shisō kenkyū* 諸子思想研究. Akatsuka Kiyoshi chosakushū 4. Tokyo: Kembunsha, 1987.

Allan, Sarah. *The Heir and the Sage: Dynastic Legend in Early China*. San Francisco: Chinese Materials Center, 1981.

Allan, Sarah, and Crispin Williams, eds. *The Guodian* Laozi: *Proceedings of the International Conference, Dartmouth College, May 1998*. Early China Special Monograph Series 5. Berkeley, 2000.

Alleton, Viviane. *Les Chinois et la passion des noms*. Paris: Aubier, 1993.

———, ed. *Paroles à dire, paroles à écrire: Inde, Chine, Japon*. Recherches d'histoire et de sciences sociales 75. Paris: École des Hautes Études en Sciences Sociales, 1997.

Ames, Roger T. "'The Art of Rulership' Chapter of the Huai Nan Tzu: A Practicable Taoism." *Journal of Chinese Philosophy* 8.2 (1981): 225–244.

———. *The Art of Rulership: A Study of Ancient Chinese Political Thought*. Honolulu: University of Hawai'i Press, 1983; rpt., Albany: State University of New York Press, 1994.

———. "Putting the *Te* back into Taoism." In *Nature in Asian Traditions of*

Thought: Essays in Environmental Philosophy, ed. J. Baird Callicott and Roger T. Ames, 113–144. SUNY Series in Philosophy and Biology. Albany, 1989.

———. "Thinking through Comparisons: Analytical and Narrative Methods for Cultural Understanding." In Shankman and Durrant, 93–110.

Aristotle (384–322 B.C.). *Rhetoric.* Trans. John Henry Freese. Loeb Classical Library 193. Cambridge, Mass.: Harvard University Press, 1926.

———. *Politics.* Trans. H. Rackham. Loeb Classical Library 264. Cambridge, Mass.: Harvard University Press, 1944.

Asano Yūichi 淺野裕一. *Kō-Rō dō no seiritsu to tenkai* 黃老道の成立と展開. Tōyōgaku sōsho 40. Tokyo: Sōbunsha, 1992.

Astington, Janet Wilde. *The Child's Discovery of the Mind.* The Developing Child. Cambridge, Mass.: Harvard University Press, 1993.

Ayscough, Florence (1878–1942). *Chinese Women: Yesterday and To-Day.* Cambridge, Mass: Riverside, 1937.

Balazs, Etienne. *Chinese Civilization and Bureaucracy: Variations on a Theme.* Trans. H. M. Wright. Ed. Arthur F. Wright. New Haven: Yale University Press, 1964.

Baoshan Chujian 包山楚簡. Beijing: Wenwu, 1991.

Baron-Cohen, S., et al., eds. *Understanding Other Minds: Perspectives from Autism.* Oxford: Oxford University Press, 1993.

Bauer, Wolfgang. *Der chinesische Personenname: Die Bildungsgesetze und hauptsächlichsten Bedeutungsinhalte von Ming, Tzu und Hsiao-Ming.* Asiatische Forschungen 4. Wiesbaden: Otto Harrassowitz, 1959.

Baxter, William H. *A Handbook of Old Chinese Phonology.* Trends in Linguistics: Studies and Monographs 64. Berlin and New York: Mouton de Gruyter, 1992.

Baxter, William H., and Laurent Sagart. "Word Formation in Old Chinese." In *New Approaches to Chinese Word Formation: Morphology, Phonology, and the Lexicon in Modern and Ancient Chinese,* ed. Jerome L. Packard, 35–76. Trends in Linguistics: Studies and Monographs 105. Berlin and New York: Mouton de Gruyter, 1998.

Bentham, Jeremy (1748–1832). *Bentham's Handbook of Political Fallacies.* Ed. Harold A. Larrabee. Baltimore: Johns Hopkins University Press, 1952.

Berlin, Isaiah. *The Proper Study of Mankind: An Anthology of Essays.* Ed. Henry Hardy and Roger Hausheer. New York: Farrar, Straus and Giroux, 1998.

Biersack, Aletta. "Local Knowledge, Local History: Geertz and Beyond." In *The New Cultural History,* ed. Lynn Hunt, 72–96. Studies on the History of Society and Culture. Berkeley: University of California Press, 1989.

Birrell, Anne. *Chinese Mythology: An Introduction.* Baltimore and London: Johns Hopkins University Press, 1993.

Blakney, R. B., trans. *The Way of Life: Lao Tzu.* New York: New American Library, 1955.

Blinn, Sharon B., and Mary Garrett. "Aristotelian *Topoi* as a Cross-Cultural Analytical Tool." *Philosophy and Rhetoric* 26 (1993): 93–112.

Bodde, Derk. *China's First Unifier: A Study of the Ch'in Dynasty as Seen in the Life of Li Ssu* 李斯 *280?–208 B.C.* Sinica Leidensia 3. Leiden: E. J. Brill, 1938.

———. *Statesman, Patriot, and General in Ancient China: Three* Shih-chi *Biographies of the Ch'in Dynasty (255–206 B.C.).* American Oriental Series 17. New Haven, Conn.: American Oriental Society, 1940.

———. *Tolstoy and China.* History of Ideas Series 4. Princeton: Princeton University Press, 1950.

———. *Essays on Chinese Civilization.* Ed. Charles Le Blanc and Dorothy Borei. Princeton: Princeton University Press, 1981.

———. "The State and Empire of Ch'in." In *The Cambridge History of China,* vol. 1: *The Ch'in and Han Empires,* ed. Denis Twitchett and Michael Loewe, 20–102. Cambridge: Cambridge University Press, 1986.

Bodde, Derk, and Clarence Morris. *Law in Imperial China.* Harvard: Harvard University Press, 1967.

Bonner, S. F. *Roman Declamation in the Late Republic and Early Empire.* Berkeley and Los Angeles: University of California Press, 1949.

Boodberg, Peter A. *Selected Works of Peter A. Boodberg.* Ed. Alvin P. Cohen. Berkeley: University of California Press, 1979.

Bradbury, Steve. "The American Conquest of Philosophical Taoism." In *Translation East and West: A Cross-Cultural Approach,* ed. Cornelia N. Moore and Lucy Lower, 29–41. Literary Studies: East and West 5. Honolulu: College of Language, Linguistics and Literature, University of Hawai'i, 1992.

Brooks, E. Bruce. "The Present State and Future Prospects of Pre-Hàn Text Studies." *Sino-Platonic Papers* 46 (1994).

Buxbaum, David C., and Frederick W. Mote, eds. *Transition and Permanence: Chinese History and Culture.* Hong Kong: Cathay, 1972.

Bynner, Witter. *The Chinese Translations.* The Works of Witter Bynner. New York: Farrar, Straus, Giroux, 1978.

———. *Selected Letters.* Ed. James Kraft. The Works of Witter Bynner. New York: Farrar, Straus, Giroux, 1981.

Cahill, Suzanne. *Transcendence and Divine Passion: The Queen Mother of the West in Medieval China.* Stanford: Stanford University Press, 1993.

Cai, Zong-qi. *Configurations of Comparative Poetics: Three Perspectives on Western and Chinese Literary Criticism.* Honolulu: University of Hawai'i Press, 2002.

Capra, Fritjof. *The Tao of Physics: An Exploration of the Parallels between Modern Physics and Eastern Mysticism.* 3d edition. Boston: Shambhala, 1991.

Carus, Paul, and D. T. Suzuki, trans. *The Canon of Reason and Virtue (Lao-tze's Tao Te King).* La Salle, Ill.: Open Court, 1913.

Chan, Alan K. L. "The *Daode jing* and Its Tradition." In *Daoism Handbook,* ed. Livia Kohn, 1–29. Handbuch der Orientalistik 4.14. Leiden: Brill, 2000.

Chan, S. Y. "Disputes on the One Thread of *Chung-Shu.*" *Journal of Chinese Philosophy* 26.2 (1999): 165–186.

Chan, Wing-tsit. "Chinese and Western Interpretations of *Jen* (Humanity)." *Journal of Chinese Philosophy* 2.2 (1975): 107–129.

———, trans. *The Way of Lao Tzu (Tao-te ching).* Library of Liberal Arts. Upper Saddle River, N.J.: Prentice Hall, 1963.

Chang, Kwang-chih [Zhang Guangzhi]. *Early Chinese Civilization: Anthropological Perspectives.* Harvard-Yenching Institute Monograph Series 23. Cambridge, Mass., and London, 1976.

———. "*T'ien kan:* A Key to the History of the Shang." In Roy and Tsien, 13–42.

Chen Anren 陳安仁. *Zhongguo zhengzhi sixiang shi* 中國政治思想史. 2d edition. Taipei: Shangwu, 1966.

Chen Dongyuan 陳東原. *Zhongguo funü shenghuo shi* 中國婦女生活史. Zhongguo wenhuashi congshu. Beijing: Shangwu, 1937; rpt., 1998.

Chen Fubin 陳福濱 et al., eds. *Ben shiji chutu sixiang wenxian yu Zhongguo gudian zhexue yanjiu lunwenji* 本世紀出土思想文獻與中國古典哲學研究論文集. 2 vols. Taipei: Furen Daxue, 1999.

Chen Guangyu 陳光宇. "Shangwang Pangeng miaohao xinjie" 商王盤庚廟號新解. *Journal of Chinese Linguistics* 29.2 (2001): 340–349.

Chen Guying 陳鼓應. "*Taiyi sheng shui* yu *Xing zi ming chu* fawei" 《太一生水》與《性自命出》發微. *Daojia wenhua yanjiu* 道家文化研究 17 (1999): 393–411.

Chen Guyuan 陳顧遠. *Zhongguo hunyin shi* 中國婚姻史. Shanghai: Shangwu, 1937.

Chen Lai 陳來. "Jingmen zhujian zhi *Xing zi ming chu* pian chutan" 荊門竹簡之《性自命出》篇初探. In *Guodian Chujian yanjiu,* 293–314.

Chen Ligui 陳麗桂. "Shi jiu jinben *Wenzi* yu *Huainanzi* de bu chongxi neirong tuice guben *Wenzi* de jige sixiang lunti" 試就今本《文子》與《淮南子》的不重襲內容推測古本《文子》的幾個思想論題. *Daojia wenhua yanjiu* 18 (2000): 200–231.

———. "*Xingqing lun* shuo 'dao'" 《性情論》說"道". In Zhu Yuanqing and Liao Mingchun, 140–151.

Chen Mengjia 陳夢家. "'Feng' 'yao' shiming—Fulun Guofeng wei fengyao" 「風」「謠」釋名—附論國風為風謠. *Geyao* 歌謠 3.12 (1937): 4–6.

Chen, Ning 陳寧. "The Problem of Theodicy in Ancient China." *Journal of Chinese Religions* 22 (1994): 51–74.

———. "*Guodian Chumu zhujian* zhong de rujia renxing yanlun chutan" 《郭店楚墓竹簡》中的儒家人性言論初探. *Zhongguo zhexueshi* 中國哲學史 1998.4: 39–46.

———. "The Ideological Background of the Mencian Discussion of Human Nature: A Reexamination." In *Mencius: Contexts and Interpretations,* ed. Alan K. L. Chan, 17–41. Honolulu: University of Hawai'i Press, 2002.

Chen Qitian 陳啟天. *Zhongguo fajia gailun* 中國法家概論. Taipei: Zhonghua, 1970.

Chen Qiyou 陳奇猷. "Han Fei yu Laozi" 韓非與老子. *Daojia wenhua yanjiu* 6 (1995): 183–191.

Chen, Shih-Hsiang. "The *Shih-ching:* Its Generic Significance in Chinese Literary History and Poetics." In *Studies in Chinese Literary Genres,* ed. Cyril Birch, 8–41. Berkeley: University of California Press, 1974.

Chen Wei 陳偉. *Baoshan Chujian chutan* 包山楚簡初探. Wuhan: Wuhan Daxue, 1996.

———. "Guodian Chujian bieshi" 郭店楚簡別釋. *Jiang-Han kaogu* 江漢考古 1998.4: 67–72.

Chen Xinxiong 陳新雄 and Yu Dacheng 于大成, eds. *Huainanzi lunwenji* 淮南子論文集. Guoxue lunwen huibian. Taipei: Muyi, 1976.

Chen, Yu-shih. "The Historical Template of Pan Chao's *Nü Chieh.*" *T'oung Pao* 82.4–5 (1996): 229–257.

Cheng, Anne. *Histoire de la pensée chinoise.* Paris: du Seuil, 1997.

Cheng Yuanmin 程元敏. "*Liji* 'Zhongyong,' 'Fangji,' 'Ziyi' fei chu yu *Zisizi* kao" 《禮記・中庸、坊記、緇衣》非出於《子思子》考. In *Zhang Yiren xiansheng qizhi shouqing lunwenji,* 1:1–47.

Cheung Kwong-yue 張光裕. *Guodian Chujian yanjiu* 郭店楚簡研究. Taipei: Yee Wen, 1999–.

Chin, Ann-Ping. Review of Stephen Mitchell. *The New Republic* 200.1 (January 2, 1989): 38–40.

Chong, Kim-Chong. "Mengzi and Gaozi on *Nei* and *Wai.*" In *Mencius: Contexts and Interpretations,* ed. Alan K. L. Chan, 103–125. Honolulu: University of Hawai'i Press, 2002.

Chow, Tse-tsung [Zhou Cezong]. "Early History of the Chinese Word *Shih* (Poetry)." In Chow, *Wen-lin,* 1:151–209.

———. "A New Theory on the Origins of Mohism." In Chow, *Wen-lin,* 2:123–151.

———. ed. *Wen-lin: Studies in the Chinese Humanities.* 2 vols. Madison: University of Wisconsin Press, 1968–1989.

Ch'ü, T'ung-tsu. *Han Social Structure.* Ed. Jack L. Dull. Han Dynasty China 1. Seattle and London: University of Washington Press, 1972.

Cicero (106–43 B.C.). *De inventione. De optimo genere oratorum. Topica.* Trans. H. M. Hubbell. Loeb Classical Library 386. Cambridge, Mass.: Harvard University Press, 1949.

Cikoski, John S. "Three Essays on Classical Chinese Grammar." *Computational Analyses of Asian and African Languages* 8 (1978): 17–152; 9 (1978): 77–208.

Clark, Donald Lemen. *Rhetoric in Greco-Roman Education.* New York: Columbia University Press, 1957.

Clarke, J. J. *The Tao of the West: Western Transformations of Taoist Thought.* London and New York: Routledge, 2000.

Coblin, W. South. *A Handbook of Eastern Han Sound Glosses.* Hong Kong: Chinese University Press, 1983.

Cole, Thomas. *The Origins of Rhetoric in Ancient Greece.* Baltimore: Johns Hopkins University Press, 1991.

Collingwood, R. G. *The Idea of History.* Ed. Jan van der Dussen. Revised edition. Oxford and New York: Oxford University Press, 1994.

Cook, Scott. "*Yue Ji* 樂記—Record of Music: Introduction, Translation, Notes, and Commentary." *Asian Music* 26.2 (1995): 1–96.

———. "Xun Zi on Ritual and Music." *Monumenta Serica* 45 (1997): 1–38.

———. "Cong lijiao yu xingfa zhi bian kan xian-Qin zhuzi de quanshi chuantong" 從禮教與刑罰之辯看先秦諸子之詮釋傳統. *Wenshizhe xuebao* 文史哲學報 53 (2000): 1–32.

———. "Consummate Artistry and Moral Virtuosity: The 'Wu xing' 五行 Essay and Its Aesthetic." *Chinese Literature: Essays, Articles, Reviews* 22 (2000): 113–146.

———. "The *Lüshi chunqiu* and the Resolution of Philosophical Dissonance." *Harvard Journal of Asiatic Studies* 62.2 (2002): 307–345.

Copi, Irving M. *Introduction to Logic.* 4th edition. New York: Macmillan, 1972.

Couvreur, S., S. J. *Li Ki ou Mémoires sur les bienséances et les cérémonies.* 2d edition. 2 vols. Ho Kien Fou: Mission Catholique, 1913.

Creel, Herrlee G. *Confucius and the Chinese Way.* 1949; rpt., New York: Harper, 1960.

———. *The Origins of Statecraft in China.* Chicago and London: University of Chicago Press, 1970.

———. *What Is Taoism? and Other Studies in Chinese Cultural History.* Midway Reprint. Chicago and London: University of Chicago Press, 1970.

———. *Shen Pu-hai: A Chinese Political Philosopher of the Fourth Century B.C.* Chicago and London: University of Chicago Press, 1974.

———. "Discussion of Professor Fingarette on Confucius." In Rosemont and Schwartz, 407–415.

Crump, James I., Jr. "The *Chan-kuo Ts'e* and Its Fiction," *T'oung Pao* 47.4–5 (1960): 305–375.

———. *Intrigues: Studies of the Chan-kuo Ts'e.* Ann Arbor: University of Michigan Press, 1964.

———, trans. *Chan-kuo Ts'e.* Revised edition. Michigan Monographs in Chinese Studies 77. Ann Arbor, 1996.

———. *Legends of the Warring States: Persuasions, Romances, and Stories from the* Chan-kuo Ts'e. Michigan Monographs in Chinese Studies 83. Ann Arbor, 1999.

Csikszentmihalyi, Mark. "Traditional Taxonomies and Revealed Texts in the Han." In *Daoist Identity: History, Lineage, and Ritual,* ed. Livia Kohn and Harold D. Roth, 81–101. Honolulu: University of Hawai'i Press, 2002.

Csikszentmihalyi, Mark, and Philip J. Ivanhoe, eds. *Religious and Philosophical Aspects of the* Laozi. SUNY Series in Chinese Philosophy and Culture. Albany, 1999.

Cui Renyi 崔仁義. "Shilun Jingmen zhujian *Laozi* de niandai" 試論荊門竹簡《老子》的年代. *Jingmen Daxue xuebao* 荊門大學學報 1997.2: 38–42.

Curtius, Ernst Robert. *European Literature and the Latin Middle Ages.* Trans. Willard Trask. Bollingen Series 36. New York, 1953.

Dai Junren 戴君仁. *Dai Jingshan xiansheng quanji* 戴靜山先生全集. 3 vols. Taipei: N.p., 1980.

Dai Zhen 戴震 (1724–1777). *Mengzi ziyi shuzheng* 孟子字義疏證. Ed. He Wenguang 何文光. 2d edition. Beijing: Zhonghua, 1982.

Darnton, Robert. *The Great Cat Massacre and Other Episodes in French Cultural History.* New York: Basic Books, 1999.

Dawson, Raymond, trans. *Sima Qian: Historical Records.* World's Classics. Oxford: Oxford University Press, 1994.

Defoort, Carine. "Is There Such a Thing as Chinese Philosophy? Arguments of an Implicit Debate." *Philosophy East and West* 51.3 (2001): 393–413.

DeWoskin, Kenneth J. *A Song for One or Two: Music and the Concept of Art in Early China.* Michigan Papers in Chinese Studies 42. Ann Arbor, 1982.

———. "Early Chinese Music and the Origins of Aesthetic Terminology." In *Theories of the Arts in China,* ed. Susan Bush and Christian Murck, 187–214. Princeton: Princeton University Press, 1983.

Di Cosmo, Nicola. *Ancient China and Its Enemies: The Rise of Nomadic Power in East Asian History.* Cambridge: Cambridge University Press, 2002.

Di erjie Shijing guoji xueshu yantaohui lunwenji 第二屆詩經國際學術研討會論文集. Beijing: Yuwen, 1996.

Di sijie Shijing guoji xueshu yantaohui lunwenji 第四屆詩經國際學術研討會論文集. Xueyuan xueshu luntan. Beijing: Xueyuan, 2000.

Diény, Jean-Pierre. *Aux origines de la poésie classique en Chine: Étude sur la poésie lyrique à l'époque des Han.* T'oung Pao Monographie 6. Leiden: E. J. Brill, 1968.

Ding Sixin 丁四新. "*Xing zi ming chu* yu Gongsun Nizi de guanxi" 《性自命出》與公孫尼子的關係. *Wuhan Daxue xuebao (Zheshe ban)* 武漢大學學報(哲社版) 1999.5: 38–41.

Ding Yuanzhi 丁原植. Huainanzi *yu* Wenzi *kaobian*《淮南子》與《文子》考辨. Taipei: Wanjuanlou, 1999.

Djamouri, Redouane. "Théorie de la 'rectification des dénominations' et réflexion linguistique chez Xunzi." *Le juste nom. Extrême-Orient Extrême-Occident* 15 (1993): 55–74.

Dong Zhian 董治安. *Xian-Qin wenxian yu xian-Qin wenxue* 先秦文獻與先秦文學. Ji'nan: Qi-Lu, 1994.

———. "*Lüshi chunqiu* zhi lun Shi yin Shi yu Zhanguo moqi Shixue de fazhan" 《呂氏春秋》之論詩引詩與戰國末期詩學的發展. *Wenshizhe* 文史哲 1996.2: 39–45.

Du Guoxiang 杜國庠. *Xian-Qin zhuzi de ruogan yanjiu* 先秦諸子的若干研究. Hong Kong: Jindai, 1958.

Du Yongming 杜永明 et al. *Hei Ershisi shi* 黑二十四史. 6 vols. Beijing: Zhongguo Huaqiao, 1998.

Dubs, Homer H. "An Ancient Chinese Mystery Cult." *Harvard Theological Review* 35 (1942): 221–240.

Duda, Kristopher. "Reconsidering Mo Tzu on the Foundations of Morality." *Asian Philosophy* 11.1 (2001): 23–31.

Dull, Jack L. "Marriage and Divorce in Han China: A Glimpse at 'Pre-Confucian' Society." In *Chinese Family Law and Social Change in Historical and Comparative Perspective,* ed. David C. Buxbaum, 23–74. Asian Law Series 3. Seattle: University of Washington, 1978.

Durrant, Stephen W. "Packaging the *Tao.*" *Rocky Mountain Review of Language and Literature* 45.1–2 (1991): 75–84.

———. "Ssu-ma Ch'ien's Portrayal of the First Ch'in Emperor." In *Imperial Rulership and Cultural Change in Traditional China,* ed. Frederick P. Brandauer and Chun-chieh Huang, 28–50. Seattle and London: University of Washington Press, 1994.

———. *The Cloudy Mirror: Tension and Conflict in the Writings of Sima Qian.* SUNY Series in Chinese Philosophy and Culture. Albany, 1995.

———. "Creating Tradition: Sima Qian Agonistes?" In Shankman and Durrant, 283–298.

Duyvendak, J. J. L. *The Book of Lord Shang: A Classic of the Chinese School of Law.* Probsthain's Oriental Series 17. London, 1928.

Dzo Ching-chuan. *Sseu-ma Ts'ien et l'historiographie chinoise.* Paris: Publications Orientalistes de France, 1978.

Emmrich, Thomas. *Tabu und Meidung im antiken China: Aspekte des Verpönten.* Münstersche sinologische Mitteilungen: Beiträge zur Geschichte und Kultur des alten China 2. Bad Honnef, Germany: Bock und Herchen, 1992.

Englert, Siegfried. *Materialien zur Stellung der Frau und zur Sexualität im vormodernen und modernen China.* Heidelberger Schriften zur Ostasienkunde 1. Frankfurt: Haag und Herchen, 1980.

Eno, Robert. *The Confucian Creation of Heaven: Philosophy and the Defense of Ritual Mastery*. SUNY Series in Chinese Philosophy and Culture. Albany, 1990.

Enoki, Kazuo. "Confucian Women in Theory and in Reality." In *La donna nella Cina imperiale e nella Cina repubblicana*, ed. Lionello Lanciotti, 1–22. Civiltà Veneziana: Studi 36. Florence: Leo S. Olschki, 1980.

Eoyang, Eugene. Review of Stephen Mitchell. *Journal of Religion* 70.3 (1990): 492–493.

Fan Shuyun 樊樹雲. "Cong da wenhua shijiao bian 'Guofeng' zhi 'feng'" 從大文化視角辨《國風》之"風". *Di erjie Shijing guoji xueshu yantaohui lunwenji*, 650–656.

Fang, Achilles. "Fenollosa and Pound." *Harvard Journal of Asiatic Studies* 20 (1957): 213–238.

Fang Shouchu 方授楚. *Moxue yuanliu* 墨學源流. Shanghai: Zhonghua, 1937.

Fields, Lanny B. "Hsia Wu-chü: Physician to the First Ch'in Emperor." *Journal of Asian History* 28.2 (1994): 97–107.

Fingarette, Herbert. "Following the 'One Thread' of the *Analects*." In Rosemont and Schwartz, 373–405.

Fleischacker, Samuel. *A Third Concept of Liberty: Judgment and Freedom in Kant and Adam Smith*. Princeton: Princeton University Press, 1999.

Forke, Alfred. *Geschichte der alten chinesischen Philosophie*. Universität Hamburg: Abhandlungen aus dem Gebiet der Auslandskunde 25; Reihe B., Völkerkunde, Kulturgeschichte und Sprachen 14. Hamburg: Friederichsen, 1927.

———. *Geschichte der mittelalterlichen chinesischen Philosophie*. Hamburgische Universität: Abhandlungen aus dem Gebiet der Auslandskunde 41; Reihe B: Völkerkunde, Kulturgeschichte und Sprachen 21. Hamburg: Friederichsen, de Gruyter and Co., 1934.

———, trans. *Lun-heng*. 2 vols. 1907; rpt., New York: Paragon, 1962.

Fracasso, Riccardo. "Holy Mothers of Ancient China: A New Approach to the Hsi-Wang-Mu Problem." *T'oung Pao* 74.1–3 (1988): 1–46.

Fricker, Ute. *Schein und Wirklichkeit: Zur altchinesischen Frauenideologie aus männlicher und weiblicher Sicht im geschichtlichen Wandel*. MOAG Mitteilungen der Gesellschaft für Natur- und Völkerkunde Ostasiens 112. Hamburg, 1988.

Friedman, Edward. "Symbols of Southern Identity: Rivaling Unitary Nationalism." In *China Off Center: Mapping the Margins of the Middle Kingdom*, ed. Susan D. Blum and Lionel M. Jensen, 31–44. Honolulu: University of Hawai'i Press, 2002.

Frühauf, Manfred W. *Die königliche Mutter des Westens: Xiwangmu in alten Dokumenten Chinas*. Edition Cathay 46. Bochum: Projekt, 1999.

Fu Wuguang 傅武光. *Zhongguo sixiangshi lunji* 中國思想史論集. Wen shi zhe daxi 29. Taipei: Wenjin, 1990.

Fukui hakushi shōju kinen Tōyō bunka ronshū 福井博士頌壽紀念東洋文化論集. Tokyo: Waseda University Press, 1969.

Fung, Yu-lan. *A History of Chinese Philosophy*. Trans. Derk Bodde. 2d edition. 2 vols. Princeton: Princeton University Press, 1952–1953.

Gao Boyuan 高柏園. *Han Fei zhexue yanjiu* 韓非哲學研究. Wenshizhe daxi 82. Taipei: Wenjin, 1994.

Garrett, Mary M. "*Pathos* Reconsidered from the Perspective of Classical Chinese Rhetorical Theories." *Quarterly Journal of Speech* 79 (1993): 19–39.

Gauthier, David. *Morals by Agreement*. Oxford: Oxford University Press, 1986.

Geaney, Jane. "Mencius's Hermeneutics." *Journal of Chinese Philosophy* 27.1 (2000): 93–100.

———. *On the Epistemology of the Senses in Early Chinese Thought*. Society for Asian and Comparative Philosophy Monograph Series 19. Honolulu: University of Hawai'i Press, 2002.

Geertz, Clifford. *The Interpretation of Cultures*. New York: Basic Books, 1973.

———. *Local Knowledge: Further Essays in Interpretive Anthropology*. New York: Basic Books, 1983.

———. *Available Light: Anthropological Reflections on Philosophical Topics*. Princeton and Oxford: Princeton University Press, 2000.

———. "The Visit." *New York Review of Books* 48.16 (2001): 27–30.

Gibbs, Donald A. "Notes on the Wind: The Term 'Feng' in Chinese Literary Criticism." In Buxbaum and Mote, 285–293.

Gibson, Roger F., Jr. "Translation, Physics, and Facts of the Matter." In *The Philosophy of W. V. Quine,* ed. Lewis Edwin Hahn and Paul Arthur Schilpp, 139–154. The Library of Living Philosophers 18. La Salle, Ill.: Open Court, 1986.

Giele, Enno. "Early Chinese Manuscripts: Including Addenda and Corrigenda to *New Sources of Early Chinese History: An Introduction to the Reading of Inscriptions and Manuscripts*." *Early China* 23–24 (1998–1999): 247–337.

Giles, Herbert A. *A History of Chinese Literature*. New York: Grove, 1923.

Goldin, Paul Rakita. "Reflections on Irrationalism in Chinese Aesthetics." *Monumenta Serica* 44 (1996): 167–189.

———. *Rituals of the Way: The Philosophy of Xunzi*. Chicago and La Salle, Ill.: Open Court, 1999.

———. Review of John Knoblock and Jeffrey Riegel, trans., *The Annals of Lü Buwei: A Complete Translation and Study*. *Early Medieval China* 7 (2001): 109–139.

———. *The Culture of Sex in Ancient China*. Honolulu: University of Hawai'i Press, 2002.

———. "A Mind-Body Problem in the *Zhuangzi?*" In *Hiding the World in the World: Uneven Discourses on the* Zhuangzi, ed. Scott Cook, 226–247. SUNY Series in Chinese Philosophy and Culture. Albany, 2003.

Grafflin, Dennis. "The Onomastics of Medieval South China: Patterned Naming in the Lang-yeh and T'ai-yüan Wang." *Journal of the American Oriental Society* 103.2 (1983): 383–398.

Graham, A. C. *Later Mohist Logic, Ethics and Science.* London: School of Oriental and African Studies, University of London, 1978.

———. *Studies in Chinese Philosophy and Philosophical Literature.* SUNY Series in Chinese Philosophy and Culture. Singapore: Institute of East Asian Philosophies, 1986; rpt., Albany, 1990.

———. *Disputers of the Tao: Philosophical Argument in Ancient China.* La Salle, Ill.: Open Court, 1989.

———. "Two Notes on the Translation of Taoist Classics." In *Interpreting Culture through Translation: A Festschrift for D. C. Lau,* ed. Roger T. Ames et al., 119–144. Hong Kong: Chinese University Press, 1991.

Granet, Marcel (1884–1940). *Fêtes et chansons anciennes de la Chine.* Paris: Ernest Leroux, 1919; rpt., Paris: Albin Michel, 1982.

———. *La pensée chinoise.* Bibliothèque de "L'Évolution de l'Humanité." Paris: La Renaissance du Livre, 1934; rpt., Paris: Albin Michel, 1999.

———. *Études sociologiques sur la Chine.* 2d edition. Collection Dito. Paris: Presses Universitaires de France, 1990.

———. *Danses et légendes de la Chine ancienne.* Ed. Rémi Mathieu. 3d edition. Orientales. Paris: Presses Universitaires de France, 1994.

Grube, G. M. A. *The Greek and Roman Critics.* Toronto: University of Toronto Press, 1968; rpt., Indianapolis and Cambridge, Mass.: Hackett, 1995.

Gu Fang 谷方. *Han Fei yu Zhongguo wenhua* 韓非與中國文化. Da sixiangjia yu Zhongguo wenhua congshu. Guiyang: Guizhou renmin, 1996.

Gu Jiegang 顧頡剛 (1893–1980). "*Shijing* zai Chunqiu Zhanguo jian de diwei" 詩經在春秋戰國間的地位. In Gu Jiegang, ed., 3:345–352.

———. "Ye you si jun" 野有死麇. In Gu Jiegang, ed., 3:439–443.

———. "Wude zhongshi shuo xia de zhengzhi he lishi" 五德終始說下的政治和歷史. In Gu Jiegang, ed., 5:404–617.

———. *Gu Jiegang gushi lunwenji* 顧頡剛古史論文集. 3 vols. Beijing: Zhonghua, 1988.

———, ed. *Gushi bian* 古史辨. 7 vols. Rpt., Shanghai: Guji, 1982.

Gu Jiegang and Tong Shuye 童書業. "Mozi xingshi bian" 墨子姓氏辨. *Guoli Beiping Yanjiuyuan shixue jikan* 國立北平研究院史學集刊 2 (1936): 151–178.

van Gulik, R. H. *Sexual Life in Ancient China: A Preliminary Survey of Chinese Sex and Society from ca. 1500 B.C. till 1644 A.D.* Ed. Paul R. Goldin. Sinica Leidensia 57. Leiden: Brill, 2003.

Guo Lihua 郭梨華. "Jianbo *Wuxing* de liyue kaoshu" 簡、帛《五行》的禮樂考述. In Chen Fubin et al., 2:511–547.

Guo Moruo 郭沫若. *Shi pipan shu* 十批判書. Minguo xueshu jingdian wenku 2. [1945]; Beijing: Dongfang, 1996.

———. *Qingtong shidai* 青銅時代. Beijing: Kexue, 1957.

Guo Qiyong 郭齊勇. "Guodian rujia jian de yiyi yu jiazhi" 郭店儒家簡的意義與價值. *Hubei Daxue xuebao (Zhexue shehui kexue ban)* 湖北大學學報(哲學社會科學版) 1999.2: 4–6.

———. "Chutu jianbo yu jingxue quanshi de fanshi wenti" 出土簡帛與經學詮釋的范式問題. *Fujian luntan* 福建論壇 2001.5: 22–30.

Guo Shaoyu 郭紹虞. *Zhongguo wenxue piping shi* 中國文學批評史. Shanghai: Guji, 1979.

Guo Yi 郭沂. *Guodian zhujian yu xian-Qin xueshu sixiang* 郭店竹簡與先秦學術思想. Shanghai: Jiaoyu, 2001.

Guodian Chujian guoji xueshu yantaohui lunwenji 郭店楚簡國際學術研討會論文集. Renwen luncong. Wuhan: Hubei Renmin, 2000.

Guodian Chujian yanjiu 郭店楚簡研究. *Zhongguo zhexue* 中國哲學 20 (1999).

Guodian Chumu zhujian 郭店楚墓竹簡. Beijing: Wenwu, 1998.

Guodian jian yu ruxue yanjiu 郭店簡與儒學研究. *Zhongguo zhexue* 21 (2000).

Hadley, Alice Ormaggio. *Teaching Language in Context.* 3d edition. Boston: Heinle and Heinle, 2001.

Hall, David L., and Roger T. Ames. *Thinking through Confucius.* SUNY Series in Systematic Philosophy. Albany, 1987.

Handlin, Joanna F. "Lü K'un's New Audience: The Influence of Women's Literacy on Sixteenth-Century Thought." In *Women in Chinese Society,* ed. Margery Wolf and Roxane Witke, 13–38. Stanford: Stanford University Press, 1975.

Haneda hakushi shōju kinen tōyōshi ronsō 羽田博士頌壽紀念東洋史論叢. Kyoto: Tōyōshi Kenkyūkai, 1950.

Hansen, Chad. *A Daoist Theory of Chinese Thought: A Philosophical Interpretation.* New York and Oxford: Oxford University Press, 1992.

———. "Qing (Emotions) 情 in Pre-Buddhist Chinese Thought." In *Emotions in Asian Thought: A Dialogue in Comparative Philosophy,* ed. Joel Marks and Roger T. Ames, 181–211. Albany: State University of New York Press, 1995.

Harbsmeier, Christoph. "Conceptions of Knowledge in Ancient China." In *Epistemological Issues in Classical Chinese Philosophy,* ed. Hans Lenk and Gregor Paul, 11–30. SUNY Series in Chinese Philosophy and Culture. Albany, 1993.

———. "Eroticism in Early Chinese Poetry: Sundry Comparative Notes." In *Das andere China: Festschrift für Wolfgang Bauer zum 65. Geburtstag,* ed. Helwig Schmidt-Glintzer, 323–380. Wolfenbütteler Forschungen 62. Wiesbaden: Harrassowitz, 1995.

———. *Language and Logic.* Ed. Kenneth Robinson. In Needham et al., 7.1. 1998.

Hardy, Julia M. "Influential Western Interpretations of the *Tao-te-ching.*" In Kohn and LaFargue, 165–188.

Hart, H. L. A. *The Concept of Law.* Clarendon Law Series. Oxford, 1961.

Hart, James. "The Discussion of the *Wu-yi* Bells in the *Kuo-yü.*" *Monumenta Serica* 29 (1970–1971): 391–418.

Hatton, Russell. "Chinese Philosophy or Chinese 'Philosophy'? Linguistic Analysis and the Chinese Philosophical Tradition, Again." *Journal of Chinese Philosophy* 14.4 (1987): 445–473.

Hawkes, David. Review of Crump, *Intrigues. Journal of the American Oriental Society* 86.1 (1966): 62–63.

He Jin 何晉. *Zhanguo ce yanjiu* 戰國策研究. Guoxue yanjiu congkan 14. Beijing: Beijing Daxue, 2001.

He Zhonghua 何中華 et al. "'Zhongguo youwu zhexue' wenti bitan" "中國有無哲學"問題筆談. *Shandong shehui kexue* 山東社會科學 2002.4: 60–71.

Henricks, Robert G., trans. *Lao-tzu Te-Tao Ching.* Classics of Ancient China. New York: Ballantine, 1989.

———. *Lao Tzu's Tao Te Ching: A Translation of the Startling New Documents Found at Guodian.* Translations from the Asian Classics. New York: Columbia, 2000.

Herman, Jonathan R. Review of Ursula K. Le Guin. *Journal of the American Academy of Religion* 66.3 (1998): 686–689.

———. "Daoist Environmentalism in the West: Ursula K. Le Guin's Reception and Transmission of Daoism." In *Daoism and Ecology: Ways within a Cosmic Landscape,* ed. N. J. Girardot et al., 391–406. Religions of the World and Ecology. Cambridge, Mass.: Harvard University Center for the Study of World Religions, 2001.

Hightower, James Robert. "The *Han-shih wai-chuan* and the *San chia shih.*" *Harvard Journal of Asiatic Studies* 11.3–4 (1948): 241–310.

Hinsch, Bret. "Women, Kinship, and Property as Seen in a Han Dynasty Will." *T'oung Pao* 84.1–3 (1998): 1–20.

———. *Women in Early Imperial China.* Asian Voices. Lanham, Md.: Rowman and Littlefield, 2002.

Hinton, David. Review of Stephen Mitchell. *The Nation* 248.25 (June 26, 1989): 893–895.

Hobsbawm, Eric. "Introduction: Inventing Traditions." In *The Invention of Tradition,* ed. Eric Hobsbawm and Terence Ranger, 1–14. Cambridge: Cambridge University Press, 1983.

Holcombe, Charles. *In the Shadow of the Han: Literati Thought and Society at the Beginning of the Southern Dynasties.* Honolulu: University of Hawai'i Press, 1994.

Holoch, Donald. "Melancholy Phoenix: Self Ascending from the Ashes of History (From *Shiji* to *Rulin Waishi*)." In *Symbols of Anguish: In Search of Melancholy in*

China, ed. Wolfgang Kubin, 169–212. Schweizer asiatische Studien: Monographien 38. Bern: Peter Lang, 2001.

Holzman, Donald. "Confucius and Ancient Chinese Literary Criticism." In *Chinese Approaches to Literature from Confucius to Liang Ch'i-ch'ao,* ed. Adele Austin Rickett, 21–41. Princeton: Princeton University Press, 1978.

Honda Wataru 本田濟. *Tōyō shisō kenkyū* 東洋思想研究. Tōyōgaku sōsho 30. Tokyo: Sōbunsha, 1987.

Howard, Jeffrey A. "Concepts of Comprehensiveness and Historical Change in the *Huai-nan-tzu.*" In *Explorations in Chinese Cosmology: Papers Presented at the Workshop on Classical Chinese Thought Held at Harvard University August 1976,* ed. Henry Rosemont, Jr., 119–131. *Journal of the American Academy of Religion* Thematic Series 50.2. Chico, Calif.: Scholars Press, 1984.

Hsiao, Kung-chuan. "Legalism and Autocracy in Traditional China." In *Shang Yang's Reforms and State Control in China,* ed. Li Yu-ning, 125–143. China Book Project: Translation and Commentary. White Plains, N.Y.: M. E. Sharpe, 1977.

———. *A History of Chinese Political Thought,* vol. 1: *From the Beginnings to the Sixth Century* A.D. Trans. F. W. Mote. Princeton Library of Asian Translations. Princeton, 1979.

Hsu, Cho-yun. *Ancient China in Transition: An Analysis of Social Mobility, 722–222* B.C. Stanford Studies in the Civilizations of Eastern Asia. Stanford, 1965.

Hu Jiacong 胡家聰. "Lun rujia Xun Kuang sixiang yu daojia zhexue de guanxi" 論儒家荀況思想與道家哲學的關係. *Daojia wenhua yanjiu* 6 (1995): 175–182.

Hu Shi 胡適 (1891–1962). "Tantan *Shijing*" 談談詩經. In Gu Jiegang, ed., 3:576–587.

———. *Hu Shi wencun* 胡適文存. 4 vols. Taipei: Yuandong, 1953.

———. *Zhongguo zhonggu sixiangshi changbian* 中國中古思想史長編. Ershi shiji guoxue congshu. Shanghai: Huadong Shifan Daxue, 1996.

Huang, Chun-chieh [Huang Junjie]. *Mencian Hermeneutics: A History of Interpretations in China.* New Brunswick, N.J., and London: Transaction, 2001.

Huang Junjie 黃俊傑 [Chun-chieh Huang]. *Mengxue sixiangshi lun* 孟學思想史論. 2 vols. Canghai congkan. Taipei: Dongda, 1991; Taipei: Academia Sinica, 1997.

Hubei Sheng Jingmen Shi Bowuguan 湖北省荊門市博物館. "Jingmen Guodian yihao Chumu" 荊門郭店一號楚墓. *Wenwu* 文物 1997.7: 35–48.

Hucker, Charles O. *A Dictionary of Official Titles in Imperial China.* Stanford: Stanford University Press, 1985.

Hughes, E. R., trans. *The Great Learning and The Mean-in-Action.* New York: E. P. Dutton, 1943.

Hulsewé, A. F. P. "The Ch'in Documents Discovered in Hupei in 1975." *T'oung Pao* 64 (1978): 175–217.

———. "Watching the Vapors: An Ancient Chinese Technique of Prognostication." *Nachrichten der Gesellschaft für Natur- und Völkerkunde Ostasiens* 125 (1979): 40–49.

———. "The Legalists and the Laws of Ch'in." In *Leyden Studies in Sinology,* ed. W. L. Idema, 1–22. Sinica Leidensia 15. Leiden: E. J. Brill, 1981.

———. "The Influence of the Legalist Government of Qin on the Economy as Reflected in the Texts Discovered in Yunmeng County." In *The Scope of State Power in State Power in China,* ed. S. R. Schram, 211–235. New York: St. Martin's, 1985.

———. *Remnants of Ch'in Law: An Annotated Translation of the Ch'in Legal and Administrative Rules of the 3rd Century B.C. Discovered in Yün-meng Prefecture, Hu-pei Province, in 1975.* Sinica Leidensia 17. Leiden: E. J. Brill, 1985.

———. "Qin and Han Legal Manuscripts." In Shaughnessy, 193–221.

Ikeda Tomohisa 池田知久. *Baōtai Kambo hakusho Gogyō-hen kenkyū* 馬王堆漢墓帛書五行篇研究. Tokyo: Kuko, 1993.

Itano Chōhachi 板野長八. *Chūgoku kodai shakai shisōshi no kenkyū* 中國古代社會思想史の研究. Tokyo: Kembunsha, 2000.

Ivanhoe, Philip J. "Reweaving the 'One Thread' in the *Analects.*" *Philosophy East and West* 40.1 (1990): 17–33.

———. "Thinking and Learning in Early Confucianism." *Journal of Chinese Philosophy* 17.4 (1990): 473–494.

———. "A Happy Symmetry: Xunzi's Ethical Thought." *Journal of the American Academy of Religion* 59.2 (1991): 309–322.

———. "The Concept of *de* ('Virtue') in the *Laozi.*" In Csikszentmihalyi and Ivanhoe, 239–257.

———, trans. *The Daodejing of Laozi.* New York and London: Seven Bridges, 2002.

Jäger, F. "Die Biographie des Wu Tzu-hsü." *Oriens Extremus* 7 (1960): 1–16.

Jakobson, Roman. *On Language.* Ed. Linda R. Waugh and Monique Monville-Burston. Cambridge, Mass., and London: Harvard University Press, 1990.

James, Jean M. "An Iconographic Study of Xiwangmu during the Han Dynasty." *Artibus Asiae* 55.1–2 (1995): 17–41.

Jensen, Lionel M. "The Genesis of Kongzi in Ancient Narrative: The Figurative as Historical." In *On Sacred Grounds: Culture, Society, Politics, and the Formation of the Cult of Confucius,* ed. Thomas A. Wilson, 175–221. Harvard East Asian Monographs 217. Cambridge, Mass., and London, 2002.

Jiang Guanghui 姜廣輝. "Guodian Chujian yu *Zisizi*—Jian tan Guodian Chujian de sixiangshi yiyi" 郭店楚簡與《子思子》—兼談郭店楚簡的思想史意義. In *Guodian Chujian yanjiu,* 81–92.

———. "Guodian Chujian yu yuandian ruxue" 郭店楚簡與原典儒學. In *Guodian jian yu ruxue yanjiu,* 263–273.

———. "Guodian Chujian yu zaoqi daojia" 郭店楚簡與早期道家. In *Guodian jian yu ruxue yanjiu,* 274–280.

Jiang Rongchang 蔣榮昌. "Zhongguo wenhua de gongsi guan" 中國文化的公私觀. *Xinan Minzu Xueyuan xuebao: Zheshe ban* 西南民族學院學報：哲社版 1998.4: 1–17.

Jiang, Yimin. *"Große Musik is tonlos": Eine historische Darstellung der frühen philosophisch-daoistischen Musikästhetik.* Europäische Hochschulschriften 36.135. Frankfurt: Peter Lang, 1995.

Jin Chunfeng 金春峰. *Handai sixiang shi* 漢代思想史. 2d edition. Sheke xueshu wenku. Beijing: Zhongguo Shehui Kexue Chubanshe, 1997.

Jin Dejian 金德建. "*Shizi* zuozhe yu *Erya*"《尸子》作者與《爾雅》. In Gu Jiegang, ed., 6:306–313.

Johnson, David. "The Wu Tzu-hsü *pien-wen* and Its Sources." *Harvard Journal of Asiatic Studies* 40.1 (1980): 93–156; 40.2 (1980): 465–505.

———. "Epic and History in Early China: The Matter of Wu Tzu-hsu." *Journal of Asian Studies* 40.2 (1981): 255–271.

Juvenal and Persius. Trans. G. G. Ramsay. Loeb Classical Library 91. Cambridge, Mass.: Harvard University Press, 1979.

Kamata Tadashi 鎌田正. *Saden no seiritsu to sono tenkai* 左傳の成立と其の展開. Tokyo: Taishūkan, 1963.

Kamenarović, Ivan P., trans. *Xun Zi (Siun Tseu) introduit et traduit du chinois.* Patrimoines: Confucianisme. Paris: du Cerf, 1987.

———. *Wang Fu: Propos d'un ermite.* Patrimoines: Confucianisme. Paris: du Cerf, 1992.

Kanaya Osamu 金谷治. *Rō-Sō teki sekai:* Enanji *no shisō* 老莊的世界：《淮南子》の思想. Saara sōsho 11. Tokyo: Heirakuji, 1959.

———. *Shin-Kan shisōshi kenkyū* 秦漢思想史研究. 2d edition. Tokyo: Heirakuji, 1992.

———. *Kanaya Osamu Chūgoku shisō ronshū* 金谷治中國思想論集. 3 vols. Tokyo: Hirakawa, 1997.

Kandel, Barbara. "Der Versuch einer politischen Restauration—Liu An von Huainan." *Nachrichten der Gesellschaft für Natur- und Völkerkunde Ostasiens* 113 (1973): 33–96.

———. *Wen Tzu—ein Beitrag zur Problematik und zum Verständnis eines taoistischen Textes.* Würzburger Sino-Japonica 1. Bern: Herbert Lang, 1974.

Kant, Immanuel (1724–1804). *Gesammelte Schriften.* Ed. Preußische Akademie der Wissenschaften, Deutsche Akademie der Wissenschaften zu Berlin, Akademie der Wissenschaften zu Göttingen. 29 vols. projected. Berlin: Georg Reimer, Walter de Gruyter, 1902–.

———. *Political Writings.* Trans. H. B. Nisbet. Ed. Hans Reiss. 2d edition.

Cambridge Texts in the History of Political Thought. Cambridge: Cambridge University Press, 1991.

Karlgren, Bernhard. "Some Fecundity Symbols in Ancient China." *Bulletin of the Museum of Far Eastern Antiquities* 2 (1930): 1–65.

———. "Legends and Cults in Ancient China." *Bulletin of the Museum of Far Eastern Antiquities* 18 (1946): 199–365.

———. *Glosses on the Book of Odes.* Stockholm: Museum of Far Eastern Antiquities, 1964.

———. "Loan Characters in Pre-Han Texts II." *Bulletin of the Museum of Far Eastern Antiquities* 36 (1964): 1–105.

———, trans. *The Book of Odes: Chinese Text, Transcription and Translation.* Stockholm: Museum of Far Eastern Antiquities, 1950.

Keane, John. "More Theses on the Philosophy of History." In *Meaning and Context: Quentin Skinner and His Critics,* ed. James Tully, 204–217. Princeton: Princeton University Press, 1988.

Keightley, David N. *The Ancestral Landscape: Time, Space, and Community in Late Shang China (ca. 1200–1045 B.C.).* China Research Monograph 53. Berkeley: Institute of East Asian Studies, 2000.

Kennedy, George A. (1901–1960). *Selected Works of George A. Kennedy.* Ed. Tien-yi Li. New Haven: Far Eastern Publications, 1964.

Kennedy, George A. (1928–). *A New History of Classical Rhetoric.* Princeton: Princeton University Press, 1994.

———. *Comparative Rhetoric: An Historical and Cross-Cultural Introduction.* Oxford and New York: Oxford University Press, 1998.

Kenner, Hugh. *The Pound Era.* Berkeley and Los Angeles: University of California Press, 1971.

Kern, Martin. "*Shi jing* Songs as Performance Texts: A Case Study of 'Chu Ci' ('Thorny Caltrop')." *Early China* 25 (2000): 49–111.

———. *The Stele Inscriptions of Ch'in Shih-huang: Text and Ritual in Early Chinese Imperial Representation.* American Oriental Series 85. New Haven, Conn.: American Oriental Society, 2000.

Knechtges, David R. "Wit, Humor, and Satire in Early Chinese Literature (to A.D. 220)." *Monumenta Serica* 29 (1970–1971): 79–98.

———. "Riddles as Poetry: The '*Fu*-Chapter' of the *Hsün-tzu.*" In Chow, *Wen-lin,* 2:1–31, 1989.

———. *Court Culture and Literature in Early China.* Variorum Collected Studies Series CS740. Aldershot, U.K., and Burlington, Vt.: Ashgate, 2002.

———, trans. *Wen xuan or Selections of Refined Literature.* Princeton Library of Asian Translations. Princeton, 1982–.

Knoblock, John, trans. *Xunzi: A Translation and Study of the Complete Works.* 3 vols. Stanford: Stanford University Press, 1988–1994.

Knoblock, John, and Jeffrey Riegel, trans. *The Annals of Lü Buwei: A Complete Translation and Study.* Stanford: Stanford University Press, 2000.

Knorringa, H. *Emporos: Data on Trade and Trader in Greek Literature from Homer to Aristotle.* Amsterdam, 1926; rpt., Chicago: Ares, 1987.

Kodama Rokurō 兒玉六郎. *Junshi no shisō—Shizen, shusai no ryō tendōkan to seiboku-setsu* 荀子の思想—自然・主宰の兩天道觀と性朴說. Tokyo: Kazama, 1992.

———. "Junshi jinseiron no shūhen" 荀子・人性論の週邊. In *Kurihara Keisuke hakushi shōju kinen tōyōgaku ronshū* 栗原圭介博士頌壽記念東洋學論集, 193–219. Tokyo: Kyūko, 1997.

Kohn, Livia, and Michael LaFargue, eds. *Lao-tzu and the Tao-te-ching.* SUNY Series in Chinese Philosophy and Culture. Albany, 1998.

Kraus, Christina Shuttleworth, ed. *The Limits of Historiography: Genre and Narrative in Ancient Historical Texts.* Mnemosyne Supplement 191. Leiden: Brill, 1999.

Kroll, J. L. "Disputation in Ancient Chinese Culture." *Early China* 11–12 (1985–1987): 118–145.

Kudō Motoo 工藤元男. "Suikochi Shinkan *Nissho* ni okeru byōinron to kishin no kankei ni tsuite" 睡虎地秦簡《日書》における病因論と鬼神の關係について. *Tōhōgaku* 東方學 88 (1994): 33–53.

Kurihara Keisuke 栗原圭介. *Chūgoku kodai gakuron no kenkyū* 中國古代樂論の研究. Tokyo: Daitō Bunka Daigaku Tōyō Kenkyūjo, 1978.

Kurita Naomi 栗田直躬. "'Kō' to 'shi'" "公"と"私". In *Fukui hakushi shōju kinen Tōyō bunka ronshū,* 371–389.

Kuriyama, Shigehisa. "The Imagination of Winds and the Development of the Chinese Conception of the Body." In *Body, Subject and Power in China,* ed. Angela Zito and Tani E. Barlow, 23–41. Chicago: University of Chicago Press, 1994.

———. *The Expressiveness of the Body and the Divergence of Greek and Chinese Medicine.* New York: Zone, 2002.

Kusuyama Haruki 楠山春樹. "*Enanji* yori mitaru *Sōshi* no seiritsu" 《淮南子》より見たる《莊子》の成立. *Firosofia* フイロソフイア 41 (1961): 41–68.

LaFargue, Michael. "Recovering the *Tao-te-ching*'s Original Meaning: Some Remarks on Historical Hermeneutics." In Kohn and LaFargue, 255–275.

LaFargue, Michael, and Julian Pas. "On Translating the *Tao-te-ching.*" In Kohn and LaFargue, 277–301.

Laloy, Louis. "Hoaī-nân tzè et la musique." *T'oung Pao* 15 (1914): 501–530.

Lao Kan. "The Early Use of the Tally in China." In Roy and Tsien, 91–98.

Latourette, Kenneth Scott. *The Chinese: Their History and Culture.* 2 vols. New York: Macmillan, 1934.

Lattimore, David. "Introduction to *The Way of Life According to Lao Tzu.*" In Bynner, *Chinese Translations,* 309–327.

Lau, D. C. "Taoist Metaphysics in the *Chieh Lao* 解老 and Plato's Theory of Forms." In Chow, *Wen-lin,* 2:101–121.

———, trans. *Lao Tzu: Tao Te Ching.* New York: Penguin, 1963.

———. *Mencius.* New York: Penguin, 1970.

———. *Confucius: The Analects.* New York: Penguin, 1979.

Lau, D. C., and Roger T. Ames, trans. *Sun Pin: The Art of Warfare.* Classics of Ancient China. New York: Ballantine, 1996.

Le Blanc, Charles. *Huai-nan Tzu: Philosophical Synthesis in Early Han Thought.* Hong Kong: Hong Kong University Press, 1985.

———. "From Ontology to Cosmogony: Notes on *Chuang Tzu* and *Huai-nan Tzu.*" In Le Blanc and Blader, 117–129.

———. *Le Wen zi à la lumière de l'histoire et de l'archéologie.* Sociétés et cultures de l'Asie. Montreal: Presses de l'Université de Montréal, 2000.

Le Blanc, Charles, and Susan Blader, eds. *Chinese Ideas about Nature and Society: Studies in Honour of Derk Bodde.* Hong Kong: Hong Kong University Press, 1987.

Le Guin, Ursula K., trans. *Lao Tzu Tao Te Ching: A Book about the Way and the Power of the Way.* Boston and London: Shambhala, 1997.

Lee, Lily Xiao Hong. *The Virtue of Yin: Studies on Chinese Women.* Sydney: Wild Peony, 1994.

Legge, James (1815–1897). *The Chinese Classics.* 5 vols. in 4. N.d.; rpt., Taipei: SMC, 1991.

Lévi, Jean. *Les fonctionnaires divins: Politique, despotisme et mystique en Chine ancienne.* La Libraire du XXe siècle. Paris: du Seuil, 1989.

———. "Quelques aspects de la rectification des noms dans la pensée et la pratique politiques de la Chine ancienne." *Le juste nom. Extrême-Orient Extrême-Occident* 15 (1993): 23–54.

———. "Quelques examples de détournement subversif de la citation dans la littérature classique chinoise." *Le travail de la citation en Chine et au Japon. Extrême-Orient Extrême-Occident* 17 (1995): 41–65.

———. "Sima Qian, Han Wudi et l'éternité." In *Hommage à Kwong Hing Foon: Études d'histoire culturelle de la Chine,* ed. Jean-Pierre Diény, 43–75. Bibliothèque de l'Institut des Hautes Études Chinoises 30. Paris, 1995.

———. "Langue, rite et écriture." In Alleton, *Paroles à dire,* 157–182.

———. *Confucius.* Chemins d'Éternité. Paris: Pygmalion/Gérard Watelet, 2002.

———, trans. *Han-Fei-tse ou Le Tao du Prince: La stratégie de la domination absolue.* Points: Sagesses 141. Paris: du Seuil, 1999.

Lewis, Mark Edward. *Sanctioned Violence in Early China.* SUNY Series in Chinese Philosophy and Culture. Albany, 1990.

———. "Warring States: Political History." In *The Cambridge History of Ancient China: From the Origins of Civilization to 221 B.C.,* ed. Michael Loewe and Edward L. Shaughnessy, 587–650. Cambridge: Cambridge University Press, 1999.

———. *Writing and Authority in Early China.* SUNY Series in Chinese Philosophy and Culture. Albany, 1999.

Li, Boqian. "A Brief Account of the Origins and Development of Chu Culture." In Allan and Williams, 9–21.

Li, Chenyang. *The Tao Encounters the West: Explorations in Comparative Philosophy.* SUNY Series in Chinese Philosophy and Culture. Albany, 1999.

Li Deyong 李德永. "Daojia lilun siwei dui Xunzi zhexue tixi de yingxiang" 道家理論思維對荀子哲學體系的影響. *Daojia wenhua yanjiu* 1 (1992): 249–264.

Li Fang 李昉 (925–996) et al. *Taiping yulan* 太平御覽. *Sibu congkan.*

Li Jiashu 李家樹. *Chuantong yiwai de Shijing xue* 傳統以外的詩經學. Hong Kong: Hong Kong University Press, 1994.

Li Jing 栗勁. *Qinlü tonglun* 秦律通論. Faxue congshu 29. Ji'nan: Shandong Renmin, 1985.

Li Jinglin 李景林. "Xifang huayu baquan xia Zhongguo zhexue xueke hefaxing zhi fansi" 西方話語霸權下中國哲學學科合法性之反思. *Xuexi yu tansuo* 學習與探索 2003.2: 20–26.

Li Ling 李零. "Guodian Chujian yanjiu zhong de liangge wenti—Meiguo Damusi Xueyuan Guodian Chujian *Laozi* guoji xueshu taolunhui ganxiang" 郭店楚簡研究中的兩個問題—美國達慕思學院郭店楚簡《老子》國際學術討論會感想. In *Guodian Chujian guoji xueshu yantaohui lunwenji,* 47–52.

———. "Cong jianbo faxian kan gushu de tili he fenlei" 從簡帛發現看古書的體例和分類. *Zhongguo dianji yu wenhua* 中國典籍與文化 2001.1: 25–34.

———. *Guodian Chujian jiaodu ji* 郭店楚簡校讀記. Beijing: Beijing Daxue, 2002.

Li Rui 李銳. "Rujia shiyue sixiang chutan" 儒家詩樂思想初探. *Zhongguo zhexueshi* 2002.1: 20–26.

Li, Wai-yee. "The Idea of Authority in the *Shi ji* (*Records of the Historian*)." *Harvard Journal of Asiatic Studies* 54.2 (1994): 345–405.

———. "Knowledge and Skepticism in Ancient Chinese Historiography." In Kraus, 27–54.

Li Weiwu 李維武. "*Liude* de zhexue yiyun chutan"《六德》的哲學意蘊初探. *Zhongguo zhexueshi* 2001.3: 64–67.

Li Xueqin 李學勤. "Cong jianbo yiji *Wuxing* tandao 'Daxue'" 從簡帛佚籍《五行》談到《大學》. *Kongzi yanjiu* 孔子研究 1998.3: 47–51.

———. *Li Xueqin juan* 李學勤卷. Dangdai xuezhe zixuan wenku. Hefei: Anhui Jiaoyu, 1998.

———. "Guodian jian yu *Yueji*" 郭店簡與《樂記》. In *Zhongguo zhexue de quanshi yu fazhan,* 23–29.

———. "Jingmen Guodian Chujian zhong de *Zisizi*" 荊門郭店楚簡中的《子思子》. In *Guodian Chujian yanjiu,* 75–80.

———. "Xian-Qin rujia zhuzuo de zhongda faxian" 先秦儒家著作的重大發現. In *Guodian Chujian yanjiu,* 13–17.

———. "The Confucian Texts from Guodian Tomb Number One: Their Date and Significance." In Allan and Williams, 107–111.

———. "Arrangement of Bamboo Slips in *Cheng Zhi Wen Zhi* and *Xing Zi Ming Chu.*" In Allan and Williams, 240.

———. "Chudu Liye Qinjian" 初讀里耶秦簡. *Wenwu* 2003.1: 73–81.

Li Yinghua 李英華. "Xunzi tianren lun de jige wenti: Jianlun Guodian zhujian *Qiongda yi shi*" 荀子天人論的幾個問題：兼論郭店竹簡《窮達以時》. *Hainan Daxue xuebao: Renwen sheke ban* 海南大學學報：人文社科版 2001.2: 13–18.

Li Yu 李漁 (1611–1680?). *Jou Pu Tuan: The Prayer Mat of Flesh.* Trans. Richard Martin from the German version by Franz Kuhn. New York: Grove, 1967.

———. *The Carnal Prayer Mat* [i.e., *Rou putuan* 肉蒲團]. Trans. Patrick Hanan. London: Arrow, 1990.

Li Zehou 李則厚. "Chudu Guodian zhujian yinxiang jiyao" 初讀郭店竹簡印象記要. *Daojia wenhua yanjiu* 17 (1999): 412–422.

Liang Tao 梁濤. "Si-Meng xuepai kaoshu" 思孟學派考述. *Zhongguo zhexueshi* 2002.3: 27–34.

———. "Zhujian *Qiongda yi shi* yu zaoqi rujia tianrenguan" 竹簡《窮達以時》與早期儒家天人觀. *Zhexue yanjiu* 哲學研究 2003.4: 65–70.

Liao Mingchun 廖明春. "Guodian Chujian rujia zhuzuo kao" 郭店楚簡儒家著作考. *Kongzi yanjiu* 1998.3: 69–83.

———. "Jingmen Guodian Chujian yu xian-Qin ruxue" 荊門郭店楚簡與先秦儒學. In *Guodian Chujian yanjiu,* 36–74.

———. "Guodian Chujian yin *Shi* lun *Shi* kao" 郭店楚簡引《詩》論《詩》考. *Jingxue jinquan chubian* 經學今詮初編. *Zhongguo zhexue* 22 (2000): 148–192.

———. *Zhou-Yi jingzhuan yu Yixue shi xinlun* 《周易》經傳與易學史新論. Zhongguo Kongzi jijinhui wenku. Ji'nan: Qi-Lu, 2001.

Liao Qifa 廖其發. *Xian-Qin Liang-Han renxing lun yu jiaoyu sixiang yanjiu* 先秦兩漢人性論與教育思想研究. Chongqing: Chongqing Chubanshe, 1999.

Liao, W. K., trans. *The Complete Works of Han Fei Tzŭ: A Classic of Chinese Legalism.* 2 vols. Probsthain's Oriental Series 25–26. London, 1939–1959.

Lin Congshun 林聰舜. *Xi-Han qianqi sixiang yu fajia de guanxi* 西漢前期思想與法家的關係. Taipei: Da'an, 1991.

Lin Qingzhang 林慶彰. "*Maoshi xu* zai *Shijing* jieshi chuantong de diwei" 《毛詩序》在《詩經》解釋傳統的地位. *Jingxue jinquan xubian* 經學今詮續編. *Zhongguo zhexue* 23 (2001): 92–118.

Lin Yaolin 林耀潾. *Xi-Han sanjia Shixue yanjiu* 西漢三家詩學研究. Rulin xuancui 1. Taipei: Wenjin, 1996.

Liu Guosheng 劉國勝. "Guodian zhujian shizi (baze)" 郭店竹簡釋字(八則). *Wuhan Daxue xuebao (Zheshe ban)* 武漢大學學報(哲社版) 1999.5: 42–44.

Liu Hainian 劉海年. "Qinlü xingfa kaoxi" 秦律刑罰考析. In *Yunmeng Qinjian yanjiu* 雲夢秦簡研究, 171–206. Beijing: Zhonghua, 1981.

Liu, James J. Y. *Language—Paradox—Poetics: A Chinese Perspective.* Ed. Richard John Lynn. Princeton: Princeton University Press, 1988.

Liu Jiyao 劉紀曜. "Gong yu si—Zhong de lunli neihan" 公與私—忠的倫理內涵. In *Tiandao yu rendao* 天道與人道, ed. Huang Junjie, 171–207. 2d edition. Zhongguo wenhua xinlun: Sixiang pian 2. Taipei: Lianjing, 1983.

Liu Lexian 劉樂賢. *Shuihudi Qinjian Rishu yanjiu* 睡虎地秦簡日書研究. Dalu diqu boshi lunwen congkan. Taibei: Wenjin, 1993.

Liu Xiaogan. "Wuwei (Non-action): From *Laozi* to *Huainanzi.*" *Taoist Resources* 3.1 (1991): 41–56.

———. "Naturalness (*Tzu-jan*), the Core Value in Taoism: Its Ancient Meaning and Its Significance Today." In Kohn and LaFargue, 211–228.

Liu Xinfang 劉信芳. *Jianbo Wuxing jiegu* 簡帛五行解詁. Taipei: Yiwen, 2000.

Liu, Zuxin. "An Overview of Tomb Number One at Jingmen Guodian." In Allan and Williams, 23–32.

Lloyd, Geoffrey E. R. *Adversaries and Authorities: Investigations into Ancient Greek and Chinese Science.* Ideas in Context. Cambridge: Cambridge University Press, 1996.

Lloyd, Geoffrey [E. R.], and Nathan Sivin. *The Way and the Word: Science and Medicine in Early China and Greece.* New Haven and London: Yale University Press, 2002.

Loewe, Michael. *Ways to Paradise: The Chinese Quest for Immortality.* London: George Allen and Unwin, 1979.

———. *A Biographical Dictionary of the Qin, Former Han and Xin Periods (221 BC–AD 24).* Handbuch der Orientalistik 4.16. Leiden: Brill, 2000.

Longgang Qinjian 龍崗秦簡. Beijing: Zhonghua, 2001.

Long Yuchun 龍宇純. *Xunzi lunji* 荀子論集. Taipei: Xuesheng, 1987.

Lu Hongsheng 魯洪生. "Guanyu 'Guofeng' shifou min'ge de taolun" 關於《國風》是否民歌的討論. In *Di erjie Shijing guoji xueshu yantaohui lunwenji,* 642–649.

Lu Kanru 陸侃如 and Feng Yuanjun 馮沅君. *Zhongguo shi shi* 中國詩史. 1931; rpt., Ji'nan: Shandong Daxue, 1996.

Lu, Xing. *Rhetoric in Ancient China, Fifth to Third Century B.C.E.: A Comparison with Classical Greek Rhetoric.* Columbia: University of South Carolina Press, 1998.

Lü Simian 呂思勉 (1884–1957). *Jingzi jieti* 經子解題. 1924; rpt., Hong Kong: Taiping, 1963.

———. *Lü Simian dushi zhaji* 呂思勉讀史札記. Shanghai: Guji, 1982.

———. *Lü Simian shuo shi* 呂思勉說史. Mingjia shuo—"Shanggu" xueshu cuibian. Shanghai: Guji, 2000.

Lundahl, Bertil. *Han Fei Zi: The Man and the Work.* Stockholm East Asian Monographs 4. Stockholm: Institute of Oriental Languages, Stockholm University, 1992.

Luo Genze 羅根澤. *Zhuzi kaosuo* 諸子考索. Hong Kong: Xuelin, 1977.

Luo Qikun 雒啟坤. Shijing *sanlun*《詩經》散論. Beijing: Shangwu, 2002.

Luo Xinhui 羅新慧. "Guodian Chujian yu rujia de renyi zhi bian" 郭店楚簡與儒家的仁義之辨. *Qi-Lu xuekan* 齊魯學刊 1999.5: 27–31.

Luo Yunhuan 羅運環. "Guodian Chujian de niandai, yongtu ji yiyi" 郭店楚簡的年代、用途及意義. *Hubei Daxue xuebao (Zhexue shehui kexue ban)* 1999.2: 13.

Ma Chengyuan 馬承源, ed. *Shanghai bowuguan cang Zhanguo Chu zhushu* 上海博物館藏戰國楚竹書. Shanghai: Guji, 2001–.

Ma Feibai 馬非百 [Ma Yuancai 馬元材]. *Qin jishi* 秦集史. 2 vols. Beijing: Zhonghua, 1982.

Ma, Yau-woon. "Confucius as a Literary Critic: A Comparison with the Early Greeks." In *Rao Zongyi jiaoshou nanyou zengbie lunwenji,* 13–45.

Maas, Paul. *Textual Criticism.* Trans. Barbara Flower. Oxford: Clarendon, 1958.

MacCormack, Geoffrey. *The Spirit of Traditional Chinese Law.* The Spirit of the Laws. Athens and London: University of Georgia Press, 1996.

Machida Saburō 町田三郎. *Shin Kan shisōshi no kenkyū* 秦漢思想史の研究. Tōyōgaku sōsho 27. Tokyo: Sōbunsha, 1985.

Mair, Victor H. "Ma Jianzhong and the Invention of Chinese Grammar." In *Studies on the History of Chinese Syntax,* ed. Chaofen Sun, 5–26. Journal of Chinese Linguistics Monograph Series 10. N.p., 1997.

———, trans. *Tao Te Ching: The Classic Book of Integrity and the Way.* New York: Bantam, 1990.

———. *Wandering on the Way: Early Taoist Tales and Parables of Chuang Tzu.* New York: Bantam, 1994.

Major, John S. "The Meaning of *hsing-te.*" In Le Blanc and Blader, 281–291.

———. "Substance, Process, Phase: *Wuxing* 五行 in the *Huainanzi.*" In Rosemont, ed., 67–78.

———. *Heaven and Earth in Early Han Thought: Chapters Three, Four, and Five of the* Huainanzi. SUNY Series in Chinese Philosophy and Culture. Albany, 1993.

———. "Celestial Cycles and Mathematical Harmonics in the *Huainanzi.*" *Sous les nombres, le monde: Matériaux pour l'histoire culturelle du nombre en Chine ancienne. Extrême-Orient Extrême-Occident* 16 (1994): 121–134.

Makeham, John. "The Legalist Concept of *hsing-ming:* An Example of the Contribution of Archaeological Evidence to the Re-Interpretation of Transmitted Texts." *Monumenta Serica* 39 (1990–1991): 87–114.

———. "Between Chen and Cai: *Zhuangzi* and the *Analects.*" In *Wandering at Ease in the Zhuangzi,* ed. Roger T. Ames, 75–100. SUNY Series in Chinese Philosophy and Culture. Albany, 1998.

Martin, François. "L'entrevue de 525 A.C.—Les joutes poético-diplomatiques dans la Chine ancienne." *Asiatische Studien* 46.2 (1992): 581–609.

———. "Le *Shijing,* de la citation à l'allusion: La disponibilité du sens." *Le travail de la citation en Chine et au Japon. Extrême-Orient Extrême-Occident* 17 (1995): 5–39.

———. "Le cas Zichan: Entre légistes et confucianistes." In *En suivant la Voie Royale: Mélanges offerts en hommage à Léon Vandermeersch,* ed. Jacques Gernet and Marc Kalinowski, 69–83. Études thématiques 7. Paris: École Française d'Extrême-Orient, 1997.

———. "La parole poétique." In Alleton, *Paroles à dire,* 51–81.

Martin-Liao, Tienchi. *Frauenerziehung im alten China: Eine Analyse der Frauenbücher.* Chinathemen 22. Bochum: N. Brockmeyer, 1984.

———. "Traditional Handbooks of Women's Education." In *Woman and Literature in China,* ed. Anna Gerstlacher et al., 165–189. Chinathemen 25. Bochum: N. Brockmeyer, 1985.

Maspero, Henri (1883–1945). "Le Roman de Sou Ts'in." *Études Asiatiques* 2 (1925): 127–141.

———. *Mélanges posthumes sur les religions et l'histoire de la Chine.* 3 vols. Publications du Musée Guimet: Bibliothèque de diffusion 57–59. Paris: Civilisations du Sud, 1950.

———. *China in Antiquity.* Trans. Frank A. Kierman, Jr. Amherst: University of Massachusetts Press, 1978.

Mathieu, Rémi, trans. *Le Mu tianzi zhuan: Traduction annotée, étude critique.* Mémoires de l'Institut des Hautes Études Chinoises 9. Paris, 1978.

Mawangdui Hanmu boshu 馬王堆漢墓帛書. Beijing: Wenwu, 1980–.

McDowell, Edwin. "Translation of Ancient Tao Text Brings $130,000." *The New York Times,* February 16, 1988, C18.

McLeod, Katrina C. D., and Robin D. S. Yates. "Forms of Ch'in Law: An Annotated Translation of the *Feng-chen shih.*" *Harvard Journal of Asiatic Studies* 41.1 (1981): 111–163.

Mei, Yi-pao, trans. *The Ethical and Political Works of Motse.* Probsthain's Oriental Series 19. London, 1929.

Meng Xiangcai 孟祥才. *Xian-Qin Qin Han shilun* 先秦秦漢史論. Ji'nan: Shandong Daxue, 2001.

Miao Fenglin 苗楓林. *Zhongguo yongren sixiang shi* 中國用人思想史. Ji'nan: Qi-Lu, 1997.

Miao Wenyuan 繆文遠. *Zhanguo shi xinian jizheng* 戰國史繫年輯證. Chengdu: Ba-Shu, 1997.

Miles, Thomas H., trans. *Tao Te Ching: About the Way of Nature and Its Powers*. Garden City Park, N.Y.: Avery, 1992.

Miller, Tracy G. "Constructing Religion: Song Dynasty Architecture and the Jinci Temple Complex." Ph.D. dissertation, University of Pennsylvania, 2000.

Mitchell, Stephen, trans. *Tao Te Ching: A New English Version*. Perennial Classics. 1988; rpt., New York: Harper Collins, 2000.

Miyamoto Masaru 宮本勝. "*Enanji* 'Shujutsu-kun' no seiji shisō to sono riron kōzō" 《淮南子》「主術訓」の政治思想とその理論構造. *Chūgoku tetsugaku* 中國哲學 4 (1966).

Miyazaki Ichisada 宮崎市定. *Miyazaki Ichisada zenshū* 宮崎市定全集. 25 vols. Tokyo: Iwanami, 1991–1994.

Mizoguchi Yūzō 溝口雄三. *Chūgoku no kō to shi* 中國の公と私. Kembun sensho 62. Tokyo: Kembusha, 1995.

Münke, Wolfgang. *Die klassische chinesische Mythologie*. Stuttgart: Ernst Klett, 1976.

Needham, Joseph, et al., eds. *Science and Civilisation in China*. 7 vols. projected. Cambridge: Cambridge University Press, 1954–.

Nienhauser, William H., Jr. "The Implied Reader and Translation: The *Shih chi* as Example." In *Translating Chinese Literature*, ed. Eugene Eoyang and Lin Yao-fu, 15–40. Bloomington and Indianapolis: Indiana University Press, 1995.

———, ed. *The Grand Scribe's Records*. 9 vols. projected. Bloomington and Indianapolis: Indiana University Press, 1994–.

Niida Noboru 仁井田陞. *Chūgoku hōseishi kenkyū* 中國法制史研究. 4 vols. Tokyo: Tōkyō Daigaku, 1959–1964.

Nivison, David S. *The Ways of Confucianism: Investigations in Chinese Philosophy*. Ed. Bryan W. Van Norden. Chicago and La Salle, Ill.: Open Court, 1996.

———. "The Key to the Chronology of the Three Dynasties: The 'Modern Text' *Bamboo Annals*." *Sino-Platonic Papers* 93 (1999).

Northrop, F. S. C. *The Meeting of East and West*. New York: Macmillan, 1946.

Numajiri Masataka 沼尻正隆. *Ryoshi shunjū no shisōteki kenkyū* 呂氏春秋の思想的研究. Tokyo: Kyūko, 1997.

Nylan, Michael. "Textual Authority in Pre-Han and Han." *Early China* 25 (2000): 205–258.

———. *The Five "Confucian" Classics.* New Haven and London: Yale University Press, 2001.

Ochi Shigeaki 越智重明. *Sengoku Shin Kan shi kenkyū* 戰國秦漢史研究. 2 vols. Fukuoka: Chūgoku Shoten, 1988–1993.

Oliver, Robert T. *Communication and Culture in Ancient India and China.* Syracuse: Syracuse University Press, 1971.

Ōshima Riichi 大島利一. "Shin Nō to nōkasha ryū" 神農と農家者流. In *Haneda hakushi shōju kinen tōyōshi ronsō,* 353–381.

Pang Pu 龐樸. "Chudu Guodian Chujian" 初讀郭店楚簡. *Lishi yanjiu* 歷史研究 1998.4: 5–10.

———. "Kong Meng zhi jian—Guodian Chujian zhong de rujia xinxing shuo" 孔孟之間—郭店楚簡中的儒家心性說. In *Guodian Chujian yanjiu,* 22–35.

———. *Zhubo* Wuxing *pian jiaozhu ji yanjiu* 竹帛《五行》篇校注及研究. Chutu wenxian yizhu yanxi congshu P009. Taipei: Wanjuanlou, 2000.

Paper, Jordan D. *The Fu-tzu: A Post-Han Confucian Text.* Monographies du T'oung Pao 13. Leiden: E. J. Brill, 1987.

Peerenboom, R. P. *Law and Morality in Ancient China: The Silk Manuscripts of Huang-Lao.* SUNY Series in Chinese Philosophy and Culture. Albany, 1993.

Pei Puyan 裴溥言. "Xunzi yu Shijing" 荀子與詩經. *Wenshizhe xuebao* 17 (1968): 151–183.

Peng Hao 彭浩. "Guodian yihao mu de niandai ji xiangguan de wenti" 郭店一號墓的年代及相關的問題." In Chen Fubin et al., 2:357–364.

———. "Guodian yihao mu de niandai yu jianben *Laozi* de jiegou" 郭店一號墓的年代與簡本《老子》的結構. *Daojia wenhua yanjiu* 17 (1999): 13–21.

Peng Lin 彭林. "*Guodian Chumu zhujian Xing zi ming chu* bushi"《郭店楚墓竹簡・性自命出》補釋. In *Guodian Chujian yanjiu,* 315–320.

Peng Wei 彭衛 and Yang Zhenhong 楊振紅. *Zhongguo fengsu tongshi: Qin Han juan* 中國風俗通史：秦漢卷. Shanghai: Wenyi, 2002.

Peng Yushang 彭裕商. "Shifa tanyuan" 謚法探源. *Zhongguo shi yanjiu* 中國史研究 1999.1: 3–11.

Petersen, Jens Østergård. "What's in a Name? On the Sources Concerning Sun Wu." *Asia Major* 5.1 (1992): 1–31.

———. "Which Books *Did* the First Emperor of Ch'in Burn? On the Meaning of *Pai Chia* in Early Chinese Sources." *Monumenta Serica* 43 (1995): 1–52.

Pi Xirui 皮錫瑞 (1850–1908). *Jingxue tonglun* 經學通論. Hong Kong: Zhonghua, 1961.

Picken, Laurence E. R. "The Shapes of the *Shi Jing* Song-Texts and Their Musical Implications." *Musica Asiatica* 1 (1977): 85–109.

Pines, Yuri. "Intellectual Change in the Chunqiu Period: The Reliability of the

Speeches in the *Zuo Zhuan* as Sources of Chunqiu Intellectual History." *Early China* 22 (1997): 77–132.

———. *Foundations of Confucian Thought: Intellectual Life in the Chunqiu Period, 722–453* B.C.E. Honolulu: University of Hawai'i Press, 2002.

———. "Friends or Foes: Changing Concepts of Ruler-Minister Relations and the Notion of Loyalty in Pre-Imperial China." *Monumenta Serica* 50 (2002): 35–74.

Pokora, Timoteus. *Hsin-lun (New Treatise) and Other Writings by Huan T'an*. Michigan Papers in Chinese Studies 20. Ann Arbor, 1974.

———. "Pre-Han Literature." In *Essays on the Sources for Chinese History*, ed. Donald D. Leslie et al., 23–35. Canberra: Australian National University, 1973; rpt., Columbia: University of South Carolina Press, 1975.

Průšek, Jaroslav. "A New Exegesis of Chan-kuo-ts'e." *Archiv Orientální* 34.4 (1966): 587–592.

———. *Chinese History and Literature: Collection of Studies*. Dordrecht, Holland: D. Reidel, 1970.

Pu Zaiyu 樸宰雨. Shiji Hanshu *bijiao yanjiu* 「史記」「漢書」比較研究. Zhongwai xuezhe xueshu congshu. Beijing: Zhongguo Wenxue, 1994.

Puett, Michael J. *The Ambivalence of Creation: Debates Concerning Innovation and Artifice in Early China*. Stanford: Stanford University Press, 2001.

———. *To Become a God: Cosmology, Sacrifice, and Self-Divinization in Early China*. Harvard-Yenching Monograph Series 57. Cambridge, Mass., and London, 2002.

Qian Cunxun 錢存訓 [Tsuen-hsuin Tsien]. *Zhongguo shuji, zhimo ji yinshua shi lunwenji* 中國書籍、紙墨及印刷史論文集. Hong Kong: Chinese University Press, 1992.

Qian Daxin 錢大昕 (1728–1804). *Nian'er shi kaoyi* 廿二史考異. *Shixue congshu* 史學叢書.

Qian Mu 錢穆 (1895–1990). *Mozi* 墨子. Wanyou wenku. Shanghai, 1930.

———. *Xian-Qin zhuzi xinian* 先秦諸子繫年. 2d edition. Canghai congkan. Hong Kong: Hong Kong University Press, 1956; rpt., Taipei: Dongda, 1990.

Qian Zhongshu 錢鍾書. *Guanzhui bian* 管錐編. 2d edition. 3 vols. Beijing: Zhonghua, 1986.

———. *Limited Views: Essays on Ideas and Letters*. Trans. Ronald Egan. Cambridge, Mass., and London: Harvard University Asia Center, 1998.

Qiu Xigui. *Chinese Writing*. Trans. Gilbert L. Mattos and Jerry Norman. Early China Special Monograph Series 4. Berkeley, 2000.

Qu Wanli 屈萬里. "Lun 'Guofeng' fei minjian geyao de benlai mianmu" 論國風非民間歌謠的本來面目. *Gu yuanzhang Hu Shi xiansheng jinian lunwenji* 故院長胡適先生紀念論文集. *Bulletin of the Institute of History and Philology* 34 (1963): 477–504.

Queen, Sarah A. "Inventories of the Past: Rethinking the 'School' Affiliation of the *Huainanzi*." *Asia Major* 14.1 (2001): 1–22.

Quine, Willard Van Orman. *Word and Object*. Cambridge, Mass.: MIT Press, 1960.

———. *Ontological Relativity and Other Essays*. The John Dewey Essays in Philosophy 1. New York: Columbia University Press, 1969.

———. *The Ways of Paradox and Other Essays*. Revised edition. Cambridge, Mass., and London: Harvard University Press, 1976.

———. *Theories and Things*. Cambridge, Mass., and London: Harvard University Press, Belknap Press, 1981.

Quintilian (b. ca. A.D. 35). *The Institutio Oratoria of Quintilian*. Trans. H. E. Butler. 4 vols. Loeb Classical Library. Cambridge, Mass.: Harvard University Press, 1920.

Rainey, Lee. "The Queen Mother of the West: An Ancient Chinese Mother Goddess?" In *Sages and Filial Sons: Mythology and Archaeology in Ancient China*, ed. Julia Ching and R. W. L. Guisso, 81–100. Hong Kong: Chinese University Press, 1991.

Rand, Christopher C. "Chuang Tzu: Text and Substance." In *Chuang-tzu: Composition and Interpretation*, ed. Victor H. Mair. *Journal of Chinese Religions* 11 (1983): 5–58.

Rao Zongyi 饒宗頤. *Zhongguo zongjiao sixiang shi xinye* 中國宗教思想史新頁. Beida xueshu jiangyan congshu 11; Tang Yongtong xueshu jiangzuo 1. Beijing: Beijing Daxue, 2000.

———. "Zhushu *Shixu* xiaojian" 竹書《詩序》小箋. In Zhu Yuanqing and Liao Mingchun, 228–232.

Rao Zongyi jiaoshou nanyou zengbie lunwenji 饒宗頤教授南遊贈別論文集. Hong Kong: N.p., 1970.

Raphals, Lisa. *Knowing Words: Wisdom and Cunning in the Classical Traditions of China and Greece*. Myth and Poetics. Ithaca, N.Y., and London: Cornell University Press, 1992.

Reding, Jean-Paul. *Les fondements philosophiques de la rhétorique chez les sophistes grecs et chez les sophistes chinois*. Bern: Peter Lang, 1985.

Richards, I. A. *Mencius on the Mind: Experiments in Multiple Definition*. London: Routledge and Kegan Paul, 1932.

Riegel, Jeffrey K. "Poetry and the Legend of Confucius's Exile." In *Sinological Studies Dedicated to Edward H. Schafer*, ed. Paul W. Kroll. *Journal of the American Oriental Society* 106.1 (1986): 13–22.

———. "Eros, Introversion, and the Beginnings of *Shijing* Commentary." *Harvard Journal of Asiatic Studies* 57.1 (1997): 143–177.

Rolston, Holmes, III. "Can the East Help the West to Value Nature?" *Philosophy East and West* 37.2 (1987): 172–190.

Rong Zhaozu 容肇祖. *Han Feizi kaozheng* 韓非子考證. Zhongyang Yanjiuyuan Lishi Yuyan Yanjiushuo dankan B.3. 1936; rpt., Taipei: Shangwu, 1992.

Rosemont, Henry, Jr. "On Representing Abstractions in Archaic Chinese." *Philosophy East and West* 24.1 (1974): 71–88.

———, ed. *Chinese Texts and Philosophical Contexts: Essays Dedicated to Angus C. Graham*. Critics and Their Critics 1. La Salle, Ill.: Open Court, 1991.

Rosemont, Henry, Jr., and Benjamin I. Schwartz, eds. *Studies in Classical Chinese Thought. Journal of the American Academy of Religion* 47.3, Thematic Issue S (1979).

Rosthorn, Arthur (1862–1945). *Geschichte Chinas*. Weltgeschichte in gemeinverständlicher Darstellung 10. Stuttgart and Gotha: Friedrich Andreas Perthes, 1923.

Roth, Harold D. "Psychology and Self-Cultivation in Early Taoistic Thought." *Harvard Journal of Asiatic Studies* 51.2 (1991): 599–650.

———. "Who Compiled the *Chuang-tzu*?" In Rosemont, ed., 79–128.

———. *The Textual History of the* Huai-nan-tzu. Monographs of the Association for Asian Studies 46. Ann Arbor, Mich., 1992.

———. "Evidence for Stages of Meditation in Early Taoism." *Bulletin of the School of Oriental and African Studies* 60.2 (1997): 295–314.

———. *Original Tao: Inward Training and the Foundations of Taoist Mysticism*. Translations from the Asian Classics. New York: Columbia University Press, 1999.

Rouzer, Paul F. *Articulated Ladies: Gender and the Male Community in Early Chinese Texts*. Harvard-Yenching Institute Monograph Series 53. Cambridge, Mass., and London, 2001.

Roy, David T., and Tsuen-hsuin Tsien [Qian Cunxun], eds. *Ancient China: Studies in Early Civilization*. Hong Kong: Chinese University Press, 1978.

Ruan Tingzhuo 阮廷焯. "Lun *Huainanzi* yu xian-Qin zhuzi yishu zhi guanxi" 論《淮南子》與先秦諸子佚書之關係. In *Rao Zongyi jiaoshou nanyou zengbie lunwenji*, 67–84.

———. *Xian-Qin zhuzi kaoyi* 先秦諸子考佚. Taipei: Dingwen, 1980.

Rubin, V. A. "Tzu-ch'an and the City-State of Ancient China." *T'oung Pao* 52 (1965): 8–34.

Russell, D. A. *Criticism in Antiquity*. 2d edition. London: Gerald Duckworth, Bristol Classical Press, 1995.

Ryle, Gilbert. *Collected Papers*. 2 vols. London: Hutchinson, 1971.

Sage, Steven F. *Ancient Sichuan and the Unification of China*. SUNY Series in Chinese Local History. Albany, 1992.

Sahleen, Joel, trans. "Han Feizi." In *Readings in Classical Chinese Philosophy*, ed. Philip J. Ivanhoe and Bryan W. Van Norden, 295–344. New York and London: Seven Bridges, 2001.

Sato, Masayuki. *The Confucian Quest for Order: The Origin and Formation of the Political Thought of Xun Zi*. Sinica Leidensia 58. Leiden: Brill, 2003.

Saussy, Haun. *The Problem of a Chinese Aesthetic*. Meridian: Crossing Aesthetics. Stanford: Stanford University Press, 1993.

———. *Great Walls of Discourse and Other Adventures in Cultural China*. Harvard East Asian Monographs 212. Cambridge, Mass., and London, 2001.

Sawada Takio 澤田多喜男. "Sen-Shin ni okeru kōshi no kannen" 先秦たおける公私の觀念. *Tōkai Daigaku kiyō bungakubu* 東海大學紀要文學部 25 (1976): 1–8.

———. "*Junshi* to *Ryoshi Shunjū* ni okeru ki" 「荀子」と「呂氏春秋」たおける氣. In *Ki no shisō—Chūgoku ni okeru shizenkan to ningenkan no tenkai* 氣の思想—中國たおける自然觀と人間觀の展開, ed. Onozawa Seiichi 小野澤精一 et al., 81–100. Tokyo: Tōkyō Daigaku, 1978.

Sawyer, Ralph D., trans. *Sun Pin: Military Methods of the Art of War*. New York: Barnes and Noble, 1998.

Scarpari, Maurizio. "Gaozi, Xunzi e i capitoli 6A1–5 del *Mengzi*." In *Studi in onore di Lionello Lanciotti*, ed. S. M. Carletti et al., 3:1275–1294. Instituto Universitario Orientale, Dipartimento di Studi Asiatici, Series minor 51. Naples, 1996.

———. "Riscrivere la storia e la cultura della Cina antica: Credenze religiose, correnti di pensiero e società alla luce delle recenti scoperte archeologiche." In *Conoscere la Cina*, ed. Lionello Lanciotti, 113–126. Contributi di ricerca. Torino: Fondazione Giovanni Agnelli, 2000.

———. *Studi sul Mengzi*. Venice: Cafoscarina, 2002.

Schaberg, David. "Social Pleasures in Early Chinese Historiography and Philosophy." In Kraus, 1–26.

———. *A Patterned Past: Form and Thought in Early Chinese Historiography*. Harvard East Asian Monographs 205. Cambridge, Mass., and London, 2001.

Schafer, Edward H. "Ritual Exposure in Ancient China." *Harvard Journal of Asiatic Studies* 14.1–2 (1951): 130–184.

Schipper, Kristofer. "Chiens de paille et tigres en papier: Une pratique rituelle et ses gloses au cours de la tradition chinoise." *Une civilisation sans théologie? Extrême-Orient Extrême-Occident* 6 (1985): 83–94.

———. "Taoism: The Story of the Way." In *Taoism and the Arts of China*, ed. Stephen Little, 33–55. Chicago: Art Institute of Chicago, 2000.

Schmölz, Andrea. *Vom Lied in der Gemeinschaft zum Liedzitat im Text: Liedzitate in den Texten der Gelehrtentradition der späten Chou-Zeit*. Deutsche Hochschulschriften 489. Egelsbach, Germany: Hänsel-Hohenhausen, 1993.

Schweitzer, Albert. *Geschichte des chinesischen Denkens*. Ed. Bernard Kaempf and Johann Zürcher. Albert Schweitzer: Werke aus dem Nachlaß. Munich: C. H. Beck, 2002.

Sellmann, James D. *Timing and Rulership in* Master Lü's Spring and Autumn Annals (Lüshi chunqiu). SUNY Series in Chinese Philosophy and Culture. Albany, 2002.

Seneca the Elder (54 B.C.–A.D. 39?). *The Elder Seneca Declamations.* Trans. M. Winterbottom. 2 vols. Loeb Classical Library 463–464. Cambridge, Mass.: Harvard University Press, 1974.

Shankman, Steven, and Stephen W. Durrant, eds. *Early China/Ancient Greece: Thinking through Comparisons.* SUNY Series in Chinese Philosophy and Culture. Albany, 2002.

Shaughnessy, Edward L. *Before Confucius: Studies in the Creation of the Chinese Classics.* SUNY Series in Chinese Philosophy and Culture. Albany, 1997.

———, ed. *New Sources of Early Chinese History: An Introduction to the Reading of Inscriptions and Manuscripts.* Early China Special Monograph Series 3. Berkeley: Institute of East Asian Studies, University of California, 1997.

———, trans. *I Ching: The Classic of Changes.* Classics of Ancient China. New York: Ballantine, 1996.

Sheng Yi 盛義. *Zhongguo hunsu wenhua* 中國婚俗文化. Yu neiwai minsuxue congkan. Shanghai: Wenyi, 1994.

Shifman, A. I. *Lev Tolstoi i vostok.* 2d edition. Moscow: Nauka, 1971.

Shuihudi Qinmu zhujian 睡虎地秦墓竹簡. Beijing: Wenwu, 1990.

Shun, Kwong-loi. *Mencius and Early Chinese Thought.* Stanford: Stanford University Press, 1997.

Sima Guang 司馬光 (1019–1086). *Zizhi tongjian* 資治通鑑. 10 vols. Beijing: Guji, 1957.

Sivin, Nathan. *Traditional Medicine in Contemporary China.* Science, Medicine, and Technology in East Asia 2. Ann Arbor: Center for Chinese Studies, University of Michigan, 1987.

———. "Text and Experience in Classical Chinese Medicine." In *Knowledge and the Scholarly Medical Traditions,* ed. Don Bates, 177–204. Cambridge: Cambridge University Press, 1995.

Skinner, Quentin. *Visions of Politics.* 3 vols. Cambridge: Cambridge University Press, 2002.

Slingerland, Edward. *Effortless Action: Wu-wei as Conceptual Metaphor and Spiritual Ideal in Early China.* Oxford: Oxford University Press, 2003.

Smith, Kidder. "Sima Tan and the Invention of Daoism, 'Legalism,' *et cetera.*" *Journal of Asian Studies* 62.1 (2003): 129–156.

Soles, David E. "Mo Tzu and the Foundations of Morality." *Journal of Chinese Philosophy* 26.1 (1999): 37–48.

Spade, Beatrice. "The Education of Women in China during the Southern Dynasties." *Journal of Asian History* 13.1 (1979): 15–41.

Spence, Jonathan D. *The Chan's Great Continent: China in Western Minds.* New York and London: W. W. Norton, 1998.

Stalnaker, Aaron. "Aspects of Xunzi's Engagement with Early Daoism." *Philosophy East and West* 53.1 (2003): 87–129.

Star, Jonathan. *Tao Te Ching: The Definitive Edition.* New York: Jeremy P. Tarcher, 2001.

Sterckx, Roel. *The Animal and the Daemon in Early China.* SUNY Series in Chinese Philosophy and Culture. Albany, 2002.

Strassberg, Richard E., trans. *A Chinese Bestiary: Strange Creatures from the Guideways through Mountains and Seas.* Berkeley: University of California Press, 2002.

Su Xuelin 蘇雪林. *Shijing zazu* 詩經雜俎. Taipei: Shangwu, 1995.

Sun Bin Bingfa 孫臏兵法. Beijing: Wenwu, 1975.

Svarverud, Rune. *Methods of the Way: Early Chinese Ethical Thought.* Sinica Leidensia 42. Leiden: Brill, 1998.

Swann, Nancy Lee. *Pan Chao: Foremost Woman Scholar of China.* Michigan Classics in Chinese Studies 5. Ann Arbor, 2001.

Taki Ryōichi 瀧遼一. *Chūgoku ongaku saihakken: Shisō hen* 中國音樂再發見：思想篇. Ed. Masuyama Kenji 増山賢治. Taki Ryōichi chosakushū 3; Academic Series New Asia 7. Tokyo: Daiichi, 1992.

Tang Junyi 唐君毅. *Zhongguo zhexue yuanlun: Yuanxing pian* 中國哲學原論：原性篇. Hong Kong: Xinya, 1968.

Tang Yijie. "Emotion in Pre-Qin Ruist Moral Theory: An Explanation of '*Dao* Begins in *Qing*.'" Trans. Brian Bruya and Hai-ming Wen. *Philosophy East and West* 53.2 (2003): 271–281.

Tay, C. N. "On the Interpretation of *Kung* (Duke?) in the *Tso-chuan.*" *Journal of the American Oriental Society* 93.4 (1973): 550–555.

Thiel, P. Jos. "Die Staatsauffassung des Han Fei-tzŭ." *Sinologica* 6 (1961): 171–192 and 225–270.

Thompson, Laurence G. "What Is Taoism? (With Apologies to H. G. Creel)." *Taoist Resources* 4.2 (1993): 9–22.

Thompson, P. M. *The* Shen-tzu *Fragments.* London Oriental Series 29. Oxford: Oxford University Press, 1979.

Thoraval, Joël. "De la philosophie en Chine à la 'Chine' dans la philosophie: Existe-t-il une philosophie chinoise?" *Esprit* 201 (1994): 5–38.

Tian Fengtai 田鳳台. *Lüshi chunqiu tanwei* 呂氏春秋探微. Zhongguo zhexue congkan 12. Taipei: Xuesheng, 1986.

Tjan Tjoe Som. *Po Hu T'ung: The Comprehensive Discussions in the White Tiger Hall.* 2 vols. Sinica Leidensia 6. Leiden: E. J. Brill, 1949–1952.

Tong Shuye 童書業. *Chunqiu Zuozhuan yanjiu* 春秋左傳研究. Shanghai: Renmin, 1980.

Tongs, Alan. "The Philosophical Basis of Geertz's Social Anthropology." *Eastern Anthropologist* 46 (1993): 1–17.

Tseu, Augustinus A. *The Moral Philosophy of Mo-tze.* Taipei: China Printing, 1965.

Tsuda Sōkichi 津田左右吉 (1873–1961). *Tsuda Sōkichi zenshū* 津田左右吉全集. 33 vols. Tokyo: Iwanami, 1963–1966.

Tu, Wei-ming. "The 'Thought of Huang-Lao': A Reflection on the Lao Tzu and Huang Ti Texts in the Silk Manuscripts of Ma-wang-tui." *Journal of Asian Studies* 39 (1979–1980): 95–110.

———. *Centrality and Commonality: An Essay on Confucian Religiousness.* SUNY Series in Chinese Philosophy and Culture. Albany, 1989.

Uchiyama Toshihiko 內山俊彥. *Chūgoku kodai shisōshi ni okeru shizen ninshiki* 中國古代思想史たおける自然認識. Tōyōgaku sōsho 31. Tokyo: Sōbunsha, 1987.

Unger, Ulrich. *Rhetorik des klassischen Chinesisch.* Wiesbaden: Harrassowitz, 1994.

Uno Shigehiko 宇野茂彥. "Enanji no sōgō to sono seigō kanken" 淮南子の總合とその整合管見. *Nagoya Daigaku Bungakubu kenkyū ronshū* 名古屋大學文學部研究論集 105 (1989): 149–159.

Van Norden, Bryan W. "What Should Western Philosophy Learn from Chinese Philosophy?" In *Chinese Language, Thought, and Culture: Nivison and His Critics,* ed. Philip J. Ivanhoe, 224–249. Critics and Their Critics 3. Chicago and La Salle, Ill.: Open Court, 1996.

———. "Method in the Madness of the *Laozi.*" In Csikszentmihalyi and Ivanhoe, 187–210.

———. "Unweaving the 'One Thread' of *Analects* 4:15." In *Confucius and the* Analects: *New Essays,* ed. Bryan W. Van Norden, 216–236. Oxford: Oxford University Press, 2002.

Van Zoeren, Steven. *Poetry and Personality: Reading, Exegesis, and Hermeneutics in Traditional China.* Stanford: Stanford University Press, 1991.

Vandermeersch, Léon. *La formation du légisme: Recherche sur la constitution d'une philosophie politique caractéristique de la Chine ancienne.* Publications de l'École Française d'Extrême-Orient 56. Paris, 1965.

Vankeerberghen, Griet. "Emotions and Actions of the Sage: Recommendations for an Orderly Heart in *Huainanzi.*" *Philosophy East and West* 45.4 (1995): 527–544.

———. *The* Huainanzi *and Liu An's Claim to Moral Authority.* SUNY Series in Chinese Philosophy and Culture. Albany, 2001.

Vasil'ev, K. V. *Plany srazhaiushchikhsia tsarstv: Issledovanie i perevody.* Moscow: Nauka, 1968.

Vorenkamp, Dirck. "Another Look at Utilitarianism in Mo-Tzu's Thought." *Journal of Chinese Philosophy* 19.4 (1992): 423–443.

Wagner, Donald B. *Iron and Steel in Ancient China*. Handbuch der Orientalistik 4.9. Leiden: E. J. Brill, 1993.

Waley, Arthur. *The Way and Its Power: A Study of the Tao Tê Ching and Its Place in Chinese Thought*. New York: Grove, 1958.

———, trans. *The Book of Songs: The Ancient Chinese Classic of Poetry*. Ed. Joseph R. Allen. New York: Grove, 1996.

Wallacker, Benjamin E. "Liu An, Second King of Huai-nan (180?–122 B.C.)." Journal of the American Oriental Society 92 (1972): 36–51.

Walters, Ronald G. "Signs of the Times: Clifford Geertz and Historians." *Social Research* 47.3 (1980): 537–556.

Wang, Aihe. *Cosmology and Political Culture in Early China*. Cambridge Studies in Chinese History, Literature and Institutions. Cambridge: Cambridge University Press, 2000.

Wang Baoxuan 王葆玹. "Shilun Guodian Chujian de chaoxie shijian yu *Zhuangzi* de zhuanzuo shidai—Jian lun Guodian yu Baoshan Chumu de shidai wenti" 試論郭店楚簡的抄寫時間與《莊子》的撰作時代兼論郭店與包山楚墓的時代問題. *Zhexue yanjiu* 1999.4: 18–29.

Wang Bo 王博. "Meiguo Damusi daxue Guodian Laozi guoji xueshu taolunhui jiyao" 美國達慕思大學郭店《老子》國際學術討論會紀要. *Daojia wenhua yanjiu* 道家文化研究 17 (1999): 1–12.

———. *Jianbo sixiang wenxian lunji* 簡帛思想文獻論集. Ed. Ding Yuanzhi. Chutu sixiang wenwu yu wenxian yanjiu congshu 5. Taipei: Taiwan Guji, 2001.

Wang Changhua 王長華. *Shilun yu zilun* 詩論與子論. Xueyuan wencong. Beijing, 2001.

Wang Chenglüe 王承略. "Cong zhuanxu de guanxi lun Shixu de xiezuo niandai" 從傳序的關係論詩序的寫作年代. In *Di sijie Shijing guoji xueshu yantaohui lunwenji*, 302–311.

Wang Fanzhi 王范之. "*Mu tianzi zhuan* suo ji gudai diming he buzu" 《穆天子傳》所記古代地名和部族. *Wenshizhe* 1963.6: 61–67 and 78.

Wang Guowei 王國維 (1877–1927). *Wang Guowei xueshu wenhua suibi* 王國維學術文化隨筆. Ed. Bi Chu 佛雛. Ershi shiji Zhongguo xueshu wenhua suibi daxi. Beijing: Zhongguo Qingnian, 1996.

Wang, Hsiao-po, and Leo S. Chang. *The Philosophical Foundations of Han Fei's Political Theory*. Monographs of the Society for Asian and Comparative Philosophy 7. [Honolulu]: University of Hawai'i Press, 1986.

Wang Keping, trans. *The Classic of the Dao: A New Investigation*. Beijing: Foreign Languages Press, 1998.

Wang Li 王力. *Tongyuan zidian* 同源字典. Beijing: Shangwu, 1982.

Wang Quchang 王蘧常. *Zhuzi xuepai yaoquan* 諸子學派要詮. Zhonghua wenshi jingkan. Beijing: Zhonghua, 1936; rpt., Shanghai: Zhonghua Shuju and Shanghai Shudian, 1987.

———. *Qinshi* 秦史. Shanghai: Guji, 2000.

Wang Shoukuan 汪受寬. *Shifa yanjiu* 謚法研究. Zhongguo chuantong wenhua yanjiu congshu. Shanghai: Guji, 1995.

Wang Shumin 王叔岷. "*Huainanzi* yu *Zhuangzi*" 《淮南子》與《莊子》. In Chen Xinxiong and Yu Dacheng, 27–40.

Wang Shuomin 王碩民. "Dui Handai *Shijing* yanjiu lishihua de pingjia" 對漢代《詩經》研究歷史化的評價. In *Di erjie Shijing guoji xueshu yantaohui lunwenji*, 376–385.

Wang, William S.-Y. "Language in China: A Chapter in the History of Linguistics." *Journal of Chinese Linguistics* 17.2 (1989): 183–222.

Wang Xueli 王學理. *Qinling caihui tong chema* 秦陵彩繪銅車馬. Shaanxi lishi wenwu congshu. Xi'an: Shaanxi Renmin, 1988.

Wang Yinglin 王應麟 (1223–1296). *Yuhai* 玉海. Taipei: Huawen, 1964.

Wang Yongxiang 王永祥 et al. *Yan Zhao xian-Qin sixiangjia: Gongsun Long, Shen Dao, Xun Kuang yanjiu* 燕趙先秦思想家：公孫龍、慎到、荀況研究. Baoding: Hebei Daxue, 2002.

Wang Yunwu 王雲五. *Xian-Qin zhengzhi sixiang* 先秦政治思想. Taipei: Shangwu, 1968.

Wang Zhongjiang 王中江. "Chuanjing yu hongdao: Xunzi de ruxue dingwei" 傳經與弘道：荀子的儒學定位. *Jingxue jinquan sanbian* 經學今詮三編. *Zhongguo zhexue* 24 (2002): 251–289.

———. "Jingdian de tiaojian: Yi zaoqi rujia jingdian de xingcheng wei li" 經典的條件：以早期儒家經典的形成為例. *Zhongguo zhexueshi* 2002.2: 48–54.

Watanabe Takashi 渡邊卓. *Kodai Chūgoku shisō no kenkyū—"Kōshiden no keisei" to Ju-Boku shūdan no shisō kōdō* 古代中國思想の研究—〈孔子傳の形成〉と儒墨集團の思想行動. Tōyōgaku sōsho 7. Tokyo: Sōbunsha, 1973.

Watson, Burton. *Ssu-ma Ch'ien: Grand Historian of China*. New York: Columbia University Press, 1958.

———. *Early Chinese Literature*. New York and London: Columbia University Press, 1962.

———, trans. *Han Fei Tzu: Basic Writings*. Translations from the Oriental Classics. New York: Columbia University Press, 1964.

———. *The Tso chuan: Selections from China's Oldest Narrative History*. Translations from the Oriental Classics. New York: Columbia University Press, 1989.

———. *Records of the Grand Historian: Qin Dynasty*. New York and Hong Kong: Columbia University Press, Renditions, 1993.

Weber, Max (1864–1920). *Roscher and Knies: The Logical Problems of Historical Economics*. Trans. Guy Oakes. New York: Macmillan, Free Press, 1975.

———. *Critique of Stammler*. Trans. Guy Oakes. New York: Macmillan, Free Press, 1977.

———. *Gesammelte Aufsätze zur Wissenschaftslehre*. Ed. Johannes Winckelmann. 5th edition. Tübingen: J. C. B. Mohr, 1982.

———. *Basic Concepts in Sociology*. Trans. H. P. Secher. New York: Citadel, 1993.

Wei Qipeng 魏啟鵬. "Si-Meng wuxing shuo de zai sikao" 思孟五行說的再思考. *Sichuan Daxue xuebao (Zheshe ban)* 四川大學學報(哲社版) 1988.4: 82–87.

———. *Jianbo* Wuxing *jianshi* 簡帛《五行》箋釋. Chutu wenxian yizhu yanxi congshu P010. Taipei: Wanjuanlou, 2000.

Whitehead, Alfred North (1861–1947). *Process and Reality: An Essay in Cosmology*. New York: Macmillan, 1929.

Wilhelm, Hellmut. "Notes on Chou Fiction." In Buxbaum and Mote, 215–269.

Wilhelm, Richard (1873–1930). *Frühling und Herbst des Lü Bu We*. Jena: Eugen Diederichs, 1928.

———. *Tao Te Ching: The Book of Meaning and Life*. Trans. H. G. Ostwald. London and New York: Arkana, 1985.

Wimsatt, W. K., Jr., and Monroe C. Beardsley. "The Intentional Fallacy." In *The Verbal Icon: Studies in the Meaning of Poetry*, 3–18. Lexington: University of Kentucky Press, 1954.

Wong, S. K., and K. S. Lee. "Ideology with a Vengeance: The *Gushibian* Interpretation of the *Shijing*." *Journal of Oriental Studies* 31.1 (1993): 28–37.

Wu Ch'i-ch'ang. "The Chinese Land System before the Ch'in Dynasty." In *Chinese Social History: Translations of Selected Studies*, ed. E-tu Zen Sun and John DeFrancis, 55–81. Washington: American Council of Learned Societies, 1956.

Wu, Hung. "Xiwangmu, the Queen Mother of the West." *Orientations* 18.4 (1987): 24–33.

Wu, John C. H., trans. *Tao Te Ching*. New York: St. John's University Press, 1961; rpt., Barnes and Noble, 1997.

Wu, Joseph S. "Western Philosophy and the Search for Chinese Wisdom." In *Invitation to Chinese Philosophy: Eight Studies*, ed. Arne Naess and Alastair Hanney, 1–18. Scandinavian University Books. Oslo: Universitetsforlaget, 1972.

Wu Wanzhong 吳萬鐘. *Cong shi dao jing—Lun Mao-Shi jieshi de yuanyuan jiqi tese* 從詩到經—論毛詩解釋的淵源及其特色. Beijing: Zhonghua, 2001.

Wu Xiaoqiang 吳小強. *Qinjian Rishu jishi* 秦簡日書集釋. Changsha: Yuelu, 2000.

Xiang Xi 向熹. "*Shijing* qiyi de fenxi" 《詩經》歧義的分析. In *Di erjie Shijing guoji xueshu yantaohui lunwenji*, 203–224.

Xiao Li 肖黎. *Sima Qian pingzhuan* 司馬遷評傳. Zhongguo lishi renwu congshu. N.p.: Jilin Wenshi, 1986.

Xiao Yaotian 蕭遙天. *Zhongguo renming de yanjiu* 中國人名的研究. Penang, Malaysia: Jiaoyu, 1970.

Xing, Wen. "Scholarship on the Guodian Texts in China: A Review Article." In Allan and Williams, 243–257.

Xu Fuchang 徐富昌. *Shuihudi Qinjian yanjiu* 睡虎地秦簡研究. Wenshizhe xue jicheng 287. Taipei, 1993.

———. "Shuihudi Qinjian *Rishu* zhong de guishen xinyang" 睡虎地秦簡《日書》中的鬼神信仰. In *Zhang Yiren xiansheng qizhi shouqing lunwenji,* 2:873–926.

Xu Fuguan 徐復觀. *Liang-Han sixiang shi* 兩漢思想史. 3 vols. Hong Kong: Chinese University of Hong Kong, 1975.

Xu Junru 許鈞儒. *Xunzi zhexue* 荀子哲學. Changyan congshu. Taipei: Daxue Wenxuan She, 1971.

Xu Xiyan 徐希燕. "Mozi xingming liji niandai kao" 墨子姓名里籍年代考. *Fudan xuebao: Sheke ban* 復旦學報：社科版 1999.1: 67–73.

Xu Zhongshu 徐中舒. "Lun *Zhanguo ce* de bianxie ji youguan Su Qin zhu wenti" 論《戰國策》的編寫及有關蘇秦諸問題. *Lishi yanjiu* 歷史研究 1964.1: 133–150.

Yan Kejun 嚴可均 (1762–1843). *Quan Shanggu Sandai Qin Han Sanguo Liuchao wen* 全上古三代秦漢三國六朝文. 1893; rpt., Beijing: Zhonghua, 1958.

Yan Shixuan 顏世鉉. "Guodian Chujian jianshi" 郭店楚簡淺釋. In *Zhang Yiren xiansheng qizhi shouqing lunwenji,* 1:379–396.

Yang Bojun 楊伯峻. *Yang Bojun xueshu lunwenji* 楊伯峻學術論文集. Changsha: Yuelu, 1984.

Yang Junguang 楊俊光. *Mozi xinlun* 墨子新論. Nanjing: Jiangsu Jiaoyu, 1992.

Yang Kuan 楊寬 [K'uan Yang]. *Zhanguo shi* 戰國史. 3d edition. Shanghai: Renmin, 1998.

———. *Zhanguo shiliao biannian jizheng* 戰國史料編年輯證. Shanghai: Renmin, 2001.

Yang, K'uan [Yang Kuan]. "Shang Yang's Reforms." In *Shang Yang's Reforms and State Control in China,* ed. Li Yu-ning, 3–99. China Book Project: Translation and Commentary. White Plains, N.Y.: M. E. Sharpe, 1977.

Yang Molei 楊沒累. "*Huainanzi* de yuelü xue" 淮南子的樂律學. In Chen Xinxiong and Yu Dacheng, 37–77.

Yang Ximei 楊希枚. *Xian-Qin wenhuashi lunji* 先秦文化史論集. Beijing: Zhongguo Shehui Kexue, 1995.

Yang Xiangshi 楊向時. *Zuozhuan fu-Shi yin-Shi kao* 左傳賦詩引詩考. Taipei: Zhonghua Congshu, 1972.

Yasumoto Hiroshi 安本博. "Tei no Shisan to Shin no Shukkō" 鄭の子產と晉の叔向. *Tōhōgaku* 東方學 44 (1972): 1–15.

Yates, Robin D. S. "Some Notes on Ch'in Law." *Early China* 11–12 (1985–1987): 243–275.

———. "Social Status in the Ch'in: Evidence from the Yün-meng Legal Documents. Part One: Commoners." *Harvard Journal of Asiatic Studies* 47.1 (1987): 211–248.

———. "State Control of Bureaucrats under the Qin: Techniques and Procedures." *Early China* 20 (1995): 331–365.

———, trans. *Five Lost Classics: Tao, Huang-Lao, and Yin-Yang in Ancient China.* Classics of Ancient China. New York: Ballantine, 1997.

Ye Shuxian 葉舒憲. *Shijing de wenhua chanshi—Zhongguo shige de fasheng yanjiu* 詩經的文化闡釋—中國詩歌的發生研究. Zhongguo wenhua de renleixue poyi 2. Wuhan: Hubei Renmin, 1994.

Yearley, Lee H. "Hsün Tzu on the Mind: His Attempted Synthesis of Confucianism and Taoism." *Journal of Asian Studies* 39.3 (1980): 465–480.

Yip, Wai-lim. *Ezra Pound's* Cathay. Princeton: Princeton University Press, 1969.

Yu, Anthony C. "*Cratylus* and *Xunzi* on Names." In Shankman and Durrant, 235–250.

Yu Dacheng 于大成. *Huainan lunwen sanzhong* 淮南論文三種. Taipei: Wenshizhe, 1975.

Yu Kunqi 于琨奇. *Qin shihuang (Ying Zheng) pingzhuan* 秦始皇(嬴政)評傳. Zhongguo sixiangjia pingzhuan congshu 13. Nanjing: Nanjing Daxue, 2002.

Yu Mingguang 余明光. "Xunzi sixiang yu Huang-Lao zhi xue" 荀子思想與黃老之學. *Daojia wenhua yanjiu* 6 (1995): 160–174.

Yu, Pauline. *The Reading of Imagery in the Chinese Poetic Tradition.* Princeton: Princeton University Press, 1987.

Yü, Ying-shih [Yu Yingshi]. "Life and Immortality in the Mind of Han China." *Harvard Journal of Asiatic Studies* 25 (1965): 80–122.

Yu Yingshi 余英時 [Ying-shih Yü]. *Lishi yu sixiang* 歷史與思想. Taipei: Lianjing, 1976.

Yuan Changjiang 袁長江. *Xian-Qin Liang-Han Shijing yanjiu lun gao* 先秦兩漢詩經研究論稿. Beijing: Xueyuan, 1999.

Zach, Erwin von, trans. *Die chinesische Anthologie: Übersetzungen aus dem* Wen hsüan. 2 vols. Harvard-Yenching Institute Studies 18. Cambridge, Mass, 1958.

Zau Sinmay. "Confucius on Poetry." *T'ien Hsia Monthly* 7.2 (1938): 137–150.

Zeng Dahui 曾達輝. "Jinben *Wenzi* zhenwei kao" 今本《文子》真偽考. *Daojia wenhua yanjiu* 18 (2000): 251–263.

Zeng Qinliang 曾勤良. *Zuozhuan yin-Shi fu-Shi zhi shijiao yanjiu* 左傳引詩賦詩之詩教研究. Wenshizhe daxi 61. Taipei: Wenjin, 1993.

Zhang Bingnan 張秉楠. *Jixia gouchen* 稷下鉤沉. Shanghai: Guji, 1991.

Zhang Chuanxi 張傳璽. *Qin-Han wenti yanjiu* 秦漢問題研究. Beijing: Beijing Daxue, 1985.

Zhang Dake 張大可. *Shiji yanjiu* 史記研究. Beijing: Huawen, 2002.

Zhang Fengqian 張豐乾. "Shilun zhujian *Wenzi* yu jinben *Wenzi* de guanxi—jian wei *Huainanzi* zhengming" 試論竹簡《文子》與今本《文子》的關係—兼為《淮南子》正名. *Zhongguo shehui kexue* 中國社會科學 1998.2: 117–125.

Zhang Guangzhi 張光直 [Kwang-chih Chang]. "Shangwang miaohao xinkao" 商王廟號新考. *Bulletin of the Institute of Ethnology* 15 (1963): 65–95.

———. "Guanyu 'Shangwang miaohao xinkao' yiwen de buchong yijian" 關於商王廟號新考一文的補充意見. *Bulletin of the Institute of Ethnology* 19 (1965): 53–69.

Zhang Haiyan 張海晏. "*Shijing* zai Handai de jiaohua gongneng—Qi Lu Han Mao sijia *Shi* xue helun" 《詩經》在漢代的教化功能—齊魯韓毛四家《詩》學合論. *Jingxue jinquan chubian. Zhongguo zhexue* 22 (2000): 334–374.

Zhang Jiewen 張傑文. "Ershi shiji ershi niandai Mozi guoji lunzhan shuping" 20世紀20年代墨子國籍論戰述評. *Dongyue luncong* 東岳論叢 2001.6: 100–102.

Zhang, Longxi. "The Letter or the Spirit: The Song of Songs, Allegoresis, and the Book of Poetry." *Comparative Literature* 39.3 (1987): 193–217.

Zhang Shunhui 張舜徽. *Zhou-Qin daolun fawei* 周秦道論發微. Beijing: Zhonghua, 1982.

Zhang Suqing 張素卿. *Zuozhuan cheng Shi yanjiu* 左傳稱詩研究. Guoli Taiwan Daxue wenshi congkan 89. Taipei, 1991.

Zhang Xiaokang 張小康 and Liu Sanfu 劉三富. *Zhongguo wenxue lilun piping fazhan shi* 中國文學理論批評發展史. Beijing: Beijing Daxue, 1995.

Zhang Xitang 張西堂. "*Shizi* kaozheng" 《尸子》考證. In Gu Jiegang, ed., 4:646–653.

Zhang Yiren xiansheng qizhi shouqing lunwenji 張以仁先生七秩壽慶論文集. 2 vols. Taibei: Xuesheng, 1999.

Zhang, Zhenhua. *Chinesische und europäische Rhetorik: Ein Vergleich in Grundzügen.* Europäische Hochschulschriften 20.333. Frankfurt: Peter Lang, 1991.

Zhao Peilin 趙沛霖. *Shijing yanjiu fansi* 詩經研究反思. Xueshu yanjiu zhinan congshu. Tianjin: Tianjin Jiaoyu, 1989.

Zhao Zhiyang 趙制陽. *Shijing mingzhu pingjie* 詩經名著評介. Zhongguo wenxue yanjiu congshu. Taipei: Xuesheng, 1983.

Zheng Liangshu 鄭良樹. *Huainanzi jiaoli* 淮南子斠理. Jiaxin Shuini Gongsi Wenhua Jijin Hui yanjiu lunwen 125. Taipei, 1969.

———. *Zhanguo ce yanjiu* 戰國策研究. Singapore: Xueshu, 1972.

———. *Han Fei zhi zhushu ji sixiang* 韓非之著述及思想. Zhongguo zhexue congkan 35. Taipei: Xuesheng, 1993.

———. *Zhuzi zhuzuo niandai kao* 諸子著作年代考. Beijing: Beijing Tushuguan, 2001.

Zhongguo zhexue de quanshi yu fazhan—Zhang Dainian xiansheng jiushi shouqing ji-

nian lunwenji 中國哲學的詮釋與發展—張岱年先生九十壽慶紀念論文集. Beijing: Beijing Daxue, 1999.

Zhou Fagao 周法高. *Zhou Qin mingzi jiegu huishi* 周秦名字解詁彙釋. Zhonghua congshu. Taipei, 1958.

Zhou Fengwu 周鳳五. "Guodian Chujian shizi zhaji" 郭店楚簡識字札記. In *Zhang Yiren xiansheng qizhi shouqing lunwenji,* 1:351–362.

———. "*Kongzi shilun* xin shiwen ji zhujie" 《孔子詩論》新釋文及注解. In Zhu Yuanqing and Liao Mingchun, 152–172.

Zhou Junfu 周駿富. "*Huainanzi* yu *Zhuangzi* zhi guanxi" 《淮南子》與《莊子》之關係. In Chen Xinxiong and Yu Dacheng, 27–30.

Zhu Bingxiang 朱炳祥. "'Feng' zhi huanyuan" "風"之還原. In *Di sijie Shijing guoji xueshu yantaohui lunwenji,* 1077–1082.

Zhu Dongrun 朱東潤. *Shiji kaosuo (wai erzhong)* 史記考索(外二種). Ershi shiji guoxue congshu. Shanghai: Huadong Shifan Daxue, 1996.

Zhu Hongbin 朱洪斌. *Zhonghua wubai xingshi yuanliu* 中華五百姓氏源流. Wuhan: Wuhan Daxue, 1999.

Zhu Qianzhi 朱謙之 (1899–1972). *Zhongguo yinyue wenxue shi* 中國音樂文學史. Shanghai: Shangwu, 1935.

Zhu Xi 朱熹 (1130–1200), ed. *Henan Chengshi yishu* 河南程氏遺書. *Guoxue jiben congshu.*

Zhu Yuanqing 朱淵清 and Liao Mingchun, eds. *Shangboguan cang Zhanguo Chu zhushu yanjiu* 上博館藏戰國楚竹書研究. Shanghai: Shanghai Shudian, 2002.

Zhu Ziqing 朱自清 (1898–1948). *Jingdian changtan* 經典常談. Dashi xiaozuo congshu. [1946]; Hong Kong: Sanlian, 2001.

———. *Zhu Ziqing shuo shi* 朱自清說詩. Mingjia shuo—"Shanggu" xueshu cuibian. Shanghai: Guji, 1998. [Contains *Shi yan zhi bian* 詩言志辨.]

Index

Note: Chinese names and terms are alphabetized by character.

About the Author

PAUL R. GOLDIN (Ph.D. Harvard University) is associate professor of Chinese thought at the University of Pennsylvania. Among his publications are *Rituals of the Way: The Philosophy of Xunzi* (1999) and *The Culture of Sex in Ancient China* (2002). He is the editor of the new edition of R. H. van Gulik's classic study *Sexual Life in Ancient China* (2003) and coeditor (with Victor Mair and Nancy Steinhardt) of the *Hawai'i Reader in Traditional Chinese Culture* (2005).